Mapping the World With Art

by Ellen Johnston McHenry

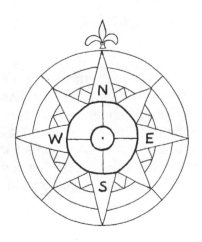

**Written, illustrated and published in
Ellen McHenry's Basement Workshop**

Mapping the World with Art
© 2009: text, step-by-step drawing lessons, and board games
Published by Ellen McHenry's Basement Workshop
State College, PA
www.ellenjmchenry.com
ejm.basementworkshop@gmail.com
Printed and distributed by Lightning Source. www.lightningsource.com

ISBN 978-0-9825377-0-1

INTRODUCTION

Writing this book was a "voyage" of discovery for me. Just when I was sure where the next chapter would lead, I was surprised when my research would take me to the other side of the globe! I've "met" people and "traveled" to places that I hardly knew existed, as well as taking a fresh look at familiar ones. Formerly meaningless shapes of landmasses are now unforgetable silly creatures. I've taken virtual vacations to places I'll never be able to actually visit. I hope that everyone who uses this curriculum—both students and teachers—will enjoy using it as much as I enjoyed creating it!

Ellen J. McHenry

NOTE ABOUT THE DRAWING LESSONS:

The drawing lessons in the middle section of this book are available on DVD. If you purchased this curriculum as either a digital download or a hard copy that did not come with DVDs, you can purchase the DVDs by going to www.ellenjmchenry.com, or you can order on Amazon.com.

TOOLS AND MATERIALS YOU WILL NEED:

Each student will need these drawing tools:

- ruler
- compass (metal is best)
- protractor (a paper one is provided in the curriculum if you don't have any other available)
- pencil with an extra eraser on the tip
- large eraser (white is best, but pink will do)
- black waterproof pen:

    I recommend either a professional quality pen such as Micron™ brand (size 02), or the brand new (as of 2009) Sharpie™ non-bleeding pen. A regular Sharpie is passable if you haven't got anything else, but if you can get the new non-bleeding pen it is well worth the trip to the store to buy it. The non-bleeding Sharpies also come in blue and red, which make them handy when you are doing the antique map projects.

    A non-waterproof felt tip pen is okay for drawings where you won't be applying anything wet.

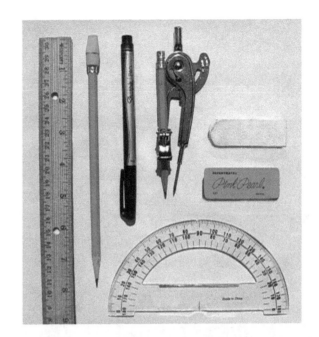

Types of paper you will need:

- white paper
- white card stock
- blue card stock (substitute white if you really need to avoid buying a ream of paper you won't use)
- calligraphy paper (also called "parchment")

General supplies to have on hand:

- colored pencils (I recommend Berol Prismacolor™. They aren't cheap, but they're worth the price)
- white glue (the regular kind, not "school" glue or washable glue)
- clear cellophane tape
- clear packing tape
- brass paper fasteners
- paint brushes of various sizes
- scissors
- dice
- toothpicks

Extra art supplies needed for specific projects:

- watercolor paints (either tube paints or pan paints): black or brown, yellow, orange, green
- acrylic paints: green, tan, white (activity 3A)
- crayons: tans, browns, greens (activities 11E and 25A)
- plastic straw, heavy thread, and metal washer (activity 4B)
- kitchen supplies, including food coloring (for cookie projects in sections 13 and 15)
- calligraphy pens: a small tip and a medium tip (for various antique maps)
- sculpting dough (for various games, one block of white "Sculpy" is sufficient)
- poster board (activity 7B, one sheet per 2-4 players)
- play dough (optional, for activity 21A)

CONTENTS

READINGS

1: The Very Earliest Maps

2: Strabo and Eratosthenes

3: Lines on the Globe

4: Claudius Ptolemy

5: The Dark Ages of Western Mapmaking

6: Marco Polo and Ibn Battuta

7: Henry the Navigator

8: Printed Maps

9: Spice Wars and Pirates

10: Christopher Columbus

11: Columbus Sails Again

12: John Cabot (Giovanni Caboto)

13: Vasco da Gama

14: Columbus's Last Voyages, Amerigo Vespucci and Juan de la Cosa

15: The New World Becomes "America"

16: Zheng He

17: Portugal Finds Malacca

MAP DRAWINGS

1: Mesopotamia

2: The Nile River

3: Greece

4: The Roman "Boot" (the Italian peninsula)

5A: The "Holy Land" of the Crusaders
5B: The Arabian Peninsula

6A: The Black Sea
6B: The Caspian Sea
6C: The Aral Sea

7: The Iberian Peninsula

8A: France
8B: Adding France to the Iberian Peninsula

9: The Indian "Subcontinent"

10: The Greater Antilles

11: The Lesser Antilles

12A: Britain
2B: Newfoundland

13: Africa

14: Central America and the Caribbean

15. South America

16: The Malay Peninsula and southern Asia

17A: Sumatra, Java and other small islands
17B: Borneo
17C: Celebes
17D: New Guinea
17E: The Spice Islands

HIGHLIGHTS OF THE ACTIVITY SECTION:

1. Make an edible Babylonian clay map, draw a local map of a room in your house or school, draw a Polynesian-style map
2. Practice using ruler, compass and protractor, play a quiz game about places above and below the equator
3. Paint a map of Greece (using acrylic paints), draw longitude lines on an egg
4. Make a star chart, make a navigational quadrant, use the quadrant
5. Fill in a review map worksheet, make a T-O map, draw weird people from the Middle Ages
6. Fill in a review map worksheet, read about Rabban Bar Sauma, watch documentaries on the Aral Sea, Ibn Batutta, and Marco Polo
7. Watch some short video clips about Henry the Navigator and Portugal, play a board game that simulates navigational techniques of the 1400s
8. Watch some short videos on printing techniques and on the country of Andorra
9. Fill in a review map worksheet, make a kamal, make a recipe for spiced meat, play the board game "Pirates of the Mediterranean"
10. Make a paper model of the Santa Maria, read Columbus in his own words
11. Watch some short videos about islands of the Caribbean, do a watercolor painting of underwater mountains, make an antique map of the Caribbean
12. Play a board game called "Viking Voyages"
13. Fill in a review map worksheet, make Africa cookies
14. Make a star clock, read how an eclipse saved Columbus
15. Learn about different types of maps and do three color-by-number maps of South America, fill in a review worksheet, make South America cookies
16. Watch a documentary on Zheng He
17. Watch a documentary on Malacca, play the "Spice Islands" board game
18. Fill in a review worksheet, watch a documentary on Magellan
19. Read a letter Verrazzano wrote to King Francis, watch an Eastern seaboard tourism video
20. Read about Anticosti Island, watch a short video on Cartier
21. Play a group game similar to "Pictionary"
22. Learn about the Svalbard Islands
23. Take a virtual tour of a globe factory, play a globe-tossing game, make a 3D octahedron paper globe
24. Watch a video clip on Henry Hudson, learn about the backstaff, download a visitor's guide to Baffin Island
25. Watch a video on Hokkaido, color a map of Japan using crayon and watercolor
26. Fill in a review map worksheet, make an antique map of Australia
27. Watch a documentary about a man who walked across the Bering Strait, fill in a review worksheet showing the entire western hemisphere
28. Make a virtual visit to the Prime Meridian, watch a grasshopper escapement in motion
29. Watch a documentary on Captain Cook, play an online quiz game, do a worksheet called "Cook's Island Match-up Challenge"
30. Download a game called "Science in Antarctica," answer review quiz questions, make an antique map of the eastern hemisphere

READINGS

NOTE: If you would like a supplemental book that gives additional information about the history of cartography and large, full-color illustrations, I recommend Mapping the World: An Illustrated History of Cartography by Ralph E. Ehrenberg, published by National Geographic. It is a 250-page book designed for adult readers, but it is very accessible to middle school and high school students, as it has just one page of text (300-400 words) per full-page illustration. The ISBN is 0-7922-6525-4.

MAPS ON THE WEB: If you would like to see more maps than "Mapping the World with Art" provides, one of the finest sites on the web is called Odden's Bookmarks; The Fascinating World of Maps and Mapping. The address is: **http:/oddens.geog.uu.nl/index.php** You have to go through a few menus to get to the maps, but don't let that put you off. They've got an incredible collection of maps, both antique and modern.

1. The Very Earliest Maps

Imagine what it would be like to live in a world without maps. How would you know what was beyond the horizon? Do you think you would be able to travel a hundred miles and find your way home again? Would you trust a neighbor's directions to get to a marketplace twenty miles away?

In ancient times, most people lived out their lives without ever seeing a map. The maps that did exist were extremely basic and showed only major land features such as rivers and mountains. It is likely that some maps were destroyed on purpose because they were intended to reveal secret routes to resources or treasures. Other maps would have been drawn in the dirt or on stones and were erased soon after they were made. The very earliest maps that are still in existence today were drawn on clay by the people of Mesopotamia (the area we now call Iraq). The one shown here, on the left, is from a place called Ga-Sur (modern day Kirkuk) and was made somewhere around 2500 BC. The lines and squiggles represent mountains and rivers. The one on the right was made in about 600 BC, when the people of that area were called Babylonians. Inside the circle is the whole world as they knew it, including Assyria and Armenia. The circle is labeled as "Bitter River" and the area outside it seems to be a sea or ocean,

2500 BC   *600 BC*

with the stars pointing to certain islands. The words on the side of the stars tell how far away these islands are. The Babylonian form of writing is called cuneiform (*cue-nee-i-form*) and looks like little wedge shapes pressed into the clay. All writing or drawing was done while the clay was wet. They also drew on stones, etching the lines into the stone with a sharp tool.

The oldest paper map still in existence is from Egypt and was drawn on papyrus somewhere around 1300 BC. It is a local map showing roads, buildings, and what look like mountains. The pharaohs were very organized about collecting taxes from their citizens and we know the tax collectors did use maps, so this map might well have been used by Egyptian tax collectors to find their way to certain neighborhoods. This map is now in a museum in Turin, Italy (the city made famous by the "Shroud of Turin"—the supposed burial shroud of Christ).

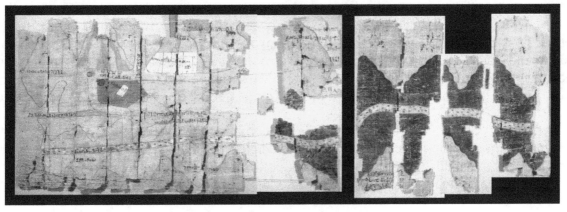

The "Turin" Papyrus is from Egypt, about 1300 BC

The ancient Polynesians made maps of the ocean from the materials they had available to them: reeds and shells. The shells marked where islands were located and the reeds often corresponded to certain latitudes or to strong currents or prevailing winds. The Polynesians were expert navigators, and with little more than these maps and the ability to sight the North Star, they could sail from island to island in their part of the world. The tool they used to sight the North Star was nothing more than a loop on top of a stick.

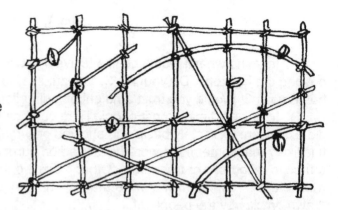

None of these ancient peoples even tried to make a map of the world because they knew that their information about the world was very limited. They understood that there was a lot more to the world than the part they lived in, but they couldn't begin to guess the true shape and size of the world. The best they could do was to make up stories. Some believed that the Earth was a great disk surrounded by water called Oceanus, and the sky was resting on four invisible pillars. The sun rose from the waters of Oceanus each morning and plunged back into them at night. Other ancient peoples guessed that the Earth was a giant cylinder or rectangle. A few guessed it might be a sphere, but only because they liked that shape. Some believed it to be supported underneath by a god, or even by a giant turtle!

Ancient peoples did get a few things right, however. They all believed that there was a huge body of water out there, much bigger than any piece of land. Many cultures believed that to north lay a land so cold that no one could live there. They also discovered many things about the sun, moon and stars that would give future mapmakers valuable information. They observed shadows made by the sun, the phases of the moon, lunar and solar eclipses, planetary motion and passing comets. They kept charts of the position of the stars at various times of the year. The Bablyonian clay tablet shown here contains a list of dates when eclipses occurred. Little did they know that their observations would lead to great discoveries about the shape of the world.

Bablyonian record of eclipses

The first ancient people that took on the task of trying to find out the shape and size of the entire world were some of the greatest thinkers of all-time: the Greeks. Aristotle was quite sure the Earth was a sphere. He gave several reasons for thinking so. First, during a partial eclipse of the moon, he said that you could see the shadow of the Earth—and it was round. Second, he pointed out that certain stars that were above the horizon in Egypt were below the horizon in Greece. If the Earth was a sphere, that's exactly what you would expect to see. Third, when you looked out to sea, you could see ships "appearing" on the horizon and anyone who had ever sailed knew that ships didn't come out of the water. Only a spherical shape could explain this phenomenon. Most people were convinced by his argument and thus, since the time of Aristotle, people have believed the Earth to be a sphere. The old story that people believed the Earth was flat until the time of Columbus isn't true at all.

The Greeks also discovered the principles of geometry. They could use basic facts about triangles to help them solve all kinds of problems. Using triangles, the Greeks figured out how large the world is. After they had figured out both the shape and size of the world, they were then ready to move on to the greatest mapping question of all time: how can you draw something round on a flat surface?

2. Strabo and Eratosthenes

In the year 25 BC, a Greek man named Strabo went to visit Alexandria, Egypt. The highlight of his trip was visiting the famous library there. Alexandria was a center for education in the ancient world. The royal library contained over half a million manuscripts collected over hundreds of years. You could read the works of Roman poets and historians, the writings of Greek philosophers and mathematicians, or the ancient charts kept by the Babylonians. Strabo was most interested in books on astronomy and geography. He read enough about both to realize that they were connected. He said, "It is impossible for anyone to attain knowledge of geography without knowledge of the heavenly bodies and the eclipses that have been observed." Tragically, the books that Strabo was able to read are no longer in existence. The great library of Alexandria has been plundered and destroyed several times since Strabo was there. The only way we know about these books is through the book Strabo himself wrote, simply called <u>Geography</u>.

Strabo was right about geography and astronomy being connected. One of the books he read there at the library was about a Greek man, named Eratosthenes, who had lived 200 years before him. Geography took a huge leap forward in about 250 BC when Eratosthenes used observations of the sun's behavior to figure out the size of the Earth. Eratosthenes was Greek, but he lived in Egypt, since Egypt had been conquered by the Greeks under Alexander the Great (hence the name of the city, Alexandria). Eratosthenes was very scholarly and he eventually became the librarian in Alexandria. Being a Greek, he was a thinker, and was particularly fond of thinking about geometry. He reasoned that if the Earth was a sphere, then the whole question of the size of the Earth just boiled down to a simple geometry problem no harder than any others he had solved in his math books. He only needed to add some astronomical observations about the sun to the rules of geometry.

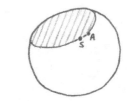

The first astronomical observation he made was in a city below Alexandria, called Syene (near modern day Aswan). He found that the sun reached its highest point (the meridian) at exactly the same time of day as it did in Alexandria. This meant that Syene must be directly south of Alexandria. (The compass as we know it today had not been invented yet so all measurements north and south had to be done using astronomy.) This also meant that if you drew a line between these two cities and kept on going, the line would trace out a perfect circle all the way around the globe. If Syene had been east or west of Alexandria, the circle they traced out would be smaller than the full distance around the Earth. Eratosthenes needed two cities that were lined up north and south of each other so that the distance between them was part of the total measurement around the globe.

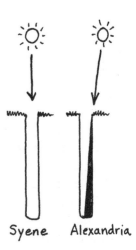

Eratosthenes' next astronomical observation was that on the longest day of the year (called the summer solstice) the sundials down in Syene cast no shadow. On this day of the year you could see to the bottom of the deepest well in Syene and there would be no shadow at the bottom. This meant that the sun's rays must be coming directly down—perfectly straight down, not even at the slightest angle. He also knew that in Alexandria the sundials <u>did</u> cast a shadow on the longest day of the year, and there <u>were</u> shadows at the bottom of deep wells. This meant that the sun's rays were coming down at an angle.

Syene   Alexandria

Eratosthenes, like all educated Greeks, was also very good at geometry. He knew that if you have a triangle with a perfectly "square" corner of 90 degrees (called a "right" triangle) you can figure out the measurement of the angles if you know the measurement of two sides. Eratosthenes simply measured how tall the gnomon was (that's the thing that sticks up and casts the shadow) and measured how long the shadow was. He then calculated the angle of the sun's rays; the angle was about 1/50 of a circle. (In other words, if you put 50 of those little angles together, you would have a complete circle.) Now all he had to do was apply one more rule of geometry and he would know how big the Earth was.

Eratosthenes drew a diagram showing a circle representing the Earth, two dots representing the cities of Alexandria and Syene, a dot at the center of the Earth, lines showing the rays of the sun coming straight down (he assumed the rays were parallel, and he was right) and a little tiny line representing the gnomon of a sundial in Alexandria.

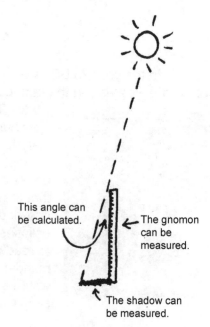

This angle can be calculated.

The gnomon can be measured.

The shadow can be measured.

RAYS OF SUN COMING DOWN

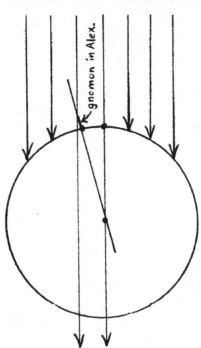

gnomon in Alex.

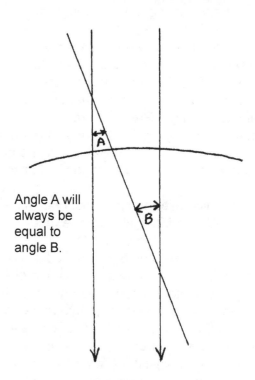

Angle A will always be equal to angle B.

The rules of geometry said that because the lines he had drawn for the rays of the sun were parallel, the angle of the shadow on the sundial (marked as angle A) had to be exactly the same as the angle marked as B. Therefore, the distance between Alexandria and Syene was 1/50 of the total distance around the Earth. He already knew that these two cities were exactly 500 miles apart. All he had to do was multiply 500 miles times 50 to get 25,000 miles. We know today that the circumference of the Earth at the Equator is 24,901.55 miles. Eratosthenes was almost exactly right! His "error" was due to the facts that Syene and Alexandria are not precisely north and south of each other (they're off by just a tiny bit) and that the Earth is not perfectly round. Neither of these facts could possilby have been known to anyone in Eratosthenes' time.

3. Lines on the globe

People living after 250 BC knew that the Earth was a sphere with a circumference of about 25,000 miles. The next question was how to map it. Once again, astronomy provided the basic answers.

You will remember that on the longest day of the year, the sundials in Syene cast no shadow at noon, and you could see to the bottom of the deepest wells. In Alexandria, this never happened. The sun never got to a point where it shone directly down. Apparently, the sun stopped its travels north somewhere around Syene, then headed south again. They decided that this was an important line (although it was imaginary, of course, and you couldn't really see it on the ground). You could find this line anywhere around the globe, just by observing the sun, so it would be a good starting point for making a map of the world. They also decided that they should go ahead and mark the equivalent line to the south, where the sun stopped traveling south and headed north again. Then there should be a line in the middle, too.

Now the lines needed names. The one in the middle was equally distant from the other two, and it divided the Earth into two equal parts, so it was named the equator. Since the people doing the naming were astronomers, names for the other lines were taken from star constellations. On the day when the sun reached its highest point in the north, the constellation Cancer, the crab, became visible on the horizon. This line was called the Tropic of Cancer. On the day when the sun reached its lowest point in the south, the constellation Capricorn, the goat, was visible on the horizon. This line became known as the Tropic of Capricorn. Now there were three fixed lines on the globe. These lines would never change, because the sun never changed. They circled the globe, staying perfectly parallel to each other.

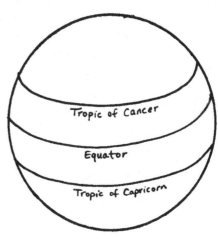

Using geometry, other lines could be drawn, perpendicular to these lines, creating a grid that divided up the globe into equal sections that could be measured and put onto maps. The lines going around the Earth like belts were later given the name "latitude" and the lines going from north to south were eventually called "longitude." Longitude lines don't have any natural starting point like the equator. Astronomy could not provide an easy and obvious answer to measurment of longitude. Measuring longitude was a puzzle that would not be solved until the 1700s.

Greek geographers realized that these lines of longitude would not act like lines on a flat surface. Because they were on a spherical surface, these lines would come closer and closer together at the poles, yet without bending. How can two lines stay perfectly straight and yet bend towards each other? It would be impossible on anything but a curved surface.

It is common to get these names mixed up and forget which is which. A simple way to remember them is to think of the lines of latitude as looking like a ladder. "Lat" and "lad" sound almost the same. You could imagine climbing up to the North Pole on a ladder of latitude lines.

You will hear a lot about latitude at first, and not very much about longitude. In fact, you may begin to think we've forgotten about longitude. This is because the problem of measuring longitude is so difficult that it was not solved until the middle of the 1700s.

The number of lines that were drawn and the distances between them were based on the ideas of the Babylonians. The astronomers and mathematicians of Babylon used a system of counting that was based not on the number 10, but on the number 60. The number 6 was used a lot, too, so they decided that a circle should be divided into (60x6) 360 parts. (They also decided that the day should be divided into (6x4) 24 hours, with each hour consisting of 60 minutes, and each minute divided into 60 seconds.) There isn't any reason that you couldn't divide a circle, into 100 parts or 63 parts or 382 parts. We use the number 360 just because everyone has since the time of the Babylonians. It's a 2500-year-old tradition. Each of the 360 parts of the circle is called a degree (not to be confused with temperature degrees) and those degrees can be broken down into smaller parts called minutes (not to be confused with minutes of time). It would have been nice if less confusing names had been chosen, rather than degrees and minutes, but it's an ancient tradition and we're stuck with it!

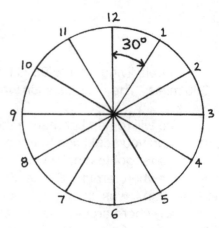

The numbers on our clocks are 30 degrees apart. (12 x 30 = 360)

According to Strabo, Eratosthenes was the first person to draw lines on a map of the world. None of Eratosthenes' maps exist any more; all we have are descriptions of them. Someone in the 1880s read those descriptions and tried to guess what Eratosthenes' map might have looked like.

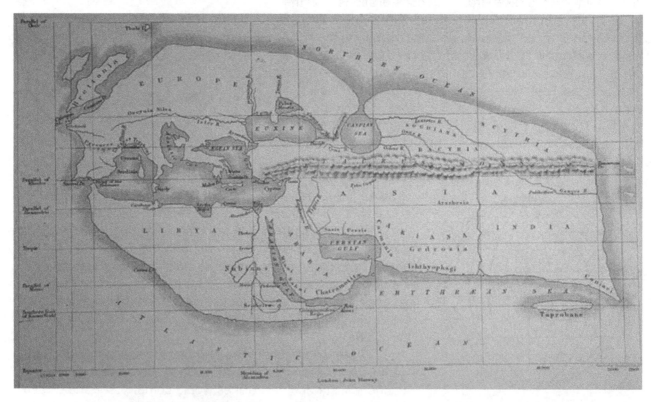

This is the entire world as Eratosthenes knew it. The line at the bottom is the equator. The lines of longitude seem to be spaced out according to sites they knew such as Alexandria, the tip of the Italian peninsula, the Straits of Gibraltar, and the tip of Portugal. There wasn't any obvious starting point for longitude, like the equator is for latitude. It didn't really matter where you started measuring. Eratosthenes was the person drawing the map and he lived in Alexandria, so Alexandria became his starting point, his "prime meridian" of longitude. (It wasn't until the 1800s that Greenwich, England, was recognized world-wide as the official Prime Meridian.)

Can you find the Persian Gulf, the Tigris and Euphrates Rivers, and the Nile River?

4. Claudius Ptolemy

Before we begin talking about yet another Greco-Roman mapmaker, we should, in fairness, give the peoples of the East their due. At the same time that Eratosthenes was making his famous calculation and Strabo was writing his books, the geographers of China were creating their own theories about the size and shape of the world. Like the Babylonians, the Chinese kept extensive astronomical records. In fact, during certain periods of history, the Chinese were the only ones keeping track of eclipses and novas. We know the Chinese did create maps of some kind but apparently every last one has been destroyed over the course of the last thousand years. There are stories of maps being embroidered onto silk fabric, with the warp and weft (up and down) fibers being used as latitude and longitude. The Chinese were probably the first to make maps of the stars and constellations. But once again, all of these very old maps were destroyed. We know about them because they are mentioned in ancient manuscripts; but the maps themselves are gone.

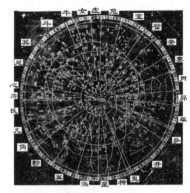

A Chinese star chart

The Greco-Roman world and the Chinese Empire were far enough apart that each one had very little knowledge of the other. Silk traders seemed to be the only ones who actually travelled far enough to learn anything of distant cultures. It is said that Julius Caesar had a silk tunic that was stunningly beautiful—so beautiful, in fact, that no one listened to his speeches while he was wearing it—they just stared at the tunic! Mostly, people in the Mediterranean circulated crazy rumors about the bizarre peoples far to the East: people with ears so long they stepped on them and headless people whose eyes and ears were in their chest!

One man who probably did not believe these stories, and who took geography very seriously, was Claudius Ptolemy. You may recognize the name "Ptolemy" as being the royal family of Egypt during the days of Cleopatra. Claudius Ptolemy lived quite a bit after that time (around 150 AD) and had no connection (as far as we know) to the royal Ptolemies. Some people in the Middle Ages did get confused about his name and drew sketches of the geographer Claudius Ptolemy wearing a crown. Although we know very little about Claudius Ptolemy, he was just an ordinary Roman citizen, as far as historians can tell.

Ptolemy wearing a crown.

Just like Strabo, Claudius Ptolemy lived in Alexandria, Egypt. Just like Strabo, he wrote a book called <u>Geography</u>. And just like Strabo, he got many of his ideas from earlier Greek and Roman writers whose books were probably on file at the Royal Library in Alexandria. Like Strabo's book, the original copies of Ptolemy's book are gone. What we have are medieval copies, not his originals.

Claudius Ptolemy set out certain rules for mapmakers. He saw that the future of mapmaking lay in being able to accurately plot positions using lines of latitude and longitude. How to make a flat map of a spherical world was a major concern for Ptolemy. He said that geographers would have to "project" the shape of the world onto a flat surface. The various ways you can do this are called "projections." Ptolemy's projection made both latitude and longitude lines slightly curved. He warned people that this would be hard to draw and would not be totally accurate. Some parts of the world would have to be stretched slightly to make them fit onto the flat surface.

Here is a copy (made in 1561) of one of Ptolemy's projected maps:

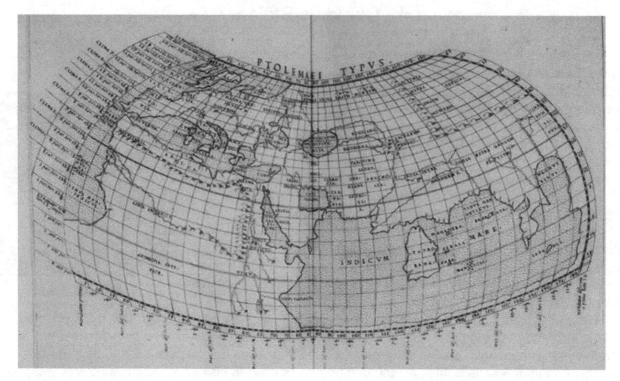

This was the whole word, as Ptolemy knew it. He guessed that there was a lot more land south of the equator, but he simply did not have enough information about it to put it on his map. Notice that at the very upper left corner, he has drawn in the British Isles, and perhaps even Iceland. There were rumors at that time of a land called Thule that was so far north that the sun never set during the summer. Ptolemy seems to have made an attempt to include this northern territory, even though many people had a hard time believing these stories.

Besides this world map, Ptolemy also made maps of smaller areas, such as the areas we now call Spain and Italy. He bound these smaller maps into a book, making the first-ever geographical atlas. He even included an alphabetical index in the back which gave the latitude and longitude coordinates he had calculated for each location. He really was the first modern cartographer (mapmaker).

In Ptolemy's book on geography, he mentioned a tool that was particularly helpful in finding angles and latitudes: the astrolabe. The astrolabe was nothing new; the Babylonians were already using them hundreds of years before Ptolemy. The astrolabe was used to measure (in degrees) how far a star was above the horizon. A star right at the horizon would be 0 degrees and a star straight overhead would be 90 degrees. To use an astrolabe, you hold it so that you are looking along the level of the straight arm. You move the arm so that it lines up exactly with a star, then you look at what degree the arm is pointing to. That's how many degrees the star is above the horizon. If you look back at the picture of Ptolemy wearing the crown, you will see that he is using an instrument very similar to an astrolabe. The instrument is called a quadrant because it consists of just one quarter of an astrolabe; but it works very much like a full astrolabe.

There was one particular star that sailors were most interested in: Polaris, the North Star. Polaris could tell you your latitude with great precision. The number of degrees Polaris is above your horizon is also how many degrees you are above the equator. Thus, finding latitude was fairly easy. Finding longitude, on the other hand, turned out to be very difficult, as it required a tool ancient civilizations could not produce: a highly accurate clock that even worked out at sea. The problem of longitude was not solved until the 1700s.

5. The Dark Ages of Western Mapmaking

Ptolemy lived in the Roman Empire before it collapsed. His world was one that took pride in its love of education and its desire for more advanced technology. Ptolemy's world came to an end by the year 500 AD. Germanic tribes had been sacking and burning their way into the Roman Empire for years. They finally completed the job and the Roman Empire was gone. The people groups that had been ruled by the Romans for centuries had no idea how to build their own governments and rule themselves. Most of Europe fell into what we call the Dark Ages.

The guardians of the libraries of Europe (many of them monks) saw the "barbarians" coming and they decided to gather up all the scrolls they could carry and head East, to a place where the scrolls would be safe—Constantinople, also known as Byzantium (now Istanbul), the center of the Christian Church of the East. Thus, knowledge and learning were drained out of Europe and transplanted into lands far to the East. (Meanwhile, back in the West, those "barbarians" converted to Christianity. Their descendants would include many great scholars of the Renaissance.)

During the Dark Ages (about 500-1,000 AD) the people of Europe went backwards in their knowledge of many things, including geography. The church grew in strength and became the unifying force that held society together. The bishops had little to read besides the Bible, since so many ancient books had gone East. They relied on the Bible not only for the plan of salvation but for their theories of science and geography, as well. The Bible talked about the "four corners of the Earth" so the Earth must be square, not round. It was absurd to think of the Earth as a sphere. People on the other side of the sphere would be standing upside down! Rain on the other side would have to fall up, not down, and that was impossible. Maps during this time were drawn from people's imaginations, always with Jerusalem, or perhaps the Garden of Eden, at the center, and

This is a medieval map of the world, showing three continents forming a T. Maps of this type are called T-O maps.

east at the top. An influential writer named Cosmas told people to take it literally when the apostle Paul said that the Tabernacle of Moses was a picture of the world. Cosmas drew a map where the Earth was shaped like a rectangular trunk with the lid as the sky and sun inside it, revolving around a giant mountain, causing day and night. The stars were "printed" on the inside of the lid.

Meanwhile, the Arabic-speaking people in and around Constantinople showed great interest in the stack of old books that had come to town. They began translating them into the Arabic language and sending out copies to Arabic scholars all over the Middle East. Thus it came to be that the learning of the Greeks and Romans was passed along to the Arabs. It was Arabic scholars who read Strabo and Ptolemy and talked about how to improve the science of geography. Unfortunately, the Arabs believed every single word Strabo and Ptolemy wrote, including their mistakes, such as believing that the Indian Ocean was a giant lake surrounded by land on all sides. The Arabs did not make a lot of advances in the field of geography during this time, but at least they kept the old Greek theories alive and well.

A Muslim map from about 1,000

The Arabs were great travellers during these days, as well as military conquerors. By the year 800, the Arabs, along with their new religion of Islam, took over all of northern Africa and even went up into Europe, into what is now Spain. The Arabs certainly made maps during this time, but the earliest ones still in existence, like the one shown here, are from after the year 1,000.

The Muslims kept coming up through Spain and were not stopped until they had almost reached the southern border of what we now call France. Even though the Europeans resented their being there and fought military campaigns to try to get them to leave, merchants and scholars from both cultures mingled together and traded both merchandise and ideas. Perhaps it was through the Arabs (and perhaps not—we don't know for sure) that the Europeans gradually began to be reintroduced to Greek and Roman ideas. Somehow or other, Europeans began gaining in architectural skill, using Roman building techniques to construct churches. By the year 1,000, they were building elaborate cathedrals.

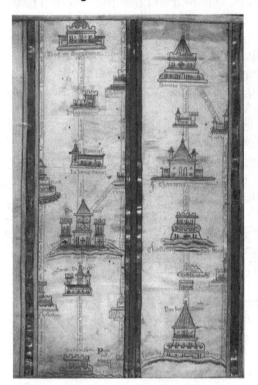

A map showing how to get from England to Jerusalem going from landmark to landmark.

Europeans began to realize that those Middle-Eastern places they read about in their Bibles were still out there, and could be visited if they were willing to make a very long journey. The thought that it was actually possible to visit the sites where Jesus did his miracles was enough to get thousands of religious pilgrims to leave Europe and head southeast, hoping to find the Holy Land. Unfortunately, there were no good maps to guide them. The map here on the left was a typical map for pilgrims going to the Holy Land. This type of map is called a "strip map." Just find each landmark on the list, in the correct order, and you'll get there.

The news these pilgrims brought back from the Middle East was discouraging: the Muslims had taken over the Holy Land, as well as many areas that had been Christian for centuries, such as Syria and Egypt. This seemed so terrible that the Pope sent out a plea for volunteers to form an army that would make war on the Muslims and take back these territories by military force.

Christians had already been fighting Muslims in southern Spain since the year 711 and everyone knew how difficult it would be to take back the Holy Land. Yet enough people volunteered to fight that a Crusade was successfully launched. In fact, many more Crusades were launched, from the years 1095 to 1272. Although some battles were won, and for a short time the Europeans controlled the Holy Land, the Crusades were essentially huge disasters and thousands of people were killed (in very nasty ways) for a cause that was pointless. All they did was stir up hatred between Jews, Christians and Muslims—hatred that continues to this day.

One of the very few good things that came out of the Crusades was a new awareness in Europe of a world "beyond their front door." The Crusaders took home stories about new plants and strange animals they had seen, and new ways of spinning and weaving. They brought back stories they had heard about exotic civilizations even farther to the East. Most importantly, they brought back samples of things that Europeans would want to buy, such as silk fabric, precious gemstones, rare spices and gunpowder. Now the Europeans had a new reason to be interested in the lands that lay to the east—there were fortunes to be made! Medieval maps of the world would be of no use to these new business men. They would need maps that were accurate and showed the world as it really was. They would need maps that could get them to foreign ports and safely back again. This desire for better maps led Europe into its golden age of mapmaking.

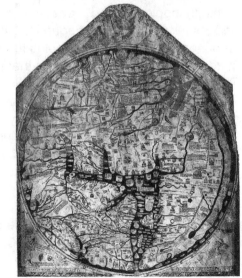

A medieval "Mappa Mundi"

6. Marco Polo and Ibn Battuta

Right at the end of the Middle Ages, just before Europe began its golden age of mapmaking, two men made history as the first world travelers. Although they did not make maps of their travels, the books they wrote about their travels greatly influenced the people who would start making maps.

One of the first merchants to leave Europe in hopes of finding adventure and fortune in the lands to the East was Marco Polo. Although Marco didn't draw any maps, he is still important in the history of maps because of all the knowledge be brought back about the lands to the east.

Marco was from a family of merchants who lived in Venice. The founders of Venice were Romans fleeing from the Germanic tribes around the year 500 AD (those same barbarians who caused the exit of all the Greek and Roman books). As these tribes were sacking and burning their way down the peninsula, one group of Romans decided to hide in a soggy salt marsh. The plan worked perfectly—the Germans had no interest in coming into the soggy marsh. Now, the only problem was to find a way to actually live in the marsh. Then someone made an important discovery: the salt in the marsh could be dried out and sold at a very good price. Salt was a precious commodity in those days because it was one of the only ways to preserve food. So the industrious Venetians began harvesting their salt and were soon one of the biggest salt producers in the Mediterranean area. At first, the Venetians lived in soggy little huts in the marsh until someone made another important discovery: the marshes could be drained and filled with logs to make dry spots that would support houses and public buildings. Thus began centuries of draining the marshes to create land that could support buildings. Today there is a whole city built on the land that used to be a salt marsh. Eventually, the Venetians began buying and selling salt from all over the Mediterranean world. They found that buying and selling things was very profitable and they decided to expand their markets to include other items, not just salt. By Marco Polo's time the Venetians were world-class merchants.

A painting of the Polos arriving in a Chinese city.

In the year 1271, Marco's father and uncle began a business trip that would take them far to the east. Marco was 17 years old then, just old enough to be allowed to go along. They went not just as merchants, but as ambassadors from the Pope. The most important ruler in the east (in what we now call China), known as the Kublai Khan (the grandson of the infamous Ghengis Khan), had requested that missionaries come to his kingdom to teach his people about Christianity. Two monks were sent along with the Polo family, although they "chickened out" half way into the trip and turned back.

The Polos made it safely to the Khan's court and Marco ended up staying 17 years with the Khan. The Khan is said to have sent Marco on important diplomatic missions and made him governor of a city. Marco's return to Europe was occasioned by his last mission: escorting a princess from her homeland in China to marry a prince in what is now western Iran. After dropping off the princess, Marco continued on his way and eventually came back home to Venice. His stories about what he saw and what he did in China were quite a sensation, and he eventually wrote a book about it.. Some of what he wrote is so fanciful it's hard to believe, but other parts of his book are accurate descriptions of the geography and cultures of Asia.

A page from a Medieval copy of Polo's book

The Polo family weren't the only ones who traveled all over Europe and Asia. The Arabic world has their own Marco Polo—a man named Ibn Battuta. He lived at about the same time as Marco, went to a lot of the same places, and also wrote a book about his travels.

Ibn Battuta was born around the year 1300 in the city of Tangier, in Northern Africa. When he was 20 years old, he made the journey that all Muslims must make: the pilgrimage to Mecca. After he got to Mecca he didn't feel like going back home again—instead, he kept on going and didn't stop until he had covered about 75,000 miles! (That's like going around the world at the equator three times.) He finally ended up back at Mecca again. He knew he really should be getting back home by now, but he just couldn't resist seeing what was up north and spent the next year traveling in the areas we now call Iraq and Iran. (This was the same area that Marco Polo had traveled through to deliver the princess to her fiancé.) Battuta returned to Mecca again and visited other holy sites along the way.

After having been to Mecca several times, he knew he really, really should be getting back home, but... there was just so much world to see out there! This time he went down the east coast of Africa. After this grand African adventure he went back to Mecca again and tried very hard to get a job and stay put for a while. But then he had this great idea! Why not work for the Muslim ruler of far-off India? (The religion of Islam had spread to quite a lot of the world by this time, including India.) To do this, he would need transportation and a translator. He figured the best place to acquire these was in the area we now call Turkey. So off he went.

He did manage to catch a caravan headed east towards India, but found that a side-trip was planned to drop off a princess in Istanbul (yet another "princess-drop-off" mission). He enjoyed this side trip immensely but eventually got back on track and made it all the way to India. He did indeed end up working for the Muslim Sultan in India, just as he had planned. However, the Sultan turned out to be crazy and Battuta decided to escape by offering to be an ambassador to China. After staying for a while in China (and living in Sumatra for a while, as well) he once again returned to Mecca.

When Battuta received news that his father had died, he knew that he really did have to go home now. It had been 25 years since he had left home. On the way home he witnessed much human suffering and death, for the plague, the Black Death, was consuming a third of the world's population. When he got home to Tangier he discovered his mother was dead as well.

After this, Battuta decided to explore a little closer to home. He went to Morocco, then back home by way of the Sahara Desert. He stayed for a time in the famous city of Timbuktu. When he returned to Morocco after this trip he never traveled again. Battuta told his stories to a scribe who wrote them all down. Not long after that, Ibn Battuta died of the plague.

He didn't leave any maps of his travels, but by his descriptions of the places he visited, we can figure out where he went.

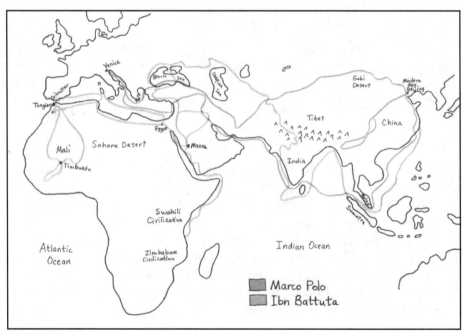

This map makes it easy to compare the travels of Marco Polo and Ibn battuta.

7. Henry the Navigator

It is now the early 1400s and the Dark Ages in Europe are over. It is now the Age of Discovery! Sailing technology and the art of mapmaking will now start improving very quickly and will take us around the world. We'll see exploration turn into a frantic race among the European countries to see who can get the farthest the fastest. One of the pioneers in this race to get around the world was a man known to the world as Henry the Navigator.

Henry wasn't a sailor as you might guess from his nickname. His real name was Prince Henrique, Duke of Viseu, the third son of King John of Portugal. Being the third son, Henry wasn't first in line for the throne, so he was allowed to dabble in whatever hobbies interested him and was given a generous allowance to do so. Sailing and exploration were of great interest to him and he provided funding and encouragement to the explorers of his day. Fortunately, Portugal already had some pretty good sailing ships. During the 1300s, a previous king of Portugal had bribed a dozen ship builders in Genoa (at the top of what is now Italy) to come over and teach the Portuguese how to build state-of-the-art ships. Now, in the 1400s, Portugal had one of the strongest navies in the world. Henry realized, however, that these naval ships were big and slow and not the ideal form of transportation for exploring the world. Henry asked his expert ship builders to design a smaller and lighter ship. These ships, called "caravels," could sail farther and faster than any of the naval ships of the time. They were the jet airplanes of their day, so to speak.

The first place Henry sent his caravels was down the coast of Africa. The farthest point south that any European had ever been was Cape Bojador, located on the coast of the country we now call Western Sahara. There was a reason no one had been south of this cape—it was here that the winds changed. The sailors of that day didn't know about global wind patterns. They believed that the sea was treacherous at this location because of giant monsters that lived beneath it. So many ships had gone down trying to round this cape that perhaps it was cursed! Henry didn't believe the fanciful stories that were told about Cape Bojador. He believed that excellent sailing technology could overcome the natural difficulties. He was right, of course, and his caravels did manage to sail around this cape. They kept going south for another 150 miles, mapping every part of the coastline of Africa as they went. They returned not only with maps, but with treasures as well: gold and (sadly) African people who would be sold as slaves throughout Europe.

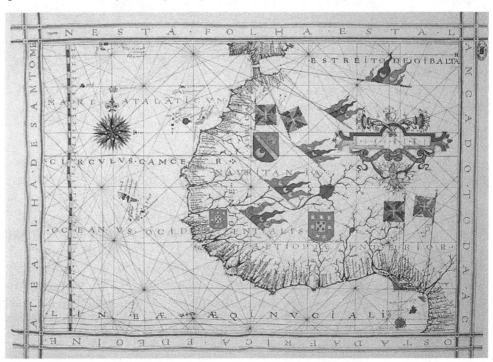

This type of map is called a "portolan" map. All the criss-cross lines are called "rhumb lines." The sailors sailed in the directions of these lines, using astrolabes and compasses to determine the right direction. This portolan map was made in Portugal in 1571. Cape Bojador is the point nearest the blue dot.

When Henry's navigators returned home, they brought back maps they had made along the way, showing the coastline they had explored. They had gone ashore at various points and found treasures such as gold and (unfortunately) natives they could take as slaves. The quest for more gold turned exploration from hobby into serious business.

Henry's navigators went west as well as south. They sailed out into the Atlantic Ocean and discovered quite a few islands: the Madeiras, the Azores, the Canaries, and the Cape Verde Islands. They claimed these islands (and more importantly, all the natural resources on those islands) for Portugal. Today, Portugal still owns the Azores and the Madeiras. Cape Verde gained its independence in 1975. The Canary Islands now belong to Spain. The picture below shows a landscape on one of the Azore islands.

These islands were important to politicians because of the ways they could enrich their treasuries. To sailors, however, these islands were important for two very practical reasons. The most important reason was that these islands could be used as a "pit stop" out in the Atlantic. Ships could take on board only a limited supply of food and fresh water. These islands were like rest stop plazas on our modern highways. Ships could pull in to these islands for a few days to restock supplies, make repairs, and allow the deck hands a few days to relax or to recuperate if they were sick. After days of eating salted meat and stale biscuits, sailors rejoiced when an island came into view. Fresh food was a special treat.

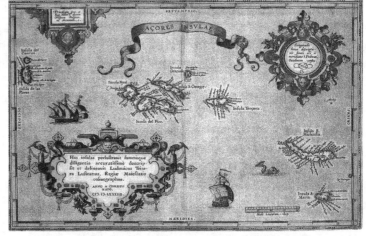

A Portugues map from the 1500s showing the Azore Islands

The second reason these islands were of great significance to sailors was the possibility of these islands being used by pirates as bases of operation. Control of these islands meant reducing the chances of your ship's being attacked while at sea. The famous Barbary pirates ranged all over the Mediterranean and the East Atlantic. Pirates couldn't stay out at sea all the time any more than regular sailors could; they needed base ports, too. If these islands were under the control of European countries, pirates had to go elsewhere (hopefully farther away from where the Europeans wanted to sail).

Henry the Navigator died before Portuguese caravels made it all the way down to the bottom of Africa. In 1488, twenty-eight years after Henry's death, a navigator named Bartholomew Dias sailed farther south than any European had ever gone. He rounded the very bottom tip of Africa, around the cape that is known today as "Cape of Good Hope," and after sailing northeast just far enough to be really sure he had indeed found the bottom of Africa, he then returned home with the grand news. The news spread quickly and soon other countries were jumping into the race to map the world.

8. Printed Maps

While the Portuguese caravels were sailing down the coast of Africa, an inventive young goldsmith from Strasbourg, Germany, was making his own important contribution to the history of maps and mapmaking. His contribution had nothing to do with gold even though he was trained as a goldsmith. He used his training in fine craftsmanship to create something that would prove to be far more valuable than gold.   His name was Johann Gutenburg and he was the inventor of the first printing press that used moveable type. "Moveable type" means using individual letter blocks which are placed side by side in a tray to form words and sentences. Previous to this invention, printing was done by chiseling the pattern of a whole page onto one piece of wood. (To be fair, it must be mentioned that the Chinese had also come up with a way to print with moveable type. There are also books in Korean printed about the same time as Gutenberg's books. But in China and Korea, printing never really caught on the way it did in Europe.)

Here is a case full of "moveable type" letters. The small tray shown sitting on top of the case has letters stuck into it very tightly so they don't fall out when the tray is turned over during the printing process. Gutenberg's letters were made of a mixture of tin, lead and antimony.

Around the year 1440, Gutenberg's press was finished and he began printing his most famous book: the Gutenberg Bible. Each letter on every page had to be set by hand, so it took him several years to print it. But when he was finished (in 1455) he had not one copy, but over a hundred and fifty copies. Gutenberg had produced more copies of the Bible in just a few years than a scribe could have written by hand in a lifetime. News of this amazing invention spread across Europe in a flash. Scribes were outraged that their jobs were at stake, but most people looked forward to a time when there would be so many books in print that they would be able to have a book of their own. Up until this time, books were things that only churches and universities and rich nobles had—and even they had very few of them. The printing press would make books available to everyone.

The demand for books was huge. Printing presses began appearing in towns all across Europe. Bibles were big sellers, but people wanted other things to read, as well. The Dark Ages were over and people were thirsty for knowledge. The spirit of the Renaissance was spreading throughout Europe, making people want to know more about their world. Printers had to scramble to find things to print. Fortunately, they discovered some "new" manuscripts that had come from faraway cities such as Alexandria and Constantinople. Because of these printers, the writings of the Greeks and Romans

would once again become part of the intellectual life of Europe. Printers made books of Greek myths and Roman poems. Aesop's fables and Euclid's geometry were rediscovered, and so were... you guessed it—the geography books of Strabo and Ptolemy! These geography manuscripts were well over a thousand years old when they were printed in Europe in the 1400s, yet they brought new ideas into Europe. Ptolemy's original maps had disappeared completely, however. Artists had to recreate Ptolemy's maps using only his written descriptions.

To print a book of maps, printers had to hire artists to engrave copies of the maps onto metal plates. The engravers could scratch the lines right into the metal or they could use acid chemicals to "etch" the lines into the metal. After the plates were done, they were rubbed with ink. The ink would go down into the scratches and stick there. When a piece of paper was pressed onto the plate, the ink in the scratches would be transferred to the paper. Perhaps the trickiest part of engraving was the fact that the design on the plate had to be backwards so that when it was printed, it would come out forwards. If they wanted to print a map with more than one color, each color required a separate plate.

The map shown below was printed sometime in the early 1400s, although the exact year is not known. A European artist read a copy of Ptolemy's geography book and used the mathematical coordinates he gave for certain cities and landmarks to create this approximation of what Ptolemy's map of 150 AD may have looked like. Can you find the Black Sea and the Caspian Sea? How much of the Caspian Sea had been explored? Did the Romans of 150 AD know about the Aral Sea? Notice the words "Indicum Pelagus." How would this be translated to English?

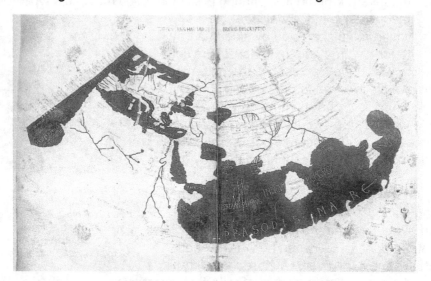

The map shown below is a page from a reprinting of Ptolemy's "Geographia," made in 1482 by a man named Johannes Schnitzer who lived in the town of Ulm. It is a woodcut, meaning the design was carved into a block of wood which was then used to make prints. The heads around the outside of the map represent the winds blowing from the four points of the compass (plus the points in between, such as northeast and southwest). People living in the 1400s no longer believed the folk tales about gods and goddesses controlling the winds, but they had grown quite fond of Greek myths. The wind gods seemed appropriate decorations for a map of the world. After all, it was the wind that drove the ships of the brave men who went out to explore and map the world.

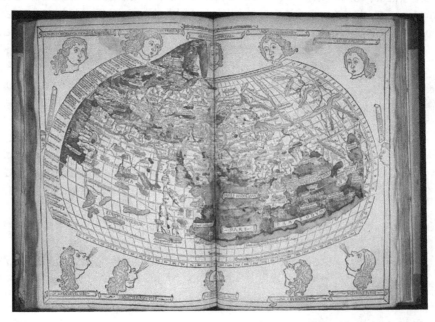

9. Spice Wars and Pirates

While wealthy merchants and craftsmen in the 1400s were busy buying and reading books, their wives were busy buying, and cooking with, strange new spices that were arriving from far-off India. Spices that seem very common to you, such as pepper and cinnamon, were hot new items in Europe in the 1400s. The list of new spices also included ginger, cumin, cardamom, coriander and saffron.

The black pepper plant is a large vine that produces small pepper "berries."

Most spices came into Europe through the city of Venice. You may remember that the original Venetians had created their city out of a salt marsh and had become rich by selling their salt. Then they started buying and selling other things, along with their salt. Now, in the 1400s, the Venetians were master merchants and practically owned the spice trade in Europe. This was partly due to their business skills, but also partly due to their location on the map. As you can see on the map below, the Venetian ships had only to sail down the Adriatic Sea, then either down to Alexandria or up through the Aegean Sea to Constantinople. At these two cities they could buy spices from Muslim traders who had gone to India. Usually the Venetians brought copper and silver to trade for the spices. These metals were mined in central Europe. The people of the Middle East were happy to trade spices for these metals or for other products made in Europe, such as woolen cloth.

An illustration from an old book about Marco Polo, showing Indians harvesting spices.

The city of Genoa, on the other side of the Italian "boot," also tried to get into the spice business. They had a little bit longer voyage, but could also stay clear of North Africa. Since Genoa was closer to France and Spain than Venice was, the plan of the Genoese merchants was to dominate the market in Spain and southern France, leaving central and eastern Europe to Venice. The rivalry between these two cities became legendary. (Over a century later, Venetian merchants would inspire Shakespeare with characters for his play "The Merchant of Venice.")

The Portuguese decided that they would like to get into the spice trading business, too. Their caravels had already discovered a form of pepper growing in West Africa. The obvious next move was to try to get spices from Asia as well as Africa. However, to get from Lisbon to Alexandria, you have to sail the entire length of North Africa.

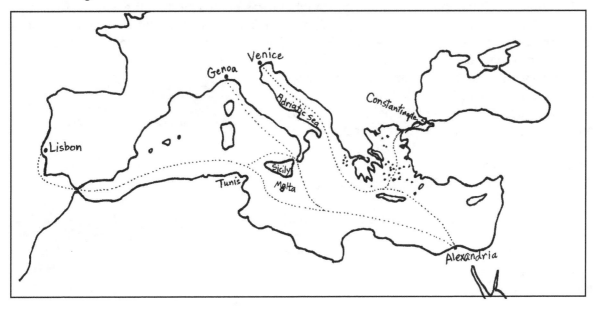

Now, what was the big deal about sailing past North Africa? Were the currents that bad? Was the water infested with sharks? No, it was something far worse: pirates! The pirates who lived along the coast of North Africa were called the "Barbary" pirates, named after the native people of North Africa, the Berbers. The Barbary pirate ships would intercept European trading vessels that were headed to Alexandria. The pirates would capture all the European sailors and force them to spend the rest of their lives chained to a rowing bench, pulling the oars of a pirate ship. Rowing was exhausting work and rowers were underfed; sometimes they starved to death. Pirate captains were cruel and would often whip the rowers. If a rower went unconscious, they'd whip him to wake him up and if he didn't respond they'd just dump the body overboard and get a replacement from the next European ship they attacked. Those were some pretty good reasons to avoid sailing near North Africa! The Barbary pirates continued to be a serious threat in the Mediterranean all the way up until the 1700s.

Venice was going to be hard to beat in the spice-trading game. Not only did they have a better sailing route, they had also worked out a deal with the Barbary pirates. Venice paid an annual "tribute" (a large sum of money) to the Barbary pirates in exchange for not being attacked.

Hayreddin Pasha, also known as "Barbarossa"

The most famous Barbary pirate wasn't a Berber at all, but a Turkish Greek born on an island in the Aegean Sea. He was known as "Barbarossa," translated into English as "Redbeard." He and his three brothers (it was actually his older brother who had the red beard) became sailors and eventually ended up working for the Ottoman Turkish rulers who wanted to expand their empire and take over all of Europe if they could. (Because Barbarossa worked for the Turks, he is technically considered a "privateer," not a regular pirate. Privateers steal and kill on behalf of politicians; regular pirates steal and kill only for themselves.) Dominating the Mediterranean Sea would be an important step for the Ottoman Turks in achieving their goal, and to this end Barbarossa and his brothers were employed to rid the Mediterranean of European vessels.

Barbarossa and his brothers had their bases of operation at various places on the coast of North Africa. Their ships (lots of them) roamed all over the Mediterranean. They also went on shore and raided the coastal towns of Italy and Spain, being especially careful to destroy their shipyards. One of the pirates' favorite places to attack ships at sea was in the narrow space between Tunis and the island of Sicily. If you look back at the map, you will see how narrow this part of the Mediterranean is. Ships had the option of sailing up and over Sicily, but sailing through the narrow strait right at the tip of the "boot" was not exactly risk-free, and the extra time it took to sail this route added expense to the trip. Not all ships got caught by pirates, so often the merchant vessels would take the risk of sailing the southern route.

Eventually, a European pirate-fighting stronghold was established on the island of Malta, right below Sicily. From here, Europeans could launch counter-attacks on the pirates. Captured Barbary pirates would spend the rest of their lives on a Spanish or Italian ship, chained to a rowing bench, proving that the Spaniards and Italians could be just as cruel as the Turks.

In the 1530s, the Spanish king (and the "Holy Roman Emperor") Charles V tried to bribe Barbarossa into switching sides and fighting for Spain. He offered Barbarossa the title of Admiral-in-chief over the entire Spanish navy! It didn't work. Barbarossa went on attacking Spanish ships.

In the late 1400s, the Portuguese decided that they would like to join in on the "fun" and get into spice trading, too. However, the part about the Barbary pirates didn't thrill them. What they needed was a way to get to India without having to go past the pirates. Their plan was to go all the way around Africa, even if it was a very long trip. Safety from pirates was worth the extra mileage.

This painting, from 1538, shows the Barbary pirates defeating a Spanish fleet.

10. Christopher Columbus

Portugal's success exploring down the coast of west Africa, especially Bartholomew Dias' discovery of the southern tip of Africa, showed that Portugal could, and would, find a way to dominate the spice trade. If Spain, Venice, and Genoa wanted to stay in the spice-trading game, they were going to have to find ways to counter these bold moves by Portugal.

Unfortunately for Venice, it was becoming increasingly difficult to get Indian spices from Middle Eastern countries. The Ottoman Turks had conquered most of the Middle East and were now refusing to trade with anyone who came from a country where Christianity was the dominant religion. Spain had the additional problem of Barbary pirates, because of its location on the western side of the Mediterranean. So why not just follow after Portugal and try to go around Africa? Well, first of all, it was not yet proven that you really could get to India by going around Africa. And secondly, there was no guarantee that Portugal would just sit by and watch other European ships go sailing down the coast. Portugal might decide to attack non-Portuguese vessels that tried to use their shipping lanes. The best possible solution was to find another option—one that didn't involve Africa or Arabs.

It was during this time that Christopher Columbus came on the scene. He was born in Genoa but lived in Lisbon during his teen years, studying at the school that Henry the Navigator had established. While in Lisbon he lived with his older brother, who worked for a mapmaker.   Lisbon was becoming a center for cartography (making maps) and Columbus would have seen the very latest maps, showing everything that was known about the world.

When he was in his twenties, Columbus sailed to various places as a representative of merchants in Genoa. He sailed all over the Mediterranean, but also out into the Atlantic and up to Ireland. Some historians believe he may even have visited Iceland. Perhaps it was on this trip out into the Atlantic that the idea of sailing west first occurred to him. However the idea came into his mind, he became convinced that you could sail around the world by going west, and he spent the next decade of his life trying to get someone to pay his expenses for a voyage that would prove his theory.

Now you'd think that with Portugal claiming the southern route around the world, the other European powers would jump at the chance to find an alternate route. The monarchs and merchants of those countries might well have hired Columbus immediately except for a couple of small problems. Spain had the problem of being out of money. Ferdinand and Isabella, the rulers of Spain, were spending their last dollars on the war against the Muslims, determined to make them leave southern Spain and go back to North Africa.   The biggest problem, however, was that whenever the monarchs or the wealthy merchants took Columbus' plans to their experts for consultation, the experts (who were mathematicians) always said that Columbus' calculations were wrong. They said that Columbus was underestimating the size of the earth. Columbus' figure for the circumference of the earth was quite a bit less than what Eratosthenes had calculated. (Columbus' error may have been partly due to reading the mileage wrong on Arabic maps. He didn't know that the Arabic mile was longer than the Italian mile.) The math experts stuck with Eratosthenes. They said that caravels couldn't possibly carry enough supplies for a journey that would go clear around the Earth. When the monarchs and merchants heard that advice from their experts, they told Columbus that they were sorry, but they couldn't risk their money on a voyage that was

"Columbus petitioning Ferdinand and Isabella" from the doors of the United States Capitol Building

doomed from the start. Had anyone known there were two huge continents on the other side of the globe, it would have been a different story. But they didn't know, so the monarchs and merchants can hardly be blamed for not wanting to finance such a dubious voyage.

Columbus didn't give up. He went on for several years trying to find a sponsor for his voyage. Then, in 1488, Dias rounded the southern tip of Africa. Portugal's success made the other participants in the spice wars start to panic. Something had to be done! Ferdinand and Isabella told Columbus they would sposor his trip if he could get half the money from somewhere else. Columbus managed to strike a deal with powers on both sides of the Mediterranean, getting half the money he needed from Genoese merchants but sailing as an admiral under the Spanish flag. He would claim all lands he discovered for Spain and become governor of those lands, receiving one tenth of all the riches that came from them. The deal was signed and sealed, and Columbus (the "Admiral of the Ocean") began his voyage in August of 1492.

Columbus' first stop was at the Canary Islands, off the coast of Morocco. Almost all ships sailing out from Spain or Portugal made a stop at the Canaries. Here they could take on fresh water and food. Then the long journey began. Columbus sailed with the winds that naturally cross the Atlantic from east to west. (Winds that generally always blow in the same direction are called "prevailing" winds.) After about two months at sea, the supplies were getting low and the sailors were beginning to think about forcing Columbus to turn the ship around and go home. Fortunately for Columbus, land was soon sighted. On October 12, 1492, Columbus and his crew landed on one of the islands we now call the Bahamas. We don't know exactly which island he landed on. Columbus decided to name the island San Salvador, but the island already had a name, "Guanahani," given to it by the native people who lived there. (The island we call San Salvador was not officially given that name until 1925.)

The coat of arms of the Canary Islands shows their national symbol: dogs. The word "Canary" has nothing to do with birds. It comes from the Latin word "canis," meaning "dog." When the Romans first discovered the islands, there was a large population of wild dogs.

The native people of the island were very friendly. After several days, Columbus and his crew left that island and went on to find others. The next one they bumped into was the island of Cuba. After that, they went farther south and landed on the island of Hispaniola.

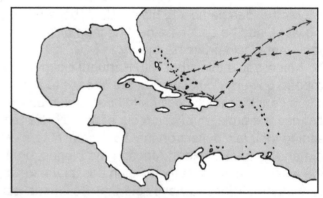

They built a fort there and called it "La Navidad," meaning "Christmas," because it was on Christmas morning that they had first landed there. Unfortunately, one of the ships sustained serious damage and had to be abandoned there at La Navidad. Columbus decided to leave 39 of his crew there on the island as the first Spanish garrison in what would eventually be called "The New World."

Columbus believed he had gone all the way around the world and discovered islands off the coast of India. His calculations of the size of the world didn't allow for the Pacific Ocean. Since he believed that these islands were near India, he called them the West Indies, a name still used today, even though we know better. He returned to Spain on March 15, 1493, with the news of all his discoveries. Even faster than printers could get it into print, this hot news item spread over Europe in a flash. Although the Portuguese were certainly impressed and perhaps even stunned by this news, they weren't convinced that Columbus had discovered India. They pressed on with their plans to go around the bottom of Africa and come up to India from the south. The spice war was still on!

11. Columbus Sails Again

The king and queen of Spain, Ferdinand and Isabella, were very happy with the discoveries of Columbus. They didn't care whether the land he had found was India or not. They were just happy with a bunch of new territory they could claim for Spain, and the possibility that the new territory contained valuable resources such as silver and gold. Columbus had brought back some very small pieces of gold but believed there was much more to be found on those islands. He also brought back a few representatives of the tribe he had encountered, the Taino tribe. We might wonder who was more bewildered at their meeting—the tribesmen or the Spaniards? Columbus also brought back brightly colored parrots and samples of new plants. One of the strangest edible plants Columbus had discovered was a plant that produced long green seed pods that, when opened, revealed a cylinder covered with yellow kernels. (Does it sound familiar to you?)

Ferdinand and Isabella wanted Columbus to go back to these islands again. In a matter of just a few months, ships were being prepared for a second voyage. This time Columbus had 17 ships in his fleet. Over 1,000 people were going with him! Spain intended to "colonize" these islands, which meant sending Spanish people to live on these islands for the rest of their lives. The Spanish people would build towns and grow crops and raise their children on these islands.

Columbus and his fleet arrived in the West Indies much farther south than the place they had landed on their first trip. They came across a very long line of small islands. Strangely enough, there were ancient legends among sailors in Europe that told of a large island out at the edge of the Western Sea (the Atlantic) called "Antillia." This legendary island even showed up on a map made in 1424, as if the mapmaker had had sufficient proof of its existence to mark its location. Most people doubted its existence but many sailors claimed

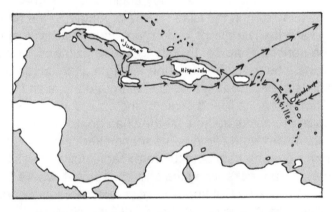

that the legend was true. When Columbus and his crew discovered these islands, their first thought must have been that they had discovered legendary Antillia, and that is why these islands are still called the Antilles to this day.

An Arawak, drawn by an artist in the 1700s

The Spanish ships now went island-hopping. It must have been great fun at first. As they went along, they gave a Spanish name to each island. Many of these names are still used today. Sometimes they named the islands after a place in Spain (Guadeloupe, Montserrat, and Antigua) or a saint (St. Kitts (Christopher), St. Martin, St. Eustatius, San Pedro, and the Virgin Islands, named after St. Ursula and her 11,000 virgins).

As they hopped along the islands, they met the people who lived on them. They already knew the Taino people, and found that there were other tribes related to them, all part of a large group called the Arawaks. The two other tribal groups of the Antilles islands were the Ciboneys and the Caribs. The Arawaks got along just fine with the Ciboneys, although they held many of them as slaves. The people to be feared were the Caribs. When they came across the water in their war boats, called canous (do you recognize that word?), it was sometimes for trade, but often for war. If they came for a battle,

A drawing of Caribs made by an artist in the 1700s.

they killed every male Arawak they could find and kidnapped the females, taking them as extra wives. Rumor had it that at their victory ceremonies, Caribs would chew on the flesh of their enemies. When Columbus learned this astonishing bit of information, he recorded it in his diary. When he wrote down the name of the tribe that did this, he wrote "Caribales," making a Spanish version of the word "Carib." Somehow or other, the word "Caribales" got translated as "Canibales" and eventually turned into our English word "cannibal."

Another word that came from the people of the Antilles is the word "hammock." The Spanish sailors were fascinated with the hanging beds of the Arawaks. They tried out the hammocks and noticed how much more comfortable they were than the hard benches they slept on. The sailors immediately adopted this new technology, and sailors have been sleeping in hammocks ever since.

Every time they stopped at an island, the mapmakers got out their equipment and started taking measurements. On land, without the constant rocking and rolling of the boat, the mapmakers could get very accurate measurements with their astrolabes, and could determine the exact latitude they were on. They could set up a sundial on the beach and do some experiments with it, adding data to their almanac charts. They could use a magnetic compass to determine the direction in which the coastline ran. If the island had a mountain in the middle of it (which many did because the islands were actually the tops of dormant underwater volcanoes), they might hike to the top to be able to see the general shape of the island, or the existence of any bays which were suitable for anchoring large ships. As for longitude—the left/right direction on a map—that was just an educated guess. If the ship's captain was willing to sail around the island, they could use dead reckoning to judge distances. (Remember, to "dead reckon," the sailors would use the speed of the boat and the time they had been sailing to calculate how far they had gone. They were using the formula $d=rt$, where *distance* equals *rate* multiplied by *time*.) The mapmakers would also be very careful to write down any observations that would be helpful to future expeditions, such as the depth of the water at low tide, the location of dangerous rocks along the shore, or places where fresh water could be found. Unfortunately, any maps made by Columbus or his crew were lost or destroyed not long after they were made. All we have from this voyage is the diary Columbus kept, in which he wrote down many navigational details.

The Spanish island-hopping fun came to a sudden halt when they reached the island of Hispaniola, the island where they had left their friends almost a year ago. The men were gone and the fort had been burned to the ground. Something had gone terribly wrong. Columbus learned that the Spanish soldiers had not behaved well. They had gone into Taino villages and stolen things, including women. The Taino men hadn't liked that at all and had decided to get rid of the Spaniards. Sadly, this event was to be the beginning of the end for the Taino people. The Spanish had their revenge; over the next several years, the Spaniards would kill and enslave thousands of Arawak and Carib people. Columbus stationed a whole garrison of soldiers on the island and left many settlers there as well, hoping for better "luck" the second time around.

After sailing north and exploring the island we now call Cuba (which Columbus named "Juana," after one of Ferdinand and Isabella's daughters), Columbus went home to Spain.

The Guadeloupe Amazon parrot is now extinct, but would have been one of the parrot species seen by Columbus.

12. Giovanni Caboto (John Cabot)

This statue of John Cabot stands on Cape Bonavista in Newfoundland, Canada.

Giovanni Caboto was born in the same town as Columbus and in the same year, too. We don't know if they knew each other as children. Giovanni's family moved from Genoa when he was eleven years old and went to live in the city that was Genoa's rival: Venice. As a young man, Giovanni sailed with Venetian merchants down to Alexandria. (You'll remember that the Venetians were the only ones who could get near Muslim ports because they paid an annual tax to the Barbary pirates.) Once in Egypt, he then hitched a ride on a Muslim boat going down the Red Sea. He visited Mecca and got to see for himself all the spices and silks that were being imported into the Middle East from China and India, and he was very impressed.

Not long after Giovanni got home, he heard some amazing news — a Spanish ship had discovered large land masses out at the far end of the Atlantic Ocean! The navigator, Christopher Columbus, believed these islands were not far from India and China. But geography aside, these islands were filled with treasures and brand new spices. And as an added bonus, the natives of these islands were harmless and seemed willing to have Europeans move right in (so the story went).

Giovanni began thinking about geography. He knew the world was round and he knew where Europe was on the globe. (Remember, by now, navigators and mapmakers were experts at latitude. They used tools like the astroblabe, and knew exactly how far everything was from the equator. It was longitude that was more of a guess.)   Giovanni knew that Columbus had sailed far to the south, dipping far below the Tropic of Cancer, almost to the equator. He also knew that since the earth was a sphere, the longest way to go around the earth would be at the equator. Columbus had attempted to go around the earth by the longest path! Giovanni then had a brainstorm of an idea: why not take a shorter path around the globe? Why not sail north for a while, then go west, then go back south again? Perhaps the best way to get to India was to go over the top of the world.

Giovanni decided to actually try out his plan. He wanted to leave from a northern port city, so he moved to England, to the port city of Bristol. Once in England, he decided to use the English form of Giovanni: John. He also dropped the final "o" on his last name, making it Cabot. From that time on he was known as John Cabot, so we'll start calling him that.

The next step was to ask the king of England for ships. Now it just so happened that the king, Henry VII, was kicking himself for not jumping at the chance to sponsor Columbus. Columbus had asked Henry to sponsor him, but Henry had been just a few days too late in sending out a reply. Just think — it could have been England that had discovered all that new land, not Spain! So when John Cabot came knocking on Henry's door, telling him about a plan to get to India faster than the Spanish or the Portuguese could, Henry took him up on it immediately.

John Cabot's adopted home town.

John Cabot left England in May of 1497. He had just a tiny ship and a crew of only 18. He sailed up and over the North Atlantic, going south of the islands he already knew about, Iceland and Greenland. When he sighted land several weeks later, he knew he had found something new. It was a New Found Land. The exact spot he landed on is not known because longitude measurements were so inaccurate in those days. It could have been anywhere on the north eastern coast of Canada. Most historians, however, will say that he was probably the first European (since the Vikings) to discover the island we call Newfoundland.

Perhaps Cabot's expedition ran into icebergs in the North Atlantic. It is likely they at least saw them from afar. The drawing on the right is how one artist imagined the scene when Cabot landed, claiming the land for England.

John Cabot didn't find any gold there, just a bunch of rocks. He picked a few plant specimens and headed back to England. King Henry wasn't upset about Cabot's not finding gold. He was happy with the discovery of new land. He immediately began planning what England could do with new territory. He made Cabot an admiral and promised him five more ships the next time he went exploring.

In 1498 he left on his second voyage. He planned to explore beyond the New Found Land, hoping to discover a sea or river that would take him west, towards India and China. Sadly, John's entire expedition was lost at sea and was never heard from again. Some historians think that Spain or Portugal may have sent out warships to destroy Cabot's fleet, to stop them from finding a better way to the riches of the East. Spain and Portugal took the "spice war" very seriously, and in wars sometimes people get killed by the enemy.

Interestingly enough, Portugal sent a few expeditions north, just to scope things out. They found their way to Newfoundland in 1501. In true Portuguese style, they captured a bunch of natives and brought them back. Legend has it that one of those natives had in his possession a piece of Venetian jewelry that had belonged to someone in Cabot's crew! The Portuguese also landed on the continent just above Newfoundland, and named it "Terra Lavrador" after the official title of their leader, João Fernandes. The Portuguese word "lavrador" means "landowner." (At some point in time, mapmakers in Europe who did not speak Portuguese changed the "v" to a "b," turning it into Labrador.) Upon his return, Fernandes followed in Cabot's footsteps, turning his back on Portugal and offering his services to Henry VII of England. Henry funded another voyage for Fernandes, but that voyage was lost at sea and never heard from again.

John Cabot left behind a grown son, Sebastian, who would become a famous explorer, just like his father. Sebastian Cabot would continue his father's plan of finding a way to India and China by going north instead of south, but he would also end up going south as well, into what we call Brazil.

Sebastian Caobt followed in his father's footsteps and became a famous explorer.

Sebastian Cabot

13. Vasco da Gama

Portugal was determined to dominate the spice trade . There was a lot of money to be made if they could find a way to out-do the merchants of Venice and Genoa. The voyages sent out by Henry the Navigator, along with the discovery of the southern tip of Africa by Bartholomew Dias in 1488, had paved the way for the Portuguese to accomplish what they were now setting out to do. Bartholomew Dias had believed that if he had kept sailing he would have come to India eventually. Other people were doubtful about it, however. No one knew for sure exactly how big the Indian Ocean was. No matter what Dias said, it was possible that India was just a peninsula jutting into a land-locked Indian Sea, as shown on the Ptolemy world map that had been recently printed. If this was true, Portugal's plans would be in vain.

The journey of Dias in 1488

Ptolemy showed the Indian Ocean as a land-locked sea, completely surrounded by Africa.

Someone had to go and find out. Someone had to sail all the way around the tip of Africa and just keep going north until they bumped into Asia or India or whatever land mass was on the other side of Africa. The navigator who was chosen for this job was Vasco da Gama.

Vasco da Gama was only ten years old when Bartholomew Dias came back with his news about the southern tip of Africa. During his teen years he heard about the discoveries of Columbus and Cabot. He decided to become a sailor and by his early twenties he had made a reputation not only for being able to captain a ship but also for being able to squelch trouble. For the Portuguese government, de Gama was the right man for the job; they were confident he could deal with anything. He set sail in July of 1497 with four ships and 170 men, determined to sail to India by going around Africa.

Vasco de Gama

Like Dias, da Gama and his crew were among the first Europeans to cross the equator. Once they were south of the equator, they found that they could no longer see Polaris. This made navigation much more difficult. They relied mostly on charts and maps made by Dias, but they also found that there was a southern equivalent to Polaris, a constellation called The Southern Cross. Using the constellation was a lot more difficult than using the single point of Polaris, however, because no one star in the constellation was in exactly the right place. You had to draw imaginary lines between the stars to determine the exact point around which the other constellations revolved.

Half a year after they left Portugal, they finally found the south African cape that Bartholomew Dias had reached in 1488. But instead of turning around and going home like Dias had done, da Gama and his crew kept on going, sailing north along the eastern coast of Africa. They stopped at various places as they made their up the coast. Da Gama found that the eastern side of Africa had been under the influence of Islam for a long time. They found Islamic sultanates (political territories) almost as soon as they had rounded the bend and started north.

One of their first stops was in the area we know as Mozambique. Da Gama disguised himself as a Muslim and went to see the ruler there. Unfortunately, he found that the native custom in those parts dictated that he bring an expensive gift to the ruler. Da Gama hadn't thought to bring along riches from Europe to hand out to Muslim sultans. He tried to scrape up some little trinkets to give away (such as glass beads, copper bowls and tin bells—things that were perfect gifts for west African peoples), but they weren't enough to please the sultan. The sultan became suspicious of da Gama and told him to leave. Da Gama didn't take rejection well—his parting gift to the sultan was a bunch of cannon balls fired into the city as the ship left the harbor.

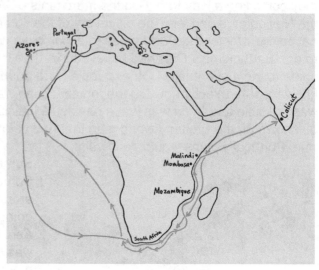

The next stop wasn't any better. When they got to what we now call Kenya (Mombasa and Malindi on this map), they were met with hostility everywhere they went. Finding that you couldn't get anywhere in this part of the world without having expenses gifts to give out, they decided to go and get some by capturing and looting unarmed Arab merchant vessels. A little further north they found a slightly friendlier reception and managed to find a navigator who could sail with them and show them how to get to India. They finally arrived in India almost a year after they had left Portugal. They landed at Calicut (not the same as Calcutta). Da Gama's main goal was to establish some kind of trading agreement with the ruler of Calicut. He got an agreement, but had to pull a fast move and leave without notice in order to avoid keeping his half of the bargain, which was to leave all the goods on his ship as collateral in case he didn't return. Da Gama left some sailors instead.

Da Gama's sudden departure meant that he had to cross the Indian Ocean at the worst time of the year. It had only taken 23 days to cross over the first time because he had been sailing with the monsoon winds. Going back, however, took 132 days! During this time, half his crew died and the other half were sick. In the end, only two of his four ships made it back to Portugal.

When da Gama got back to Portugal he was knighted by the king and made "Admiral of the Indian Seas," a title which came with many privileges and great wealth. He was also scheduled for a return trip—this time with a fleet of 20 warships. The Portuguese weren't going to take "no" as an answer from anyone. If they had to use force to get their spices, then so be it. Da Gama didn't wait for opposition, either. He engaged in quite a bit of piracy, raiding and looting numerous Arab merchant vessels. He once locked a wealthy Arab merchant inside his unarmed ship and set fire to it.

The Portuguese managed to conquer and colonize quite a few port cities along the east African coast. (Little wonder they were successful if you compare European and African military technology at that time.) They used these east African ports as pit stops and repair shops for ships going on to India to pick up spices. Once in India, they established trading centers by holding spice growers at gunpoint (or cannon point) until they agreed to trade with Portugal . Thus, in the end, Portugal did indeed achieve what they set out to accomplish. They dominated the spice trade and became big winners in the spice war. (Needless to say, the coming of the Europeans was not seen as a good thing by the Arabs, most of whom were Muslim. The behavior of the Portuguese gave the Muslims a legitimate reason to hate the so-called "Christians.")

Da Gama's commemorative tower on the cape of S. Africa.

As for da Gama, after he returned from his second voyage he stayed at home in Portugal for a while. He got married and had seven children. Years later, in 1524, the king requested that he return to India to "fix" some problems there (da Gama fixed problems using guns and cannons) and so he eventually made a third journey to India. It was on this voyage that he caught malaria in India and died on Christmas Eve of 1524.

European maps changed forever after da Gama's first journey. Ptolemy's map became a piece of ancient history, never again to be consulted by navigators.

14. Columbus's last voyages,
Amerigo Vespucci, and Juan de la Cosa

In 1498, Columbus made a third voyage to the Antilles. This time he ended up even further south, landing on the island of Trinidad, not too far from the mainland of South America. He then landed on the mainland and explored the coast of what we now call Venezuela. He went down the coast until he came across the huge river delta of the Amazon, but failed to realize what a good clue this was as to the size of the landmass he was standing on.

After this, he sailed north to visit Hispaniola again, to see how the Spanish colony was doing. It wasn't a pleasant visit. There was a lot of arguing and fighting, partly because everyone was so disappointed (and therefore a bit angry) at not finding enough gold. There was indeed some gold to be had, but not nearly the quantities of it they had hoped for. When a ship sailed back home and told Queen Isabella about all the unhappiness that was going on in the colony, she sent a man named Bobadilla to take Columbus' job as governor. When Bobadilla arrived, he sent Columbus home.

Vespucci appears as a detail in this Italian Renaissance painting.

In 1499, one of the ship captains from Columbus' first voyage, Juan de la Cosa (pilot of the *Santa Maria*), set sail with another Spanish captain, Alonso Hojeda. Also sailing with them was an Italian merchant named Amerigo Vespucci, an agent of the famous Medici family of Florence. He was probably going along to scope out any investment opportunities for the Medici, but in the course of the journey Vespucci discovered how much he loved astronomy and navigation— interests that would change his life. This expedition headed west to find out more about what lay beyond all the islands Columbus had discovered. Everyone still hoped that there might even be a way to get through all the islands and keep sailing all the way around the world.

They landed on the north coast of South America, probably near the mouth of the Amazon River. The size of this river delta was impressive, and Vespucci saw it as a clue to the landmass that lay behind it. Even a fairly large island could never contain the number of rivers it would take to create a delta region this large. Vespucci began to suspect that what they had discovered was not an island. They sailed along the coast for quite a while without finding any way to get around it, adding support to Vespucci's theory that they had discovered not an island but an entire continent. Vespucci took notes on many other details of the voyage: new plants and animals, new stars and constellations, and new races of people. The expedition covered the coastlines of the modern countries of Brazil, French Guyana, Suriname, Guyana, Venezuela and Columbia.

When Vespucci returned home, he wrote letters to Lorenzo Medici telling details of the trip, as well as his theory about having discovered an entirely new continent. He also began making plans to go back again, this time to discover the exact size and shape of this new continent.

When Juan de la Cosa got back home, he decided to make a map. He took all the information they had gathered on this journey, and put it together with everything he knew about all other voyages of discovery to the "New World," including that of John Cabot. In 1500, he created what was destined to

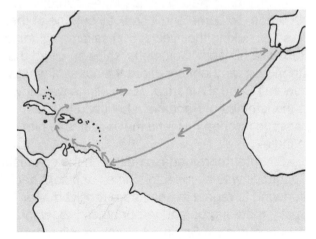

become a famous map. He painted it on a sheep skin, giving it a strangely-shaped outline. You can see where the sheep's head was, on the left.

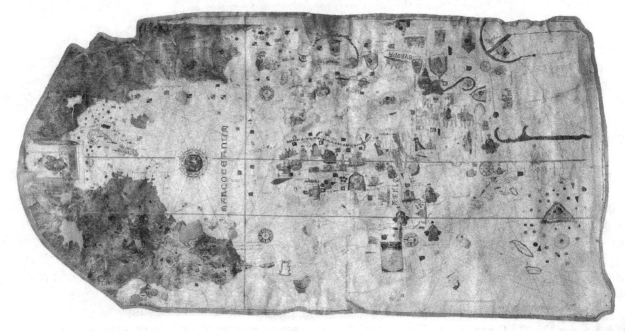

   This was the first map to show the all the discoveries made in the late 1400s, including those of Columbus, da Gama and Cabot. The shape of Africa isn't perfect, but it's a continent that can be sailed around. In fact, you can see little ships going up the east coast of Africa, all the way to India. It also clearly shows the New World as a continent with islands to the east of it. You will notice that this is a portolan chart made for sailors, with thin lines criss-crossing all over it. There are two horizontal lines marked, possibly representing the Tropic of Cancer and the equator, although they are a bit too far south. Since latitude could be determined fairly accurately by this time, these lines might represent something else. The green longitude line could be Juan's prime meridian, or it could mark the beginning of what Spain saw as "their" territory in the west. Spain and Portugal were already fighting about who owned what in the New World. In 1493 the pope (who was Spanish) had signed a law that gave Spain everything west of a certain line of longitude. Perhaps this green line shows how much of Brazil the Spaniards were willing to give to Portugal!
   Amazingly enough, even after that disastrous third voyage, Columbus made a fourth, and final, voyage. When he got to Hispaniola, no one was pleased to see him. Bobadilla wouldn't let him come on shore even though Columbus told him there was a hurricane on the way. Bobadilla scoffed at any advice from Columbus and went ahead and launched 30 ships to take gold back to Spain. Columbus anchored his ships in the harbor. The hurricane did come and it sank all but one of the 30 ships, taking the lives of 500 sailors, including Bobadilla himself. Columbus' ships survived the storm and went on to explore the coast of what we now call Central America, going all the way down to the isthmus of Panama. He hoped to find a passage through this land that would take him on to India.

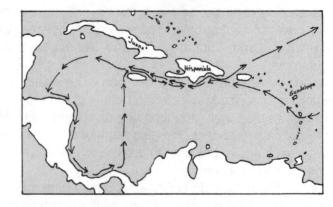

   After more unhappiness with the colonists, Columbus was accused of crimes and sent back to Spain as a prisoner. He lived out the rest of his life trying to regain the honor he received after his first voyage. When he died, his body was buried in Spain, then dug up and re-buried on Hispaniola, then dug up and re-buried in Cuba, then dug up and re-buried back in Spain. He kept traveling even after he died!

15. The New World Becomes "America"

After Vasco da Gama proved that it was possible to sail from Portugal to India by going around Africa, this route became a major "highway" for Portuguese ships. One of the first follow-up voyages after da Gama was a voyage headed up by a man named Pedro Cabral. In March of the year 1500, he took 13 ships and 1500 men (one of whom was Bartholomew Dias) and headed for India.

A Cuban stamp honoring Cabral.

On the first leg of the voyage, going around the western part of Africa, they wanted to make sure they steered clear of all the troubled waters around the capes (the very ones that had made sailors before the days of Henry the Navigator think that they were coming to the end of world and were being warned to turn around). In fact, they steered so far away from the African capes (and with some additional help from bad weather) that they hit land far to the west of Africa, accidentally discovering the existence of what we now call Brazil. They explored the coast of Brazil for about two weeks, claimed the land for Portugal, then decided to get back on track and continue their journey to India.

When they rounded the bend at South Africa they encountered terrible storms and lost four of their ships, including the one on which Bartholomew Dias was sailing. As they went up towards Mozambique, there was another storm and one of their ships got blown over the island we now call Madagascar—accidental discovery number two! At least some of the ships actually made it to India. They managed to do what they came to do (load their ships full of expensive spices) then they left the harbor in typical Portuguese fashion, with a round of cannon balls fired back at the city.

The Portuguese felt that they owned the sea route around Africa. Any European competitors would face an attack by Portuguese war ships. The Portuguese also claimed chunks of land on the east coast of Africa as well as some islands in the Indian Ocean. But his wasn't enough. They felt they had the resources to control not only these territories, but expand to the west, as well, claiming territory in the New World. The key resource that allowed Portugal to be so dominant was their superior ship building technology. The legacy of Henry the Navigator was still with them.

It was perhaps the superior vessels of the Portuguese that caused Amerigo Vespucci to decline an offer from the Spanish king to sponsor a return voyage to the New World. Vespucci chose instead to sail under the Portuguese flag, and with three of the best and fastest ships in the world at his command, Vespucci set off in 1501 to find out more about the new continent he had discovered. Before heading out into the Atlantic, Vespucci sailed down the coast of Africa. When he stopped at Cape Verde to take on fresh supplies, who should he meet but two of Cabral's ships, limping back from their voyage to India! After catching up on the latest news from India, Vespucci headed west.

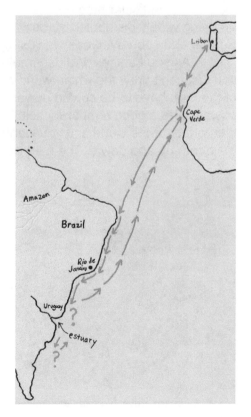

Vespucci's ships landed on the coast of Brazil and began to make their way south. They sailed all the way around Brazil, down to where the modern city of Rio de Janeiro is. Vespucci's journal clearly describes the bay at Rio de Janeiro, then goes on to say that they went further south where the weather began to turn cold and stormy. We don't know exactly how far south Vespucci went. His journal doesn't mention the huge estuary beneath the area we call Uruguay, yet it clearly describes weather typical of the southern tip of South America. (An estuary is an enclosed body of water on a coastline that has one or more rivers flowing into it. The name comes from the Latin word "aestus" meaning tide. An estuary has a free and open connection to the ocean so that it is affected by tides. The main part of an estuary is salt water but it is likely to have areas of fresh water around the edges, where the rivers are flowing into it.) Estuaries would have been of particular interest to Vespucci since they give clues to what the land is like far away from the coast. Modern scientists are even more intestested in estuaries than Vespucci was because here you find very specialized ecological "niches" where unusual plants and animals live.

When Vespucci got back home from this expedition, once again he wrote letters to Lorenzo Medici in Florence (Italy) describing all of the amazing new things he had discovered. After Lorenzo died, these letters ended up in the hands of the lawyers and scholars of Florence. These men were so excited about the information these letters contained that they decided everyone in Florence should read them. They had the content of the letters set in type and printed on a printing press. Some modern historians believe that in the process of getting the letters ready for publication, someone adapted them a bit, adding things that were not in the original letters or exaggerating the details a bit.

Soon copies of these letters made their way out of Florence, all the way north to Germany.

A mapmaker named Martin Waldseemüller read these letters and in 1507 decided to make a world map that would include these new lands. He had to put a name on them, so he chose to name them after the man who wrote the letters about them: Amerigo Vespucci. Waldseemüller adapted Amerigo's name and wrote "America" on the map. This particular map ended up being widely distributed across Europe and soon everyone was using the term "America."

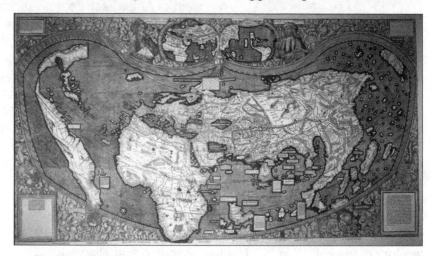
The Waldseemüller map of 1507 was the first to name "America."

As you can see, Waldseemüller was dealing with the same problem that Ptolemy wrote about: you just can't draw the whole world on a flat page. Since the world is actually a sphere, the edges of the map have to be curved upward so that the shapes don't get too distorted. Curving the map upward was a good temporary solution, but what would happen when more discoveries were made at the bottom of the world and you wanted to include those on your map, as well? You can't curve the map both up and down! The man who would come up with the best possible solution to this problem wouldn't be born until 1512, five years after the Waldseemüller map was printed.

The map shown here at the left was also printed in 1507. It's an updated version of Ptolemy's old map. (People just didn't want to give him up, did they?!) The New World has been added, as well as the sea route to India. The shape of the map might remind you of an ice cream cone that has been slit down the side and opened up. Using a cone shape is one way you can create a map of the world.

Johannes Ruysch printed this map in 1507.

16. Zheng He

Before we go on with more European exploration, we need to stop and backtrack just a bit. Let's find out about exploring and mapping that was going on in Asia between the years 1300 and 1500.

Ghengis Khan

During the days of Marco Polo and Ibn Battuta, the Mongol Empire reached its peak, stretching from China and Korea in the east, to Turkey and the border of Poland in the west. It was the largest empire in history, larger than the Roman Empire. The Mongols came from the area north of China, modern day Mongolia. Their leader, Ghengis Khan, founded the empire in 1206. His success was based on state-of-the-art military technology of that day (including trebuchets and catapults), skillful archers, a highly organized army, and a policy that tolerated the customs and religions of the people he conquered. It is likely that Ghengis Khan had some kind of maps to help him organize his empire, but none have survived, so we can only guess what they may have been like.

Within China, the Mongol Empire was called the Yuan Dynasty. Maybe the Mongols hoped that the Chinese would accept it as just another Chinese dynasty. (Interestingly enough, the Mongols were profoundly affected by the Chinese culture and found themselves becoming more and more Chinese as time went on.) It was during this Yuan Dynasty of Mongol rule that Marco Polo visited China.

Since the Mongols were tolerant of all religions, their empire included Buddhists, Christians, Jews, and Muslims. Islam was the dominant religion in most of southern and western China. Many of the Muslims living there were descendants of Arabs, Turks or Persians who had come to China as merchants or missionaries, and some of them had originally been

The Mongol Empire is yellow. The orange areas are Hui Chinese. The Hui were part of the Mongol Empire.

Christian (the Nestorian branch of the church) and later converted to Islam. These Muslims living in China became known as "Hui Chinese" and they are still known by that name today. Eventually the Mongol Empire started to fall apart, as all large empires are destined to do. The Khans became weaker and the people groups they ruled became stronger. The Chinese, in particular, wanted their country back. In 1370 the Chinese succeeded in defeating the Mongols and established their Ming Dynasty.

Just one year after the Ming Dynasty began, Zheng He was born in southern China. His great-grandparents had come to China from Uzbekistan, so he was Hui Chinese. As a boy he was captured during a Mongol revolt and taken prisoner by the Chinese army. Just like in the Biblical story of Daniel, Zheng He was taken to the royal capital, not to be tortured or killed but to be educated and trained to be an important government official. Zheng He grew to be an intelligent and capable young man and served the Chinese emperor very well. He was eventually made the admiral of a fleet of

A Chinese treasure ship compared to a European ship.

very large ships—perhaps the largest wooden ships ever built in the history of the world. Marco Polo and Ibn Battuta both wrote about Chinese "treasure ships" that had nine masts and were five times as long as European ships of their day, requiring a crew of 500 to 1,000 men. European scholars have been slow to acknowledge these accounts as being accurate, because of the unbelievable size described. But there are several written accounts of these boats and they all say the same thing. Apparently the ships really were this big!

Zheng He took a large number of these treasure ships across the Indian Ocean to Africa, India and Arabia. He traded Chinese luxury items such as silk, porcelain and gold for exotic animals such as zebras, camels, ostriches and giraffes. The goal of the Chinese emperor wasn't just trade. He wanted to show off Chinese military power, particularly naval power, so that no one would challenge them for control of the Indian Ocean and all the waterways in and around Indonesia. Zheng He was told to "walk like a tiger." He was to silently go about the oceans as long as he was not challeged, but if someone dared to challenge him, he was to react swiftly and lethally.

Another mission that Zheng He used his ships for was to transport entire communities of Hui Chinese to locations further south, even as far south as the tip of the Malay Peninsula and the Island of Sumatra. No one knows if this was to spread Islam, or just to give the Hui more land. Zheng He was known to participate in Buddhist rituals as well as Muslim. He was probably most interested in the economic success of his people, and perhaps he understood that being on the Malay peninsula would give them the opportunity to participate in the lucrative (money-making) spice trade. They established a city called Malacca (or Melaka), which became the most popular trading center in the east. Malacca had a superb location—it was right on the edge of a strait. It was like being the only road stop on a major highway. Arabs and Indians would come from the west and Chinese and Japanese would come from the east and they would meet halfway at Malacca and exhange their goods. (What do you think will happen when the Europeans find out about Malacca?)

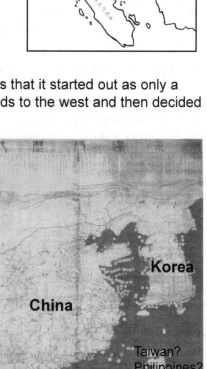

The only map surviving from this time period is dated 1402. It was made before Zheng He's travels. It is very likely that Zheng He used this map to navigate around the coastline of China. As you can see, it's not what we would consider very accurate. Where are India and the Malay peninsula? Historians think what may have happened is that it started out as only a map of China. The mapmaker may have heard about strange new lands to the west and then decided to update his map and simply add them onto China.

Below is a sea chart made by Zheng He. The words tell compass directions, depth of water, sailing times, astronomical calculations, and notes about currents and wind speeds. It was printed and published in 1621.

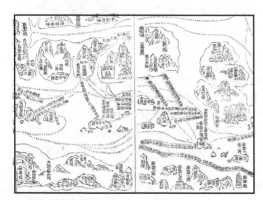

This sea chart was taken from the following webpage: http://en.wikipedia.org/wiki/File:Zhenghe-sailing-chart.gif

Zheng He might have used this map to mavigate around his part of the world.

17. Portugal Finds Malacca and the Spice Islands

Portugal dominated the spice trade in Europe by the early 1500s. Venice and Genoa could sail no farther than the eastern side of the Mediterranean Sea. Portugal was now going all the way to India. The Indian merchants were selling spices grown in India but they were also selling spices they had imported from a location even farther east, a place called Malacca. When the Portuguese found out about Malacca, they immediately started making plans to attack and capture it. Their ultimate goal was to control the spices right at their source, without any "middle man" between them and the spice farmers.

Unfortunately for the Hui Chinese living in Malacca, the Chinese government had changed its foreign policy right after Zheng He's death in 1434. The Ming emperor wanted China to decrease its contact with other countries. Perhaps they thought that if they ignored the world, it would go away and leave them alone. So the Chinese let their navy dwindle and gave up on controlling the waterways.

In 1509 the Portuguese came sailing into the Strait of Malacca. When they attacked the city, they found the Malaccans to be stronger and better prepared than they had anticipated. This first attempt at conquering Malacca failed and many Portuguese sailors were taken prisoner by the sultan of Malacca. The Portuguese retreated and spent two years planning their next attack. In 1511, they made a second attempt, this time sailing in with a fleet of at least 14 ships and somewhere around 1,000 men. (If you read different accounts of this battle you will find that each account will

Magellan doesn't look much like a fighter in this portrait.

give different numbers of ships and men. Some say 14 ships, others say as many as 18. Some say 900 men, others say as many as 1,200.) One of these Portuguese soldiers was a man named Ferdinand Magellan, a member of the Portuguese nobility who was out to seek adventure and fortune. He was a brave fighter, and a determined man. With enough men like Magellan, and with the advantage of European cannons, the Portuguese were able to capture Malacca. The sultan fled, crossing the Strait of Malacca, and found refuge on the island of Sumatra. (The sultan would have been pleased to know that the Portuguese ship carrying all the plunder they had stolen from Malacca ended up sinking in the Indian Ocean!) Over the next two decades, armies from Sumatra would besiege the Portuguese settlement at Malacca, trying to get it back, but they would never succeed.

Once the Portuguese were established at Malacca, they learned that Malacca wasn't actually producing all the spices it sold. The ultimate source for spices lay even farther to the east! They still had many miles to go if they wanted to reach the legendary Spice Islands. They immediately sent a small fleet out to the east to search for these islands. The fleet returned with the news that they had discovered a small archipelago called the Banda Islands, which did indeed contain many spices. But natives of Banda had told them that even larger spice islands lay to the north. One of these islands was said to be the only place in the entire world where nutmeg grew. These northern islands were known by their Arabic name, "the Moluccas," meaning "the land of many kings." The Arabs were used to sultans who ruled large territories. In these islands, each little island has its own king. (Don't confuse Malacca with the Moluccas. It's unfortunate that these words are so similar, but that's the way it is. Perhaps it would help to pronounce each "a" in Malacca like the "a" in "ax," making the two words sound as different as possible.)

Nutmeg— a spice to die for?!

Magellan may or may not have been on this exploratory journey to the Bandas. We don't have historical records accurate enough to determine this fact. We can be certain, however, that Magellan knew about the discovery, and this knowledge would shape the rest of his life. He would take this

One of the Banda Islands, by an artist in 1724

knowledge back to Europe and present a plan to the King of Portugal, then to the King of Spain, to find the Spice Islands by travelling west.

With a fort established at Malacca, and a fleet of warships in the harbor, the Portuguese were able to control the shipping traffic going through the Strait of Malacca, which was the major "highway" for spice merchants. The Portuguese could stop Arab and Indian ships from getting to the Spice Islands, forcing them to buy the spices at Malacca at prices determined by the Portuguese. This disruption of the Arab and Indian spice routes was yet another way to prevent any competition back in Europe, since merchants such as the Venetians and Genoese depended on the Arabs and the Indians to bring spices into Mediterranean ports.

While in Malacca, Magellan bought a slave, a 13-year-old boy who had come from the island of Sumatra, just below Malacca. Magellan named him Enrique ("*En-ree-kay*") although he was often called "Black Henry" by the other sailors, since his skin was so much darker than theirs. Enrique learned to speak Spanish and Portuguese and traveled with Magellan everywhere he went. He would eventually become Magellan's closest companion. Magellan wrote in his will that after he (Magellan) died, Enrique was to be given not only his freedom, but a large sum of money as well.

Magellan spent seven years in, or near, the Malay peninsula, then he went to Morocco (with Enrique by his side) to fight the Moors. While in Africa, two important events happened to Magellan. The first was that he was severely wounded in his left knee, causing him to limp for the rest of his life. The second was that he was accused of striking bargains with the Moors behind the backs of the Portuguese. He denied that he had done anything wrong and went back to Portugal to explain his side of the story to the king. At the royal court, the other nobles had already decided what they wanted to believe about the case, and they made sure that Magellan was shut out of all their social circles. The last straw was when the king publicly humiliated Magellan. From that day on, Magellan no longer considered himself Portuguese. He packed his bags and moved to Spain, taking Enrique with him.

Meanwhile, the Portuguese fleet in the east continued to look for the Molucca Islands. In 1512, Captain Francisco Serrão ("*Sare-ow*") landed on the southernmost Moluccan island: Ambon. He was able to establish diplomatic ties with the ruler of the island. Then he went north and finished discovering the rest of the Moluccas. Right off the coast of the biggest island were two tiny islands called Ternate and Tidore. These two islands were often at war with each other. Serrão decided to take advantage of this conflict and join one side, choosing to side with Ternate. The ruler of Ternate was happy to have Portuguese help in defeating his enemy on Tidore. Thus, the Portuguese were able to establish a fort on Ternate.

Just wait until Spain finds out that Portugal has discovered the Spice Islands and taken control of some of them! Will Spain give up the Spice War?

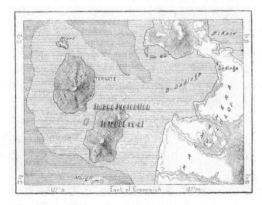

Ternate and Tidore are volcanic islands. As you can see, they are not much more than a volcano sticking out of the water. They are active volcanoes even to this day.

18. Magellan and Elcano

Even though Portugal now owned the spice trade, Spain was not willing to give up yet. The spice war was still as hot as ever. Spain knew that the only way to stay in the game was to keep trying to go east. Then along came Magellan (with faithful Enrique at his side). Magellan presented himself to the king of Spain, Charles V (who was also the Holy Roman Emperor at that time) with a proposal for a voyage to find a western route to the Spice Islands. As an added incentive, Magellan told the king that he believed the Spice Islands to be on the Spanish side of the "line of demarcation" drawn by the pope in 1494 (the Treaty of Tordesillas) dividing up the world between Spain and Portugal. That line theoretically went all the way around the world, cutting the globe in half. On the far side of the world, that line would be pretty close to where the Spice Islands were. Magellan believed that the Spice Islands were on Spain's side of the line. (Actually, Magellan was off in his calculations and the Spice Islands were still on the side of the world claimed by Portugal, but there was no way for anyone to prove him wrong since calculations of longitude (east-west distances) were just rough guesses, and could not be measured accurately.) He told the Spanish king that the islands were already his and all they needed to do was go and find them.

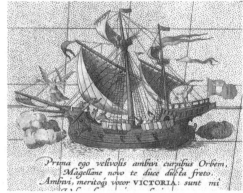

The ship Magellan sailed on—the Victoria

The king was quite happy to sponsor Magellan. However, the Spanish nobles distrusted Magellan because he was Portuguese, and insisted that all the officers who went along with him would be Spanish. Charles granted Magellan five ships and over 200 men for the crew. The crew was quite international, with sailors from Spain, Portugal, England, France, Italy, Germany, Africa and Malaysia. (Enrique was the Malaysian.)

Magellan and his five ships set sail in 1519. The king of Portugal heard about the voyage and sent some warships out to try to stop him. Magellan evaded the war ships, however, and arrived safely at the customary Atlantic pit stop, the Canary Islands. He then headed for the coast of Brazil, which all the sailors believed to be their destination. Magellan had kept the voyage's true destination a secret, even from his other captains. He knew that most sailors would not volunteer to go on a voyage into the unknown. But when Magellan ordered the ships to turn south and head down the coast of South America they knew something was up. It didn't take the other captains long to realize exactly what this mission was about: finding a passage around South America and then on to India. And they didn't like it one bit.

Magellan kept the fleet sailing south, looking for any inlet that might be a passage through to the ocean on the other side. The huge estuary at the Plata River fooled him. It was so large that by the time Magellan realized they were heading into a river, they had already spent several weeks sailing into it and would have to spend several more weeks sailing back out of it. The disappointment was immense. The captains of the other ships wanted to turn around and go home. When Magellan directed them to press on southward, they rebelled. One of them even began plotting assassination. Magellan had to take drastic measures. He managed to get one captain to change his mind, and the others he executed or marooned. With the trouble-makers dispatched, the voyage went on.

The weather was increasingly bad as they journeyed farther and farther south. Magellan was always watching for any inlet that might turn out to be a passage. The only clue Magellan used to tell him whether a waterway was likely to be a true passage, or simply a river going into the interior of the continent, was whether the water was salty. If the water became fresher as they sailed into it, then it was not a passage to the ocean on the other side.

After months of sailing, winter began setting in. They would have to find a spot where they could "winter over" until the weather became warm enough to sail once again. The coast was cold and rocky, not a very fun place to spend seven months. Magellan named this coast "Patagonia" because the natives apparently wore shoes that looked like animal paws. The crew called it "the land of the giants." They had seen some native Patagonians and they seemed very tall. Their actual height was only about six feet, but since the average Spaniard during that century was only a bit over five feet tall, the Patagonians seemed like giants. While they were waiting out the winter in Patagonia, one of their ships was dashed to pieces on the rocks.

Spring finally came, and they set sail again. Magellan soon discovered a water passageway that tasted salty. This was the strait that was to be named after him: the Magellan Strait. It cut through the bottom tip of South America. This strait was very long and narrow and full of twists and turns that were dangerous for large sailing ships. There was no guarantee that they would ever make it to the other side. One captain finally decided that he had had enough. He made his ship lag behind to get out of sight of Magellan, then he headed back to Spain. Unfortunately, this was the ship that had been carrying all the supplies Magellan had packed for the rest of the journey! Magellan kept going, though, and eventually found his way out to the ocean again. After all they had been through, the ocean on the other side seemed so calm that Magellan named it "Pacific," meaning "peaceful."

Heading northwest, they sailed for months with no sight of land. Many sailors died of scurvy (lack of vitamin C) or starvation. They ate the ship's rats along with pieces of fabric and wood. Finally, the lucky survivors sighted land. They had found the archipelago we now call the Philippines. They knew these were not the famous Spice Islands but they were grateful to be on land once again. Magellan claimed the islands for Spain (of course) and made contact with the tribal chief, Humabon, using Enrique as his interpreter. He told Humabon that he must convert to Christianity and submit to Spanish rule. Seeing the Spanish cannons in action, Humabon agreed—but on the condition that the Spanish would favor him over other tribal chiefs. Magellan agreed to this bad foreign policy and struck the bargain. Not long after, Humabon asked Magellan to help him attack one of the neighboring tribes. Magellan brought his ships into the bay without realizing it was low tide. The ships could not get close enough to the shore to be within firing range. Magellan would not be able to rely on cannons and crossbows to back up his ground force. The neighbor-chief, Lapu-Lapu, was ready for Magellan, with an army of 1,000 men. Magellan and his crew didn't stand a chance. Magellan was chopped to pieces (literally) as he was wading to shore. The Spanish crew fled and returned to the safety of their ships. The man who took Magellan's place as commanding captain was Juan Sebastian Elcano. It would be Elcano who would finish the journey around the world.

According to Magellan's will, his slave Enrique was now free. However, Magellan had a relative among the crew who told Enrique that he would not set him free. He ordered Enrique to speak to Humabon. Enrique did so, and as a result the Spanish crew was invited to a feast. The Spaniards walked right into the trap. The natives ended the feast by turning on the Spaniards and killing as many as they could. Enrique escaped and was never seen again.

There were not enough crew left to sail the three remaining ships, so they left one behind. The two remaining ships found their way to the Spice Islands, the Moluccas. Then one of the ships sprang a leak. The captain of the leaky ship told Elcano he'd just go back the way they had come after the repairs were complete. Elcano would keep going west and complete the trip around the world.

When Elcano finally made it back to Spain, there were only 18 men left from the original crew of 270. (The leaky ship never made it home. It was captured by the Portuguese.) In Spain, Elcano is the hero who gets credit for being the first person to circumnavigate the world. In truth, the first person to go all the way around the globe was probably Enrique, who would have arrived back home on Sumatra long before Elcano got back to Spain.

19. A Forgotten Navigator and a Forgotten Map

Have you ever heard of Giovanni da Verrazzano? Very few people have, yet he was the first European to set foot on the part of North America that eventually became North Carolina, Virginia, New York, and Massachusetts. Why is he so unknown? Nobody knows! Verrazzano was born near Florence, Italy, in 1485. As a young adult, he moved to the northern part of France and became a navigator for ships sailing in the Mediterranean Sea. Very little else is known about his life before his famous (or not-so-famous) voyage to America.

Right about this time, the king of France decided that he'd like to get into the Spice Wars, too. There might yet be an undiscovered route to the Spice Islands—a passage to the north and west of Europe. It was true that the English were out looking for it, too, but perhaps the French could beat them to it. So King Francis I went out looking for a navigator he could hire to look for what would become known as the Northwest Passage. Verrazzano was recommended to Francis for this job.

In 1524, Francis launched Verrazzano on a journey to North America, to explore the area of land no European had yet been to: the area between Florida and Newfoundland. The Spanish were actively taking possession of Florida and the English and Portuguese had been to Newfoundland (and perhaps to the area of Nova Scotia, as well). There was a vast section of land between those places. There wasn't any reason why the passage through the continent couldn't be in this area. And there was only one way to find out.

Verrazzano landed at what we now call Cape Fear, North Carolina. Cape Fear got its name much later, in 1585, when English explorers ran into the dangerous shoals in front of the cape. (A cape is a piece of land with water on three sides. A shoal is a very shallow place where ships can easily get stuck.)

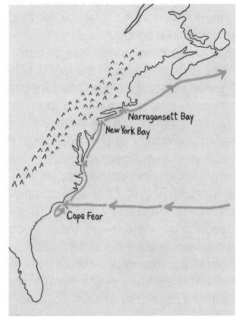

Next, Verrazzano sailed north and discovered a huge lagoon, the largest one on the eastern coast of the United States. (Lagoons are shallow places that are separated from the ocean by a long line of sandbanks or coral reefs. Lagoons don't have to be tropical.) This lagoon was so large that Verrazzano wondered if he had discovered the Pacific Ocean. Going farther north, Verrazzano discovered what we call the Chesapeake Bay and the Delaware River. Somewhere along these shores he made contact with the Native Americans. As far as we know, his meetings with the natives were peaceful. He wrote a long letter to Francis describing in detail what the natives were like, as well as information about the plants and animals found along the coast. Verrazzano knew Francis was an avid hunter and told him about the great abundance of deer in these places. Verrazzano continued north and saw the places we call New York Bay, the Hudson River, Long Island, Narragansett Bay, Maine, and Nova Scotia. After going past Newfoundland he headed back to France.

Even though Verrazzano was the first to see so much of North America, many people have never heard of him. He does have some bridges in America named after him, though. The Verrazzano-Narrows Bridge connects Staten Island to Brooklyn in New York Harbor, and the Verrazzano Bridge in Maryland connects Assateague Island to the mainland.

Now that we've learned about a "forgotten" navigator, let's take a look at a forgotten map. This map was lost for over 400 years! It was discovered in 1929 in Istanbul, Turkey, in an old palace that was being cleaned out to be converted to a museum. When the museum curators read the Arabic inscriptions on the map, they were stunned to find out that the map was from the year 1513 and that the mapmaker, a Turkish admiral of the Ottoman navy named Piri Ries, claimed to have used maps drawn by Columbus for his information about the shape of the coastline of the Americas. Since there are no known maps by Columbus that match this one, it then became obvious that Columbus had made more maps than anyone had previously thought. The existence of "lost maps of Columbus" excited the imagination of cartographers everywhere. They hoped that possibly these maps would show up someday. Alas, they never have.

This map has become famous for several reasons. The first is obvious—it was lost for 400 years. The second is that this is the first map in history to show the coastline of South America lined up correctly with the coastline of Africa. In other words, the lines of latitude are consistent across the map. The third is that it brought to light the lost maps of Columbus.

The last reason is that it has created controversy among scholars because of Charles Hapgood's theory (published in 1966) that the coastline on the bottom edge of the map shows Antarctica. Most map experts believe that the bottom coastline is either the bottom edge of South America, curled up to fit on the parchment, or else it is a representation of what medieval and Renaissance mapmakers called Terra Australis Incognito, or "Unknown Southern Land." You'll remember that medieval sailors had tales of a land called Antilles out in the western ocean. They knew, or guessed, that there was something out there long before the Americas were discovered. In the same way, scholars as far back as ancient Greece seemed to have believed that there was a large land mass on the bottom of the world. The Greeks, masters of logic, said that there <u>had</u> to be a land mass down there, in order to balance out the land on the top half of the world. The navigators of the Renaissance era perhaps picked this up from the Greeks and developed the idea so thoroughly that it became common practice to show this Terra Australis Incognita on world maps, even though no one knew for sure if it even existed. This modern controversial scholar believed that Piri Ries was using information gathered from very ancient sources that told of actual voyages made to Antarctica thousands of years ago. No records of such ancient voyages exist, however.

Look carefully at the map. What do you think the bottom coastline represents? How accurate is the representation of the Caribbean and its islands? Can you find the Lesser Antilles?

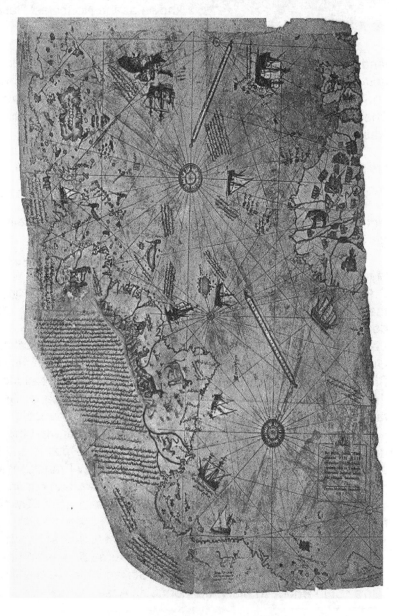

20. Jacques Cartier

A portrait of Cartier painted in 1844

Upon Verrazzano's successful return from America, the king of France, Francis I, decided it was worthwhile to send out at least one more expedition to do further exploration of this part of America. The main goal, of course, was still to find a way to break into the spice market by finding a passage through the continent that led to the Pacific Ocean (and the Spice Islands) on the other side. Francis chose a navigator who had probably been on Verrazzano's voyage. Unlike Verrazzano, this navigator would not be forgotten. His name was Jacques Cartier (*Car-teey-ay*) and he was the first in a long line of French explorers who would explore the land we now call the country of Canada.

Cartier left France in 1534 and landed somewhere in northern Newfoundland. He then sailed through the strait right above Newfoundland (Belle Isle Strait), and down into what we call the Gulf of St. Lawrence. Here he discovered a tiny island covered with birds. On this island the crew re-stocked their meat supply by killing about 1,000 great auks. Sadly, these large, penguin-like birds would become extinct by the 1800s. Today this island is a bird sanctuary and a primary nesting site for many species of sea birds.

Cartier and his crew landed at several places in the Gulf of St. Lawrence and briefly met with representatives of a native tribe called the Micmacs. The Micmacs indicated that they were interested in trading and brought animal skins to trade for iron tools. At another stop farther south, Cartier met the inhabitants of a village called Stadacona. The chief was named Donnacona and he had two sons named Domagaya and Taignoagny (just pronounce all the letters). The natives watched as Cartier planted a large cross on the shore bearing the words, "Long Live the King of France." It is unknown how much of this ceremony the natives understood, but certainly they had suspicions that something was up. Willing to trust the Europeans, however, the natives obliged when invited to come on board the ship. While on the ship, Domagaya and Taignoagny were held against their will and told they must agree to visit France.

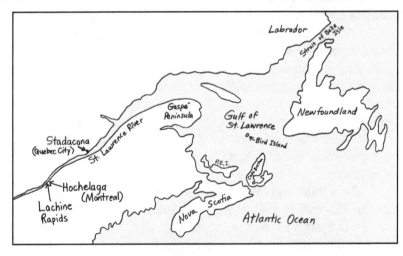

Cartier promised the chief that his two sons would return safely the following year. Chief Donnacona grudgingly agreed, but no doubt he suspected he would never see them again. Cartier then sailed back to France. Can you imagine what it would have been like for those two young men—going from a "Stone Age" culture into the height of the European Renaissance?!

Cartier kept his promise to Donnacona and the following year he sailed again, taking the two young men home to their father. The information they brought back to their village would have seemed almost unbelievable. Certainly Chief Donnacona was given a glimpse of the future—one that did not bode well for his people. The Europeans far outnumbered them and had military forces and weapons that were beyond their comprehension. During this second voyage Cartier and his crew spent the winter with the natives. (The Europeans were shocked to see the natives wearing nothing but leggings and a loin cloth, even in the dead of winter.) Cartier had plenty of time to draw maps of the area. He asked Donnacona what the name of the place was called and Donnacona said

"Canada." Cartier wrote the word "Canada" on his map.

Donnacona offered to take Cartier to a larger town that was down the river a bit. Cartier was eager to learn more about this new land and gladly accepted the offer. This larger town was called Hochelaga and, indeed, it was much larger than Donnacona's village. Over a thousand Iroquois came to the river bank to see the light-skinned strangers. Cartier could sail no farther than this town because the river turned into rapids at this point. Amazingly enough, Cartier still thought that this river was part of a passage that would eventually lead to the

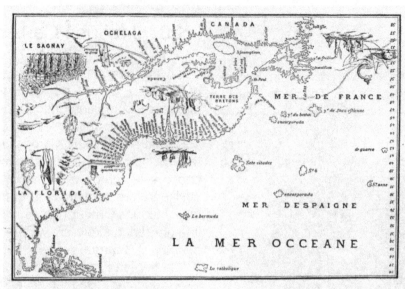

THE "DAUPHIN MAP" OF CANADA, CIRCA 1543, SHOWING CARTIER'S DISCOVERIES

Pacific Ocean and to China. Even though he had to turn around, that spot in the river was named La Chine, the French word for China. Today the town of Lachine is part of the city of Montreal. Nearby, the Jacques Cartier Bridge stretches across the St. Lawrence River.

During the long winter, both Europeans and natives began to come down with scurvy. Fortunately, Domagaya, one of the chief's sons, discovered a remedy that saved many lives. He knew of a certain tree (which scientists now believe was the *arbor vitae*, a bush-like tree commonly planted in yards all over North America) from which a brew could be made, one that would cure scurvy. Because of this help from Domagaya, the majority of the Frenchmen survived the winter.

When spring came and it was time to go back to France, Cartier managed to persuade Chief Donnacona to go with him. Other Iroquois went as well. The natives were treated well in France and Chief Donnacona was asked to speak to the king and tell him the Iroquois legend of a land farther to the north that contained gold and precious gemstones. Donnacona was unwittingly sealing the fate of his people. These tales made the French even more determined to press on into Canada and some day colonize it. Sadly, none of the visiting Iroquois lived long enough to return to their native land; they all died of European diseases. When Cartier returned to Canada for a third voyage (in 1541), he told the natives that their Iroquois friends were having such a good time in Europe that they had decided not to return.

This third and last trip to Canada was bittersweet for Cartier, as he had been replaced as captain. Captain Roberval was taking Cartier along as a guide and advisor. On this voyage, Roberval planned to start a French colony in Canada. Upon reaching Iroquois territory, the French built a fort, released the cattle they had brought over, and planted gardens of cabbage, turnips and lettuce. As they investigated their surroundings more thoroughly, they discovered mineral deposits containing what appeared to be diamonds. Even more surprising was the discovery of what appeared to be gold! They began gathering these rocks as fast as they could and loading them onto one of the ships. Perhaps France, not Spain, would be the lucky country that found the riches of the New World! At the very time Cartier and his men were gathering these minerals, the Spanish were systematically killing and conquering the natives of Central America in vain hopes of discovering the ultimate source of gold.

When Cartier's shipment of "diamonds and gold" reached France, the gemstone experts identified these minerals as quartz crystals and "fool's gold" (iron pyrite). A new figure of speech entered the French language as a result of this incident: "As false as Canadian diamonds."

Cartier's exploring came to an end after this voyage. He lived out the rest of his life on his estate in the town of Saint-Malo, occasionally offering his services as an interpreter.

21. Spain Explores the West Coast of America

While Cartier and his entourage were exploring the Gulf of St. Lawrence, Spanish explorers were busy conquering and exploiting the people and the natural resources of Central America. They were known as "Conquistadors" fighting for the honor of their religion and their country, both of which they believed would be helped out considerably by the discovery of vast amounts of gold. It is beyond the scope of this curriculum to go into the atrocities committed by the Spaniards during this era. Men such as Balboa, Alvarado and Cortés were honored in their day by their fellow Spaniards, but today we see them as villains. They destroyed civilizations that had existed for thousands of years. Much of the destruction was deliberate, but some was accidental. The Spaniards unknowingly brought European diseases to Central America. Countless numbers of native Americans died of smallpox. If you are interested in the details of the conquest of Central America, you can read more on your own. Our interest in this lesson is in what the Spaniards learned about the shape of North America and how this knowledge helped mapmakers to improve their maps of the world.

Cortés as a young man

Cortés didn't just stay on the coasts of Central America, as most previous explorers had done; he went deep inland. His mission was ambitious: he wanted to conquer all of Central America and open it up for Spanish colonization. He headed for the capital of the Aztec empire, and along the way he managed to gain many extra soldiers from tribes who considered the Aztecs to be enemies. Cortés was received in honor by the Aztec king, Montezuma, and returned the favor by kidnapping him. The city was plunged into chaos and the casualties were high on both sides. Disease eventually killed enough Aztecs that Cortés was able to gain control of their empire.

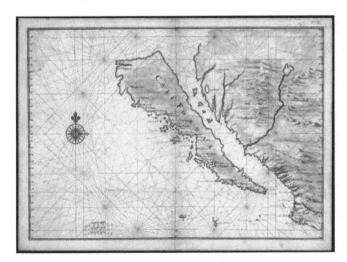

After all the conquering was done, the government of Spain ordered Cortés to yield control of the empire to other governors. Left with nothing better to do, Cortés headed out to do more exploring. He sailed up the west coast of what we now call Mexico, and discovered a large body of water that was originally named after him: "the Sea of Cortez." It was eventually renamed "the Gulf of California." Many people who live around the Gulf of California still call it the Sea of Cortez. He also discovered the peninsula we now call Baja California, although Cortés believed it to be a large island and named it the Island of California. This name came from a book written in 1510, not a book about geography but a romance novel! In this popular Spanish novel one of the characters describes an island not far from Paradise, inhabited only by women. The name the author gave to this island was the Island of California. It is doubtful that Cortés really thought the desert climate of Baja California looked like Paradise, and the peninsula cannot have been populated just by women, but he applied this fanciful name anyway.

In 1539 Cortés sent one of his men, Francisco Ulloa, on a voyage to explore the Sea of Cortez, going as far north as possible. If California really was an island, Ulloa would eventually find the top of the island and be able to sail around it. If California was a peninsula, he would find the northern edge of the

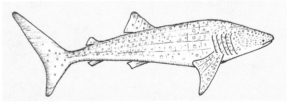

The whale shark is the largest animal in the Gulf of California.

sea, and perhaps a river flowing into it. What Ulloa discovered was, of course, the northern shore of the sea, and also a river (the Colorado River) flowing into the sea. When this new information about California reached the mapmakers back in Europe, California was thereafter shown as a peninsula.

A few years after the discovery that California (Baja California) was a peninsula, another former Conquistador was sent on a voyage of discovery. Juan Cabrillo was to sail up the west side of the peninsula. We know that he sailed up past modern San Diego, through what we call the Santa Barbara Channel, and didn't turn around until he had reached the river that is now called the Russian River. (In the past, this river has been called the Ashokawna, the Bidapte, the Misallaako, the Rio Grande, and the Slavyanka.) He stopped for a while to look for gold in the area that was to become San Francisco but wasn't very successful. Little did he know there would someday be a gold rush in that same area! On his way back down, he stopped at various islands. The ship needed repairs so he chose to spend the winter (it wasn't that cold but the weather was terrible for sailing) at the island we know as Santa Catalina. Unfortunately, Cabrillo stumbled on jagged rocks and cut his leg very badly. Gangrene set in and he died shortly after. No one knows where he is buried.

In the late 1500s a few Spanish explorers came across the Pacific Ocean from the Philippines and landed, or wrecked, on the coast of what is now Oregon, but they didn't stay and they didn't make maps of it. This area of North America remained largely unexplored by Europeans until the days of Lewis and Clark in the early 1800s.

Look at the map below and compare how much was known about the northeast compared to the northwest. This map was made around 1650. This mapmaker hadn't yet heard that California wasn't an island (remember, this was still the age where maps of the world were top secret documents), but look at how much was known about the St. Lawrence Gulf and the icy lands to the north! It's fairly impressive considering that this map was made when the landing of the Pilgrims was still recent history.

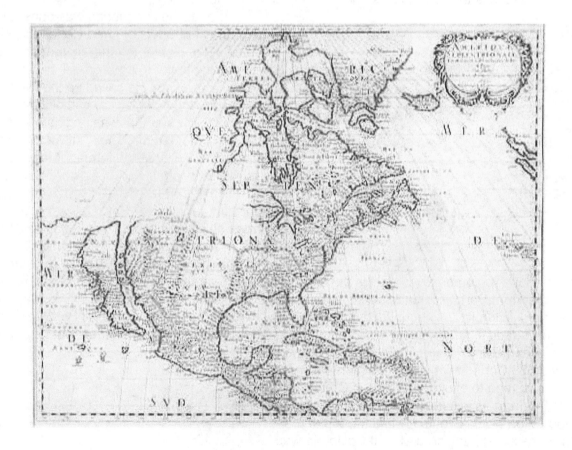

22. The Northeast Passage

There was only one direction that no one had yet tried as a passage to the Orient. The Portuguese had claimed the southeastern route (around Africa), Columbus had opened up the southwestern route (to the Caribbean), and England and France were trying the northwestern route over the top of the Atlantic and (hopefully) through North America. There was still one direction left. Why not go northeast? Because it was horribly cold—that's why! Finding a northeast passage to the Orient would require going up and over Norway and Siberia. Even in the 1500s, people knew enough about the world to know that it was deathly cold up there. (So far, the northwestern explorers had not gone far enough north to get into serious icebergs. The northwest passage would prove to be almost as cold and difficult as the northeastern one, but they didn't know that yet.) Europeans were so desperate to get their valuable spices and silks from the Orient that a few brave sailors and navigators were willing to try going up over Norway.

The first captain of the first northeast voyage was Englishman Sir Hugh Willoughby, in 1553. (If you keep in mind that this was still the Renaissance era, just barely past the time of the infamous King Henry VIII, you'll agree that it was truly amazing for these men to attempt a voyage like this—one that is still difficult even for us modern folks with all our advanced polar survival gear.) Willoughby launched with great confidence. He was so sure about finding this route to the Indies that he had the hulls of his five ships covered in lead to protect them from the wood-eating marine worms of the Indian Ocean. Needless to say, none of his ships even came close to tropical waters. Four of the ships (including the one Willoughby was on) were caught up in a storm as they were going over the top of Norway and were forced to land on the Kola peninsula. They explored the coastline for

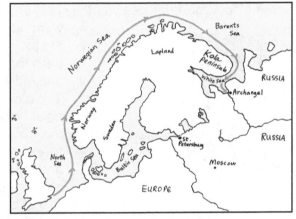

a while, then prepared to spend the winter in the Arctic. A year later, Russian fishing vessels found the ships with all the crew dead and frozen inside. Modern scholars believe their death was caused primarily by carbon monoxide poisoning from their coal stoves, not by the cold temperature.

One ship made it all the way over the top and down to the coast of Russia. The captain of this ship, Richard Chancellor, found overland transportation down to the city of Moscow and met the Russian czar, Ivan the Terrible. A trade agreement was signed and this began England's Moscow Trading Company. Chancellor made it back home and managed to take a second northeastern voyage, but on his return he died as his ship was wrecked off the coast of Scotland.

The next major northeast expedition was in 1594. Holland was on the rise as a new competitor in the Spice Wars. A Dutch seaman, Willem Barents, decided to take a shot at finding the

Willem Barents

northeast passage. Barents loaded his ship with trade goods to take to the Indies, and set sail for the Arctic. He made it up and over Norway and past the point where the English expedition had stopped. He made it all the way to the island of Novaya Zemlya (which means "new land"). This island, however, is very long—as long as the island of Britain. It would take quite a bit of sailing to find a way around it, and sailing conditions in the Arctic make for slow going. Barents could not find a way to get past this land mass, so he went home before the Arctic winter set in. He made a second trip the following year and tried again. He sailed to the south and would have discovered the strait he was seeking, but his ship got stuck in pack ice. After returning home from his second voyage he made his third, and final, expedition in 1596.

On his third voyage, Barents decided to go north of Norway, instead of heading east. The first island he came to he named Bear Island because of polar bears seen there. (Little did Barents know, but these bears of the Arctic would become a daily threat to his crew in the near future.) He sailed even farther north and discovered a large group of islands, which today is called the Svalbard Archipelago. He sailed all the way around the Svalbard islands, then headed to the place he had been to twice before and was determined to get around: Novaya Zemlya. Once again, he was defeated by the polar winter. He got stuck in ice floes and could not sail past this island. Fortunately, the crew had come prepared to spend some time in the Arctic. They had brought timbers with which to build a shelter, and enough food to last until spring. They built a cozy lodge that was impressively large: 20 feet by 33 feet. It had a tall chimney that could also serve as an emergency exit in case of extreme snowfall, bunk beds for the crew, and even a bathtub made from a wooden barrel. To keep

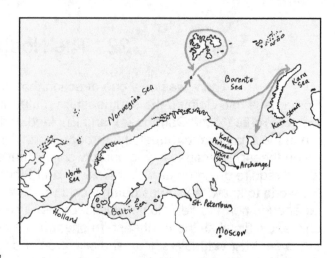

warm at night, they slept with stones or cannon balls they had heated in their stoves. The crew dined on ham, bacon, beef, fish, peas, barley, biscuits, beer and wine. They even had vinegar and mustard for their meat! Lack of food was not a problem. The crew's biggest problem was their next door neighbors—the polar bears. The Europeans had never encountered such ferocious animals. The sailors managed to kill quite a few bears (using very long lances) and used their fat as fuel for their lamps and their skins as extra blankets. In their free time the sailors also caught foxes by making elaborate wooden traps.

The Dutch sailors had expected that by June the ice would have melted enough for them to cut their ship free and sail away. The reality was that in June their ship was still stuck fast in the ice. They all began to suffer from scurvy and knew they had to attempt an escape before they became any weaker. They decided to set out in the lifeboats and try to land on the coast of Russia, where they knew they would eventually find Russian fishermen or fur trappers who could get them back to civilization. Sadly, after only a week at sea in the lifeboats, Barents died. When the lifeboats were rescued by a passing Russian ship, only 12 out of 16 crew members were still alive. Those men did eventually make it back to Holland.

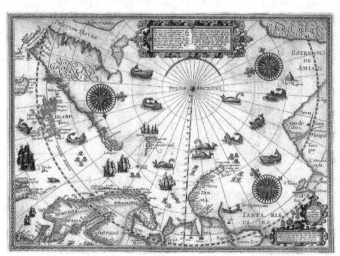

This map was made in 1599, using information brought back by the survivors. This was a new kind of map—the world as seen from the pole.

The lodge where Barents and his men wintered over was discovered by Norwegians in 1871. Many items had been left behind, such as cooking pots, chests, tools, and clothing. From these items, historians have gained much information about the explorers and how they survived.

The Dutch gave up trying to find the northeast passage and left polar exploration to the Russians and the Norwegians. (The first explorer to make it all the way over Asia and down into the Pacific Ocean was the Norwegian navigator Nils Nordenskjold in 1878.) The Dutch decided to go southeast, instead, right into the heart of the Portuguese empire!

23. Gerard Mercator

Now that explorers were reaching into the very far north, mapping was becoming increasingly difficult. Maps of the world usually had the equator in the middle. This was fine for mapping the areas of the world most often traveled, such as the Mediterranean, the Caribbean, Europe, Africa, India, and China. This was not so fine for the areas far to the north. As you went farther and farther north, the lines of longitude (going up and down) came closer and closer together until they finally converged at the north pole. All the way back to the time of Ptolemy, mapmakers had been curving their lines of longitude as they went north.

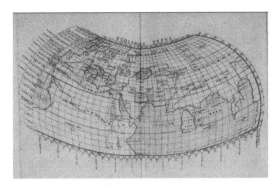

Remember Ptolemy's map?

There were two main problems with this mapping technique. First, the lands in the north tended to look "squinchy" and smaller than they really were. Second, these maps could not be used by navigators. Navigators had to have straight lines to sail by. Curved lines were useless. Navigators needed a world map on which all lines of latitude and longitude were straight .

The first mapmaker to produce such a map was a man named Gerard Mercator (born as Gérard de Crémère). Mercator was from Flanders (what we now call the country of Belgium). Mercator was a scholar who was also an excellent craftman. He began making precision brass tools, such as astrolabes, and hand-crafted globes. His tools and globes soon commanded high prices. He once made a special set of globes for Emperor Charles V of Spain. The outer globe was made of crystal and showed the heavens (stars and constellations). The inner globe represented the earth, and although it was made of just wood and paper, the artwork was so beautiful that everyone marveled at it. Mercator's skill became known throughout Europe. So many people wanted to buy his globes that he invented a technique for mass-producing them. He made hollow paper-mâché spheres instead of solid wooden ones. He then printed the map onto flat paper, but in wedge-shaped sections, like sections of a peeled orange. The sections were then glued to the paper-mâché globe, with the seams tightly pressed and sealed. (This is basically the same technique used in mass production of globes today.) Twenty-two of these Mercator globes are still in existence.

This photo is from Wikimedia: posted by Paul Hermans.

The one shown here is in the Mercator Museum in Sint-Niklass, Belgium. Many modern globe companies sell reproductions (copies) of these famous Mercator globes. It might seem strange that someone today would want a globe that has outdated geography, but that just shows how incredible his workmanship was—people still value it even today.

Mercator also made regular maps. His first big seller was a map of Palestine. Europeans read their Bibles every day and were interested in the geography of the Bible lands. After that, he produced an exquisite map of Europe that included some of the northern lands that Willoughby had explored just a few years earlier.

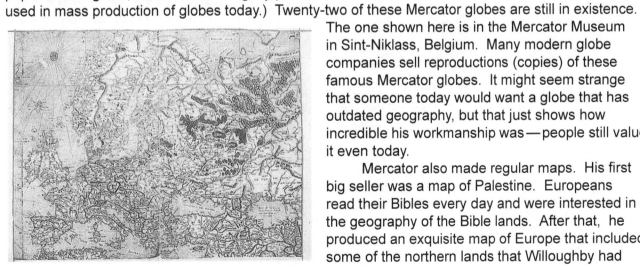

Mercator's map of Europe

Mercator was also a mathematician. His mathematical ability led him to investigate the geometrical problem of how to project the spherical surface of the Earth onto a flat page. Mercator realized that there was more than one way to flatten the globe onto a map and that each way would have its advantages and disadvantages. One possibility was to simply glue the wedge-shaped sections of his globe onto pieces of flat paper. Each section would be highly accurate, and the map would show the whole world, but how many people would want a map that looks all chopped up? Then there was Ptolemy's idea of making the lines of longitude and latitude curve toward the poles. This kind of map would look nice and would show the shapes of the continents very well, but it would be useless to navigators who needed straight lines. What about two circles, each showing one half of the world? Once again, this type of map would look nice hanging on a wall but it would be useless to navigators. For whom should Mercator design a map?

Mercator decided that navigators needed world maps more than anyone else did. After all, they risked their lives sailing across the oceans. Mercator knew that navigators needed straight lines, so he created a map just for them. He knew that doing this would make very strange things happen to the shapes of the polar land masses, but he hoped navigators wouldn't care what the shapes looked like as long as the directions on the map were correct for navigation. Mercator chose to favor correct directions, knowing that he would have to sacrifice accurate shapes.

To make his map, Mercator imagined the Earth inside a cylinder. If the Earth was inflated like a balloon its sides would begin to push against the inside of the cylinder. Soon, the Tropics of Cancer and Capricorn would be pressed against the cylinder. If you kept inflating it, eventually even the Arctic Circle would be pressed like a giant ring around the inside of the

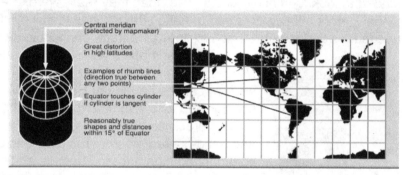

cylinder. If you pricked the globe at the poles, you could allow it to open up completely. The north and south poles, which are actually single points, would become straight lines at the top and bottom of the map! Finally, you could cut the cylinder open and lay it out flat.

What Mercator had done was to "project" a spherical surface onto a flat surface. This was only one way to project the Earth onto a map. Since the time of Mercator, mapmakers have found dozens of ways to project the Earth onto a flat map. Mercator's method of projecting the globe into a cylinder, then rolling it out flat, has become known as the "Mercator projection."

Mercator published his first world map in 1569. It was a huge success, although at first sailors

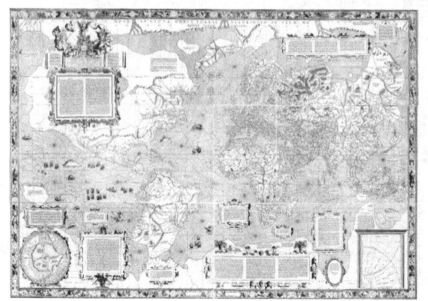

were a bit nervous when they saw how large Greenland looked in comparison to South America. They knew Greenland wasn't the same size as South America. But as they used the map they found it to be very accurate for navigation. The Mercator projection became the most popular type of world map for the next 400 years.

Mercator placed his prime meridian (the zero point for longitude) in the Azores, off the coast of Spain. This was because sailors reported that their compasses never varied from true north at this location.

24. The Continued Search for the Northwest Passage

Finding the Northeast Passage had proven to be difficult, if not impossible. Soon after rounding Norway, ships always ran into trouble. Europeans had a pretty good idea of how large Russia was and they realized that if they were getting stuck by the time they reached Novaya Zemlya, this route just wasn't going to be a viable (do-able) way to get to the Orient. The Northwest Passage, however, was still a great unknown. It seemed much more likely that a way could still be found through North America. Therefore, the English and French governments were willing to spend more money sending out explorers to Canada.

The next explorer who tried to find the Northwest Passage was an Englishman named Martin Frobisher. In 1576 he set sail with three ships. One of these ships was lost in a storm when the expedition landed on the southern tip of Greenland. The sailors from the wrecked ship piled into the

two other ships and they all kept sailing. They went past Labrador and kept sailing north, looking for an inlet that would lead west. They did find an inlet and sailed into it, but it turned out to be a dead end. They named it Frobisher Bay and sent a five-man welcoming party ashore to meet the natives. The Inuit (Eskimo) natives were less than thrilled with their visitors and kidnapped some of them. Frobisher tried to find and rescue his men, but was not successful. Inuit natives who live in that region today have a legend about five strange men who built a homemade boat and tried to escape the island, drowning in the attempt.

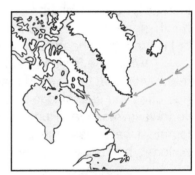

Martin Frobisher's voyage to the bay where he found his Fool's Gold.

Frobisher brought home some rocks that had gold flecks in them. This was enough for the queen to sponsor a second trip. The second voyage brought back huge quantities of gold-flecked rocks which Frobisher took to a refinery where the gold could be extracted. The English mineral experts at the refinery told Frobisher the same news that Cartier had received about his rocks: they were not gold-bearing rocks at all. The gold flecks were merely iron pyrite—Fool's Gold! Frobisher proved himself worthy of his "gold" when he launched a <u>third</u> trip to that same bay, bringing back even more of the useless stuff! Frobisher then retired from polar exploration and joined Sir Francis Drake's fleet sailing to the Indies to fight the Spanish Armada.

The next voyager to sail west was John Davis. In 1585 he followed much the same course as Frobisher, only he went farther north. Above Frobisher Bay was another inlet. Would this be the inlet that led to a passage across to the Pacific? No, it was another dead end. Apparently, the Arctic was full of dead ends! Davis made two more trips back to this area and explored all the way up the western coast of Greenland, but did not discover anything that looked like a passage to the west. The best thing that Davis did on his journeys was accurately mapping all the coastlines he traveled and keeping detailed records of every new plant, animal, and mineral he discovered. The body of water where he spent all his time exploring is now known as Davis Strait. Eventually, Davis invented an improved instrument for finding latitude. It was called the backstaff because you stood with your back to the sun. Navigators were glad to stop squinting into the sun!

Next up was Henry Hudson, probably the best-known Arctic explorer from this time period. His first trip was to the northeast, not the northwest. The Dutch East India Company said they would pay his expenses if he would make one more attempt at finding a passage over the top of Norway and Russia. Sailing under the Dutch flag, he headed north. After rounding the top of Norway and getting stuck in ice, he decided it was no use and turned around. Hearing rumors of how nice it was on the mid-Atlantic coast of America (Virginia and North Carolina), he decided not to return to Holland but to continue on for more exploration. He crossed the Atlantic and landed near Nova Scotia. He began working his way down the coastline and eventually discovered the river that would be named after him: the Hudson River. He sailed a considerable way into the river, before he decided that it was not going to be the hoped-for passage through the continent. (If he had used Magellan's technique of tasting the water, he would have discovered this as soon as he turned into the

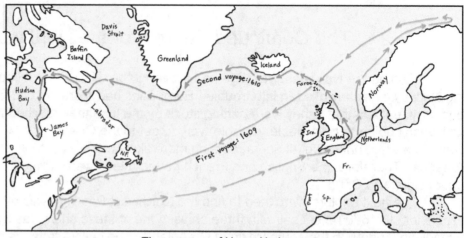

The voyages of Henry Hudson.

mouth of the river.) He did the "meet-the-natives-and-exchange-goods" thing, claimed some territory for Holland, then headed back home.

When the British East India Company found out that Hudson had sailed for Holland, they determined that they would make him a funding offer that he couldn't refuse. Hudson did accept their offer and set sail again in 1610, leading yet another expedition that would search for the elusive Northwest Passage. Hudson was convinced that the mid-Atlantic region of North America did not contain a water passage, so he went much farther north. He discovered a waterway that previous explorers had not yet discovered—a large waterway that looked like it could possibly lead to the

much-hoped-for western passage. The crew's hopes were high as they sailed south into a body of water so large that it looked to them like an ocean (if only they had used Magellan's taste test!). They sailed around the bay (now called Hudson Bay) all summer doing exploring and mapping. When November came, winter started to set in quickly and the crew realized they would be spending the winter in Canada. They survived fairly well and when spring came, Hudson announced that they would pick up where they left off in the fall and continue mapping and exploring the bay. The crew, however, wanted to go home. They took over the ship and forced Hudson, his teenage son, and some sick crew members into a life boat. The mutineers sailed the ship back to England and Henry Hudson was never seen or heard from again.

Right after Hudson's ill-fated journey, an explorer named William Baffin made yet another attempt at finding the Northwest Passage. In 1616 he sailed to the Hudson Strait and made detailed charts of it, studying the tidal patterns and making the astronomical observations necessary for determining points of latitude. The following year, he made another trip west, this time visiting the area that Frobisher and Davis had explored. But Baffin went even farther north, going all the way up to the place where Greenland almost touches the northern Canadian island of Ellesmere. He decided that it was impossible to sail north beyond this point. He formally declared the route along the coast of Greenland to be a dead end. After returning to England, he did the same thing that Frobisher and Davis had done: he sailed east to the Indies and died fighting for the English empire in the east.

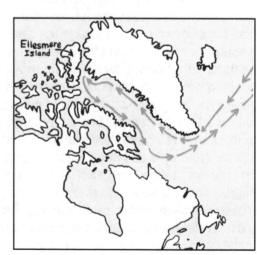

Baffin found the dead end to the north.

25. The Dutch in Japan

In the late 1500s, the power of the Portuguese was beginning to fade. You may have wondered how such a small country could have dominated so many parts of the world. The way they accomplished it was by putting almost all of their national effort into their navy. Young boys growing up in Portugal expected that they would become sailors or navigators. The number of farmers and craftsmen started to decline. Agriculture in Portugal began to suffer. There weren't enough people at home to grow and prepare all the food needed by the seafarers. As Portugal struggled to maintain its empire, another tiny country was on the rise to power: Holland.

Holland had fought bitterly for its independence from Spain in the late 1500s. After years of intense battles for freedom, they finally won. In the early 1600s they began a century of relative peace and prosperity that has become known as the Golden Age of Holland. This is the century in which Rembrandt and Vermeer lived. Holland was a center for art, science, philosophy, trade, and freedom of religion. The country grew incredibly wealthy in a very short amount of time. This wealth allowed it to build a strong navy, and to construct many merchant ships as well. The Dutch began to realize that they were becoming strong enough to challenge Portugal and Spain for control of trading ports in the Far East (such as Malacca and the Spice Islands). Wealthy businessmen started the Dutch East India Company, which funded voyages to places like the Spice Islands. As the 1600s progressed, the Dutch were indeed able to oust Portugal from many trading ports in the East.

The Dutch fleet consisted of five ships. The names of the ships were Hope, Love, Faith, Loyalty, and Good Tidings.

One of the first Dutch explorers of that century wasn't Dutch by birth. Englishman Will Adams was hired by the Dutch East India Company in 1598 to be the captain of a fleet of five ships that would attempt to go to the Spice Islands the way Magellan did: around the tip of South America and across the Pacific Ocean. The crossing of the Pacific resulted in the death of over half the crew (mostly because of malnutrition). When land was finally sighted (in April of 1600), only one of the five ships was left and fewer than ten men were well enough to stand on their feet. The land they had sighted was the coast of Japan. When they came into the harbor of the well-populated city of Kyushu, they were very surprised to be greeted not by Japanese natives, but by Portuguese missionaries who had been living there for some time. (One of the first European missionaries to go to Japan was Francis Xavier, in 1549.) The Portuguese monks were alarmed at seeing a Dutch vessel sail into what they considered Portuguese territory. They told the Japanese rulers that the Dutch were pirates and should be executed immediately. The local Japanese ruler, Ieyasu, ordered that the Dutch sailors be imprisoned in Osaka castle while he decided their fate.

The castle of the daimyo of the city of Hirado

Fortunately, Ieyasu was a sensible man and thought he should talk to the prisoners before executing them. He found Will Adams to be a very likeable person. By using a Japanese interpreter who had learned Portuguese, the two men were able to have a constructive conversation. (Will knew a bit of Portuguese, as did many European sailors of his day.) Will explained that he and his men had come only for the purpose of friendly trade, not to threaten Japan in any way. He drew a map to show where Holland was and how they had sailed across the Pacific Ocean. Ieyasu asked if Holland fought wars and Will replied that they only fought in self-defense against the Spanish and the Portuguese. Will emphasized that Holland was a peace-

A Japanese "Red Seal" ship from 1634

loving country and would respect Japan as an independent country. Will's words impressed Ieyasu so much that not only did he free the Dutch crew, but he demanded that Will stay in Japan to teach the Japanese how to build Western-style ships.

Will Adams did indeed teach the Japanese how to construct ships. He learned Japanese very quickly and soon was able to speak without an interpreter. Ieyasu was so pleased with Will that he granted him privileges normally reserved for the Japanese nobility. Ieyasu eventually made Will his personal advisor and insisted that he be adopted into Japanese society as a samurai. Will was given a mansion on a large estate, and almost a hundred servants. As if that wasn't enough, Ieyusu also insisted that Will complete his entry into Japanese society by marrying a Japanese woman. When Will told Ieyasu he already had a wife and children back in England, Ieyasu thought of a clever way around this problem. He changed Will's name to Miura Anjin. Ieyasu said that according to their customs, the man "Will Adams" no longer existed. Therefore "Miura Anjin" had just been born and was free to pursue a new life. Since Ieyasu was a powerful man and could have ordered Will's execution at any time, Will got married.

Because of Will Adams, Japan was willing to begin trading with European countries. The Dutch established a trading center at the town of Hirado. Soon, ships from other European countries began to arrive in Japanese harbors. In 1613, the first English ship arrived. The English captain met with Will Adams and was horrified at how "Japanese" Will had become. Will wore Japanese clothing, spoke Japanese fluently, and had many Japanese friends. The English captain was not pleased. Like many Europeans of his day, he had disdain for cultures that were very different from his own. (Will lived out the rest of his life in Japan, dying there in 1620 at the age of 55.)

It wasn't long until the Japanese began to feel uneasy about the growing number of Europeans in their country. There were still quite a few Portuguese missionaries in Japan, and these Catholic missionaries resented the presence of Protestants (the Dutch and English). Soon there began to be unrest in Japan. Some of the Japanese who had converted to Catholicism were beginning to side with the Europeans and see things from their point of view. When quarrels and riots finally broke out, the Japanese rulers decided that the Europeans had outstayed their welcome and must be banished. In 1638, all Europeans were forced to leave Japan...

Will Adams is shown on this map of Japan made in 1707.

except for the Dutch. A small group of Dutch merchants were allowed to stay, thanks to the legacy of Will Adams. However, even the Dutch were restricted. The Japanese built a man-made island in the harbor of Nagasaki. The Dutch were to remain on this island, surrounded by a tall fence with metal spikes at the top. The Dutch now felt like prisoners. Only once a year were Dutch ships allowed in or out of the harbor, and upon entrance they had to surrender all weapons and religious items. The Dutch were willing to put up with this inconvenience to gain access to exclusive trading rights with Japan, and they gained much wealth by it.

The Dutch moved on past Japan and took control of many Portuguese trading centers in the Malay archipelago. (They still have strong connections to Indonesia today.) The Dutch also established colonies in South Africa and North America. The city of New York started out as a Dutch colony called New Amsterdam. The English captured it and renamed it after the English city of York.

26. The Dutch Find Australia;
The Golden Age of Maps

The seventeenth century (the 1600s) was the Golden Age of Holland. Their rivals, Spain and Portugal, were becoming less able to control their territories on the far side of the world. Somehow, the small country of Holland was able to take over many of these territories and expand to new ones, as well. The Dutch had plenty of money to invest in exploration.

The first Dutch captain to discover a whole new area of the world was Willem Janszoon, in 1606. He was sailing along the coast of New Guinea when he decided to turn south and find out what was down that direction. He didn't see the strait between New Guinea and Australia, so when he discovered land (the peninsula at the top of Australia) he thought it was the southern part of New Guinea. He sailed along the coast and mapped it, without ever realizing he had discovered a new continent.

The strait that Janszoon missed was discovered by a Spanish explorer, Luis de Torres, in that same year, 1606. The strait was later named the Torres Strait, in his honor. Torres merely sailed through the strait and made a note of it in his diary. He had no way of knowing that the southern edge of the strait was the tip of a great continent. He didn't have the time to go and explore it (he was on a business trip) so it was just as well he didn't know what he was missing.

There were several more Dutch expeditions to this area in the early 1600s. An expedition in 1623 explored and mapped the Gulf of Carpentaria and named it in honor of the Governor of the Dutch East India Company, Pieter de Carpentier.

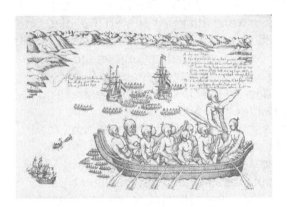

The next European expedition to Australia was in 1642 under the leadership of Abel Tasman. His plan was to discover and map the bottom of whatever landmass it was that Janszoon had discovered in 1606. He therefore headed south—way, way south. In fact, he went so far south that he missed Australia altogether! He landed on the island that would eventually be named after him: Tasmania. After sailing around it and determining that it was too small to be a new continent, he headed northeast and discovered the islands that would eventually become known as New Zealand. The natives on these islands, the Maori, didn't like visitors; they killed several of Tasman's men. Tasman named that place Murderer's Bay. (Fortunately, the name was later changed to Golden Bay, which sounds more like a place that future tourists would want to visit.)

Tasman then went on to discover the Tonga Islands and the Fiji Islands. The natives of Tonga were the opposite of the Maoris—they were extremely friendly. In fact, they were too friendly. The Tongan women wanted to flirt with the Dutch sailors and Tasman had to order the men not to leave the ship!

Tasman was sent out on a second voyage of discovery, in hopes of proving the existence of a large southern continent, if there was one. This time he decided not to go so far south. He went too far north, however, and ended up charting much of the same territory that Janszoon had already been to on the northern coast of Australia. And just like Janszoon, Tasman completely missed the Torres Strait. For years, the Dutch maps showed the northern coast of Australia connected to the island of New Guinea!

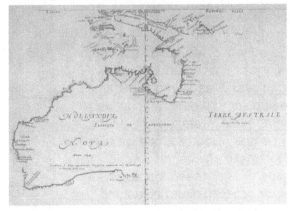

A map showing Australia connected to New Guinea.

While Dutch sailors were busy establishing trading centers all over southeast Asia, the mapmakers back home in Holland were busy turning mapmaking into a fine art. One of the first mapmakers to achieve world-wide fame was Abraham Ortelius. In 1570 he published what is considered to be the first modern atlas: *Theatrum Orbis Terrarum*. (The modern definition of an "atlas" is a bound book containing a general map of the world followed by a collection of maps that are all the same size and provide the reader with a close-up view of each part of the world.) The first editions were written in Latin, but it was soon translated into all the major European languages. The *Theatrum* was incredibly popular and continued to be printed and purchased well into the 1600s.

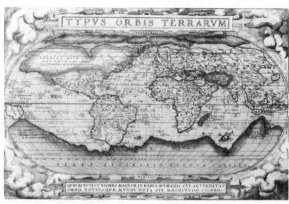
A world map by Abraham Ortelius

Mercator published his own collection of maps in 1585 and called his collection an "atlas." He was the first person to ever use the word "atlas" to describe a collection of maps. This atlas, however, was not a complete survey of the whole world, the way Ortelius' atlas was.

"The Belgian Lion" by Hondius

A mapmaker known for being especially artistic was Jodocus Hondius. One of his most famous maps shows the Low Countries in the shape of a lion. (On this map, north is to the right. You can see the Frisian Islands in the lion's tail.) Hondius also did portraits, his most famous being a portrait of the explorer and navigator Francis Drake. Hondius loved maps and was a great admirer of Mercator's world atlas. After Mercator died, Hondius was able to purchase many of Mercator's original printing plates. Hondius continued to improve the atlas and added many of his own beautiful maps to it, as well. The Mercator/Hondius atlas was one of the best-selling books in Holland during the 1600s.

Probably the most famous Dutch mapmaker of all was a man named Willem Janszoon Blaeu. Blaeu was a mapmaker extraordinaire and produced some of the finest maps in the history of the world. He had a huge warehouse in Amsterdam that functioned as a mapmaking factory, with 15 flatbed printing presses and many separate rooms for all kinds of jobs: setting type, cleaning type, editing, proof-reading, etching, printing, storing and selling. Not only were Blaeu's maps as accurate as he could make them (which depended on the information brought back by the explorers) but they were also highly decorated with pictures of Greek gods and goddesses (especially the wind gods), the seven wonders of the ancient world, famous people from history, or native peoples of the Americas. Blaeu's maps became so popular that other mapmakers began to decorate their maps the same way. Soon Europe was filled with amazingly beautiful world maps. Today, these maps are highly collectible and command high prices.

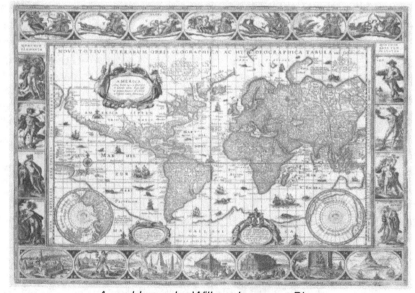
A world map by Willem Janszoon Blaeu

27. Vitus Bering and Alaska

In the 1700s, Russia began to explore the northernmost reaches of its country. No one in Russia knew how far east Asia went. They knew about the countries of China and Japan, but what lay to the north of them was a complete mystery.

In 1694, Peter the Great became czar over Russia. Peter was quite unlike any of the previous czars—they had not been interested in anything beyond their front door. Peter looked to the west and saw the European nations exploring the world and inventing new technologies, and he wanted Russia to catch up to them. One of Peter's strongest personal interests was shipbuilding. He traveled throughout Europe to meet the best ship builders and learned their trade secrets. When he came home he gave orders for the construction of a state-of-the-art navy.

This painting shows Peter the Great looking at the Baltic Sea and thinking about building a city on the shore.

Next, Peter needed more seaports in which to put all his new ships. Russia had only one outlet to the ocean and it was filled with ice half the year. Peter ordered his army to go south and take the Sea of Azov (the top part of the Black Sea) away from the Ottoman Turks. The Russian ships could then sail across the Black Sea, through the strait at Constantinople, and into the Mediterranean. (Ever since then, Russia has fought to maintain control of the Black Sea.) Peter also sent his army to the west to fight against the Swedes and gain a port on the Baltic Sea, as well.

With these new seaports secured, Peter began thinking about the eastern side of his country. In that direction there wasn't really anyone to fight. To the northeast lay the cold wilderness of Siberia, and beyond that was uncharted territory. Peter decided to send explorers to map eastern Russia.

This well-known portrait of Vitus Bering might not be him. It could be another member of the Bering family.

One of the explorers that Peter sent out was a Danish man named Vitus Bering. Vitus had left Denmark early in his life and decided to live in Russia instead. He fought in the Russian army during the battles for the ports on the Black Sea and the Baltic Sea; then he retired from the army and started exploring.

In 1725, Vitus Bering crossed Asia and arrived at the town of Okhotsk, on the edge of the Sea of Okhotsk. He had brought along carpenters and tools for building a ship, and using local lumber they built a ship right there on the edge of the Sea of Okhotsk. They set sail and went east, not knowing what they would find. They soon ran into land again: the Kamchatka peninsula. They left their boat behind and crossed the peninsula on foot. When they ran into water again, they had to build another boat! When the boat was built, they set sail into the unknown once again. Bering decided to go north, and see how far they could go before they hit land. For all Bering knew, this was just another giant sea, like the Sea of Okhotsk. They sailed farther and farther north, but never came to any land. Presumably, they must have gone through what we now call the Bering Strait—otherwise they would have hit land. They eventually turned around and went back to Russia, and Bering reported his findings to czar Peter.

Peter thought it was worthwhile to fund another expedition east. Vitus traveled very much the same route he

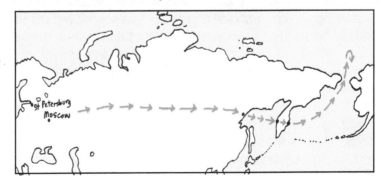

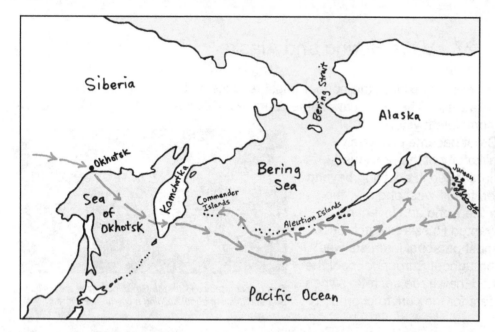

The native peoples of southern Alaska carved totem poles

had on the first trip, but this time when his expedition launched from the coast of Kamchatka, they went east instead of north. This direction headed them straight towards southern Alaska. They sighted mainland Alaska but landed on an island off the coast, now called Kayak Island. (Russian explorers named this island "Kayak" because the shape of the island reminded them of the Eskimo kayak boats.) Vitus had two ships at this time, and the second one was sent south along the coastline. This ship discovered a large group of islands which were later named the Alexander Archipelago. (The Russians gave them this name in 1867 in honor of their czar, Alexander.) This island group contains over 1,000 islands, which are covered with dense forests and are full of wildlife. The modern capital of Alaska, the city of Juneau, is on the mainland, not far from these islands. The native people of these islands are called the Tlingits. They still live in the area and have a unusual relationship with the American and Canadian governments—in some ways they are considered citizens, and in other ways they retain their sovereignty as an independent people.

Bering headed back to Russia, and on the way he discovered the Aleutian Islands. This long trail of islands forms an arc that reaches from Alaska almost all the way to the Kamchatka peninsula. Most of these islands are volcanic and form the northern edge of the Pacific "ring of fire." The name "Aleutian" refers to the native peoples of these islands: the Aleuts.

At this point in the voyage, the expedition had been at sea for a very long time and, as usual, scurvy began to set in. The men became weak and their health began to fail. When a sailor died, he was buried on one of the Aleutian Islands. Finally, Vitus Bering himself became so ill that he died. He had made it all the way to the last group of islands in the chain (which now belong to Russia and are called the Commander Islands). The ship was getting torn apart by storms so they landed on one of the islands to try to make repairs. Bering died on this island, and the sailors named it Bering Island in his honor. Twenty-eight other men died during the course of the return voyage. Fortunately for the survivors, the ship's carpenter was among those who did not die, and he managed to build a smaller ship using lumber from the first one. This tiny ship (less than 40 feet long) arrived back at Kamchatka and all the survivors eventually made it back to their homes in Russia.

Vitus Bering has been well-remembered in history (unlike poor Verrazzano!) and has five things named after him: an island, a strait, a sea, a glacier, and a land bridge. The two biggest problems Bering faced on his voyages were scurvy, which had been killing sailors for hundreds of years, and longitude, which strangely enough, could be just as deadly as scurvy. Miscalculations of longitude could cause a ship to sail right into a dangerous coastline at night and be wrecked on jagged rocks. Both of these problems, scurvy and longitude, were soon to be solved by men from the nation that dominated the seas in the 1700s: England.

28. Longitude

The inability to calculate longitude (east-west distance) continued to plague navigators right into the middle of the 1700s. Ships were still unable to pinpoint their location at sea, and mapmakers were still unable to determine the exact location of places around the world.

The key to determining longitude was accurately measuring time. If a navigator could keep track of exactly what time it was back home and compare that to what time it was in his present location, he could calculate exactly how far east or west he had traveled. Since the earth takes 24 hours to rotate, and there are 360 degrees of longitude around the earth, one hour equals 15 degrees of longitude. If it is noon at your present location and it's three o'clock back home, you are 45 degrees of longitude away from home. If you know your exact latitude (easily determined by sighting Polaris) you can then calculate the mileage for 45 degrees and know how many miles you are from home. Any cheap modern wristwatch is accurate enough to accomplish this task, but in past centuries, accurate time-keeping seemed almost impossible.

At the end of the 1500s, the problem of calculating longitude finally came to the attention of European monarchs. They realized that the inability to calculate longitude was causing disputes over their territories, as well as losses to their shipping industries. In 1598, King Philip III of Spain announced that he would award a huge sum of money to anyone who could solve the problem of longitude. Soon, other countries began announcing similar contests and prizes. One of the first scientists to come up with a solution was Galileo. He discovered that the moons of Jupiter could be used as a clock, and devised a method of using this "heavenly clock" to determine longitude. He wrote a letter to King Philip, describing his method, but unfortunately King Philip's staff had been deluged by letters from all over Europe, and Galileo's ideas were set aside as being "interesting but not practical." (Truth be told, Galileo's idea was a bit tricky to use. Galileo could make it work, but your average sailor wasn't exactly Galileo!) Galileo wrote letters to other heads of state around Europe, and finally got at least a little credit for his idea: Holland said he was a genius and gave him a gold chain.

Galileo Galilei

The idea of using astronomical observations as "clocks" wasn't new with Galileo. You'll remember that Columbus carried with him charts giving the exact times of eclipses. Vespucci wrote that by observing the paths of the planets you could make calculations of longitude. These methods enabled the early explorers to determine with at least some accuracy the location of places such as Brazil and Cuba. The problem with these astronomical methods was that you had to wait for astronomical events to happen. The world needed a method that could be used anywhere, anytime.

The Royal Observatory in Paris

In the mid 1600s, King Louis XIV (the famous "Sun King" of France) decided to outshine the other monarchs by announcing not just a longitude prize, but also a new Royal Academy of Science in Paris (complete with a brand-new observatory) designed to attract the best and brightest minds from all over Europe. The plan worked, and one of the bright minds who came was a Dutchman named Christian Huygens. He brought along his most famous invention: the pendulum clock. (Galileo was the first to suggest that pendulums be used as time-keepers, but it was Huygens who made the idea actually work and created the first pendulum clock.) Louis sent out surveyors with pendulum clocks all over Europe to make measurements of longitude. They determined the exact borders of countries and the exact longitude and latitude coordinates of cities and towns. (Of course, they used the Paris Observatory as the starting point of longitude—the Prime Meridian.) When they got back to Paris they plotted these on a 24-foot diameter map of the world drawn on the floor of the observatory. When the work of the Royal Academy became known around the world, scientists and cartographers from faraway places began trying to help out by sending coordinates for their cities. Soon the map on the floor was the most accurate map in the history of the world!

Pendulum clocks did have drawbacks, however. Their biggest problem was that they had to be perfectly level to work properly. Pendulum clocks were useless on ships. To be able to calculate longitude while at sea, an entirely new type of time-keeping device would have to be invented. In 1713, England's Parliament announced a reward of 20,000 pounds to anyone who could invent a time-keeping device that would not lose more than 2 minutes per day, even at sea. The man who was eventually given the prize money was a simple clockmaker named John Harrison. His entire life was devoted to perfecting that timepiece and to demonstrating to Parliament that he was worthy of the prize.

Harrison used a spring to power his device. The mechanical energy stored in the spring was released gradually by a trigger mechanism called a "grasshopper escapement." He found that when he added this escapement to a regular clock, it would become accurate to within one second per month. After five years of work, he finished a portable clock that was ready for a trial at sea. This famous first model has become known as "H1." Harrison and H1 sailed on a ship bound for Lisbon, and on the return trip they plotted the ship's position more accurately than the ship's navigator. H1 was a huge success. Harrison was awarded enough money to be able to build a smaller version of H1. (H1 wasn't exactly a wristwatch—it weighed 72 pounds!)

Harrison built H2 but wasn't satisfied with it and immediately started H3. After H3 came his most famous clock: H4. By the time he had finished H4, Harrison was 68 years old. Harrison's son, William, was sent along with H4 on a voyage to Jamaica in 1761, to prove that H4 would pass the tests required for winning the longitude prize. When H4 returned home after 5 months, it had lost only one minute and 53 seconds. The rules of the contest said the winning device had to lose no more than 2 minutes. H4 had passed the test.

H4

John Harrison in 1767

Despite this amazing performance and the obvious fact that H4 had won the contest, Parliament's Board of Longitude was unwilling to announce Harrison as the winner of the contest. Some of those board members had spent large sums of their own money on other contestants, and they didn't want to lose their investments. So they gave lame excuses for several years, then finally demanded that to receive the award Harrison would have to turn over to them all four clocks AND all the plans he used to make them! (They weren't going to steal any technology, of course...) The public became outraged, and even the king demanded that Parliament hand over the prize money to Harrison. So Parliament backed down and graciously gave Harrison—half the money. Harrison was forced into "loaning" H4 to them, and, as you might predict, it wasn't long before a set of plans for a similar device was published.

Harrison was told to make an H5 if he wanted the rest of the prize money. He did start work on H5, but by now he was 78 years old and his eyes were getting weak. Harrison decided he had no choice but to petition the king for help in getting the rest of his prize money. George III was very willing to take up Harrison's cause and threatened Parliament that they had better hand over the money. Parliament grudgingly gave Harrison the rest of his money, but never did make any official announcements about anyone winning the contest.

The question of which line of longitude would be the Prime Meridian was not settled until the International Meridian Conference of 1884, held in Washington D.C. Everyone knew ahead of time that it was likely to come down to a choice between the Royal Observatory of France and the Royal Observatory of England. After much discussion, the English Royal Observatory in the town of Greenwich ("*Gren-itch*") was chosen by a vote of 22 to 1. The French delegate refused to vote, and France would not officially recognize this international decision until 1911.

29. Captain Cook's Island Adventures

While John Harrison was working on H2, a young man named James Cook was beginning his training as a sailor and navigator. James had been apprenticed to a shopkeeper, but his boss found him constantly looking out the shop windows, gazing longingly at the sea. The boss decided there was nothing for it but to take James to the nearest port city and apprentice him to a ship captain. James then spent three years learning how to sail and navigate, as well as learning mathematics and astronomy. After completing his apprenticeship he worked for a short time aboard trading vessels in the Baltic Sea.

When war broke out in Europe, Cook joined the English Royal Navy. The war spread to the colonies in North America, and Cook ended up spending several years in and around Newfoundland. He had learned to do surveying, as well as navigating, so while he was there, he decided to make a new and highly accurate map of Newfoundland. This map was so accurate that Cook's skill came to the attention of the Royal Society.

In 1766, the Royal Society hired Cook to lead a voyage to the other side of the world to observe and record an astronomical event that happens only twice each century: an "eclipse" of the planet Venus as it passes in front of the sun. Timing how long it takes for Venus to go across the face of the sun would enable the Royal astronomers to

Cook's 1775 map of Newfoundland

calculate the distance between the Earth and the sun. Cook was to sail to the middle of the Pacific Ocean and find a suitable island where he could set up his equipment for observing Venus. Cook landed on the island of Tahiti and made his observations there.

As far as the sailors knew, they had completed their mission and could return home. Cook, however, knew that the voyage had only begun. Cook had been given secret orders from the British government to keep sailing west in the South Pacific, attempting to find what had for centuries been called "Terra Australis Incognita," the unknown southern continent. Going back to the time of the ancient Greeks, there had been geographers who strongly believed that there was a large landmass in the southern hemisphere (to "balance off" the northern landmasses). In the 18th century, the European

This map shows Terra Australis Incognita. Here it is called Magallanica, after Magellan.

nations were still trying to expand their empires, and one of the best ways to do this was to discover new places around the globe that had not yet been claimed by any other empire. Britain no doubt hoped to discover a vast continent it could add to its overseas colonies. Cook was to sail south to 40 degrees below the equator, then keep sailing west until he discovered land.

After weeks at sea, land was finally sighted. Everyone aboard the ship was certain they were making history. The land they had discovered, however, turned out to be the north island of New Zealand, discovered and mapped by the Dutch many years earlier. Cook now knew where they were. He had seen Dutch maps showing the west coast of Australia (which the Dutch called New Holland) and also the western side of New Zealand. He knew that any land that lay west of New Zealand was most likely to be the eastern side of New Holland. He was probably a bit disappointed to realize that there wasn't any unknown continent to be discovered, but he made the best of it and decided that mapping the eastern side of New Holland (and claiming it for Britain, of course) was certainly a worthwhile project, so they sailed west.

Cook's ship, the *Endeavor*, anchored in a bay that was surrounded by exotic plant life. The botanists aboard ship had such a fabulous time collecting and recording plant specimens that Cook named the bay "Botany Bay." They collected so many specimens to take back to England that the ship became a floating greenhouse and zoo.

When they arrived back in England, after having been at sea for two years, it was reported that not a single member of the crew had died of scurvy—an almost miraculous occurrence for that time period. During the voyage, Cook had been experimenting with various cures for scurvy. The most famous of these experimental cures was a food that the sailors didn't particularly like: sauerkraut.

Cook sometimes had to punish the sailors to get them to eat it. Vitamins had not yet been discovered during Cook's time, so he had no way of knowing that the high level of vitamin C in the cabbage was the reason it seemed to be a cure. Some of the crew members tried drinking lemon juice, which provided even faster relief from the bleeding gums and open sores caused by scurvy. Perhaps the best thing that this voyage did was to improve the diet of the sailors in the Royal Navy, preventing future deaths from scurvy.

The geographers and scientists of Britain were still not convinced that the unknown southern continent did not exist. They hired Cook to make a second voyage to look for it. On this second voyage, Cook was given a timepiece called K1 (made by Larcum Kendall), a copy of Harrison's H4, which enabled Cook to navigate and to map more accurately than anyone ever had.

Cook's portrait from 1775

In the southern part of the Atlantic Ocean, Cook landed on South Georgia Island and claimed it for Britain. He also discovered islands even farther south than South Georgia. He sailed down below the Antarctic Circle, and if he had gone just a bit more south, he would have sighted the coast of Antarctica. He never found out about Antarctica, however, turning back north and heading for Tahiti in order to resupply the ship. He then sailed all over the South Pacific in order to be sure that there really wasn't a continent there. While doing all this sailing, he discovered the Tonga Islands (which Cook called the Friendly Islands), Easter Island, Norfolk Island, New Caledonia Island and the Vanuatu Islands. Several of these islands had been visited by Europeans before Cook found them, and all of them had native populations. When Cook got back to England, he published his journals so that everyone in Europe (and in America) could learn about these exotic and faraway places.

Cook's third, and final, assignment was to look for the elusive Northwest Passage. Believe it or not, geographers still thought there might be a way to cross North America by ship. If anyone could find this passage, surely Cook would be the man to do it. Cook headed for the Pacific Ocean again, but this time he turned north instead of south. On his way north he discovered what we now call the islands of Hawaii. Cook named them the Sandwich Islands after the Earl of Sandwich. (Sandwich is the name of a town in England.) He left Hawaii and sailed east, landing on the shores of California. He sailed up the coast, accurately mapping everything from California to Alaska. Cook proved once and for all that there was no Northwest passage anywhere below Alaska.

Cook then headed back to Hawaii to reprovision his ship for the return trip. Unfortunately, he ran into trouble with the natives. Some of the tribesmen stole one of the ship's small boats. Cook decided that to get the boat returned he had to take something that belonged to the natives and hold it for ransom until the boat was returned. Unfortunately, the thing he decided to take from the natives was their king. As Cook and his men attempted to kidnap the king, the native Hawaiians killed them on the beach. In all his travels, Cook had never mistreated any natives, and it was unlikely that any harm would have come to the Hawaiian king. The

A painting showing the death of Captain Cook

natives had actually gotten along fairly well with Cook and his men, previous to this event.

Two of Cook's officers would go on to make more sailing history. William Bligh would become the captain of a ship called the *Bounty*, made famous by the book *Mutiny on the Bounty*, and George Vancouver would do more exploring on the western coast of North America, giving his name to the large island of Vancouver, now part of Canada.

30. The Polar Regions

Captain Cook had proven that Terra Australis Incognita, the unknown southern continent, didn't exist. Explorers stopped looking for it. New Holland eventually became known as Australia, but it wasn't thought of as THE unknown land that everyone had been looking for. What began to draw people to the southern end of the world was (believe it or not) business opportunities. The spice wars were a thing of the past because spice growers had figured out how to transplant spice trees to other parts of the world. In the 1700s and 1800s, two "hot" items were seal furs and whale oil. The cold waters at the bottom of the world were where seals and whales were most abundant. British and French companies set up whale and seal processing stations on cold, desolate islands such as South Georgia Island, the South Orkney Islands and the Kerguelen Islands. Dead whales would be brought to these stations for boiling, in order to extract the precious oil. With so many European ships doing business in these waters, it was inevitable that one of them would eventually sight Antarctica.

The first recorded sighting of the continent of Antarctica was by a Russian named Fabian Gottleib von Bellinghausen, in the year 1820. A year later, in 1821, an American seal hunter named John Davis is recorded as having actually set foot on the continent. The Davis Sea was named in his honor. After these landmarks, there were many more sightings and brief landings. Every time a different part of the coast was sighted, the sighter felt he had the right to name it. Thus, Antarctica's coasts have names like Wilkes Land, Enderby Land, Queen Maud Land, Adelie Land and Marie Byrd Land (the last two being named after wives).

You might think that people would have immediately identified Antarctica as the infamous Terra Australis Incognita (for, in a way, it really was!), but they didn't. The legendary Terra Australis Incognita was supposed to be a lush, habitable land. Antarctica was too cold for anyone to live on. Antarctica was a bit of a disappointment. What was it good for? The only people really interested in it were extreme explorers.

In 1841, James Ross came to Antarctica. Ross had already done quite a bit of polar exploration and had been the first to discover the magnetic north pole—the place all compasses point to. Now he was looking forward to tackling this new southern frontier. Ross's ship, the *Erebus*, sailed into what would eventually be called the Ross Sea. As they sailed along the coast they sighted a massive volcano belching smoke and fire. Ross named the volcano Erebus, after his ship. Then they discovered another massive feature of Antarctica: an ice shelf the size of France! It formed a flat wall that rose up in front of them anywhere from 30 to 80 feet above the water. Ross likened it to the white cliffs of Dover, back in England. They could sail no farther south.

After Ross left Antarctica, several decades went by before anyone tried again to explore it. In 1899, a Norwegian explorer named Carsten Borchgrevink became the first person in history (along with his small crew of men) to spend the winter in Antarctica. Then, in 1911, Roald Amundsen and Robert Scott raced to see who could be first to get to the geographic South Pole (not the magnetic one). Amundsen beat Scott by a few weeks. Sadly, Scott and his men then froze to death on their way home. Amundsen attributed his own success to survival skills he had learned from the Eskimos. Amundsen had more than a

Roald Amundsen at the South Pole

decade of polar navigation and survival experience behind him. In 1903 he had been the first person to sail over the top of Canada, from the Atlantic to the Pacific, thus transversing a northwest passage. (The Northwest Passage at last!)

Since the days of Scott and Amundsen, many research bases have been established all over

Antarctica, including one at the South Pole. America's largest base, McMurdo, is located in the area that James Ross explored. McMurdo provides housing, labs and offices for thousands of scientists. No one is officially allowed to "live" on Antarctic however. In 1961, an international treaty was signed by all major nations of the world, agreeing that Antarctica was to be used for research purposes only. No one would be allowed to live there permanently and no country would ever be allowed to use any part of the continent for war-related activities. Recently, oil has been discovered under Antarctica, which could possibly make it a very controversial part of the world in the future.

Peary and crew at the "North Pole"

The North Pole turned out to be a little more difficult to get to than the South Pole. Some of the same men that explored Antarctica went north to participate in the race to the North Pole. A big difference between the South Pole and the North Pole is that the South Pole is on land and the North Pole is over nothing but water (though the water is frozen most of the year). The first person to claim to have been to the North Pole was Robert Peary in 1909. He went by dogsled to the area around the North Pole and came back claiming to have reached it. Upon examining his travel records, however, it became obvious that he had not travelled far enough.

After being the first person to the South Pole, Roald Amundsen decided he'd like to be the first person to the North Pole, as well. Since the North Pole was over water, his first plan was to sail to it, even though he knew it might take several years to work his way through the polar ice. His plan didn't work as well as he had hoped, and after several years of being stuck in the ice, he gave up.

In 1925, Amundsen decided a better plan would be to fly an airplane over the pole. It took him two attempts, but he finally did it. He flew from the Svalbard Islands to Alaska, crossing over the spot where the North Pole is. He saw with his own eyes that (as he had guessed) there is no land at the North Pole, only frozen water. Three years later, the pilot from this mission would try the stunt again, but this time it would end in disaster, and Amundsen would lose his life attempting to rescue them.

The race to the poles got a lot of public attention because it sounded so exciting. But much more important than getting to the poles was the work still being done by hardy explorers who were willing to fight for survival in the vast frozen wildernesses of Siberia and Canada, in order to finish the job of mapping the world. These hardy explorers were able to finish charting the most northern coastlines on the globe.

So what's left? Has the world been totally explored and mapped? On the surface, yes. With modern technology such as GPS satellites and digital photographs taken by space shuttle missions, there really isn't any uncharted territory left. Every part of the globe has been seen and mapped. Even the land under the oceans has been charted to a large degree. Underwater exploration isn't finished by any means, but we basically know where all the underwater mountains and plains are. The surface of the earth is constantly changing, however, so there will always be a need for mapmakers to keep up with it. For instance, a totally new island came into being during the 1960s. Surtsey Island, off the coast of Iceland, was formed by an underwater volcano. Where there used to be only water on the map, now there is an island!

Surtsey in its early stages in the 1960s.

View of Surtsey Island, 1999
(from en.wikepedia.org, originally uploaded from iceland.world-traveler.org.)

M.AP DRAWINGS

PLEASE NOTE: The purpose of these drawings is not to be an all-inclusive source of geography knowledge. You won't learn every river, desert or mountain on the planet. They are intended to give the students a very basic knowledge of each area, and the ability to draw it from memory. You are welcome to add as many extra details as you wish.

These pages can be used by the instructor as guidance for in-class demonstrations, or they can be copied and handed out to the students.

You can watch these drawing lessons on DVDs! If you purchased this curriculum as an individual book (no DVDs included) and you would like to purchase the set of DVDs, they can be ordered at www.ellenjmchenry.com, or on Amazon.com.

MAP DRAWING 1: Mesopotamia

Mesopotamia means "between the rivers." ("Meso" means "middle" and "potam" means "river.") Mesopotamia is located in the modern country of Iraq.

At the very northern reaches of Mesopotamia was the territory of Assyria, with its capital at Nineveh. (This is the city that Jonah was sent to in the famous Bible story.) Assyria rose to power first, then the Babylonians conquered them, then both of them were overtaken by the Persians, coming from the area we now call Iran.

The ancient cities of Nineveh and Babylon are completely gone. The modern cities of Mosul and Baghdad are now the largest cities in those regions.

Here is a way you can remember which river is which: the <u>T</u>igris is on <u>T</u>op. Both words start with the letter "T." (Perhaps you can think of another way to keep them straight. Whatever works for you is fine.)

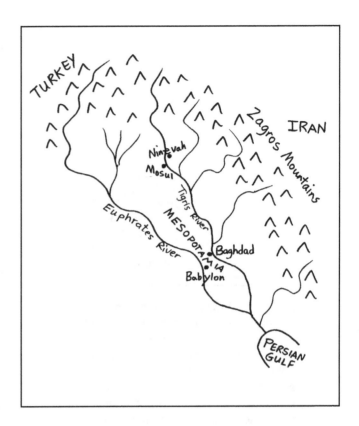

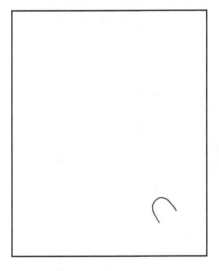

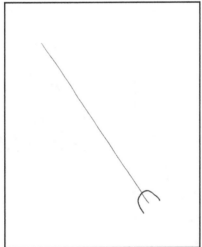

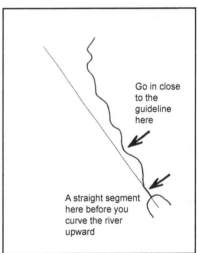

Go in close to the guideline here

A straight segment here before you curve the river upward

STEP 1: Draw a tilted arch. This will be the top of the Persian Gulf. In this drawing you will see only the top of the gulf. You can label the gulf now, or you can wait until the end, in step 7.

STEP 2: Draw a very light guideline up from the tilted arch. You will be erasing this line soon, so make it light. The guideline is just to help you gauge where to draw the lines for the two rivers.

STEP 3: Start right at the top of the Persian Gulf and begin to draw the Tigris River. Draw along the straight guideline to make a short, straight segment, then make the river curve away from the guideline. Bring the river back in again, almost to the guideline, then curve it out and away again, making a few ripples before it fades off.

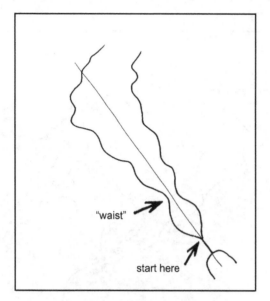

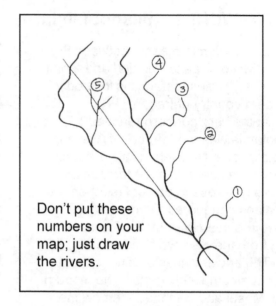

Don't put these numbers on your map; just draw the rivers.

STEP 4: Draw in the lower river (the Euphrates), starting at the top of the first little straight part. You can see that this river also comes in toward the guideline right at the place the top one did, making sort of a "waist" (shown by the arrow). Continue the river on up and fade it off in the same direction as the first one.

STEP 5: Now add five smaller rivers. These smaller ones are called tributaries. Don't worry about making them the exact shape you see here. The important thing is to know that they are there and to understand that it's the water from these tributaries that creates the larger rivers. (Don't write the numbers on your map.)

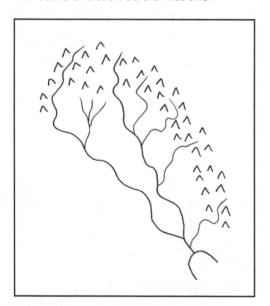

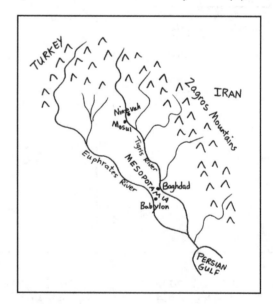

STEP 6: Erase your guideline now and draw in some mountains. (You may want to draw over your good lines with pen before you erase your guideline.) Tributaries almost always flow out of a mountain range. Snow and rain from the mountains drain down into the valleys and create streams. These streams feed into larger streams which then feed into rivers. We will see this pattern again and again as we map the world. Tributaries flow out of mountains.

STEP 7: Now it's time to label. The Tigris River is on the Top, and the Euphrates is the lower one. The cities of Baghdad and Babylon are right at the "waist." The cities of Nineveh and Mosul are above the highest tributary. Label the Persian Gulf if it isn't already labeled. You may want to label the mountains on the right as the Zagros Mountains. The area between the rivers is Mesopotamia. Optional: Label modern countries of Turkey and Iran, which border Iraq.

MAP DRAWING 2: The Nile river

The Nile River flows from south to north, a fact which surprised European explorers and mapmakers. The reason that the river flows north is obvious when you look at the overall geography of the river. We see tributaries flowing out of the mountains in the south. The tributaries join together to make the Nile, and it flows towards the nearest sea: the Mediterranean.

On this map we will draw and label the Tropic of Cancer. Knowing where certain geographical features cross the Tropic line will help you later, when you try to draw a large portion of the world from memory.

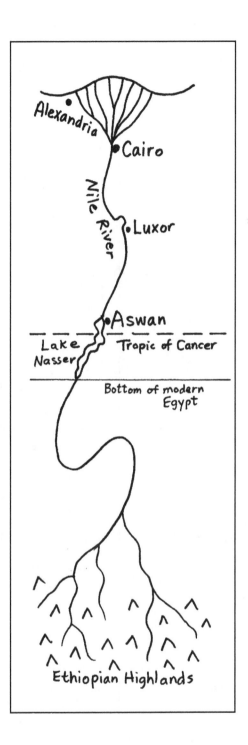

STEP 1: Draw a curvy line at the top. Make sure the curve goes up in the middle and down on each side.

STEP 2: Draw lines converging to form an upside-down triangle. This is the "delta" region of the river. A delta is where a river splits into smaller branches as it flows towards the sea.

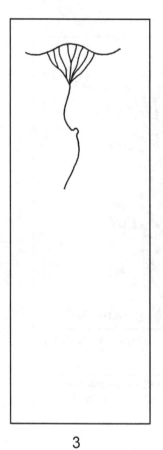

3

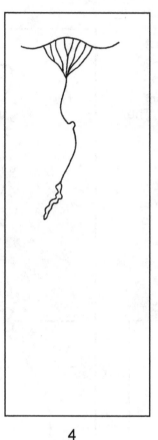

4

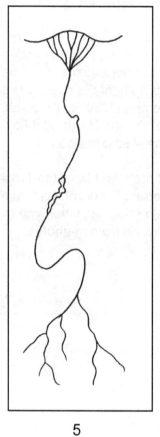

5

STEP 3: Draw a shallow "S" shape (one that doesn't curve too much). If you want to be more accurate, add a little bump right in the middle. (This bump is the location of the Valley of the Kings, at Luxor. This is where you go if you want to see King Tut's tomb.)

STEP 4: Add a narrow "squiggle" lake just below the shallow "S."

STEP 5: Now make a very curvy "S" shape. At the bottom of this "S," add tributaries going off to the south.

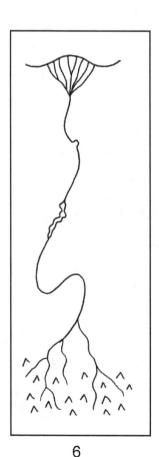

6

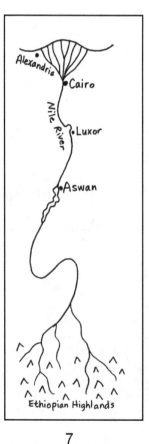

7

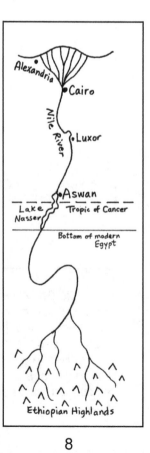

8

STEP 6: Add mountains in and around the tributaries. These mountains provide all the water for the Nile River.

STEP 7: Label the mountains "Ethiopian Highlands." Label Lake Nasser and four cities: Aswan, Luxor, Cairo and Alexandria. At Aswan, there is a huge dam that controls the flow of the Nile River. Cairo is where you go to see the famous pyramids of Giza.

STEP 8: Draw a line right below Aswan, cutting across the top of Lake Nasser. Label it as the Tropic of Cancer. You may also want to draw a line showing the bottom of modern Egypt, at the bottom of Lake Nasser.

MAP DRAWING 3: Greece

Ready for a challenge? Great! This map of Greece will certainly be a challenge, but if you follow the directions step by step, you will be surprised how easily you can learn to draw it. (Don't worry— map drawing 4 will be a lot easier than this one!)

To begin, you will need to do some preparation steps that you didn't have to do with the first two maps. For this map, you will create the basic shape using your hand. When you draw around your hand, make your lines as light as you possible can, because they are only guidelines, not actual lines on your map.

NOTE: **The sketched-in lines below look much darker than your lines will. Your lines should be so light you can hardly see them!**

Preparing your paper:

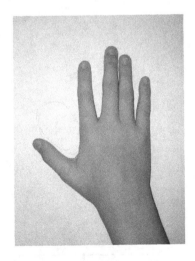

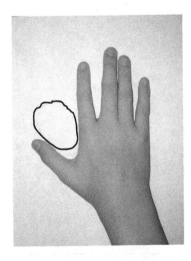

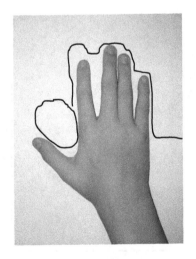

STEP 1: Lay your right hand on your paper, right in the center, so that it looks just like the one shown here. You need to have a space between your index finger and the other fingers.

STEP 2: With your left hand, use a pencil to sketch in an egg shape between your thumb and your hand. Draw VERY LIGHTLY as you will eventually erase this line.

STEP 3: Use a pencil to sketch a "mitten" around your hand, going well up over your index finger and going down into the dip between the fingers. Go off the paper at the bottom knuckle of the pinky, as shown here.

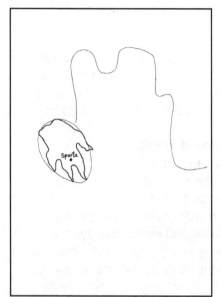

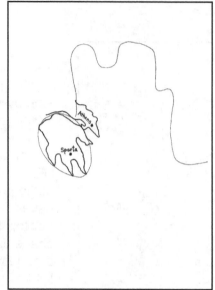

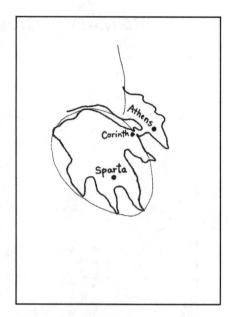

STEP 4: Draw a weird 3-fingered hand inside the egg shape. The pinky is bent and the fingers have long skinny nails. Try to copy the shape you see here as accurately as you can, or use an atlas to look at the real shape. (Maybe it's a dragon's foot, belonging to the dragon in the next step?) Label "Sparta."

STEP 5: Does this next shape remind you of the backside of an animal? Maybe it has its head buried in the sand? (With its lumpy back, does it look a bit like a dragon?) Draw a foot shape that touches the thumb of the hand, then draw a stubby tail and a lumpy back. Extend the line up over the back of the hand, too. Label "Athens."

STEP 6: Now you need to connect these first two shapes. Erase the lines where they touch (which will be a very small area) and adjust the lines so that there is a tiny land bridge connecting the two land masses. The correct name for this feature is an "isthmus." (That's a very strange word, isn't it?) Label the city on the isthmus "Corinth."

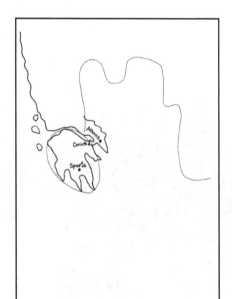

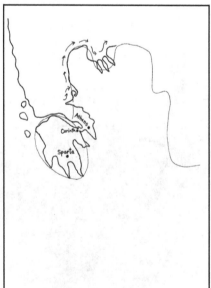

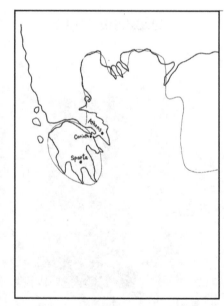

STEP 7: Pick up where you left off on the back of the dragon/animal and draw up the coastline, forming the sleeve that the weird hand came out of. Draw three islands off the coast. You can make up what these might be, according to your own imagination.

STEP 8: Continue the coastline on the other side. Draw up along your guide line. When you come to the dip between your fingers, draw a cow's udder with three very skinny teats leaning off to the right.

STEP 9: Continue along your guide line, then draw another peninsula in the shape you see here. Notice how there is still some of your guideline left below this peninsula.

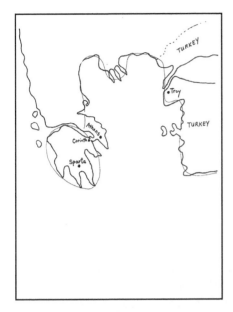

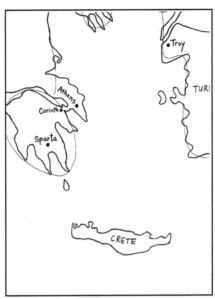

STEP 10: Draw in the land mass below the peninsula and label it "Turkey." Notice the hand reaching out from Turkey to snatch the island? (Or maybe you think it looks like something else.) Put in the dotted line where the top of Turkey is, and label the location of the ancient city of Troy.

STEP 11: Make a "drip" just below the index finger of the hand. Then imagine a line going straight down from the thumb—this is where the head of Crete will be. Draw in Crete and label it. We think Crete looks like a Martian with two short antenae and a bulbous nose, lying on his back, with one leg chopped off. (Maybe the dragon got him?) What do you think?

STEP 12: Greece has hundreds of small islands. The islands behind the dragon look like they are strung out in long lines. Make sure you get the long skinny island right above the back end of the dragon (marked with the arrow). The big island on the far right is Rhodes. It had a huge statue on it (called The Colossus), which was one of the Seven Wonders of the Ancient World.

STEP 13: Label these bodies of water: the Aegean Sea (remember it's "ae" then "ea," and it's pronounced *Uh-GEE-an*), the Ionian Sea, and the Mediterranean. ("Medi" means "middle" and "terra" means "earth." The Greeks believed this sea to be in the middle of the world.)

STEP 14: Erase your light pencil guidelines. (You may want to trace over your good lines with pen before you erase your guidelines.) If you want to make the coastlines more accurate, you can consult an atlas for the exact shape. Now trace over your "good" lines with a black pen, then erase all pencil lines.

STEP 15: Optional: Label the Sea of Marmara and the Dardanelles Strait. If this step is one too many, just skip it. We'll learn these later on, too.

MAP DRAWING 4: The Roman Boot

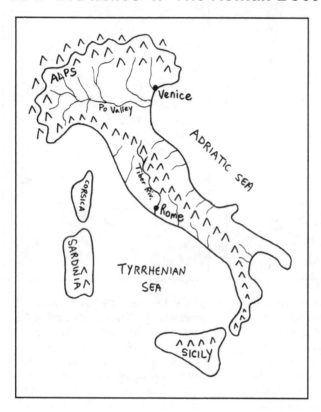

Do you think this peninsula looks like a boot? Most people see it as either a tall boot or a leg. It looks as though the island of Sicily is getting kicked by the foot. (To remember which island is Sicily, think of it as the "sissy" getting kicked around by the foot.)

Ptolemy was a Roman citizen even though he lived in Alexandria. The Roman Empire was huge, but it was centered in the peninsula we now call Italy. From the city of Rome, the Emperor controlled the entire Mediterranean region.

The proper name for this peninsula is the Italian peninsula. Nowadays we also call this peninsula "Italy" but until the 19th century, there was no country of Italy. The peninsula was a collection of small territories called "city states."

The Tyrrhenian Sea (*Tie-REE-nee-an*) is named after Tyrrheus (*Tie-REE-us*), a shepherd from a story in Roman mythology whose pet stag was killed by the Trojans.

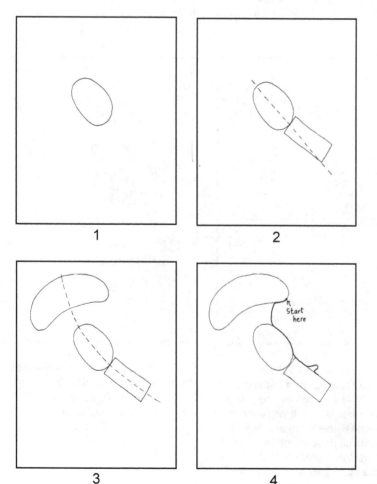

STEP 1: Draw an oval. This is a guideline and should be very light. You wil be erasing the oval as soon as you have your "good" lines drawn in.

STEP 2: Draw a long rectangle below the oval. The rectangle should be about the same length as the oval. A center line for the oval is shown here so that you can see that the rectangle is adjusted just slightly upward. You don't have to draw this center line.

STEP 3: Draw a large flatish kidney bean shape above the oval. Once again, a center line has been sketched in so that you can see that these three shapes are sort of lined up on a curve. You may sketch in the line, or you can decide not to. It's up to you.

STEP 4: Now begin your outline of the peninsula. Start where it says, "Start here" and begin drawing down the side as shown here. When you come to the middle of the rectangle, draw a "spur." (It might remind you of a rooster's spur if you've ever seen one.)

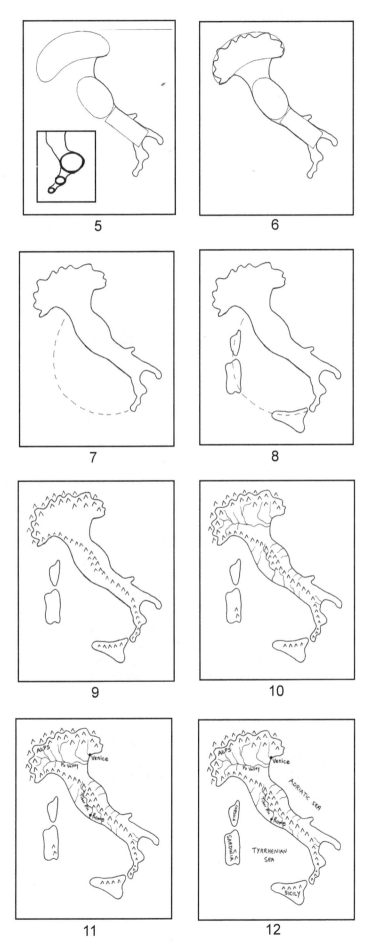

5

6

7

8

9

10

11

12

STEP 5: Now make a very long heel on the boot. The distance it sticks down is about the same as the width of the rectangle. The big toe starts out like the heel, making a line going almost straight down from the rectangle. But then you draw out to the left, to form the toe. Notice that there are bumps that look like knuckles along the toe. The inset picture shows that you can make three balls—large, medium and small—along the toe.

STEP 6: Finish drawing up along the left side, then continue over the top, making the edges of the kidney-bean shape very wavy.

STEP 7: Draw an arc from the tip of the toe to the inward curve at the top. This will be your guide for placement of the islands.

STEP 8: Draw a triangular-shaped island right at the toe. (This is Sicily. Perhaps Sicily is the sissy getting kicked by the foot?) Draw the other two islands; they are fairly close together. These are the islands of Sardinia and Corsica. You can label the islands now, or you can wait until step 12.

STEP 9: Add mountains all along the wavy top as well as running down the middle of the peninsula. The mountains go right down the toe and even onto the triangular island.

STEP 10: You might be able to guess where rivers would go on this peninsula—coming out of the mountains and flowing down into the sea. The large valley at the top, with all the rivers flowing through it, is a prime agricultural region (meaning plants grow really well).

STEP 11: Label the Alps at the top, and the Po Valley along the river. Label the Tiber River and the city of Rome (which is located on the river). Also label the city of Venice. Venice will be an important location for European explorers and mapmakers.

STEP 12: Label the three islands: Sicily, Sardinia and Corsica. Label the seas on each side of the peninsula: the Adriatic and the Tyrrenhenian. (The name Adriatic is heard much more frequently than Tyrrenhenian. If you only remember one of them, remember the Adriatic.)

MAP DRAWING 5A: The "Holy Land" of the Crusaders

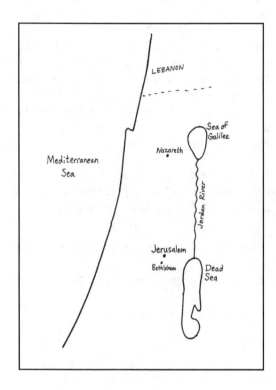

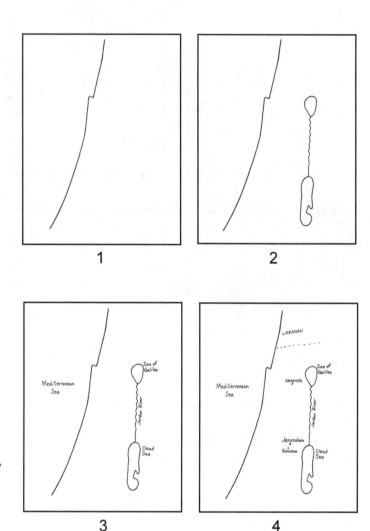

This area of the world is known by three names: Palestine, the Holy Land, and the land of Israel. The word Palestine comes from its ancient inhabitants, the Philistines. The Crusaders called it the Holy Land because it was the land where Jesus lived. In modern times, most of the land west of the Jordan River has been claimed by the modern state of Israel, founded in 1948.

STEP 1: Draw a slanted line down the page, giving it a small bump about two-thirds of the way up the coast.

STEP 2: Draw a lake to the east of the bump on the coastline, a river going down from it, then a long lake at the bottom.

STEP 3: Label the bodies of water: the Sea of Galiliee, the Jordan River, the Dead Sea (also called the Salt Sea), and the Mediterranean Sea.

STEP 4: Label the cities that were of most interest to the Crusaders: Jerusalem (where the Jewish temple used to be), Bethlehem (where Jesus was born) and Nazareth (the town where Jesus lived until he began his public ministry).

OPTIONAL: Draw a dotted line across the top and label the land above the line Lebanon. This area has been known as Lebanon as far back as 1000 BC. Today it is the modern country of Lebanon.

Wow— this one was easy! Since you've got a little mental energy left over, let's do another map. Let's draw the Arabian peninsula.

MAP DRAWING 5B: The Arabian peninsula

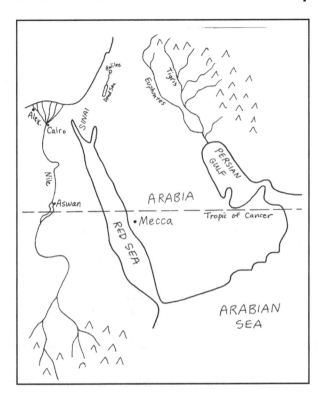

Arabia is the land where the religion of Islam originated (around 600 AD). The central city of Islam, Mecca, is located here.

The Arabian peninsula looks a little bit like a boot, but a rugged hiking boot, nothing like the fancy Roman boot. This boot looks like it had some serious tread on the soles.

The addition of Arabia will let us bring together three other maps: the Nile River, the "Holy Land," and Mesopotamia. After learning Arabia, you will be able to draw large chunk of the Middle East.

You will need to do three easy steps to prepare your paper, then you will be ready to draw.

To prepare your paper:

STEP 1: Put a dot 3" (7.5 cm) from the bottom of the paper, right in the middle.

STEP 2: Draw a rectangle 5" (12.5 cm) tall by 2 1/2" (6.25 cm) wide, going up from the dot, at a 25 degree angle. Draw a dividing line right in the middle, making two squares.

STEP 3: Draw a semi-circle going out from the bottom square.

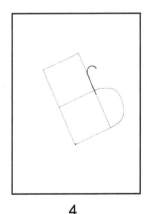

1

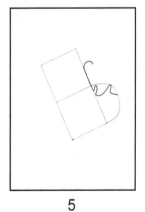

2

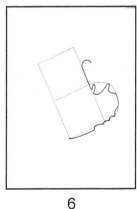

3

To begin your map:

STEP 4: Draw a candy cane going up from the dividing line between the squares. Make the hooked end about halfway up the top square.

STEP 5: Draw two long skinny bumps inside the top of the semi-circle, as shown here. (Maybe these are loops from the laces of the boot?)

STEP 6: Draw along the bottom rim of the semi-circle and onto the bottom of the lower square. Make three treads (you might want to call them spikes) on the sole before you get to the heel (but don't make them too spikey).

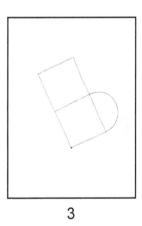

4

5

6

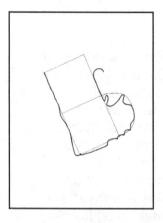

STEP 7: Draw a line up the back of the boot. Make a bump at the heel and another bump halfway up, right at the dividing line.

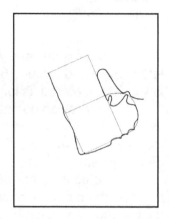

STEP 8: Go back over to the "candy" line and pick up the line where you left off. Draw down to the point on the shoe, then go around it, as shown here. You have just made the Persian Gulf. You can label it now, if you wish, or you can wait till the end, like we did. Either is fine.

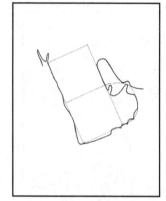

STEP 9: Now go back to the other side again and pick up the line at the top of the boot, making two tall, skinny bumps that form a tri-angle shape in between them.

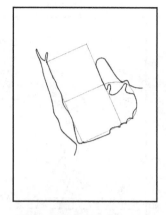

STEP 10: Draw down the side, parallel to the back of the boot. You have just drawn the Red Sea. What does it look like? A skinny fish? A long slug? What do you think? You can label the Red Sea now, or you can wait and do all the labeling at the end.

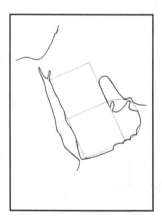

STEP 11: This is an easy step. Just draw a wavy line at the top, like you see here. This is the coastline along the edge of the Mediterranean Sea. Make sure you get the bump that will turn into the Nile River delta.

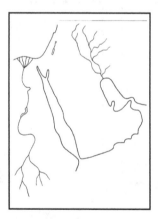

STEP 12: Now it's time to fill in with some things you already know. Draw in the Nile River, the Tigris and Euphrates, the Sea of Galilee, the Jordan River and the Dead Sea. (Note that Aswan—the top of the lake on the Nile—should be about even with the "shoe string" bumps on the top of the boot.)

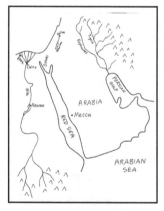

STEP 13: Now it's labeling time! Fill in everything you already know. You are welcome to label more than what is shown here. Then add the Red Sea, the Persian Gulf, the Arabian Sea, and the city of Mecca.

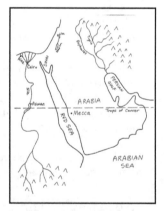

STEP 14: Here's a bonus step: put in the Tropic of Cancer. Knowing where this line goes will be helpful when you are mapping the whole world later on. The tropic line runs through the top of Lake Nasser, just above Mecca, and just below those little "shoe string" peninsulas that stick up.

MAP DRAWING 6A: The Black Sea

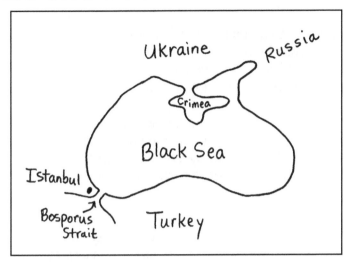

People have been living on the shores of the Black Sea for at least 6,000 years. These ancient peoples from around the Black Sea spread out and eventually populated all the areas we now call Europe, Russia, India and Iran. One reason we know this to be true is that the languages spoken in these areas have many similarities, suggesting that all these languages (English, French, German, Italian, Spanish, Norwegian, Greek, Latin, Russian, Hindi, Persian, and many more) came from one original language, which linguists call Proto-Indo-European.

The Turks have controlled the south shore of the Black Sea for about a thousand years. The Turks came to this region from central Asia, east of the Aral Sea.

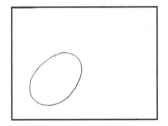

STEP 1: Draw an egg. This is just a sketchy guideline so make it very light and easy to erase. (Make the next two circles very light, as well.)

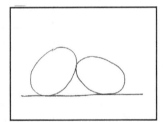

STEP 2: Draw a line representing the table top and then draw another egg leaning on the first one. Notice that this second egg is leaning more than the first one.

STEP 3: Draw a small cirlce on top of the second egg. Make sure the circle isn't any higher than the first egg.

STEP 4: Begin your outline of the sea. First, draw a "finger" pointing out from the small circle. This finger points toward Russia, a country which has fought bloody battles to gain control over the Black Sea).

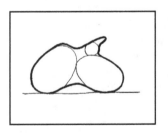

STEP 5: Draw the rest of the outline. Notice how on the bottom you don't go all the way in to where the eggs touch, just part way.

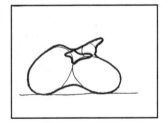

STEP 6: Draw in a T-shaped land mass right at the intersection of the three egg cirlces.

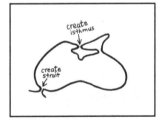

STEP 7: With your eraser, create a tiny isthmus, making the T-shape into a peninsula. Also create an inlet to the Black Sea so ships can sail in. As you can imagine, whoever controls this strait controls commerce in the Black Sea.

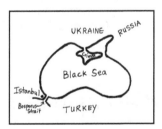

STEP 8: Label your map. The peninsula is called "The Crimea" or "The Crimean Peninsula." There are a few other countries that touch the Black Sea, but right now learn just these three. Label the city of Istanbul and the Bosporus Strait. (The large map at the top of the page shows the labeling more clearly.)

MAP DRAWING 6B: The Caspian Sea

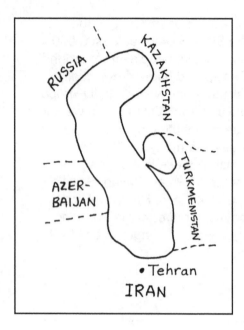

The Caspian Sea has become important in the modern world recently because of the discovery of vast amounts of crude oil under the sea floor. The countries that touch the Caspian Sea all want as much of the oil as they can get.

The little circle on the right of the sea is extremely shallow. It is mainly used to evaporate the salty water to produce salt crystals. Historically, salt has been an important trade item for countries that can produce it.

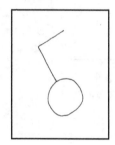

STEP 1: To begin, make these light guidelines: an upside-down L with a circle stuck onto the bottom.

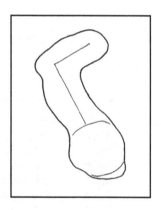

STEP 2: Draw an outline that stays well away from the corner shape but goes right next to the circle.

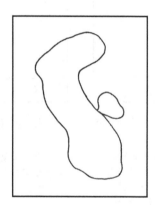

STEP 3: Add the little extra sea on the eastern side. It almost makes it look like the letter F. This sea is extremely shallow.

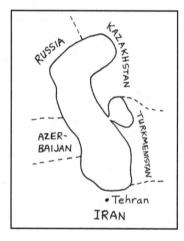

STEP 4: Label the Caspian Sea, the city of Tehran, Iran, and the surrounding countries. All of these five countries would like to have exclusive rights to the oil under the sea, but Russia and Iran have more political power than the other three countries.

MAP DRAWING 6C: The Aral Sea

To make the Aral Sea, just draw an egg-shape with a wiggly outline. It doesn't matter exactly what shape it is because the shape of the Aral Sea is changing all the time—it's getting smaller and smaller every year. It used to be the size of Lake Superior and by the year 2020 it will be just about gone! The reason it is shrinking is that the Communist government decided to change the course of the rivers that fed into the sea. They used this water to irrigate cotton fields. When the sea is completely gone, the name will officially be changed to the Aral Desert. The two countries that have inherited this ecological disaster are Uzbekistan and Kazakhstan.

Check out a current satellite image to get an exact shape.

MAP DRAWING 7: The Iberian Peninsula

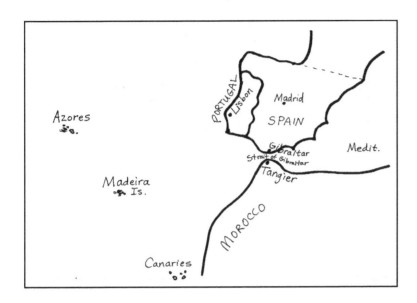

This part of Europe is called the Iberian peninsula. It is made up of the countries of Spain and Portugal. Notice how close Spain comes to Africa.

Portugal owns two groups of islands: the Azores and the Madeira Islands. It used to own another group, the Cape Verde Islands, but they were given their independence in 1975.

The new geography word you will learn in this lesson is the correct term for a group of islands: "archipelago." ("*ark-i-PELL-ah-go*")

Your three preparatory steps:

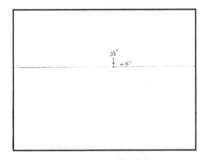

STEP 1: Draw a line across your paper 3 1/2" (9 cm) down from the top. Put a dot on the line 5" (12.5 cm) in from the right end.

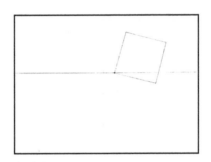

STEP 2: Draw a box that is 2 1/2" (6.25 cm) on each side and is tilted 15 degrees down from the line.

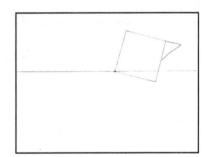

STEP 3: Draw a small triangle on the side of the box, as shown here.

Now, start drawing the map:

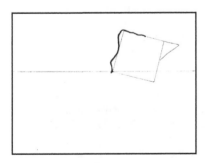

STEP 4: Begin to outline the peninsula. Start in the middle of the top of the square and go counter-clockwise, rounding the first corner quite a bit. Make a significant bump right before you get to the seond corner. The city of Lisbon will sit on this bump. Come to a point at your original dot (the one in step 1).

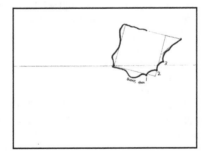

STEP 5: Continue to draw around the square, making a bulge in the middle of the bottom of the square. After making the bulge, go up at an angle, as shown, making three "spiked" points, just like you did when you drew the botttom of Arabia. Then, continue on up to the corner.

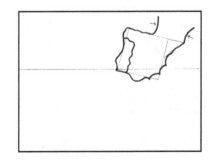

STEP 6: Continue your line up past the corner Then go over to where you started, and pick up the line again, curving it upward. (These two lines are shown with arrows.) After you have drawn these two lines, mark out where Portugal is, as shown here.

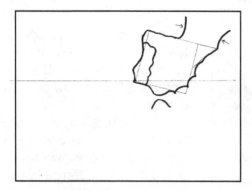

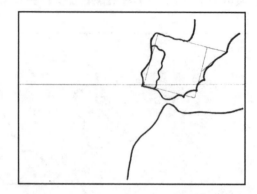

STEP 7: Draw a bump right below Spain's bump. This new, matching bump will be the other side of the Strait of Gibraltar.

STEP 8: Draw in the rest of the coast of Africa, something like you see here—just two simple curved lines.

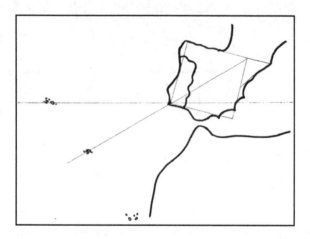

STEP 9: Now we need to add islands. These islands are arranged in small groups. A group of islands is called an "archipelago." (This word comes from the Greek words "archi," meaning "most important" and "pelagus," meaning "sea." It is likely that this was the original name for the Aegean Sea. Since the Aegean Sea is filled with islands, over time the meaning of the word shifted to refer to the islands, not the sea.)

Draw your first group of islands right on your preparatory line. The distance they are out from land is the same distance as the measurement from your original dot to the farthest-away point of the small triangle you drew in step 3. You can use your pencil to take an estimated measurement of this distance catty-corner across the peninsula, then make the islands that same distance out in the ocean.

To make the second group of islands, draw a line through the corners of your square and extend it out into the ocean. Now measure the distance from corner to corner on your square and make the islands that same distance out into the ocean.

The third group of islands is right at the bottom of your paper, just off the coast of Africa.

STEP 10: Now it's time to label. Write in the names of the countries of Spain and Portugal. The borders of these countries haven't changed much over the centuries. Make a dot in the center of Spain and label it Madrid. Make a dot on the bump on Portugal and label it Lisbon. (You might want to make a dotted line across the top of Spain, also, showing where its northern border is.)

Label the country of Morocco and mark the city of Tangier. (Can you remember what explorer was born in Tangier?)

Label the Strait of Gibraltar. You may also want to label the city on the Spanish side, Gibraltar. The city of Gibraltar is a narrow peninsula consisting of a rock the size of a mountain. This city/peninsula is actually owned by Great Britain!

Label the groups of islands. The top ones are the Azores, the middle ones are the Madeira Islands, and the ones on the bottom are the Canary Islands. Portugal owns the top two, the Azores and the Madeiras. Spain owns the Canary Islands.

You may also want to label the Mediterranean Sea and the Atlantic Ocean.

MAP DRAWING 8A: France

This map drawing will be a little different from the others we've done. In this exercise you will try to learn a shape by tracing over it many times and learning to "feel" the shape with your pencil.

As you can see, France has been placed inside a circle with numbers around the outside as if it were a clock. This will help you get all the points and curves in the right places when you go to draw it on your own. But first, you will trace this shape right here.

Begin by placing your pencil at either the six or the twelve (six is recommended). Choose whether you will go clockwise (following the numbers in order) or counter-clockwise. Then trace right over the outline, noticing how the curves and shapes feel as you go along. Find a rhythm to the shapes and let your pencil stop and start with those rhythms. Trace the outline at least ten times. Yes, that's right. At least ten times!

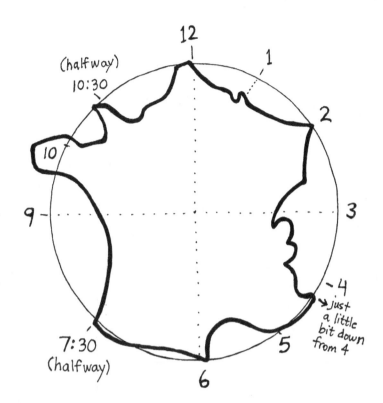

Now you can try drawing it on your own:

STEP 1: Make a circle with your compass. Make it at least 4" (10 cm) in diameter (that means set your compass for a radius of 2 inches). The exact size of the circle is not important, however. It can be larger.
STEP 2: Mark off 3, 6, 9 and 12, then mark 1, 2, 4, 5 and the halfway points of 7:30 and 10:30.
STEP 3: Start at the same place you did when you traced the shape above. Draw the outline, keeping your pencil down on the paper the whole time. You may look at the drawing above while you draw, to help you remember the shapes.
STEP 4: Trace over your good line in pen, then erase the pencil lines. Label the capital city, Paris, and the city of Strasbourg, where Gutenberg lived. Label the regions that are known as Brittany and Normandy. These regions are quite significant in the history of Europe and it's worth knowing where they are. Also, you may want to dot in the sections in the north eastern corner of the country, as shown, and label them Alsace and Lorraine. The territories of Alsace and Lorraine (also known by their combined name Alsace-Lorraine) have gone back and forth between France and Germany for hundreds of years. The last time they changed hands was right after World War II, when they went back from Germany to France. You can label them separately, or you can label the whole corner as "Alsace-Lorraine". In the days of Gutenberg, the city of Strasbourg considered itself independent. The modern countries of France and Germany didn't exist yet.

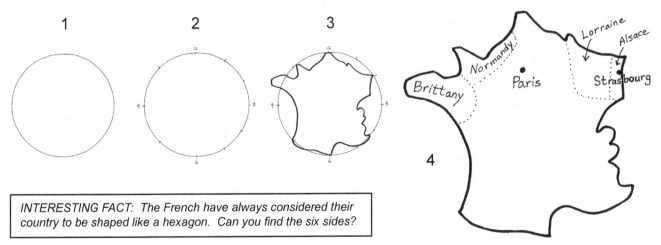

INTERESTING FACT: The French have always considered their country to be shaped like a hexagon. Can you find the six sides?

MAP DRAWING 8B: Adding France to the Iberian peninsula

Now that you've drawn France, let's put it into its proper place above the Iberian peninsula.

STEP 1: Begin by drawing a line 3" (7.5 cm) from the bottom of your paper. Then make a dot (on the line) that is 1" (2.5 cm) in from the left side.

STEP 2: Make a square that is 3 inches on each side and tilted a bit (the tilt should be something between 10 and 15 degrees—you can estimate it with your eyes if you'd like, instead of using the protractor). Don't forget to add the little triangle on the side, too.

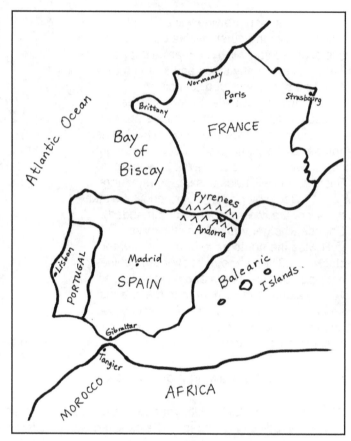

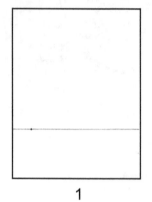
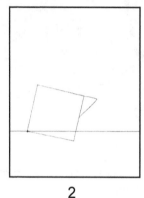

1   2

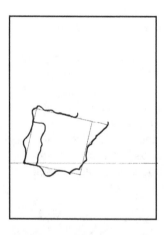
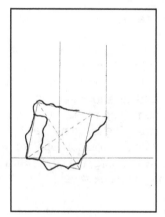
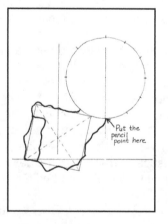

STEP 3: Draw in the outline of Spain and Portugal, just like you did in drawing 7. If you can't remember how to do it, go back and check the directions again.

You can add Africa at this point, if you want to, or you can wait until you've drawn France.

STEP 4: Connect the corners inside the box in order to find the center. Draw a line up from the center dot. Make sure the line is parallel to the edge of your paper (in other words it goes up perfectly straight). This line will mark the edge of Brittany. Also draw a line straight up from the point of the little triangle. The center of your circle will be right on this line.

STEP 5: Set your compass so that it measures the same distance as from the center of the square to one corner (this will be about 2 1/8 inches). Put the pencil point of your compass on the end point of the little triangle (right where your line leaves off) and then set the pointed end down on the line that goes straight up. Then draw the circle with your compass.

STEP 6: Draw little dashes where the numbers would go on the clock. Use your protractor if you have any question about getting the numbers 3, 6, 9 and 12 placed correctly. Then draw your outline of France.

STEP 7: Label the map as shown above. Add the Bay of Biscay, the Balearic Islands, the Pyrenees Mountains, and the tiny country of Andorra.

MAP DRAWING 9: The Indian "subcontinent"

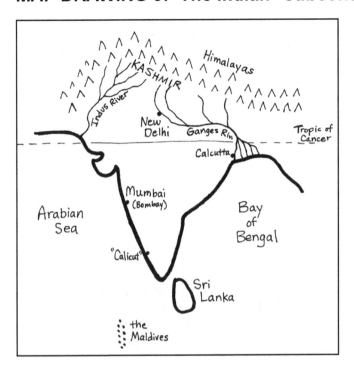

The Indian peninsula is easy to identify and easy to draw. This region is called a "subcontinent" for several reasons. First, the word "sub' means "under" and this peninsula is under Asia. Second, most geologists believe that India used to be a separate continent until it crashed into Asia, forming the Himalaya mountains in the process.   Third, the mountain ranges separate the peninsula geographically from the rest of Asia. The land and the people groups of India are different from the rest of Asia. The plants that grow in India produce many of the world's most popular spices: pepper, cinnamon, ginger and coriander.

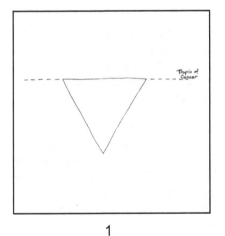

1

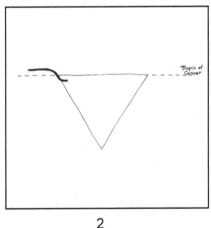

2

STEP 1: Draw a line across your paper and label it "Tropic of Cancer." Then draw a triangle hanging from the line.

STEP 2: Start your outline a little above the Tropic line, then curve it down along the triangle. Just a tiny bit down the side of the triangle, make the line go in a bit.

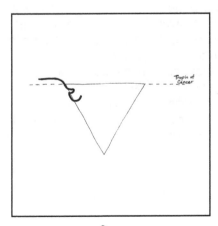

3

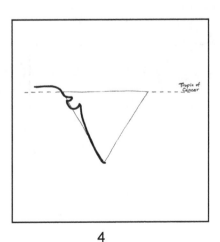

4

STEP 3: Make a curvy "tongue" shape, ending your line well inside the triangle.

STEP 4:   Now extend your outline down to the the bottom of the triangle.

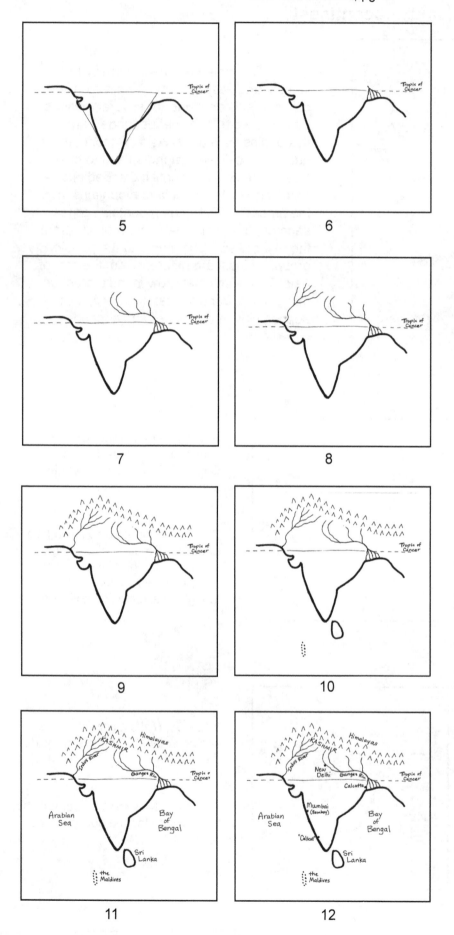

STEP 5: Continue the outline up the other side of the triangle but don't go up to the Tropic line. Curve over and down before you get to the Tropic line.

STEP 6: This map will have a delta region, just like the map of the Nile River. Draw the delta as shown here.

STEP 7: Now draw in the Ganges River and its tributaries. There are four main tributaries stretching to the north. The last two look almost like C shapes, curving back around to the east a bit.

STEP 8: India has another large river, on the other side. This is the Indus River. It starts just a little above the Tropic line and goes northeast. Add tributaries at the end of it.

STEP 9: These tributaries start out in the mountains above India. Melting snow fills streams that run into the river. Put the mountains in above the tributaries. (These are the Himalaya Mountains.)

STEP 10: Add the island of Sri Lanka at the tip of the triangle, and also add a long, thin archipelago made of very tiny islands. These islands are called the Maldives. They were a stopping point for Europeans coming across the Indian Ocean.

STEP 11: Label the Arabian Sea, the Bay of Bengal, the Ganges River, the Indus River, the Himalaya Mountains, the island of Sri Lanka (which used to be called Ceylon) and the Maldives. Label Kashmir, the area between the tributaries of the two rivers. Kashmir is famous for its textiles (you may have heard someone say they have a Kashmir sweater or a Kashmir scarf).

STEP 12: Label these cities: Mumbai (used to be Bombay), New Delhi (the capital), Calicut (where the Portuguese landed—now called Kozhikode) and Calcutta, a HUGE modern city.

MAP DRAWING 10: The Greater Antilles

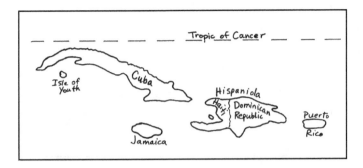

This group of islands is called the Greater Antilles. The islands are bigger (and therefore "greater") than all the other islands in the Caribbean Sea..

We are going to do something really silly in this lesson, but you'll find that it helps immensely with remembering the shapes of these islands. As you can see in the cartoon drawing to the left, we are going to imagine these islands to be bizarre forms of sea life, like something from the dark depths of the ocean. We'll call them the Cuban Vacuum Cleaner fish and the Haitian ("Hay-shun") Gulper fish. Each has a tiny baby following it, and both of them are going after a cookie that a careless human accidentally dropped overboard. The Haitian Gulper is eating a crumb while swimming toward the cookie. Baby Puerto Rico swims as fast as he can to keep up with his mother.

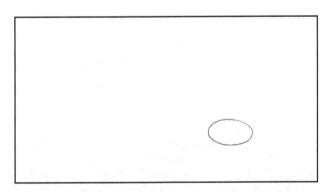

STEP 1: Lightly sketch an oval in the bottom right corner of your paper. This oval will become the body of the Haitian Gulper.

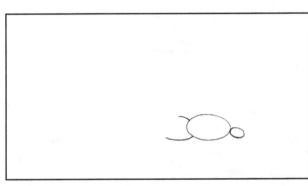

STEP 2: Add a little curved line for the upper jaw and a larger curved line for the lower jaw. These are just sketchy guide lines! Then add a small oval at the back.

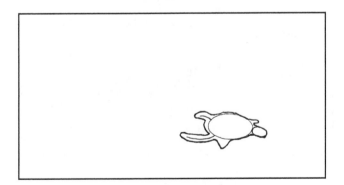

STEP 3: Now use the guidelines to guide you as you create the outline. Don't forget to add two fins—a large one down below and a tiny one peeking out from behind the tail.

STEP 4: Give the Gulper a baby following behind. The baby is just an elongated blob, without too much shape. It doesn't really look like a fish. Also add a tiny food particle going into the Gulper's mouth.

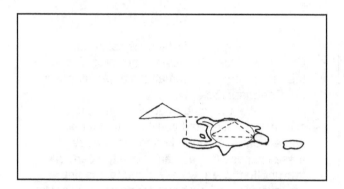

STEP 5: Draw a fairly flat triangle— one that would fit exactly inside the first oval you drew. The bottom of the triangle should be even with the very top of the Haitian Gulper fish, and the lower right corner of the triangle should be right above the end of the lower jaw. (The dashed lines show how to line it up.)

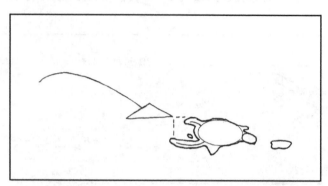

STEP 6: Put your pencil on the left side of the triangle and draw a slightly curved line going up and out to the left. It's like the body and handle of an upright vacuum cleaner. This long line will be a central guideline, sort of like the backbone of the fish. Your outline won't ever touch this backbone line.

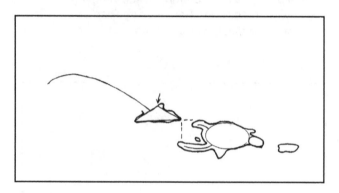

STEP 7: Begin your outline where indicated by the arrow. Draw in the eye first, then go around the triangle, making the edges nicely rounded.

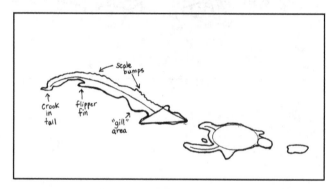

STEP 8: Continue the outline, making sure not ever to go too close to the backbone line. Make a bump for the gill area, then a long bump with a tiny flipper/fin thing on the end, then the tail (making sure to put a little kink in the end!), then all along the upper back, putting in some scaly bumps along the way.

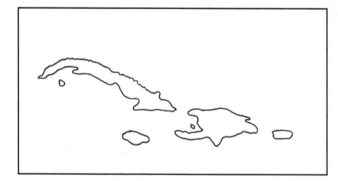

STEP 9: Add a tiny "baby" right under the Cuban Vacuum Cleaner fish's tail. It's much smaller than the Haitian Gulper's baby (maybe it's still an egg?). Lastly, add the cookie blob. It sort of forms the corner of an imaginary rectangle with the faces of the two fish. Now you may erase all your guidelines.

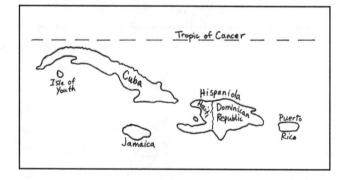

STEP 10: Label your drawing with the real names of the islands: Cuba and its tiny "Isle of Youth" (in Spanish it's "Isla de la Juventud"), Jamaica (an independent country), the island of Hispaniola which is divided into Haiti and the Dominican Republic (both independent countries), and Puerto Rico (a territory of the United States). You might also want to add the Tropic of Cancer, just above Cuba.

MAP DRAWING 11: The Lesser Antilles and the Bahamas

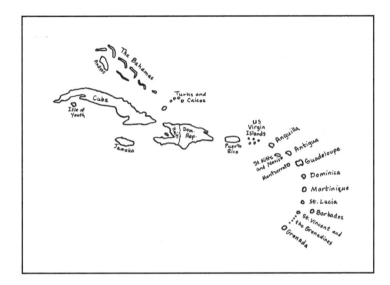

This is really an addition to map drawing 10. You will have to draw the Greater Antilles as your preparatory step, then add all these extra islands.

There are actually more islands than the ones we will draw. We've chosen only the larger and best-known islands (and still, it's a lot of islands!). If you would like to add more islands to your drawing, consult an atlas to see where additional little islands are. (We will be learning the islands along the coast of South America, such as Trinidad and Aruba, in a later lesson.) If there are too many names for you to remember, just choose a few of the names that you like the sound of, and remember those.

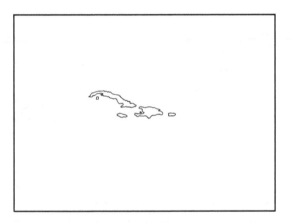

STEP 1: Draw the Greater Antilles in the center of your paper, fairly small like you see them here. There should be plenty of empty space around them.

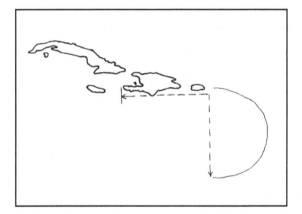

STEP 2: Draw a semi-circle right behind Puerto Rico. The diameter of the semi-circle should measure about the same as the distance from the tip of Jamaica to the tip of Puerto Rico.

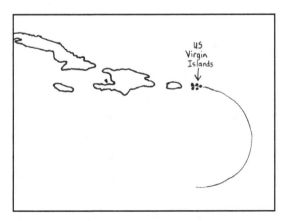

STEP 3: Make some little dots right behind Puerto Rico and label them as the "U.S. Virgin Islands." (The major islands are named St. Croix, St. Thomas and St. John, but you don't have to label them separately.)

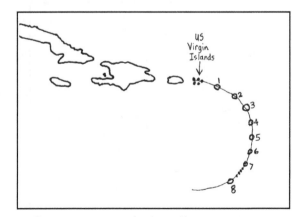

STEP 4: Draw seven islands going down the semi-circle, then some little tiny dots and then an eighth island.

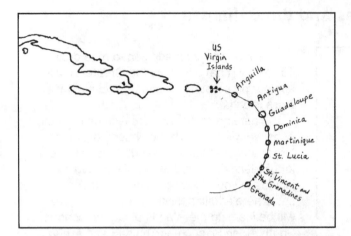

STEP 5: Write the names next to the islands: Anguilla, Antigua, Guadeloupe, Dominica, Martinique, St. Lucia, St. Vincent and the Grenadines (those tiny dots are the Grenadines) and Grenada. If you can't remember all these names, don't worry. Just pick out a few of them to remember.

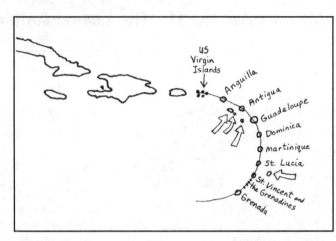

STEP 6: Add three tiny islands inside the semi-circle, right where the arrows are pointing. Also add a fourth island down between St. Lucia and St. Vincent.

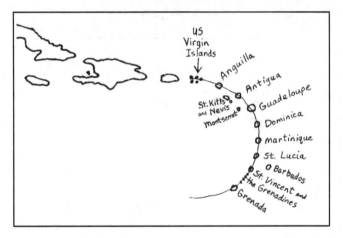

STEP 7: Label the islands from step 6 as (top to bottom): St. Kitts and Nevis, Montserrat (which is famous for its active volcano) and, way down below (between St. Lucia and St. Vincent), the island of Barbados.

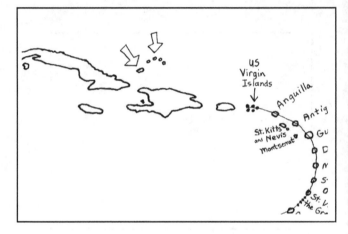

STEP 8: Add some "bubbles" over the head of the Haitian Gulper fish. They form kind of an arch. The first bubble on the left is the largest; the others are tiny.

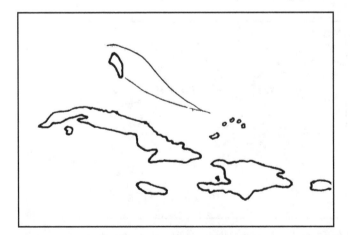

STEP 9: Draw a V shape going up from the bubbles you just drew. At the top of the lower prong of the V, draw in a fairly large island, looking somewhat like a chopped-off finger (maybe the fisherman in the next step was careless while chopping worms to feed the fish!).

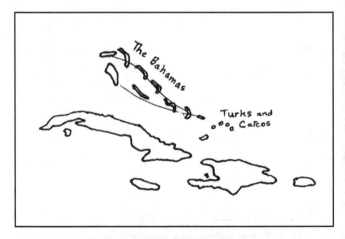

STEP 10: Draw some "worms" that a fisherman dropped overboard to attract these fish. Draw the skinny worms along the V lines. They generally look like backwards C's or long lines. Label the islands on the V as The Bahamas. Label the "bubbles" as the Turks and Caicos Islands.

MAP DRAWING 12A: Britain

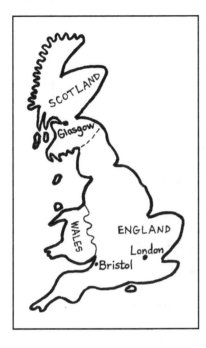

Here's another map where we will remember the shapes by drawing some weird animals. (You are welcome to substitute your own ideas, if your ideas work better for you.)

The rooster on top looks pretty normal; he's about to eat some seeds (or worms?). The creature under the rooster looks like something from mythology: sort of a half-dragon, half-wolf. He's sitting on an ice cube, which belongs to the mutant elephant-nose penguin on the bottom. Next to them there is a penguin chick hatching out of an egg.

STEP 1: Draw a very long oval in the lower right corner of your paper. (The oval should be long enough to fit three circles inside it.)

STEP 2: Draw a "flipper" on the bottom side of the oval, right in the center. Then draw a circle just to the left of the oval.

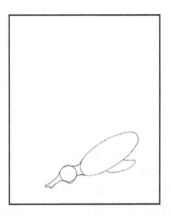

STEP 3: Using the circle as a guide, draw in the head and long nose of the elephant-nosed penguin. Make the end of the nose look like the end of an elephant's trunk, with short "fingers."

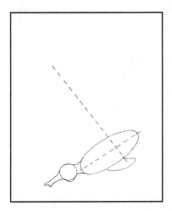

STEP 4: Draw a guideline through the center of the oval. Then draw a guideline that is perpendicular to this one.

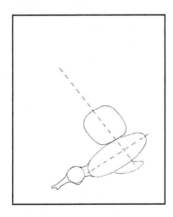

STEP 5: Draw an ice cube that is as tall as the distance from the top of the penguin's back to the bottom of its flipper. Make the ice cube slightly rounded on the corners.

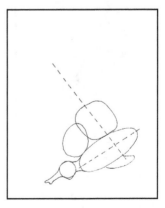

STEP 6: Draw an egg leaning onto the ice cube, overlapping it slightly. The egg should barely clear the penguin's head.

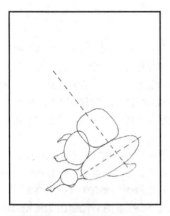

STEP 7: Now draw a little penguin head and a flipper beginning to hatch out of the egg.

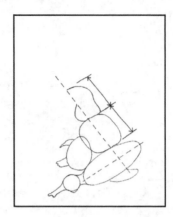

STEP 8: Draw the animal above the ice cube. Make the head as tall as the ice cube. Draw the back of the neck, then bring the underside of the neck in to the dotted line.

STEP 9: Draw in the rest of the head, including a ruffly lip, two fang teeth, and an ear. Make the ear end right at the dotted line, where you began the neck.

STEP: 10: Make the rooster's beak, right above the animal's ear. Curve the lower beak right over the ear. It will almost touch.

STEP 11: Make the rest of the rooster's head.

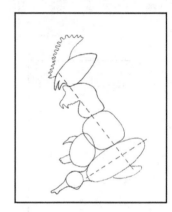

STEP: 12: Make the rooster's comb. The top should be very wiggly.

STEP 13: Draw around the outside of all the animal shapes to create the contour of Britain. After you have the outline finished, erase all the guidelines.

STEP 14: You may want to add these little islands. If your brain feels full and you don't think you'll remember the islands, at least add the ones that the rooster is about to eat.

STEP 15: Label the countries that Britain is divided into: England, Scotland and Wales. Label these cities: London, Bristol, and Glasgow.

MAP DRAWING 12B: Newfoundland

No one is sure exactly where John Cabot landed. It could have been anywhere on the eastern coast of Newfoundland. (Some scholars even claim it was farther south, on the coast of Nova Scotia.) To commemorate his discovery (wherever it was) there is a large statue of him on the cape at Bonavista and there is a tower named after him at St. John's.

To draw Newfoundland, we will think of it as a slice of pizza with a couple of bites taken out of it and cheese dripping off the end, in the shape of the letters "i" and "w."

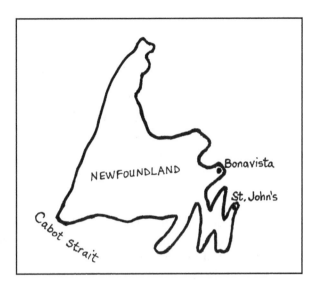

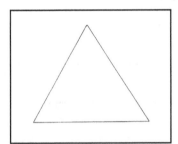

STEP 1: Draw an equilateral triangle (a triangle with sides of equal length).

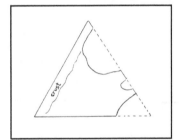

STEP 2: Imagine the left side of the triangle to be the crust. Draw a large bite taken off the tip, plus a large and small bite on the top side, where shown.

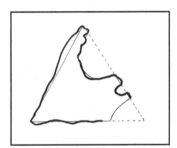

STEP 3: Draw an outline around the pizza, like this.

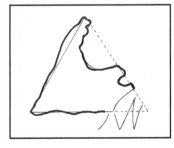

STEP 4: Draw guidelines that look like the letters "i" and "w" just like they are shown here. Notice how the middle and right side of the "w" go all the way up to the top edge guideline.

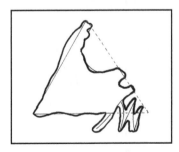

STEP 5: Draw an outline around the "i" and "w."

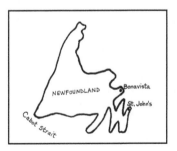

STEP 6: Erase all the guidelines and label the cities of Bonavista and St. John's. You may also want to include the strait named after Cabot.

MAP DRAWING 13: Africa

Africa is a fun shape to draw. We've already seen the northern coastline appear in several of our previous maps. You know the cities of Tangier, Tunis, Alexandria and Cairo (but watch out for Barbary pirates!).

This is a very basic and much simplified map of Africa. You probably know cities or geographical features that are not shown here. If you would like to add more features to your map when you are finished, you are welcome to do so.

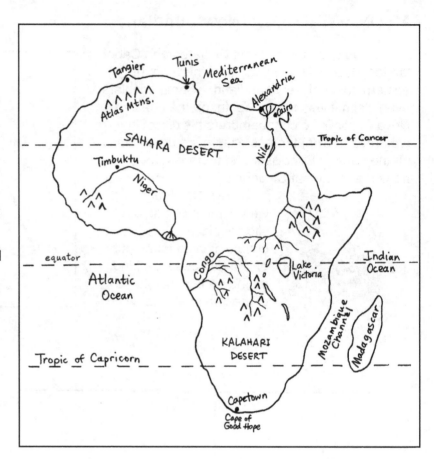

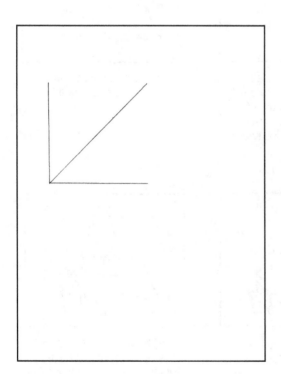

STEP 1: Draw an L-shape on the upper part of your paper, with the bottom of the "L" about halfway up the page. Then draw a line that is at a 45° angle (halfway between the two lines you just drew.

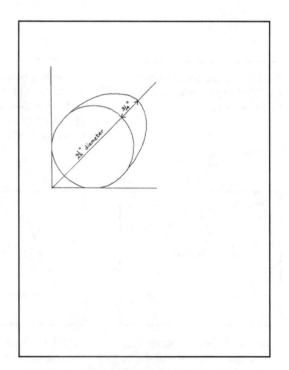

STEP 2: Use your compass to draw a circle that touches the edges of the "L" (about 2 1/2" (6.5 cm) in diameter). Then make it into an egg shape, with the extra extension being about 3/4 inch beyond the circle.

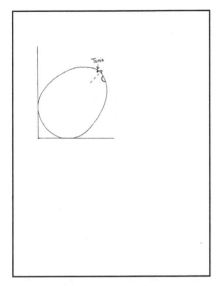

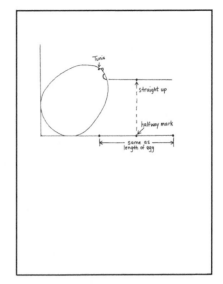

STEP 3: Draw a tiny peninsula (you might imagine it as the tip of a beak hatching out?) right at the end of the 45° angle line. Put a dot to the left of the peninsula and label it Tunis. Then draw a small semi-circle (a crack in the egg?) just underneath.

STEP 4: Draw very light guidelines (which you will erase later) down from Tunis and put a dot right where this line touches the lower line. Then draw a line out from the lower edge of the crack in the egg.

STEP 5: Measure out from the dot right below Tunis, going the same distance as the length of the egg, then put a dot. Now mark a halfway point of this distance, put a dot, then draw a line straight up from that dot until it hits the top line and make a dot there.

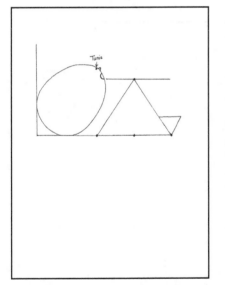

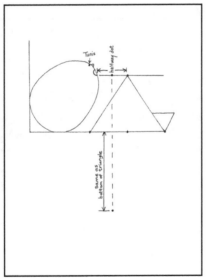

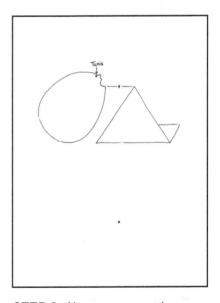

STEP 6: Make a triangle using the three dots, as shown here. Then make a smaller triangle sticking off the large one, as shown here.

STEP 7: Measure the distance between the top of the large triangle and the side of the egg and make a dot at the halfway point. Then extend a line down from this point, going well below the triangle. Make the measurement between the bottom of the triangle and the bottom point of the line the same as length of the bottom of the large triangle.

STEP 8: Now we are ready to begin drawing the outline of Africa. If you want to erase some of the extra guidelines, you may. Just make sure you leave the lines and dots shown in this picture.

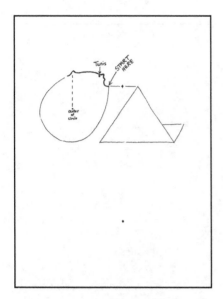

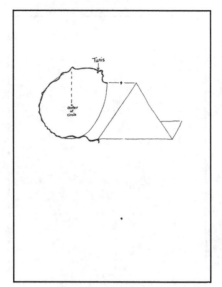

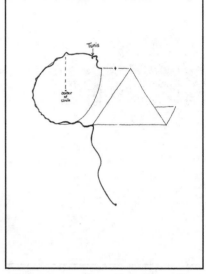

STEP 9: Start your outline at the point indicated, right at the bottom of the crack. Follow the outline of the crack and the peninsula next to Tunis, then go over and draw a bump where Africa will go up and almost touch Spain (at Gibraltar).

STEP 10: Continue the outline along the western coast of Africa, making little bumps here and there to represent the capes that those early European sailors were afraid to sail beyond. Make a bump (a cape) between the egg and the triangle, and a bay right at the point of the triangle.

STEP 11: After making a bay going in at the point of the triangle, start down the coast, heading for that point down below. Along the way, make the line wave inwards in the middle, as shown.

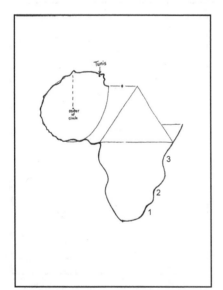

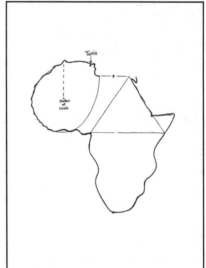

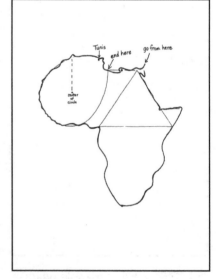

STEP 12: Now you are ready to round the cape at the bottom (make it fairly flat—not pointed) and head up the east coast. As you go up the coast, head for the little triangle. Make three shallow bays as you go up, each one just slightly bigger than the last.

STEP 13: Continue your outline around the small triangle, giving it a few slight ripples. Make a small inlet right when you reach the edge of the large triangle. Go up the side of the large triangle (this is the coast of the Red Sea). At the top, make a small "V" (this is the SInai peninsula).

STEP 14: Start a new line above the "V" of the Sinai peninsula. Make a curvy hump over the tip of the triangle (where the Nile delta will be) and continue on towards the dot. Make the line swivel around the dot, in an S shape, as shown here. Then bring the line to where you originally started. The outline is done!

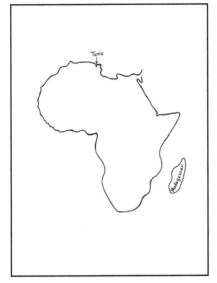

STEP 15: Erase the rest of your guidelines. Add the island of Madagascar.

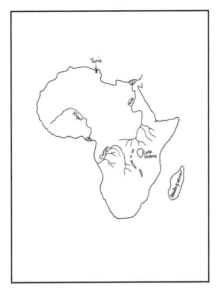

STEP 16: Add the major bodies of water. You already know how to draw the Nile River. The Niger River also has a delta region. The Congo doesn't have a large delta. Add Lake Victoria and the other smaller lakes.

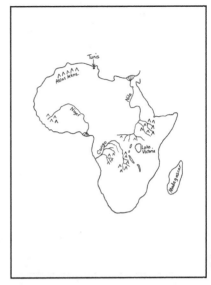

STEP 17: Add mountains in and around the tributaries. These mountains provide the water for the rivers. Also add the Atlas Mountains.

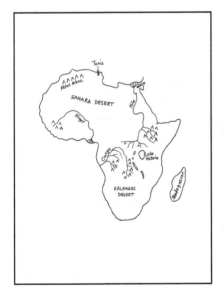

STEP 18: Label the two largest deserts: the Sahara and the Kalahari.

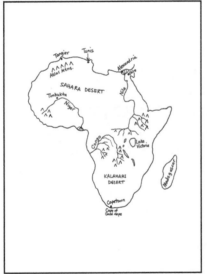

STEP 19: Add the cities of Cairo, Alexandria, Tangier, Capetown, and Timbuktu.

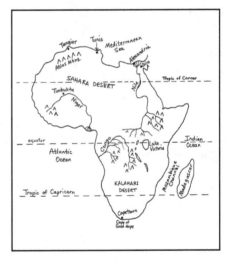

STEP 20: Label the Indian Ocean, the Atlantic Ocean, and the Mozambique Channel. Add lines for the equator, the Tropic of Cancer and the Tropic of Capricorn. You might want to make these lines a bright color such as red or yellow.

MAP DRAWING 14: Central America and the Caribbean

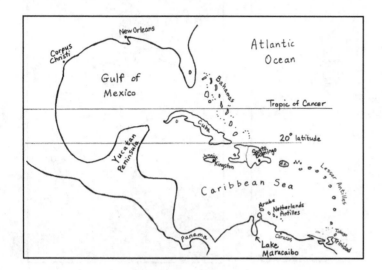

By the year 1500, most of the Caribbean had been explored by Europeans. In 1513, a Spaniard named Balboa crossed the isthmus of Panama and saw the Pacific Ocean, naming it the South Sea.

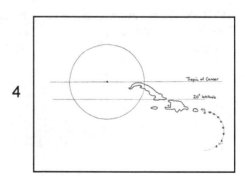

We are going to imagine the Yucatan peninsula as the head of a seal. The seal is on a rock, with waves splashing below. A type of seal that lives in the Caribbean is the Caribbean monk seal.

Caribbean monk seal

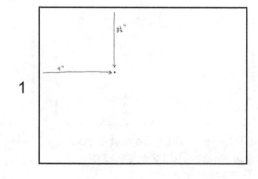

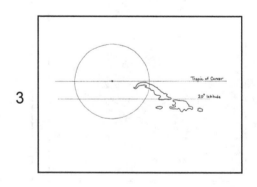

STEP 1: Make a dot that is 4" (10 cm) in from the left side of the paper and 3 1/2" (9 cm) down from the top.

STEP 2: Make a circle around this dot, 4" (10 cm) in diameter. Draw a horizontal line through the center of the circle. Label this line the Tropic of Cancer. Then draw another horizontal line through the circle halfway between the middle and the bottom. You can label this line 20 degrees north.

STEP 3: Draw in Cuba, Hispaniola, Puerto Rico and Jamaica. You already know how to draw these. Make sure the tail of Cuba is just below the Tropic line. Notice how far into the circle Cuba goes. The leg of the Cuban fish is just inside the circle. These islands (the Greater Antilles) stretch out into the sea about the distance of the diameter of the circle.

STEP 4: Draw in the semi-circle for the Lesser Antilles and add dots for the islands. Don't worry too much about getting every last island correctly placed. The goal of this drawing is to get the whole Caribbean area blocked in.

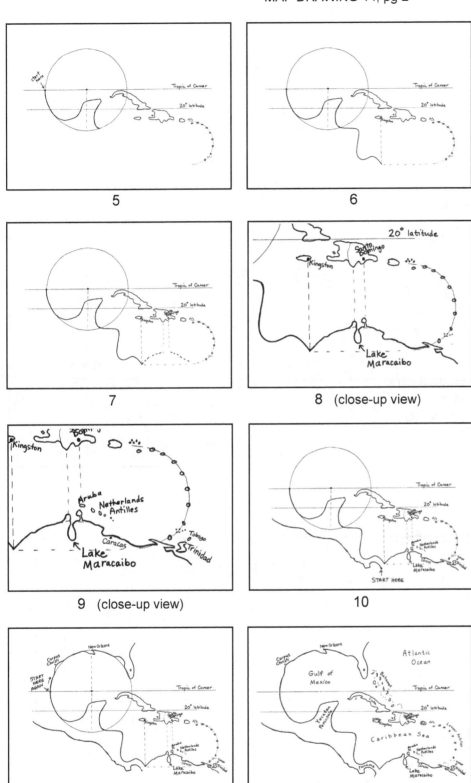

5

6

7

8 (close-up view)

9 (close-up view)

10

11

12

STEP 5: Make a light line straight down from the center of the circle. Then, put your pencil right on the midpoint of the left side of the circle, where the dot is shown in the picture. Go downwards, then make the seal head, noticing where it crosses the vertical center line of the circle.

STEP 6: Make the "rock" the seal is sitting on, as shown, then a little wave below that, ending at a point that is directly under Kingston, Jamaica, and is even with the bottom of the semi-circle.

STEP 7: Make a very light upside-down semi-circle. This will be just a guideline. Label the capital of Jamaica, Kingston, and draw a light line down from it. Also draw a line down from the "fin" of our Haitian Gulper fish. These lines will show you where to put the peninsulas in the next step.

STEP 8: Make the north coast of the continent, as shown here. Draw and label Lake Maracaibo. Note that the peninsula above the lake looks really strange—almost like a cartoon tree. Right below the Lesser Antilles there is a plate-like peninsula. Weird!

STEP 9: Add the islands of Aruba and the Netherlands Antilles, plus Trinidad and Tobago (way over on the right side). Also label the capital city of Venezuela: Caracas.

STEP 10: Start a new line right at Panama (where it says "start here") and draw the underside of Central America.

STEP 11: Continue your line upwards, drawing a slight dip in at Corpus Christi, a bulge out at New Orleans, and a dip in at the top of Florida. (You can add Lake Okeechobee or you can leave it out at this point.) Take special note of the distance between Florida and Cuba.

STEP 12: Draw in the Bahamas and label them. Label the Yucatan Peninsula, Panama, the Gulf of Mexico, the Atlantic Ocean, the Caribbean Sea and any other cities or names of islands you want to add.

MAP DRAWING 15: South America

South America is easy to draw if you put it into a rectangle. We don't even have to imagine any strange creatures.

In our time, South America is famous for its huge rain forest, located mainly in the modern country of Brazil. The "Amazon basin" is the flat area all around the river and its main tributaries. This area is filled with lush plant and animal life.

In chapter 16 we will see that the explorer Magellan finds a secret passage through the southern tip of the continent so that he does not have to go all the way around it (where the seas are choppy and dangerous). This narrow passageway was named after him: The Magellan Strait. It is not shown on this map, but you may add it if you want to. You can draw it as a very thin channel cutting across right near the pointy tip. (You'll learn how to draw this strait in lesson 18A.)

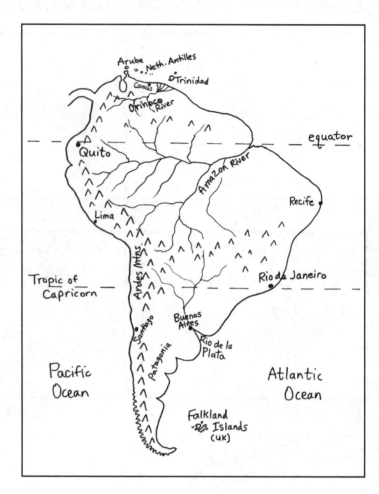

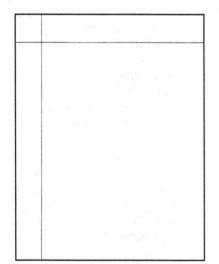

STEP 1: Draw lines on the top and left sides of the paper, 1 1/4 inches from the edge.

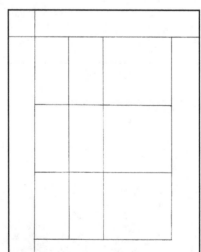

STEP 2: Using these two lines as two sides, make a 9 by 6 inch rectangle, divided into three equal parts of 3 inches. Then divide this area in half vertically, then divided the left half in half again.

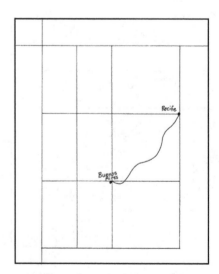

STEP 3: Make a dot where indicated here and label it as the city of Recife. Head diagonally down that square, making a bulge in the middle and then dipping slightly below the bottom line before ending up right at the intersection marked Buenos Aires.

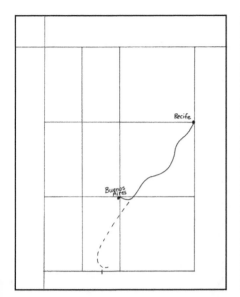

STEP 4: Make a small mark at the halfway point at the bottom of the rectangle shown here. Then make a light, sketchy line, continuing the general diagonal direction from step 3. Make it hooked on the end, like a candy cane, not quite touching the bottom line.

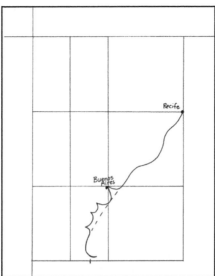

STEP 5: Put your pencil down at Buenos Aires again, and make the coastline have a large initial bulge, then going inward, creating three sharp points in, then finishing by following along right on top of the candy cane line.

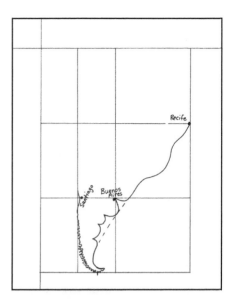

STEP 6: Round the tip of the candy cane, then head upward. As you go up, make lots of little intricate squiggles (even adding some tiny islands). The squiggles even out by the time you get to the intersection where Santiago is. Make a slight indent for Santiago (the capital of the country of Chile).

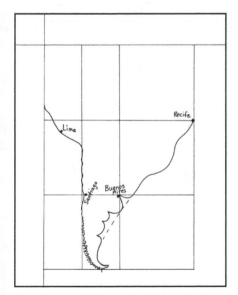

STEP 7: Pick up again at Santiago and continue north, staying right on the vertical line. When you get about two thirds of the way to the next intersection, turn left and go diagonally, as shown. After you finish the line, go back and label the city of Lima (the capital of Peru).

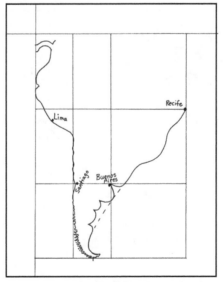

STEP 8: This will be the hardest block to draw. You might imagine the next squiggle as a mouth kissing the side of the rectangle. Or not. Make the curve of Panama snaking in from the left, as shown. This is where South America will eventually connect to our Caribbean map.

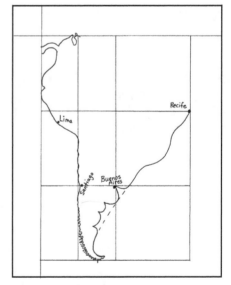

STEP 9: Lake Maracaibo and the two peninsulas above it fit into the remaining space at the top of this box. The tree-shaped peninsula will seem very small in comparison to the rest of the map, because South America is so large.

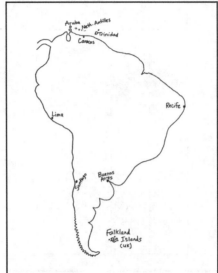

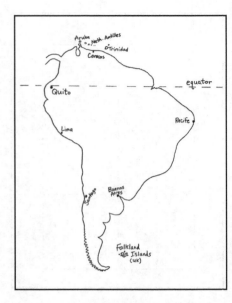

STEP 10: Head down towards Re-cife, making a bulge where shown and making an indent right after the bulge. This indent will be the mouth of the Amazon River. The Amazon doesn't have a proper delta, but it does have a bit of an estuary. Then go back and label Caracas, the capital of Venezuela.

STEP 11: Add the islands around South America: the Falklands off the southern tip (which are now owned by the United Kingdom) and Aruba, the Netherlands Antilles, Trinidad and Tobago. (All of these except the Falklands were on previous maps.) You can erase your guidelines now, or wait till the end.

STEP 12: Draw in the equator right at the Amazon River inlet. On the west coast, right under the equator, put in the capital city of Ecuador, Quito (*KEE-toe*).

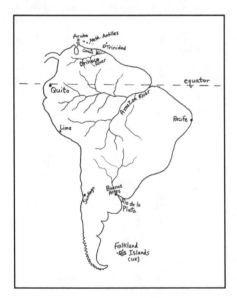

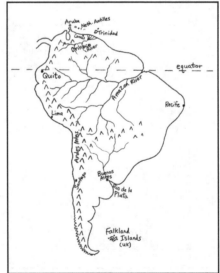

STEP 13: Add the three major rivers: the Amazon, the Orinoco and the Plata. Notice that only the Orinoco has a proper delta region. Notice that the Amazon's tributaries cover almost all of the top half of the continent.

STEP 14: Add the mountains which create the water for the tributaries. Label the Andes Mountains, running the whole way down the west coast.

STEP 15: Draw in the Tropic of Capricorn, running right through the bottom of the bulge where Rio de Janeiro is. Just estimate where this line goes, observing this map carefully. Label Rio de Janeiro. Label the desert area called Patagonia. Label the Atlantic and Pacific Oceans.

MAP DRAWING 16: Southeast Asia basics

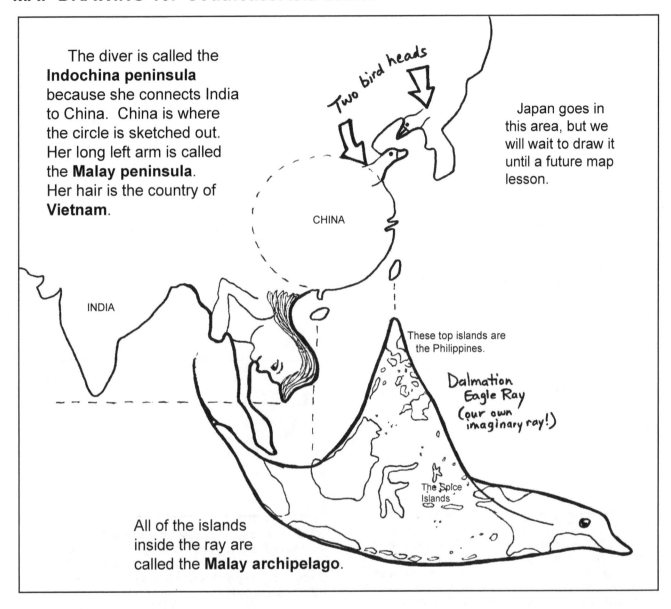

The diver is called the **Indochina peninsula** because she connects India to China. China is where the circle is sketched out. Her long left arm is called the **Malay peninsula**. Her hair is the country of **Vietnam**.

Two bird heads

Japan goes in this area, but we will wait to draw it until a future map lesson.

CHINA

INDIA

These top islands are the Philippines.

Dalmation Eagle Ray (our own imaginary ray!)

The Spice Islands

All of the islands inside the ray are called the **Malay archipelago**.

Our "Dalmation Eagle Ray" is not a real ray. There are many kinds of eagle rays, but none are called "dalmations." The spots of real eagle rays are always circular. Our ray's spots look a bit like a dalmation's spots so the name "Dalmation ray" seems like a good name for it. If you can think of a better name, you are welcome to rename the ray!

Notice that in our drawing, you only see one of the fins (which looks more like a wing than a fin). The other fin is behind it—you just can't see it.

Spotted Eagle Ray

Here is a picture of a real spotted eagle ray. It lives mainly in the Atlantic, not the Pacific. Notice the shape of the nose. It's almost the shape of a dolphin's nose or a dog's nose.

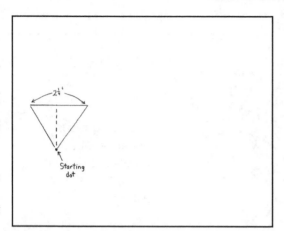

STEP 1: Draw a starting dot 3" (7.5 cm) up from the bottom and 2" (5 cm) in from the left side. Then draw a line up from the dot, 1 3/4" (4.5 cm) up. Draw a perpendicular line across the top, 2 1/4" (5.75 cm) across. Draw two more lines, making it into a triangle.

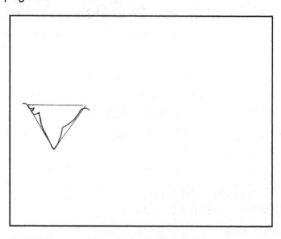

STEP 2: Draw the outline of India inside this triangle, just like you did in lesson 9.

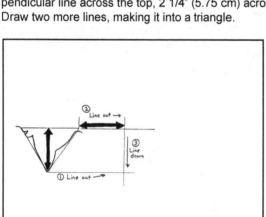

STEP 3: Draw a line out from the bottom of India (parallel to the bottom of the page). Then continue the top line of the triangle. Lastly, measure a distance on this top line that is equivalent to the distance of the height of the India triangle. After marking this distance, draw a line straight down at that point.

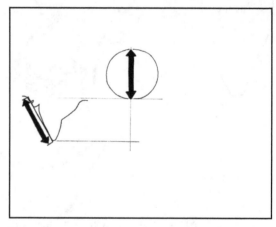

STEP 4: Measure the distance of one side of the India triangle and make a line straight up from your vertical line in step 3. Then use this distance as the diameter of a circle. You can draw the circle freehand or use a compass.

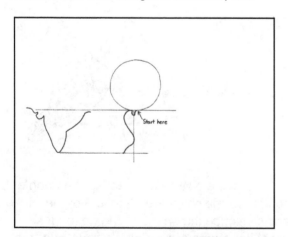

STEP 5: Make a tiny squiggly peninsula right at the bottom of the circle, then make a not-too-curvy "S" shape, coming down to a point. (You may want to look at this shape on the finished map to see where to end on the bottom line.)

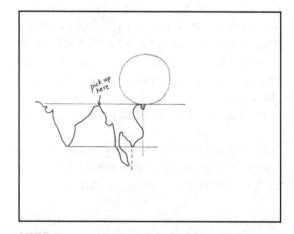

STEP 6: Go back and pick up your line where you stopped drawing India. Now continue this line on down, making the diver's right hand (which is barely showing), then making the long left arm and hand. Notice that the left hand never goes further right than where the pointy tip of the hair is.

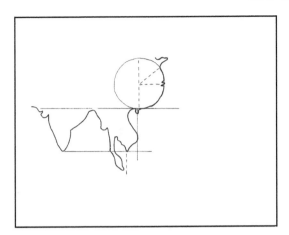

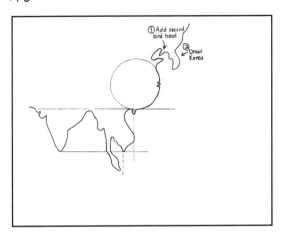

STEP 7: Now go back to where you left off at the bottom of the circle. Start at the tiny peninsula at the bottom and then draw up the side of the circle until you get halfway up. Make two small indentations (river inlets), then continue up until halfway up to the top, where you will make a peninsula in the shape of a duck's head. Perhaps this is Peking Duck?!

STEP 8: Keep going up from the duck's head, around the inside of a bay, then make a slender bird's head (perhaps a pigeon or dove?) on the other side, just a little bit higher than the duck head. Continue on down and make the Korean peninsula, with a bump for North Korea and a bottom area for South Korea. Then continue the line up and off the page.

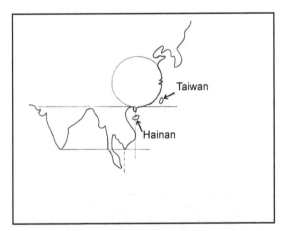

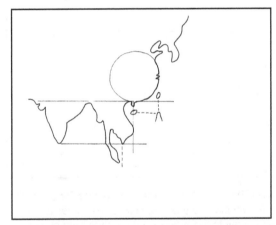

STEP 9: Add the islands of Taiwan and Hainan. You can label them now, or wait until step 17.

STEP 10: Draw guidelines down from Taiwan and over from Hainan. Where they meet, drsw what will become the top of the ray's fin.

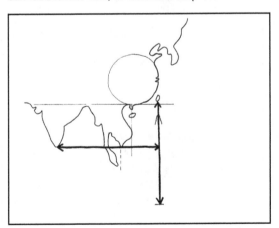

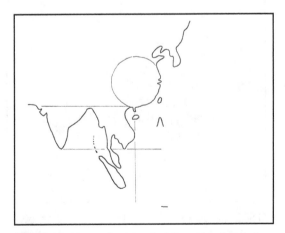

STEP 11: Measure the distance from the tip of India to a line drawn straight down from Taiwan. (You don't need to use a ruler—you can just mark the distance on your pencil or with a piece of paper.) Now measure this same distance down from Taiwan and make a guideline mark. This mark will show you where the bottom of the ray will be.

STEP 12: Draw the island of Sumatra, just below the hand of the diver. Sumatra looks like a fish that the diver is trying to touch. You can also draw a line of islands (an archipelago) going in a curved line from the end of Sumatra up towards the diver.

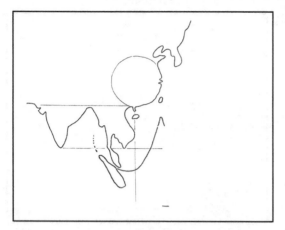

STEP 13: Draw a curved line (this will be a light guideline that can later be erased) up from Sumatra, to connect with the "fin tip" of your imaginary ray.

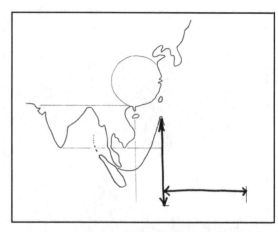

STEP 14: Draw a very light line down from the tip of the "fin" to the bottom mark. Then measure the length of this line and mark the same distance out to the right of the line and put a mark. This mark will be the very tip of the ray's nose.

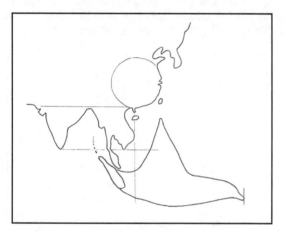

STEP 15: Draw in the curved lines for the ray's underside and topside, making your lines go all the way to the marks on the bottom and on the right side, but not beyond them.

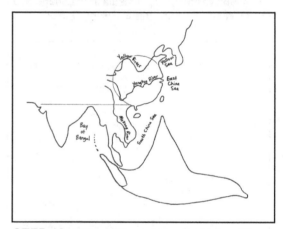

STEP 16: Draw in three rivers, the Yellow River, the Yangtze River and the Mekong River, as shown here, using the circle as a guide for the rivers in China.

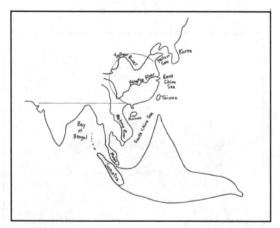

STEP 17: Label the seas into which the Yellow and Yangtze Rivers flow: the Yellow Sea and the East China Sea. Then label the South China Sea and the Bay of Bengal. Also, label the islands of Taiwan, Hainan and Sumatra. Label the Malay peninsula and the Korean peninsula.

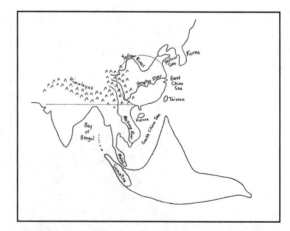

STEP 18: Put in the mountains whose streams feed into the major rivers. Label the Himalayas. Leave the body of the ray empty. The next map lesson will tell you what to draw inside it.

MAP DRAWING 17: Indonesia and the Spice Islands (the Maluku Islands)

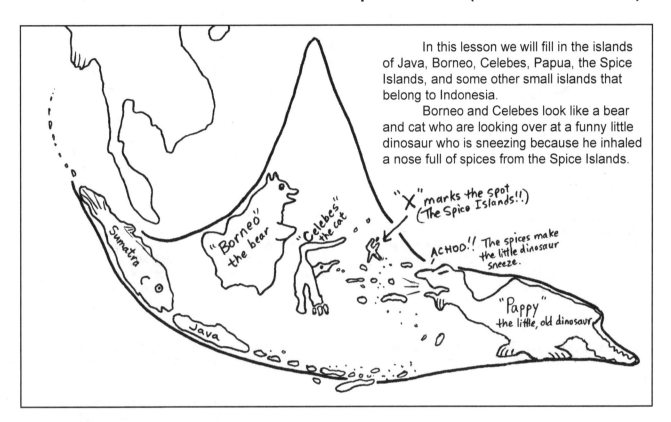

In this lesson we will fill in the islands of Java, Borneo, Celebes, Papua, the Spice Islands, and some other small islands that belong to Indonesia.

Borneo and Celebes look like a bear and cat who are looking over at a funny little dinosaur who is sneezing because he inhaled a nose full of spices from the Spice Islands.

17A: Java and the other small islands on the bottom

STEP 1: Draw Java to look like the smaller fish that Sumatra is chasing. Label it and add the capital city of Jakarta.

STEP 2: Add a long line of smaller islands along the bottom line of your eagle ray. The first one after Java is Bali. All the other islands have long complicated names, except for Timor. Timor sticks out the bottom a bit.

STEP 3: Put a dot right at the end of the Malay peninsula. This is Singapore.

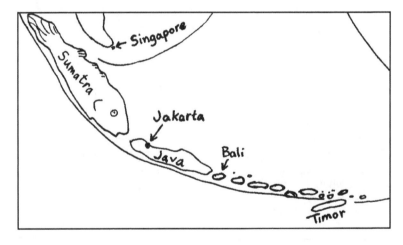

17B: Borneo (the Bear)   Use the large picture at the top of this page to get Borneo in the right place.

STEP 1: Draw a circle for the body, then a smaller circle for the head.

STEP 2: Start at the back of the head, go in at the neck, over the back, and end with a big, stubby tail. (Okay, so maybe Borneo is a mutant bear.)

STEP 3: Give Borneo some very stubby feet.

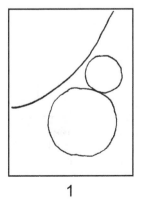

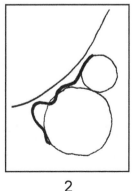

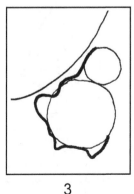

1   2   3

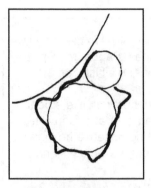

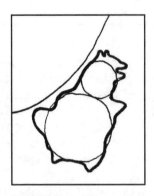

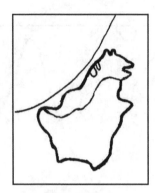

STEP 4: Come up around Borneo's chest and give him a stubby arm.

STEP 5: Draw Borneo's muzzle, giving him an open mouth. Then finish his head with two very small ears that stick straight up.

STEP 6: Borneo has a stripe along his back. Perhaps his back is a different color from his chest. He also has two little spots on his neck.

STEP 7: The whole island is called Borneo. The bottom part belongs to Indonesia and the top part belongs to Malaysia, except for the spots, which are a country called Brunei.

17C: Celebes (the Cat) Celebes is pronounced "**Sell**-eh-bess." Use the large map to get Celebes in the right place. Notice that Celebes is right under the tip of the eagle ray's fin. You'll want to leave plenty of room to the right of Celebes for drawing the Spice Islands and New Guinea.

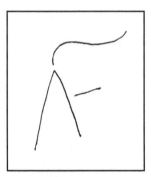

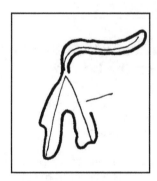

STEP 1: Draw an upside down V. Add a curvy line where the tail will be. Draw a straight line out from the middle of the V.

STEP 2: Draw around the outside of the curvy line to create the tail.

STEP 3: Draw the legs using the V as your guide. Make the right leg a little shorter to allow room for drawing the paw in step 5.

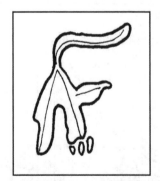

STEP 4: Draw a very skinny (almost anteater-like) head. Make the nose long and skinny. (Okay, so the cat has a mutant head. Maybe it's what you get when you cross a cat with an anteater?)

STEP 5: Draw in three footpads where the back of the right foot would be.

STEP 6: Label the island and add the Celebes Sea right above it.

17D: New Guinea ("Pappy," the little old dinosaur who is sneezing)

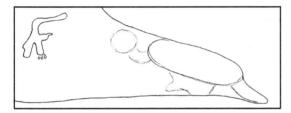

STEP 1: Draw in these rough shapes to get the basic body outline in the right place. Remember to leave enough space for the Spice Islands!

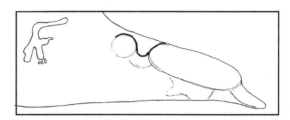

STEP 2: Start at the top of the back and draw down the droopy neck and up over the head.

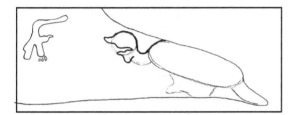

STEP 3: Draw a pointy nose, a mouth (whose point goes way back to the center of the head circle), and a pointy beard under the chin.

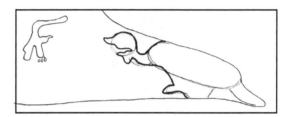

STEP 4: Finish drawing the droopy neck, then draw down the chest and then on to the feet. The feet look almost like a pedestal.

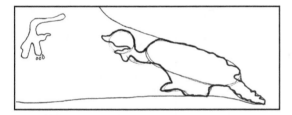

STEP 5: Make Pappy's tail fill out the eagle ray's nose area. The tail is very bumpy. You can give Pappy a hump right at the top of the tail, then finish drawing the back, making your line bumpy.

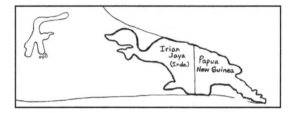

STEP 6: Draw a line down the middle of the island, cutting it in half. The eastern side is Papua New Guinea. The western side is called Irian Jaya and it currently belongs to Indonesia.

17E: The Maluku Islands (the correct name for the legendary Spice Islands)

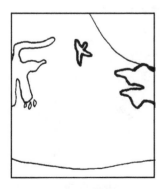

STEP 1: Draw in the largest island, Halmahera. It looks like the letter "X" doing a ballet kick.

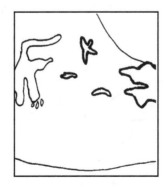

STEP 2: Draw two long islands down below Halmahera.

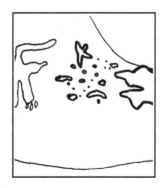

STEP 3: Draw in a bunch of smaller islands, including some that are so small that they are just dots.

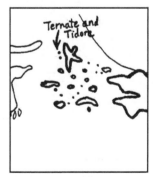

STEP 4: Draw two dots to the left of Halmahera and label them Ternate and Tidore. You can also label Halmahera if you wish.

MAP DRAWING 18A: The Magellan Strait

How did Magellan ever manage to navigate through this twisting, narrow passage?! He could have made a wrong turn at many points. Magellan named the largest island "The Land of Smoke" but the name was eventually changed to "Land of Fire" ("Tierra del Fuego"). The smoke Magellan saw was probably from large fires built by the native people who lived on the island.

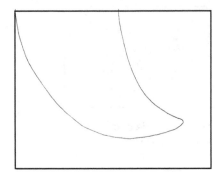

STEP 1: Draw a guideline for the curvy tip of South America. Draw lightly as this is only a guideline.

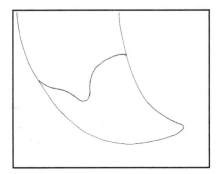

STEP 2: Draw a guideline as shown above.

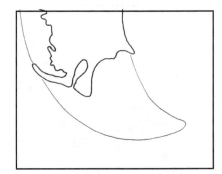

STEP 3: Do your best to make a shape that looks like this. Don't worry if yours isn't identical.

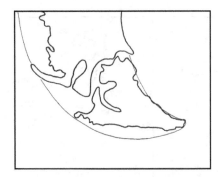

STEP 4: Draw the large island of Tierra del Fuego. It's a really strange shape so no one will notice if yours isn't excatly like this one.

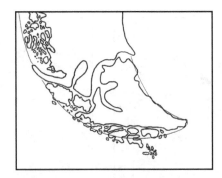

STEP 5: Draw lots of islands in the empty spaces you have left. Some are large and some are as tiny as a dot. Once again, don't worry that your islands are identical to these. The main point is that you know there are a lot of little islands here.

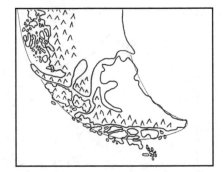

STEP 6: Draw mountains along the left side. This is the very bottom of the Andes Mountain Range.

STEP 7: Label Cape Horn, Tierra del Fuego, Patagonia and the Strait of Magellan, as shown on the map at the top.

MAP DRAWING 18B: The Philippines

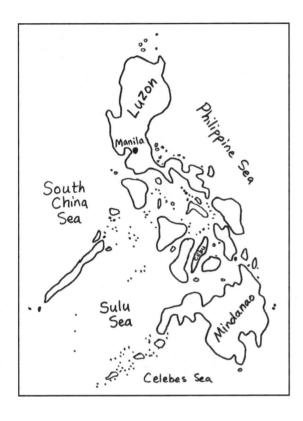

The Philippines go in this blank area at the top of the eagle ray's fin.

What do the Philippines look like? This time it is your turn to imagine a shape! Look only at the main islands, not every little dot. What are they?

The most important features of this map (the ones relevant to this book) are the largest island, Luzon, the capital city, Manila, and the island where Magellan died, Cebu. The ocean waters around the Philippines are some of the deepest in the world. Where the words "Philippine Sea" are written, the depth reaches 10,000 feet (twice as deep as the rest of the Pacific).

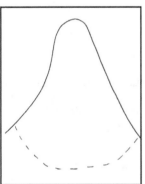

STEP 1: Draw a bottom guideline.

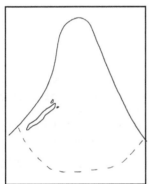

STEP 2: Draw the long, skinny island at the left.

STEP 3: Draw the large island on the top. Label it Luzon and label the city of Manila.

STEP 4: Draw the large island at the bottom and label it Mindanao.

STEP 5: Draw the island of Cebu, where Magellan was killed in battle.

STEP 6: Draw the 7 medium-sized islands around Cebu.

STEP 7: Add tiny islands. Don't worry about getting all of them exact.

STEP 8: Label the seas around the Philippines.

MAP DRAWING 19: The eastern coast of North America

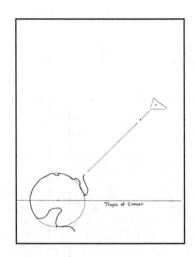

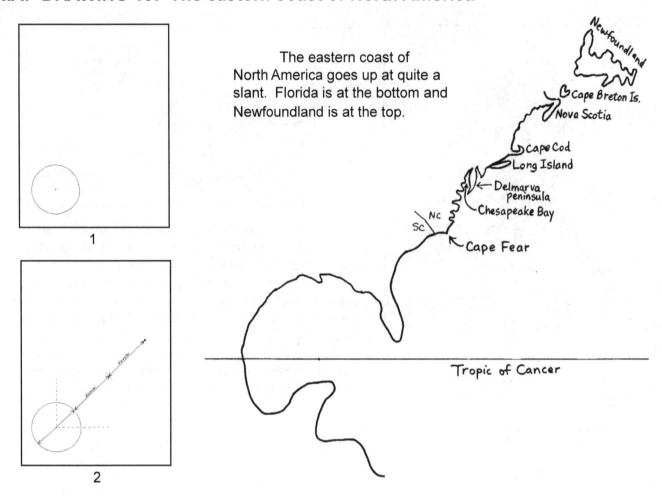

The eastern coast of North America goes up at quite a slant. Florida is at the bottom and Newfoundland is at the top.

Newfoundland

Cape Breton Is.
Nova Scotia

Cape Cod
Long Island
← Delmarva peninsula
Chesapeake Bay

Sc NC

← Cape Fear

Tropic of Cancer

STEP 1: Draw a circle in the bottom left corner of your paper. Make the center of the circle about 2 1/2" (6 cm) from each side, and make the diameter about 2 1/2 inches also. (This will be your Gulf of Mexico circle.)

STEP 2: Draw two light guide lines coming out of the center of the circle: one line straight up and one line straight out to the right (so they form a perfect corner). Then draw a bisecting line that goes up at about a 45 degree angle. The distance the line goes out from the cirlce is equal to two diameters. Put a dot at the end of the line.

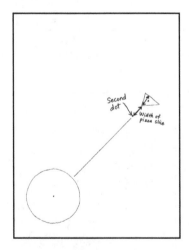

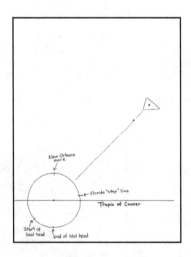

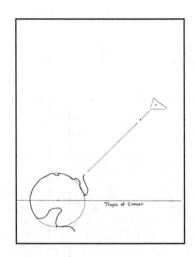

STEP 3: Sketch in a triangle around the end dot. This will be your "pizza slice" guide for New-foundland. Put a second dot on the line that is one pizza-width down from the pizza.

STEP 4: Put your guide marks around the Gulf circle: New Orleans at the top, the bottom of Florida a little up from the Tropic of Cancer, and the start and stop points for the Yucatan seal head.

STEP 5: Draw in the features around the edge of the Gulf of Mexico, as you learned in map drawing 14.

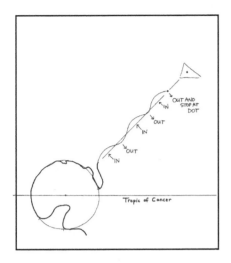

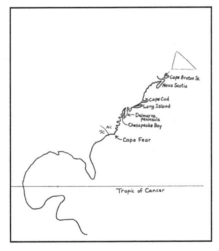

STEP 6: Draw a wavy line from the circle up to the dot that is below the triangle. Do three sets of "in" and "out." You might even want to say them as you draw: IN, OUT, IN, OUT, IN, OUT. Make sure your last "out" ends at the dot.

STEP 7: At the top of the first "out" make a slight point and label it "Cape Fear." If you want to, you may add a line showing where North and South Carolina are in relation to Cape Fear. After Cape Fear, the wavy line gets very "lacy." Make the "lace" go in even a little further than the second "in" wave.

STEP 8: Make two pointy "icicles" hanging down from the inside of the underside of this curve. (This may actually be the trickiest part of the whole drawing.) The upper one is smaller than the lower one. Label the lower peninsula "Delmarva peninsula." "Del" is for Delaware, "mar" is for Maryland, and "va" is for "Virginia." Also label the Chesapeake Bay.

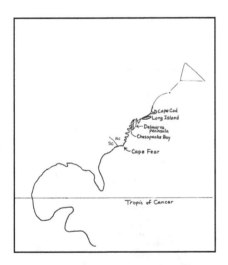

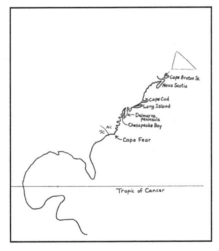

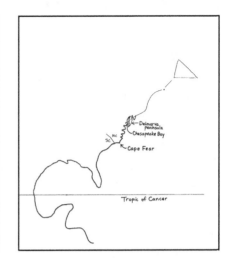

STEP 9: Add a long island that is so close to the continent that it looks like the end is actually touching the continent. Label it "Long Island." Right above Long Island, draw a hook sticking out (right where the "out" wave is out the most) and label it "Cape Cod."

STEP 10: Draw right up the inside of the last curve until you get to the dot. Draw a peninsula (or hotdog shape if you'd prefer to think of it that way) hanging down under the dot. Draw up and over the dot, then let your line trail off to the left. We won't finish that part of the map in this drawing. Label the peninsula "Nova Scotia."

STEP 11: Draw a heart-shaped island at the tip of Nova Scotia and label it "Cape Breton Island." Then draw in Newfoundland as you learned in map drawing 12B.

NOTE: YOU WILL BE ADDING TO THIS MAP IN MAP DRAWING 20.

MAP DRAWING 20: Gulf of St. Lawrence and Labrador

Above Newfoundland sits the part of Canada called Labrador. The Vikings were probably the first Europeans to visit Labrador, but the first European to put it on a map was the Portuguese explorer João Fernandes in 1498. The Portuguese word "Lavrador" means "land-owner." Fernandes had apparrently been granted this title and wanted his name to be associated with it. The first time Labrador was drawn on a map it was labeled "Terra Lavrador," meaning "land of the landowner."

The Gulf of St. Lawrence was named by Jacques Cartier in honor of a Catholic saint, St. Lawrence. The biggest islands in the gulf are Prince Edward Island and Cape Breton.

NOTE: THIS DRAWING IS A CONTINUATION OF DRAWING 19.

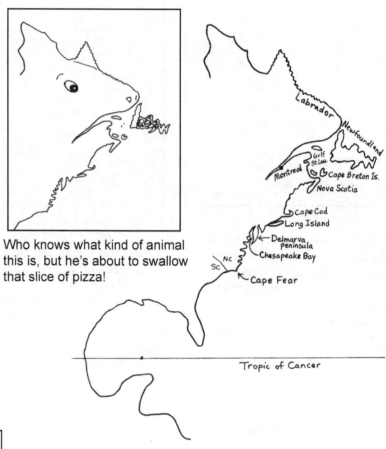

Who knows what kind of animal this is, but he's about to swallow that slice of pizza!

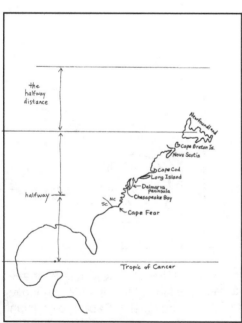

STEP 1: Draw a line out from the middle of Newfoundland to the left side of your paper. Measure the distance from the Tropic of Cancer to this line. Divide that distance in half and draw a second line that is that "half-distance" measurement above the line you just drew.

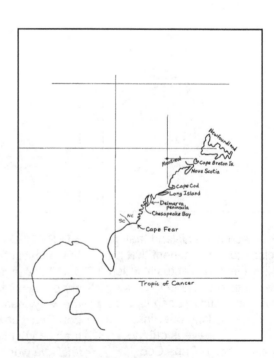

STEP 2: Draw a guide line up from the base of Cape Cod and over from Cape Breton Island. Put a dot where these lines cross and label it "Montreal."

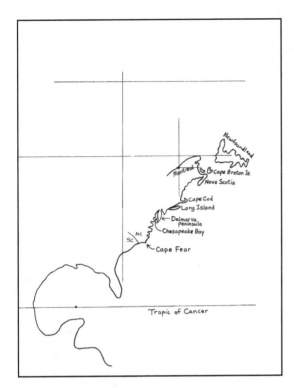

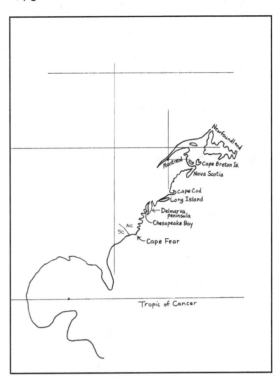

STEP 3: Starting below Montreal, draw a line up through the dot, then up and around in a tongue-like curve, ending at the place where you stopped drawing right above Nova Scotia. Draw a banana-shaped island inside this curve. If you can print extremely small letters, you can label this island "Prince Edward Island," or just "PEI."

STEP 4: Go back to where you began drawing below the Montreal dot and start again, this time taking your line in a gently sweeping curve up towards Newfoundland. You have now created the Gulf of St. Lawrence. Add an island at the top of the gulf. This is Anticosti Island. (This island was

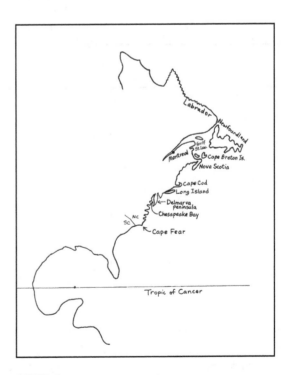

STEP 5: Add the "ears" to our creature. The first ear is located right over Montreal. (Make sure it stays under the top line.) The second ear is taller and goes above the top line, but stays to the right of the line going up from Florida.

STEP 6: Label the nose of the creature as "Labrador."

MAP DRAWING 21: The west coast of America

This part of America was explored by Cortés at the end of his career. The exploration was relatively peaceful in comparison with his other conquests. In the time of Cortés, Baja California was simply known as California. When the name California was used for the area we now know as the state of California, the peninsula had to be designated as Baja (lower) California.

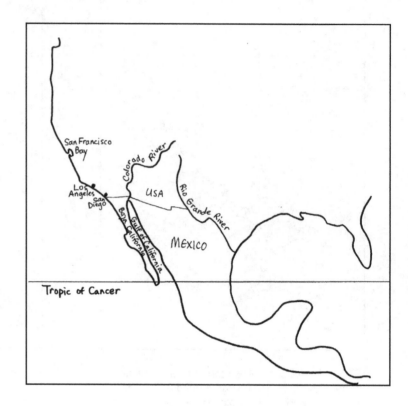

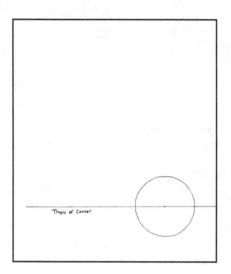

STEP 1: Draw a circle whose diameter is about 2 1/2" (6 cm) and whose center is about 2 1/2" (6 cm) from the bottom and the right side of the paper. Draw a line across the page through the center of the circle and label it the Tropic of Cancer.

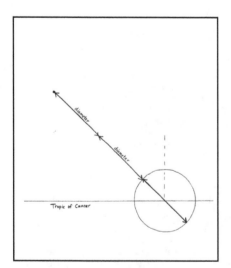

STEP 2: Lay a straight edge at a 45 degree angle and measure off a distance of two circle diameters—in this case, 5" (13 cm) —and put a dot right at that spot. (You don't need to draw along the straight edge. A dot is fine.)

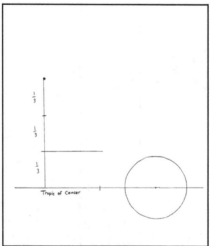

STEP 3: Draw a line straight down from the end point of the line. Then make a halfway mark on the bottom line, halfway between the vertical line and the center of the circle. Divide the vertical line into thirds, with a line stretching out from the bottom "third mark."

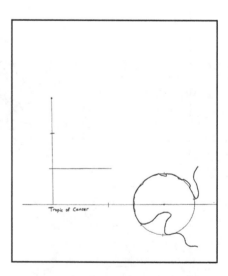

STEP 4: Draw in the Gulf of Mexico. You may want to put the guide marks in before you draw (same as you did in the last drawing).

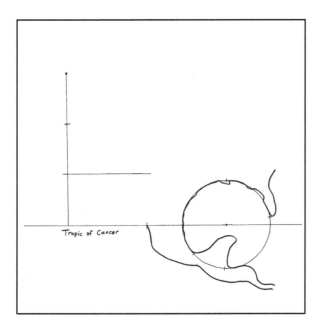

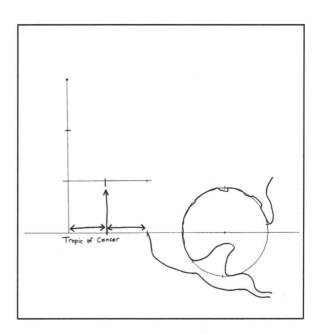

STEP 5: Start at the halfway mark on the bottom line and draw a wavy line that goes in right where the seal starts and goes in again under the seal's rock. This is the bottom of Mexico.

STEP 6: Make a mark on the bottom line that is halfway between the vertical line on the left and the place you started drawing Mexico. Then go straight up and make a mark on the short line.

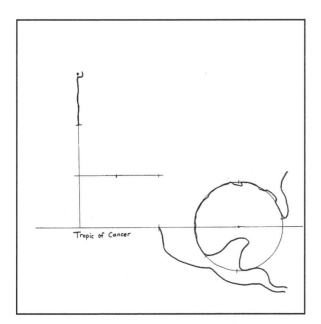

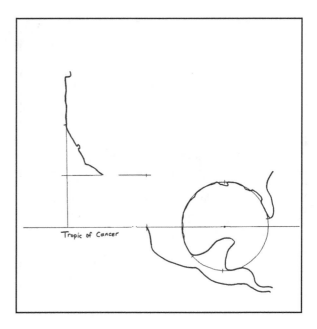

STEP 7: Go to the top of the vertical line and start just to the right of the dot. Draw around the dot in a backwards "L" shape. Then continue on down the vertical line until you come to the first mark.

STEP 8: Draw a slanted line heading down toward the mark you made on the short line. Make a little inlet halfway down. Before you get all the way to the dot, curve your line in sharply. If you've ever looked carefully at a map of California, you will recognize this little dip inwards.

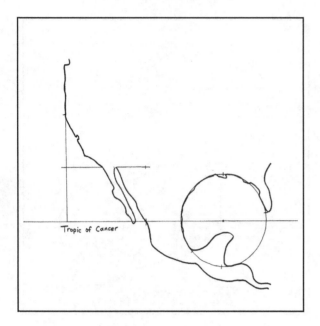

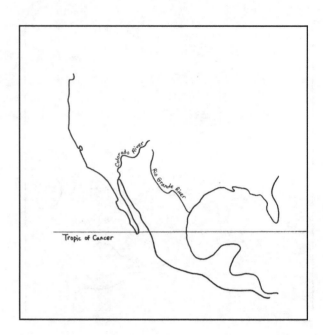

STEP 9: This is the trickiest part of the drawing. Words can't really describe the shape of the peninsula. Just make sure you go all the way down and all the way back up to your guidelines, ending at the point where you stopped drawing the bottom of Mexico.

STEP 10: Draw in the Colorado River and the Rio Grande River. The shape of the Rio Grande is more important to copy as well as you can because it forms the border between the U.S. and Mexico. (It should look like the bottom of Texas.)

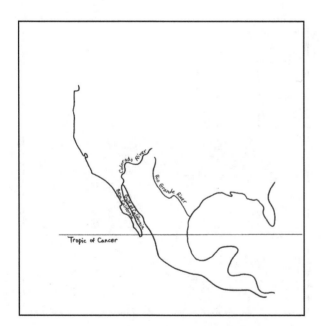

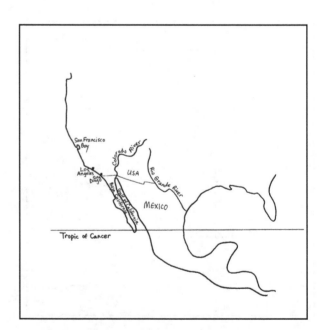

STEP 11: Label the Baja Peninsula and the Gulf of California. If you can't fit the letters inside of them, you could write the words out in the ocean, then make an arrow going from the word to the correct feature.

STEP 12: Label San Francisco Bay (which is, of course, where the city of San Francisco is located) and the cities of Los Angeles and San Diego.

MAP DRAWING 22: Scandinavia

The term "Scandinavia" refers to the area occupied by the countries of Norway, Sweden, Finland and Denmark. The Svalbard Islands and Bear Island belong to Norway. Novaya Zemlya belongs to Russia, but since it was featured in our history lesson we will include it in our map.

Denmark is the smallest part of Scandinavia and is attached to the main part of Europe. Denmark used to own all of its peninsula, but as you can see, Germany has managed to claim the base of the peninsula.

We haven't been emphasizing the political boundaries between countries, but on this map it seems appropriate since the term "Scandinavia" is defined using the names of the countries.

Remember, Norway is the spoon, Finland is the fish, and Denmark is the poor little head about to be devoured by the gaping jaws above it. Or perhaps you can think of a better story. What do you think they look like?

1

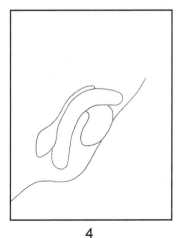

2

STEP 1: Draw a spoon with a bent handle. The end of the handle should be about in the middle of your page. Make sure your handle is really long! You might want to sketch very light guidelines first, so your spoon ends up in the right place on the page (not too far up or down).

STEP 2: Draw a long hotdog shape under the spoon. The bottom end of the hotdog should drop below the oval of the spoon.

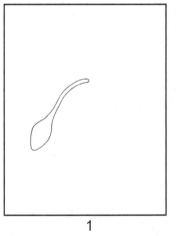

3

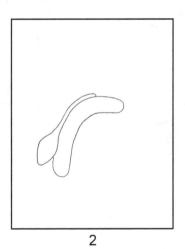

4

STEP 3: Draw a fat sock shape under the hotdog. The sock should stay inside the curve of the hotdog. After you draw your sock, you might want to compare it to this picture and make corrections if it sticks out too far away from the hotdog.

STEP 4: Draw a bottom guideline as shown in the picture. The line should touch the bottom of the sock, but should stay well below the hotdog and the spoon.

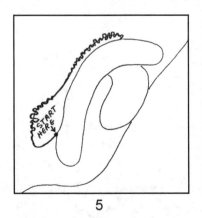

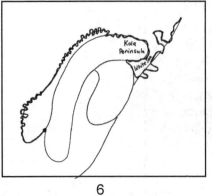

5

6

STEP 5: Begin where indicated by the dot and start outlining the spoon. Make a bunch of frills along the side of the oval, then again as you go up over the top.

STEP 6: Continue your outline around the end of the hotdog, making the line a bit wavy so it looks like a natural landform, not the end of a hotdog. When you get to the baseline, turn and follow it upward, creating some small peninsulas, including one that looks like an ax. Label the Kola Peninsula and the White Sea.

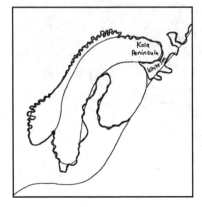

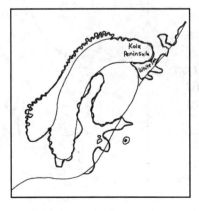

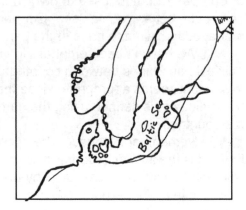

STEP 7: Go back to your original starting point. Draw around the bottom end of the hotdog, making a little rectangle hanging off the bottom. Make two slight swellings on the inside of the hotdog. Finish tracing around the edge of the sock, making the line a bit wavy.

STEP 8: Imagine a parrot-like face under the sock. The beak is open and is gobbling up two little crumbs. (You don't have to draw the eye—you can just imagine it.)

STEP 9: Imagine a goose-like head sticking up into the mouth-like gap above it. (You don't have to draw the eye!) Add 4 islands to the right of this peninsula. Label the Baltic Sea and add an island in the middle of it.

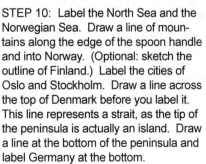

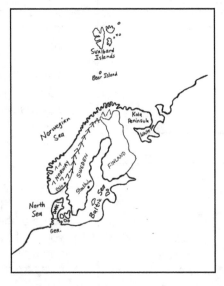

STEP 10: Label the North Sea and the Norwegian Sea. Draw a line of mountains along the edge of the spoon handle and into Norway. (Optional: sketch the outline of Finland.) Label the cities of Oslo and Stockholm. Draw a line across the top of Denmark before you label it. This line represents a strait, as the tip of the peninsula is actually an island. Draw a line at the bottom of the peninsula and label Germany at the bottom.

STEP 11: Draw and label Bear Island. Draw and label the Svalbard Islands as best you can. Use the picture on the previous page if this one is not large enough to see. There are three main islands.

STEP 12: Add the island of Novaya Zemlya. You might also want to put a dividing line between Russia and Europe, and label them.

MAP DRAWING 23A: Coastline connecting France to Scandinavia
(the "Low Countries" where Mercator lived)

Mercator lived in the area of Europe that we now call the country of Belgium. In Mercator's day it was known as Flanders. Both Belgium and the Netherlands make up the region known as the Low Countries. This area is called "low" because it is at sea level. (The word "nether" means "low.")

This part of the coastline connects two areas we have already drawn: France and Scandinavia. Once you've learned this bit of coastline you should be able to outline all of Europe.

NOTE: You may want to use the worksheet on page 99 of the activity section to get you started on this drawing. You'll draw France and Britain, then fill in the Low Countries (and Ireland).

1

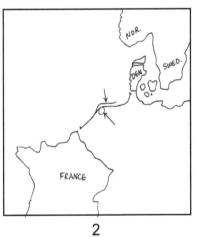

2

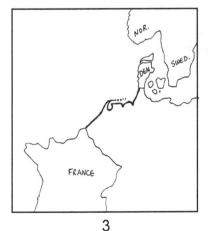

3

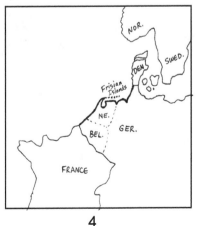

4

STEP 1: Draw a very wide up-side-down "V" between France and Denmark. Then make the line turn and go up steeply under Denmark, to form the bottom of the peninsula.

STEP 2: Draw an extra line on the top of the first line, as shown. Also add a circle on the inside of the wide angle. Make both these lines very light, as you will be tracing final lines over them.

STEP 3: Make these lines into a curved, pointy peninsula with a bay below it. Make some little islands trailing off the tip of the peninsula.

STEP 4: Mark off sections for Belgium and the Netherlands. Also label Germany (although we will not show the complete political boundary around Germany). You might also want to label the little islands (trailing off the peninsula) as the Frisian Islands.

MAP DRAWING 23B: Ireland

We need to finish up the parts of Europe we haven't drawn already, so we can put all the pieces together to make a complete map.
The island is divided into two separate countries: Ireland and Northern Ireland, each with its own capital city. Northern Ireland is a part of the United Kingdom, along with England, Scotland and Wales.

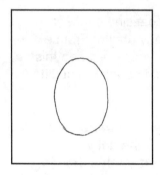

STEP 1: Draw an oval.

STEP 2: Start at the point indicated and add two blobs sticking out to the left. The bottom one has lots of fingers.

STEP 3: Continue on up the back and make a "head" off the right, finishing up where you started.

STEP 4: Make a dotted line across the top right portion. The island is divided into two countries.

MAP DRAWING 23C: Iceland

The island of Iceland is out in the North Atlantic Ocean, somewhat distant from the rest of the European countries, but it is considered a part of modern Europe. Iceland has museums, parks, schools, and even its own symphony. And it's not quite as cold as its name makes it sound. The climate is similar to Canada's.

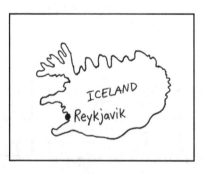

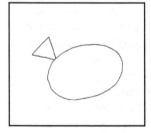

STEP 1: Draw an oval that is tipped on its side.

STEP 2: Add a triangle sticking off the side, as shown here.

STEP 3: Make the triangle very lacy, with long "fingers."

STEP 4: Continue around the outside, making it ripply. Add the country label.

MAP DRAWING 24A: Greenland

You rarely get to see Greenland's true shape unless you look at a globe. Poor Greenland is always getting stretched in one way or another. It seems that each projection has its own way of warping Greenland out of shape! In this drawing we will draw it properly, but on future maps, especially your final world map project, Greenland won't look just like this. Your starting shape—the parallelogram—may end up being more like a trapezoid or a square.

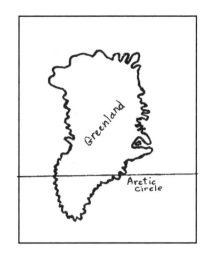

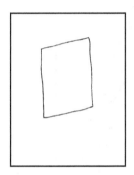

STEP 1: Draw a parallelogram.

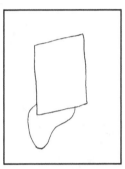

STEP 2: Add a triangular section to the bottom left corner of the parallelogram, as you see here. (It might remind you of India just a bit.)

STEP 3: Start your final outline by making a bulge at the top left corner. Then go down the side, make it very "lacy" with lots of in's and out's.

STEP 4: Finish the outline. At the bottom right corner of the parallelogram there are two "arms" with an island inside. Make long in's and out's at the top.

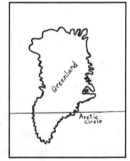

STEP 5: Erase your guidelines. Draw a line for the Arctic Circle (well below those two "arms"). Label Greenland.

MAP DRAWING 24B: Baffin Island

What does Baffin Island look like? A crab? A creature with a long body running on all fours? This one is for you to decide.   The body of water between Baffin Island and Greenland is called Baffin Bay. The crack between those bottom "fingers" is Frobisher Bay, the place where Martin Frobisher found all that iron pyrite (Fool's Gold).

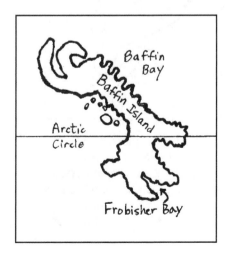

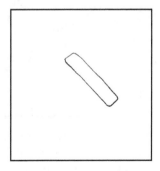

STEP 1: Draw a long rectangle going down at an angle, as shown.

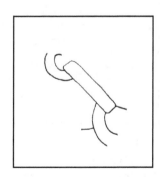

STEP 2: Add curved "legs" as shown here. These will be guides for you to draw around.

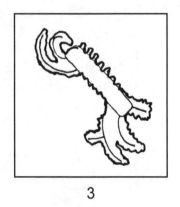

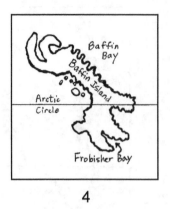

3

4

STEP 3: Draw around the outside of the guidelines. Make your lines ripply in most places. (Along the top of the rectangle the in's and out's get fairly deep.)

STEP 4: Erase your guidelines. Add the islands (crumbs for the crab to eat?) and draw a line for the Arctic Circle and label it. Label the island and also label two bays: Baffin Bay and Frobisher Bay (where all the Fool's Gold came from).

MAP DRAWING 24C: Hudson Bay

Hudson Bay is right on the back of Labrador's large ear. We will draw just the bay right now, but in a later drawing you will put Hudson Bay into its place right behind Labrador.

Hudson Bay is bigger than all five Great Lakes put together, but it's still only about half the size of the Caribbean. (Beware of Mercator projection maps—they show Hudson Bay as being much larger than the Caribbean, due to the intense stretching of the map as you near the poles.)

As you can see, there are many rivers feeding into Hudson Bay. The area around Churchill is known for its many polar bears.

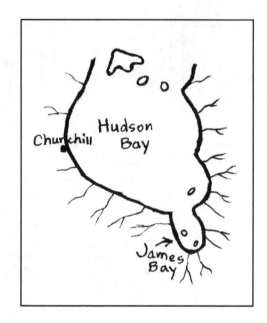

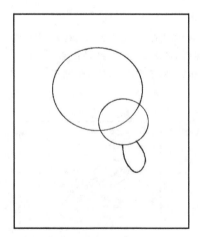

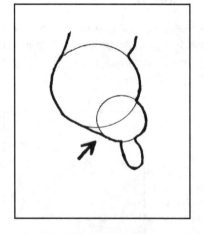

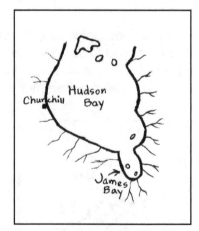

STEP 1: Draw a circle, then draw a smaller circle (about half the size of the first one) overlapping it as shown. Then add a long oval extending below the small circle.

STEP 2: Draw an outline around the edges of the circles. Notice that you want to stay out of the corner, so to speak, at the place indicated by the arrow.

STEP 3: Add many rivers coming into the bay. Add some small islands and one big one, as shown here. Label Hudson Bay and James Bay. If you want to label a town, add Churchill.

MAP DRAWING 25: Japan

The island of Japan is surrounded by the Pacific Ocean, where many strange marine creatures live. In this drawing, we'll use a real creature and an imaginary one. The real creature is the manta ray. If you don't believe that the top island really looks like this, check it on a map. It really does! Our imaginary creature is a type of seahorse thing.

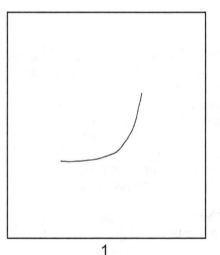

1

2

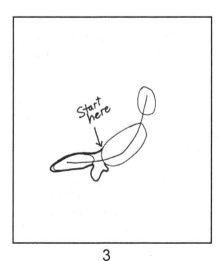

3

4

STEP 1: Draw a bow-shaped line as shown.

STEP 2: Make guidelines in the form of a ball for the head, a long oval for the body, and a fat gecko-like tail.

STEP 3: Start where indicated and draw around the outside of the tail guideline. Then make the mitten-like bottom flipper (or paw, or whatever it is).

STEP 4: Keep drawing the under-side and make two fins—one little one, then a slightly larger one that hangs down a bit.

NOTE: The actual outline of Japan just a little bit more complicated than shown in these instructions. There are some additional tiny peninsulas and bays. (All the major ones are shown here, though.) If you would like to add ALL the in's and out's of Japan, consult a good atlas or download a map from the Internet.

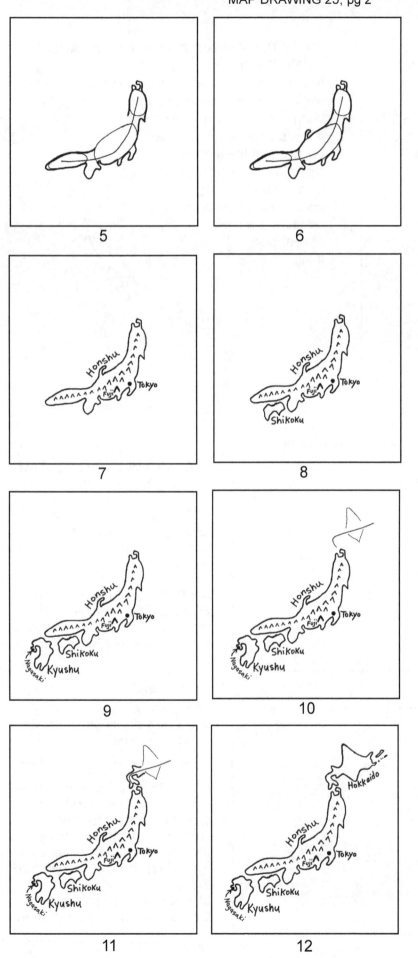

STEP 5: Continue up the neck and head and make a pointed nose. Add two little antennae-like things on top of the head. The forward one points backward.

STEP 6: Continue drawing down the back, adding a skinny bump right on the middle of the back.

STEP 7: Erase your guidelines and then add some mountains going up the middle of the island. Note which island is Mount Fuji. Label the island as Honshu, and also add the capital city of Tokyo.

STEP 8: Add the tiny island of Shikoku right under the "tail." It's like the critter's little baby.

STEP 9: Add another island at the end of the tail. This island is slightly larger than Shikoku and has a lot of in's and out's. (It has been simplified here.) Don't worry if you can't remember the shape perfectly. The point is knowing that it is there and knowing about the important city of Nagasaki, which you should label.

STEP 10: Draw a light guideline for the manta ray. Make the curve first, then add the triangle.

STEP 11: Draw in the forked tail and also the small flaps at the base of the fins.

STEP 12: Draw the fins and add the head with the two flaps that stick out in front of the mouth. Add a fish between the flaps. The manta is probably hunting this fish. You might also want to add some little islands extending from the lower flap. Label this island as Hokkaido.

MAP DRAWING 26A: Australia

The shape of Australia can vary from map to map, depending on which projection the cartographer used. Both the Australia outlines shown above are correct; they just represent different projections. You can see that you don't have to be overly concerned about getting the outline "perfect." If your drawing is a little longer or taller or wider, don't sweat it — just tell everyone it's your own projection!

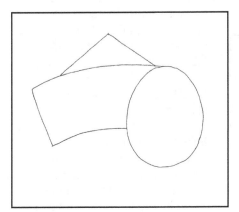

1

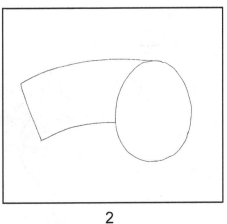

2

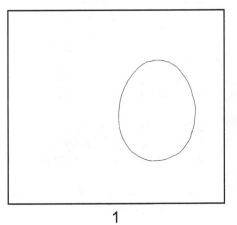

3

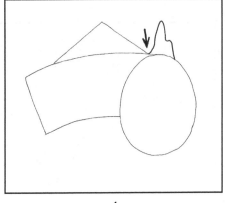

4

STEP 1: Draw an egg in the middle of your page, but to the right a bit.

STEP 2: Add a curvy flag-like shape going out from the egg.

STEP 3: Add a pointed roof-shape on top. Take careful note where the ends of the roof touch the egg and the flag. (The roof doesn't go all the way to the end of the flag.)

STEP 4: Believe it or not, your guideline steps are done, and you can begin the official outline. Start at the point where the roof, flag, and oval all meet, and make a tall peninsula. Is it a mountain? A chimney? A termite mound? Whatever it is, make sure it has an extra hump on the right side.

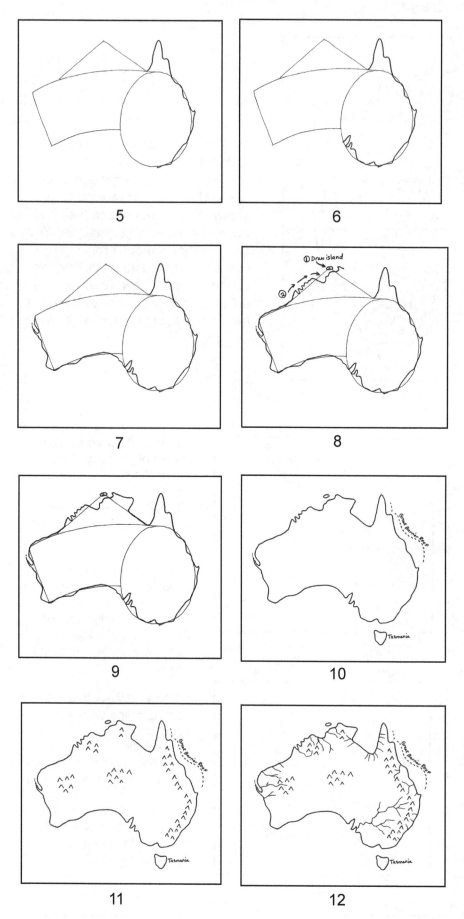

STEP 5: Continue down the side of the egg, making it a bit ripply, like a real coastline would be.

STEP 6: Go around the bottom of the egg, making an indent right at the bottom. (This will be the harbor at Melbourne.) Then as you come up the other side, make two skinny indents.

STEP 7: Don't go all the way into the corner—create a smooth curve over to the bottom of the flag. Continue along the underside of the flag, round the corner (make a bulge), and start up the vertical side. In the middle of the vertical side, there is a formation almost identical to the one you drew on the Netherlands: a long peninsula that comes to a point, with a trail of islands that get smaller and smaller.

STEP 8: First, draw an island right at the top of the roof point (Melville Island). Second, pick up your line again and go up the side of the roof, making a bulge with some inlets in it, then dropping below the island.

STEP 9: Make the last bulge at the top, then drop straight down to the roof top and trace right along it until you get back to your starting point. The outline is done, so you can erase your guidelines.

STEP 10: Add some dots or dashes along the right side and label it "Great Barrier Reef." Also add an island at the bottom and label it "Tasmania."

STEP 11: Add mountains in the areas shown.

STEP 12: Add some rivers coming out of the mountains. Notice the large river at the bottom. We aren't going to label it because each part of it has a different name.

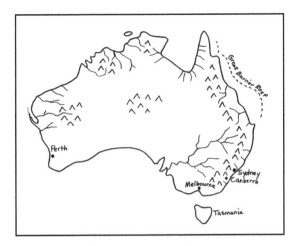

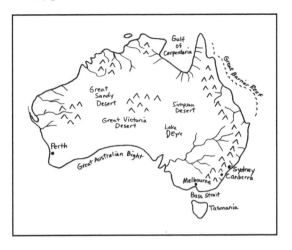

STEP 13: Label these major cities: Perth, Melbourne, Sydney, and the captial, Canberra.

STEP 14: Label the bodies of water: the Gulf of Carpentaria, Bass Strait, and the Great Australian Bight. (A "bight" is a bay that is just a slight, bow-shaped curve.)

MAP DRAWING 26B: New Zealand

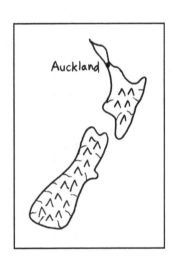

New Zealand was discovered by Europeans at the same time Australia was. The Maori natives are still alive and well in New Zealand today, although they have struggled immensely to keep their native language and culture alive.

New Zealand consists of two large islands which are simply called the northern and southern islands. The northern island is the same distance below the equator as the U.S. state of Virgina is above the equator. The southern island is equivalent to Maine.

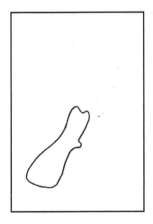

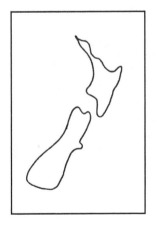

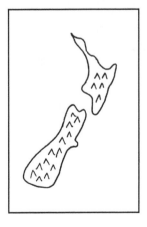

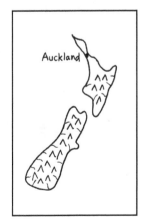

STEP 1: Draw an elongated shape with a spur on the underside and a dent in the upper end.

STEP 2: Draw a boot shape (a bit like the Italian boot, but upside down) and make the toe very pointy.

STEP 3: Add lots of mountains.

STEP 4: Add some rivers running out from between the mountains, and label the city of Auckland.

MAP DRAWING 27A: Alaska

Maybe this is one of the gold miners that came to Alaska during the Gold Rush of the 1890s?

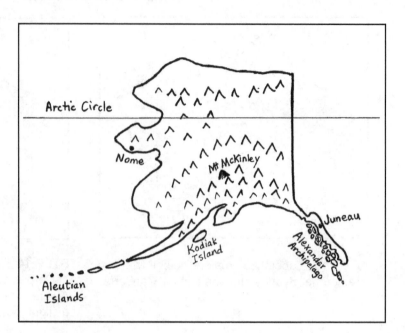

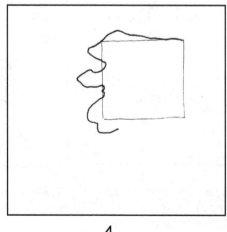

1

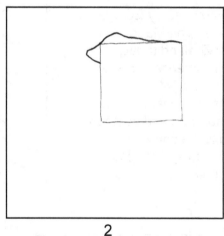

2

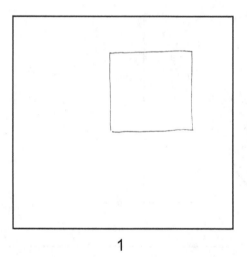

3

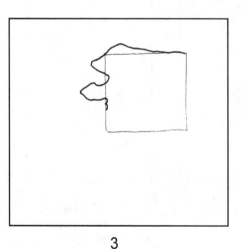

4

STEP 1: Draw a square in the upper right corner of your page. This is the only guideline you'll need for this drawing!

STEP 2: Start at the upper right corner of your square. Draw to the left along the top edge, sloping the line up as you go. Go way out around the corner, making the miner's tuft of hair sticking out.

STEP 3: Make the miner's bulbous nose. It should stick out farther than the tuft of hair. When you come back to the square, make a very small point right under the nose; this will indicate the upper lip.

STEP 4: Draw a huge beard going way out around the bottom left corner. The beard actually has two lobes.

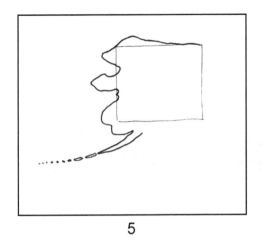

5

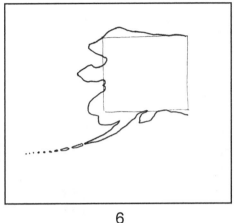

6

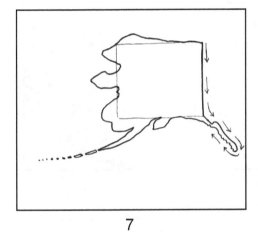

7

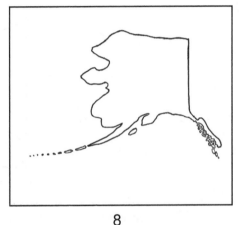

8

STEP 5: Add another part to the beard—a very long and very skinny extension. Make little islands trailing off the end of it.

STEP 6: If you can remember it, add an extra little bump under the beard.

STEP 7: Go back up to where you started, and draw a line straight down the side of the square. At the bottom, draw a diagonal extension, making it very bumpy as you come up the other side of it. Your outline is done.

STEP 8: Add a lot of very tiny islands next to the diagonal extension you just drew. Also add an island under the very skinny part of the beard.

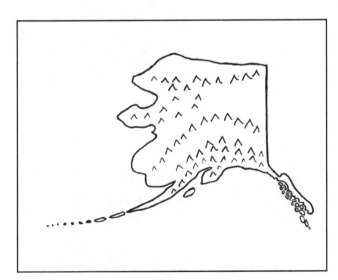

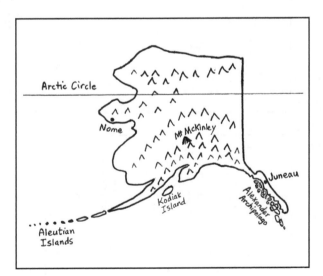

STEP 9: Add mountains in the places shown. The bottom mountain range contains the tallest peaks in North America. These mountains are the northern-most part of the Rocky Mountains, but in Alaska they are called the Alaska Range.

STEP 10: Label one mountain as Mt. McKinley, the tallest peak. Label the Aleutian Islands, Kodiak Island, the Alexander Archipelago, and the cities of Nome and Juneau (which is the capital). Draw a line right through the place where the eye would be and label it as the Arctic Cirlce.

MAP DRAWING 27B: Kamchatka peninsula and the Sea of Okhotsk

These two places take the prize for being the hardest names to remember! If you look at them carefully, you will see that they really aren't that hard to spell or pronounce. Just follow the basic rules of phonics and sound them out. They just sound very foreign to those of us who speak English.

This drawing will begin with the preparatory step of drawing Alaska. We will bridge the gap across the Bering Strait, "connecting" North America and Asia.

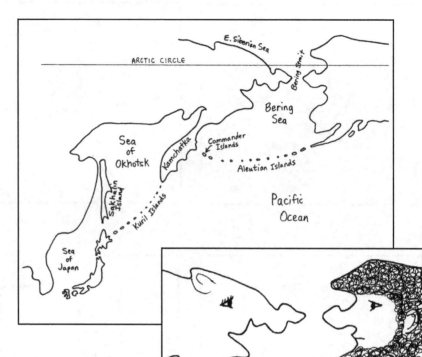

The face that is looking across the Bering Sea at Alaska is a very humorous one. The Asian side looks like a laughing piggish-elephant-thing. Apparently, Alaska isn't amused...

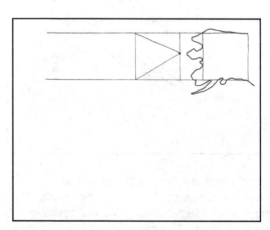

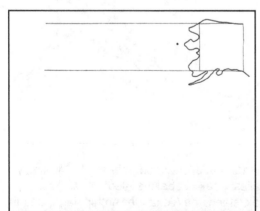

1

2

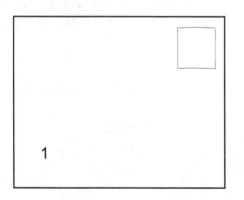

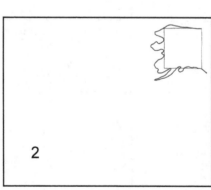

STEP 1: Draw a square that is 1 inch from both the top and the right side of the paper, and is 2 inches (5 cm) on a side.

STEP 2: Draw Alaska around the square, as you learned in drawing 27A.

STEP 3: Draw two parallel lines going out to the left from the top and bottom of the box. Then put a dot in front of Alaska's "nose" (about 1/4 inch).

STEP 4: Draw another 2-inch square so that the right side of the square goes through the dot. Then draw lines from the dot to the top left and bottom left corners of the square, making a triangle.

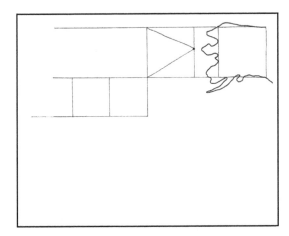

STEP 5: Extend the left side of the second square downward, 1 1/2 inches (4 cm). Use this 1 1/2 inch line as the starting point for making two squares sitting next to each other, each of them 1 1/2 inches on a side.

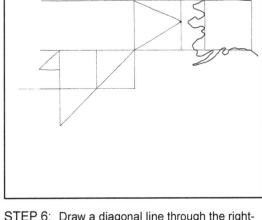

STEP 6: Draw a diagonal line through the right-hand square, then keep the diagonal line going to create another triangle under the lefthand square. Also make a triangle sticking out from the square on the left (looks like a pennant flag).

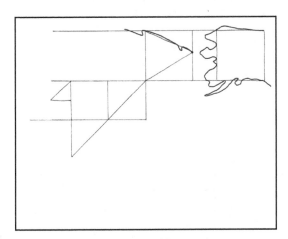

STEP 7: Now start your final outline. Start at the dot at the point of the triangle (in front of Alaska's "nose"). Make the outline go up the triangle, with one major indent near the tip.

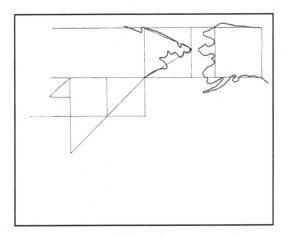

STEP 8: Next will be the bottom of the "head" that is facing Alaska. Whereas Alaska's "face" is very serious-looking, this one will be have an open, laughing mouth.

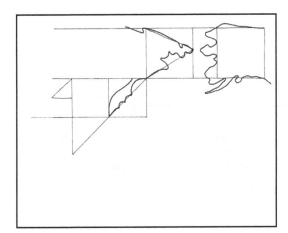

STEP 9: Now it's time for the Kamchatka peninsula. Notice that there are three spikey bumps on the bottom, just like Arabia. (Be sure to make a large arch before you start the three spikes.)

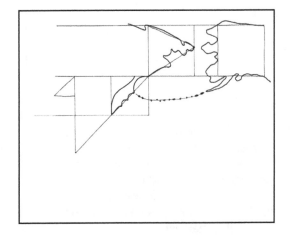

STEP 10: Draw a smooth curve from the pointy tip of Alaska's beard to the first spike on Kamchatka. Turn this line into a long archipelago of islands (the Aleutians).

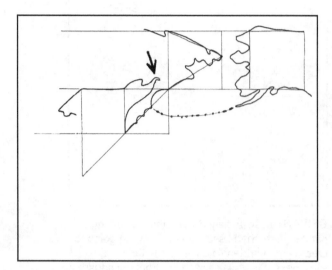

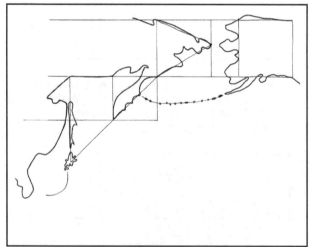

STEP 11: Go back and pick up your line where you left it at the top of the Kamchatka peninsula. Go up and make a shape like a little bird's head, as you see here, then another hump, then down to the top of the square. Draw right along the top of the square, then down the side of the pennant triangle and along the bottom of the triangle, making an extra bump, and stopping before you get to the side of the square.

STEP 12: Draw downward, making the very large bump indicated by the arrows. At the bottom, make Korea (a shape you have already drawn—when we did the map that had China on it).

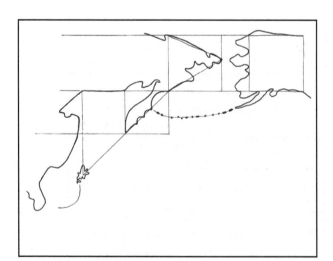

STEP 13: Now do a drawing that you have done before—Japan. Make the curvy backwards "L" shape, then draw the Hokkaido ray at the top. The center of the ray's body should be right at the corner of the triangle. Your temptation will be to make the ray too big. Keep it small. (It's surprising how small Japan looks on this map, isn't it?)

STEP 14: Next, make a very long and skinny fish, going straight up and down right above Hokkaido. This island is called Sakhalin Island. It is part of Russia.

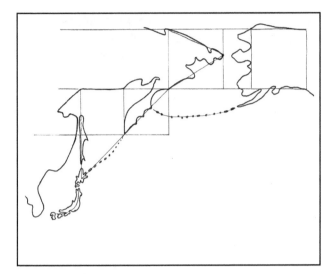

STEP 15: Finish drawing the islands of Japan.
Then draw a long line of islands going from
the head of the Hokkaido ray to the tip of the
Kamchatka peninsula. These islands are called the
Kuril Islands.

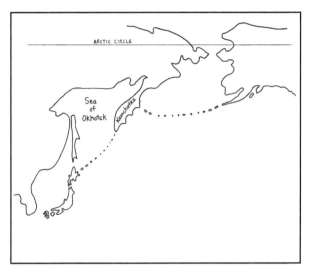

STEP 16: Now it's time to erase your guidelines
and begin labeling. First, put in a line for the Arctic
Circle. Remember, the Arctic Circle always goes
through the eye on Alaska's face (just above the
nose). Also in this step, the Okhotsk Sea and the
Kamchatka peninsula have been labeled.

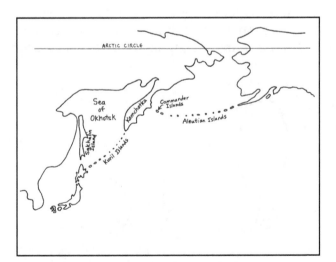

STEP 17: Label all the islands: the Aleutian
Islands, the Commander Islands (where Bering
died), the Kuril Islands, and Sakhalin Island.

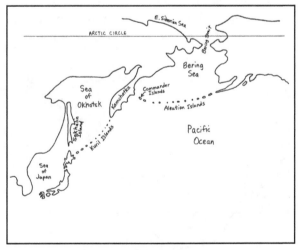

STEP 18: Label these seas: the East Siberian
Sea, the Bering Sea, the Sea of Japan. Also label
the Bering Strait and the Pacific Ocean.

MAP DRAWING 28A: The rest of North America

Before you start drawing the top of Canada, you need to carefully observe the pictures below. Each of these views of North America is correct. Look at Greenland in each drawing. What a difference! Which of these drawings is closest to the truth? What does North America really look like?

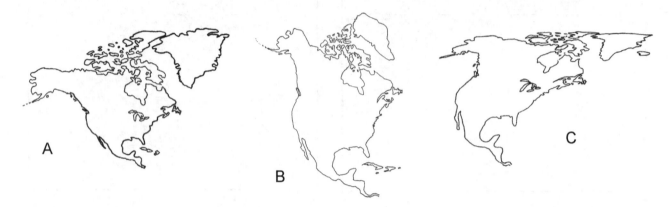

Most of the drawings we've done so far are of places near enough to the equator that projecting them onto a flat surface hasn't caused any major issues. There has been a little bending and stretching going on here and there, but chances are you've probably not even been aware of it. It's only when we start going toward the poles that we begin having difficulty. Scandinavia and the Svalvard Islands are the closest we've been to the poles, but when we did that map, we drew a narrow enough slice of the world that we didn't have to see what was going on off the sides of the page. The drawing was designed to avoid major projection issues.

Now we are going to draw a wide enough area of the world that we just can't avoid those issues any longer. So here's what we are going to do. In this lesson, we will be drawing the shapes of the islands and northern landmasses as they would look on a globe. Later, when we draw them on a worksheet, or on our final world map, we may have to squish them or stretch them a bit. Just be prepared ahead of time that you may not be able to draw these forms exactly like we will in this lesson.

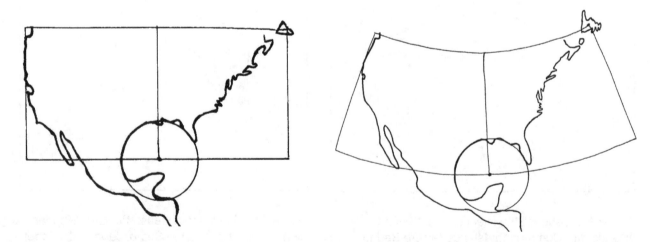

In previous lessons, we learned to draw the east and west coasts of America. If we had put the two drawings together, it would have looked like the drawing shown here on the left. The guide-lines were straight and square. This is a Mercator-type projection with straight lines of latitude and longitude. If we were to continue drawing Canada on top of it, the resulting map would resemble map A at the top. Greenland and the northern islands would be much too large. Map B is what we will get if we draw Canada on top of the map shown here at the right, with latitude and longitude lines curved and slanted to imitate the curved surface of the globe. Our drawings in this lesson will use invisible lines that are curved and slanted, so Canada will resemble the actual shapes you will see on a globe.

First, we will draw North America as shown in map A on the previous page. Since the goal is to complete North America, you will need to start out by drawing the parts of it you already know. You may draw it from scratch, or you may use the pattern pages following this lesson. After you have finished the map, there is another set of identical pictures showing how the same drawing will look if you use a more Mercator-type projection.

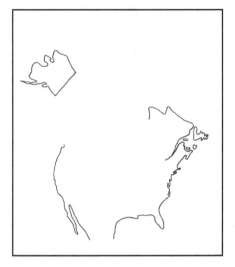

STEP 1: Start with this much of North America already drawn. You can draw it from scratch, or use a copy of the following pattern page (conical projection).

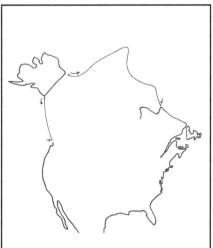

STEP 2: Draw in light guidelines over the top (with the point tilted to the right a bit, then down to meet the small ear) and also from the bottom of Alaska to the top northwest corner of America.

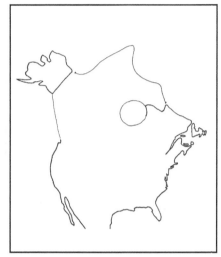

STEP 3: Draw a circle behind the larger of the two Labrador ears. Check to make sure your circle isn't a lot larger or smaller than this one. Look back and forth from your paper to this picture and compare them.

STEP 4: Draw a smaller circle that overlaps the one you just drew, as shown. Then, draw something that looks like a peninsula (although it will be water, not land) coming down from that smaller cirlce.

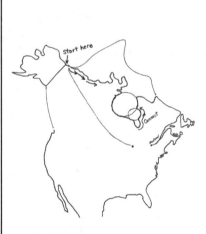

STEP 5: Draw in the top of the main continent. The line is very hard to describe, so you'll have to just imitate what you see here. For a larger version, look at the final drawing on the next page. Just before you get to the top of the Hudson Bay, there are two "bunny ears." (It's very windy and the bunny's ears are swept back.)

STEP 6: Make a guideline for Baffin Island. It fits right under the curve and will almost touch the bunny ears and Labradors' largest ear.

CLOSE-UP VIEW:

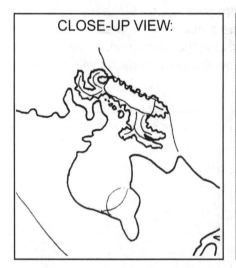

CLOSE-UP VIEW:

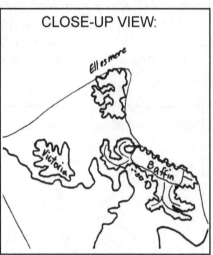

CLOSE-UP VIEW:

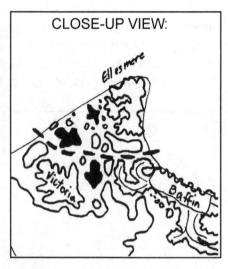

STEP 7: Draw around the outside of the Baffin guidelines, making it into the weird-looking crab eating crumbs (islands).

STEP 8: Draw two more large islands: Victoria and Ellesmere. Victoria looks like a mutant bird with a wide open beak and several wings on either side. Ellesmere isn't very easy to imagine into something, except maybe a backwards "E." It's always covered with ice, so no one ever really sees its real outline, anyway.

STEP 9: Draw a lot of smaller islands. Three of these smaller islands look a bit like birds (the ones that are colored black—but don't make yours black). The one between Ellesmere and Baffin sort of looks like a boot. The others are just blobs or dots. The dotted line indicates a clear passage where there are no islands. This is called Parry Channel. (You don't have to draw the dotted line—it's just there to show you where the channel is.)

CLOSE-UP VIEW:

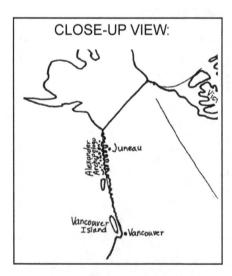

STEP 10: Draw in the outline of the coast from Alaska down to America. You've already done part of this in the Alaska drawing. Add a larger island under the Alexander Archipelago, and add a large, long island just above the "notch" (where Washington State is) and label it Vancouver Island.

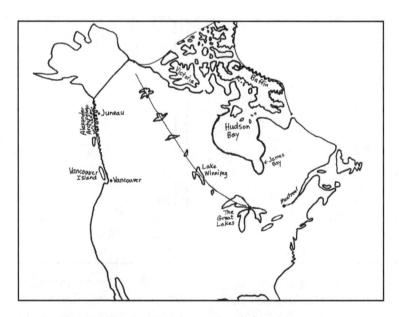

STEP 11: Draw some lakes along the line that crosses the continent. At the bottom dot, draw in the Great Lakes. Don't worry about getting them perfect, you just need to know their location.

STEP 12: Add the Rocky Mountains and the Appalachian Mountains.

STEP 13: Add the Mississippi River, the Colorado River and the Rio Grande River.

STEP 14: Add Greenland and Iceland.

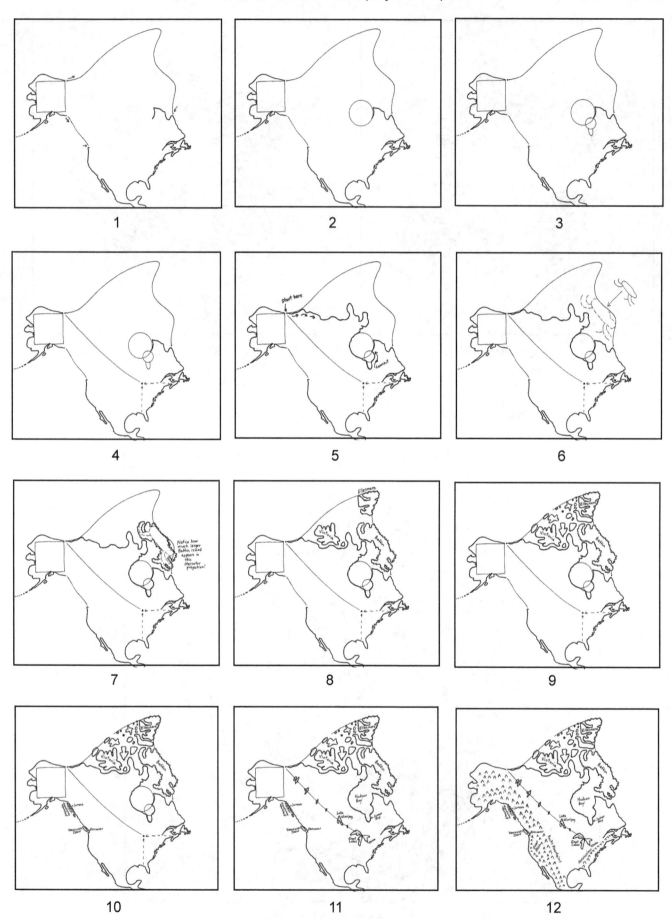

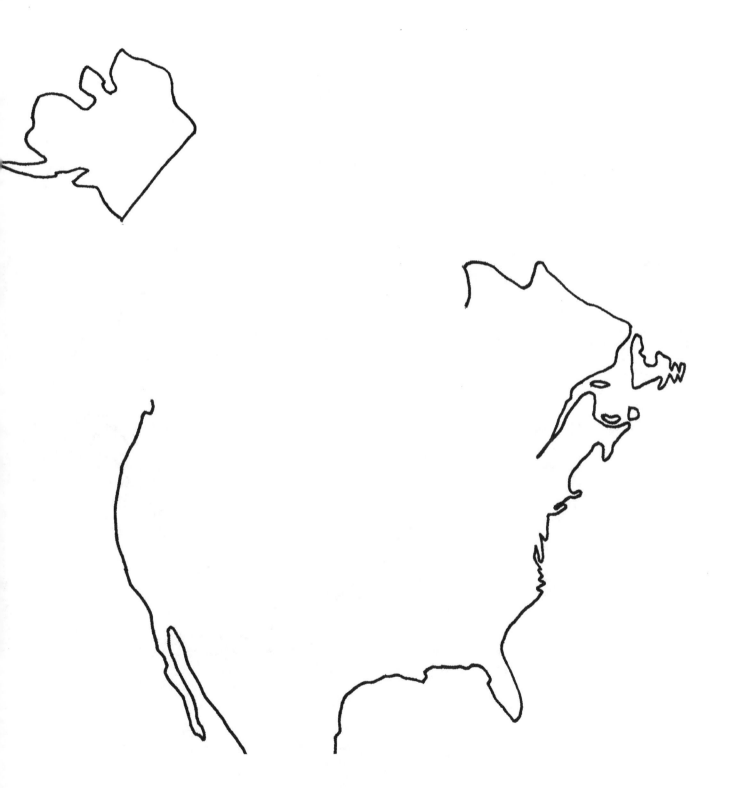

CONICAL PROJECTION (for 28A)

MERCATOR PROJECTION (for 28A)

MAP DRAWING 28B: The top of Asia

The other continent that gets stretched at the top is Asia. Although the word "Asia" may bring to mind images of pagodas and rice paddies, the top half of Asia is so cold that it is almost uninhabitable. Russia owns this cold wasteland. During the Soviet era they used it as a huge jail. Being sent to Siberia was as good as a death sentence.

The best way to remember how to draw the top of Asia is to think of a series of animals, all of which have bubbles (or balls?) over their heads. The first animal is "Yamal the Camel" (whose real name is the Yamal Peninsula). Then comes a cat-like thing who is poking at a bubble with a very long, skinny claw. Next comes a rhino with three bubbles over his head, and lastly there is a hamster who also has three bubbles. (Hamsters are native to Siberia, so our hamster should be comfortable in this landscape.)

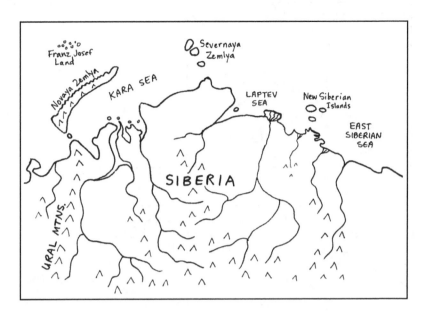

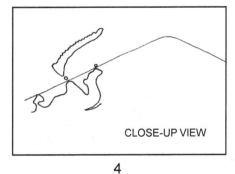

("Yamal the Camel")

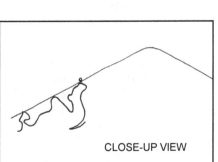

1

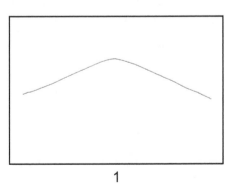

2

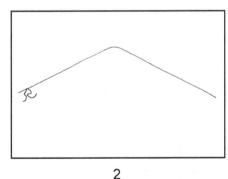

3

CLOSE-UP VIEW

4

CLOSE-UP VIEW

STEP 1: Draw a very wide upside-down "V." (The depth of the V depends on the projection you are using. The V shown here is basically a Mercator projection, but flattened just slightly.)

STEP 2: Draw a hatchet just below the guideline. You'll remember that the explorers had to use hatchets and axes to chop their way through the ice along this coast. (This is review from map drawing 22: Scandinavia.)

STEP 3: Draw Yamal the Camel. After finishing his head, add the little island above the tip of his nose.

STEP 4: Draw Novaya Zemlya right above the camel's hump. Put a little island between the hump and Novaya Zemlya.

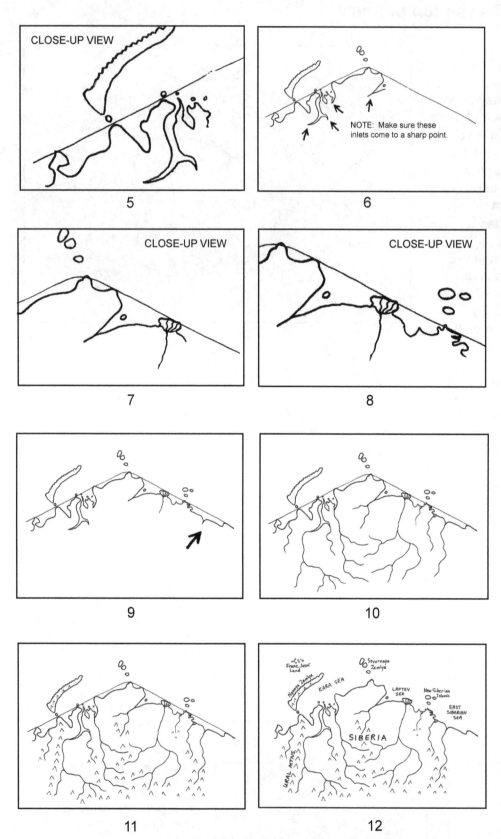

CLOSE-UP VIEW

5

NOTE: Make sure these inlets come to a sharp point.

6

CLOSE-UP VIEW

7

CLOSE-UP VIEW

8

9

10

11

12

Franz Josef Land

Novaya Zemlya

KARA SEA

Severnaya Zemlya

LAPTEV SEA

New Siberian Islands

EAST SIBERIAN SEA

SIBERIA

URAL MTNS

STEP 5: Next is the cat-like animal. This is the hardest part of the whole drawing. Don't worry too much about getting the shape exactly the same as this one. (If you want to get the shape exactly right, consult an atlas.) Just make sure it has an arm with a long, skinny, curved claw at the end, an open mouth, and an ear. Draw a tiny island at the end of the claw, and also above the nose and over the head.

STEP 6: Now it's time to draw the rhino. Don't forget to draw an ear before drawing the large nose. Don't make the horn too long. Put three islands over his nose. (Or maybe those are "thought bubbles" like in the cartoons and you can imagine what he is thinking about.)

STEP 7: Next comes a bump that is a delta. (A delta in the frozen north?! Seems strange, doesn't it?) Draw the delta area and the first part of the river. We will finish the river in step 10.

STEP 8: Draw the tail of the Siberian hamster (make it pointier than a real hamster's tail) then draw its ears and an open mouth. Finish with a paw. Add three bubbles over its head, just like the rhino.

STEP 9: Draw the last little bit of the coastline—it has one V-shaped dip inward.

STEP 10: Draw rivers going inland from every place where the coastline makes a pointed inlet. Also, finish the river connected to the delta.

STEP 11: You know where to put mountains by now, right? Everywhere there are tributaries, there are mountains that drain rainwater into them. Pay special attention to the mountain range that runs down below the camel's hump. These are the Ural Mountains. They are the official dividing line between Europe and Asia.

STEP 12: Add the archipelago called Franz Josef Land (above Novaya Zemlya), then label the Ural Mountains (for which Europe is named) and Siberia. After that, it is up to you what else to label. If you know that you will never remember all these names, just choose a few that might be easy to remember (such as the East Siberian Sea or the Kara Sea) or names that sound interesting to you. Look at the big map on the previous page while labeling—the larger size is easier to read.

INTRODUCTION TO 29A- 29G:

There are thousands of islands in the Pacific Ocean; several hundred are large enough to have people living on them. Obviously, this lesson can't expect you to memorize the location of hundreds of islands. We have chosen just a handful of islands to draw—islands that are either very well known or have been featured in our history lessons. If you would like to learn more, there's no limit to what you can teach yourself if you simply study a map and practice sketching what you see. Try to find imaginary guidelines that can help you remember the location of the islands. For instance, observe what is directly to the north or south of the islands, or how far above or below the equator they are. Look for imaginary diagonal lines that connect groups of islands. Also, it helps if the islands are more than just names on a page. Research a bit about the islands and find out the history of the land and the people. (The people of Vanuatu practice a strange custom of "bungy jumping" from wooden towers with nothing but a vine tied to their ankle!) The more real a place is to you, the more likely you are to remember where it is.

MAP DRAWING 29A: New Britain, New Ireland and the Solomon Islands

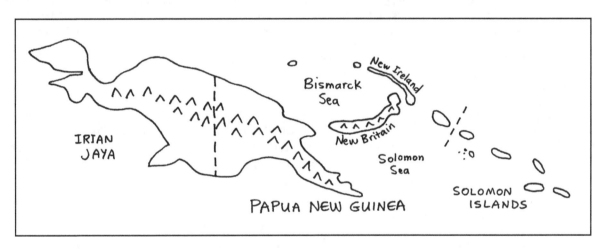

New Britain and New Ireland are part of the country of Papua New Guinea (which is the eastern half of the island of New Guinea). These islands were discovered by the Dutch in the 1600s but were thought to be part of New Guinea, not separate islands. In the early 1700s the British discovered them and gave them their English names. Germany briefly ruled the islands in the late 1800s. They gave them German names and named the Bismarck Sea after their kaiser. During World War I, the islands were taken from the Germans by the Allies and given to Australia. The names of the islands were changed back to their English names, but interestingly enough, the name of the Bismarck Sea remained.

The Solomon Islands are named after King Solomon in the Bible. The first Spanish explorers to come to these islands found flakes of gold at the mouth of one of the rivers. For unknown reasons, the Spaniards decided that these islands must have been where Solomon acquired a lot of his gold. The Solomon Islands were a key location in World War II, with one of the most intense battles occurring at a place called Guadalcanal, where 38,000 soldiers died.

The first step to drawing the islands is to draw New Guinea. The islands will then be added.

Preparatory steps (review of New Guinea)

These three preparatory steps are shown on a full sheet of paper that is turned sideways. If you don't want to use a full sheet of paper, you can skip step 1. Step 1 is given so that you have reference points that will make sure your New Guinea is approximately the right shape. Since the islands are drawn using points on New Guinea as reference points, having New Guinea as correct as possible is a good idea.

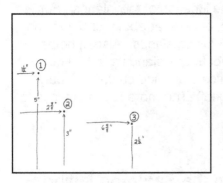

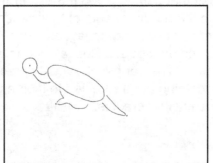

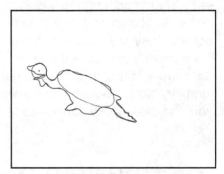

STEP 1: Put three dots on the page. The first dot should be 1 1/2 inches (3.75 cm) from the left side and 5 inches (12.5 cm) up from the bottom. The second dot should be 2 3/4 inches (7 cm) from the left side and 3 inches (7.5 cm) up from the bottom. The third dot should be 6 5/8 (16.75 cm) inches from the left side and 2 1/2 inches (6.25 cm) up from the bottom.

STEP 2: Draw a circle around the first dot, approximately 7/8 inches (2.25 cm) in diameter. Draw a long oval between the circle and the third dot. Draw in guidelines for the "neck," the "feet" and the "tail."

STEP 3: Draw around the outside of the island, adding features like the mouth, the beard, and the bumps on the tail.

> **NOTE:** In the rest of the drawings, only the middle of the paper will be shown. This will save space and allow a more close-up view of the islands.

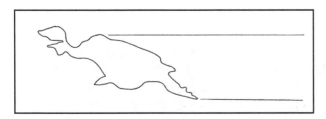

STEP 4: Draw horizontal lines out from New Guinea's feet and from the top of the back. (These are guidelines so make them light!)

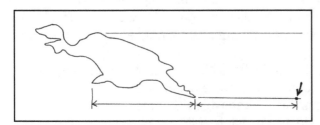

STEP 5: Put a dot on the bottom line. The dot should be the same distance from the end of the tail as the end of the tail is from the tip of the front foot.

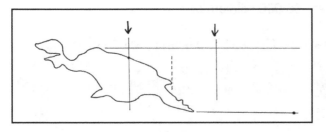

STEP 6: Draw two vertical guidelines. The left one should cut through the middle of the back—exactly at the middle. Then imagine a line where the dotted line is, right at the end of the little bump at the top of the tail. Now put in the right line so that it is the same distance from the dotted line as the left line is. Sounds complicated using words, but it's really pretty easy to do.

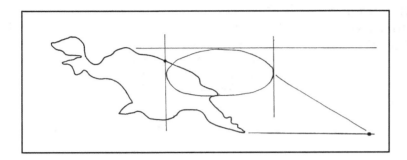

STEP 7: Draw an oval that is just slightly long and flat. The top of the oval should touch the top guideline. The bottom of it should go to the bottom of that bump at the top of the tail. The sides of the oval should touch the vertical guidelines. After you finish the oval, draw a line from the middle of the right side down to the dot on the bottom line.

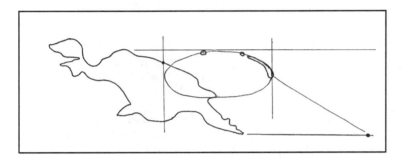

STEP 8: Draw in New Ireland. It is very long and thin, slightly curved, and having a bulge at the southern end. Some people describe the shape as a rounded musket. Others see it as a very long gourd. You can imagine it to be whatever you want.

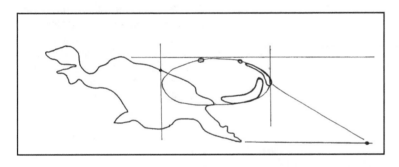

STEP 9: Draw in New Britain. It's like a banana sitting right inside the oval. Notice how the top of New Britain goes inside of where New Ireland sits. If you want to make the shape more accurate, look at the shape shown in the final drawing. It has two bulges and narrow places at the northern end.

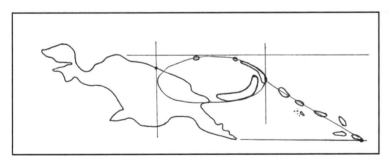

STEP 10: Draw in the Solomon islands. They lie approximately along the diagonal line. The island at the bottom is right at the dot. The next two islands up from it go on either side of the line, Then the rest of the islands are pretty much on the line. There is one little additional group of very small islands right under the second island from the top.

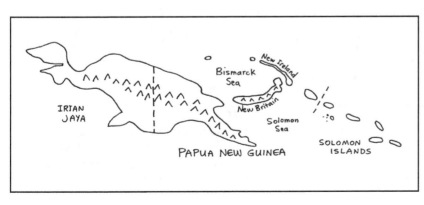

STEP 11: Erase your guidelines. Add mountains along the middle of New Guinea and New Britain. (New Ireland is also mountainous, but is too small to draw on.) Label the Bismarck Sea and the Solomon Sea. Make dotted lines where shown—these represent the east and west boundaries of Papua New Guinea. (Notice that it owns the top Solomon Island.) Label the islands and countries.

MAP DRAWING 29B: Hawaii

As you know, Hawaii is part of the United States of America. It is the most southern state, lying just below the Tropic of Cancer.   Hawaii has 4 main islands and 4 smaller ones.

Pearl Harbor is famous because the Japanese bombed it on December 7, 1941, causing the U.S. to enter World War II.

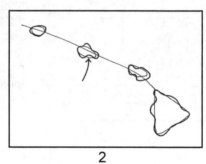

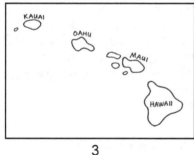

1

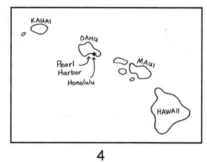

2

STEP 1: Draw a triangle, then make a guideline going up diagonally to the left. Make three ovals along the guideline.

STEP 2: Draw a wavy outline around the triangle, making it look more like an island and less like a triangle.

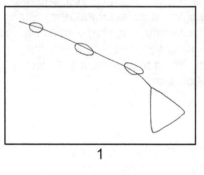

3

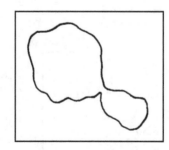

4

STEP 3: Label the islands (from the bottom up): Hawaii, Maui ("*Mow-ee*"), Oahu ("*Oh-wah'-hu*") and Kauai ("*Kay'-oo-wah'-ee*"). Add three little islands off the coast of Maui and one little island off the coast of Kauai. (To remember which island is Maui, think of it as the baby right behind mother Hawaii. Maui is saying, "Ma! Ma! There are three little fish nibbling at me!")

STEP 4: Label Pearl Harbor and

MAP DRAWING 29C: Tahiti

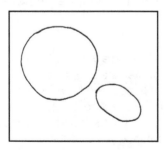

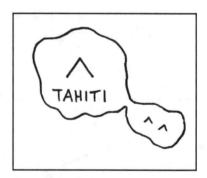

STEP 1: Draw a circle, then draw an oval next to it, right about where the number 4 would be on a clock.

STEP 2: Draw an outline around the outside of the circle and oval. Make it wavy so it looks like an island.

STEP 3: Indicate a large mountain in the center of the circle, and some little hills in the oval. These mountains are actually volcanoes, of course. Label the island as Tahiti.

MAP DRAWING 29D: Vanuatu

The island group called Vanuatu (just pronounce all the letters, making the "a" say "ah") is fairly easy to identify because the islands are arranged in a narrow "V." Not all island groups in the Pacific are so easy to spot. It's a nice coincidence that the word Vanuatu begins with a "V."

Vanuatu is located south and east (down and to the right) of the Solomon islands and is part of the same underwater mountain range. There are some very long mountain ranges in the Pacific Ocean.

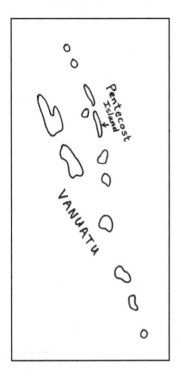

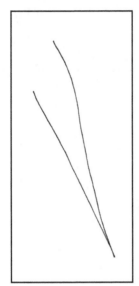

STEP 1: Draw a very narrow V. It almost looks like an upside down pair of tweezers.

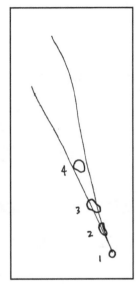

STEP 2: Draw 4 islands, starting at the point of the V. The islands get larger and farther apart as you go up.

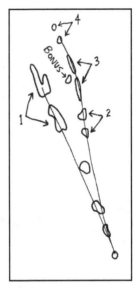

STEP 3: Draw in 4 pairs of islands, as shown here. Notice that both islands in pair 3 are long and skinny.

STEP 4: Label the Vanuatu Islands and Pentecost Island. Pentecost Island was discovered and named by Europeans on Pentecost (a Christian holiday) in the year 1768. The natives of Pentecost are famous for their dare-devil feats of jumping from very tall towers with only a vine attached to their ankle.

MAP DRAWING 29E: Fiji

Fiji lies to the east of Vanuatu. These islands are among the largest in the Pacific. The larger island is approximately the size of Connecticut.

MAP DRAWING 29F: New Caledonia

Caledonia is an ancient name for Scotland. New Caledonia lies south of Vanuatu, on a different mountain range. It is a territory of France.

MAP DRAWING 29G: Placing the islands in the Pacific

Now that you can draw some Pacific Islands, you need to know where they belong in the ocean. You won't be drawing on a blank sheet of paper for this drawing. Instead, you will need a copy of the following pattern page, showing the outline of the Pacific Ocean.

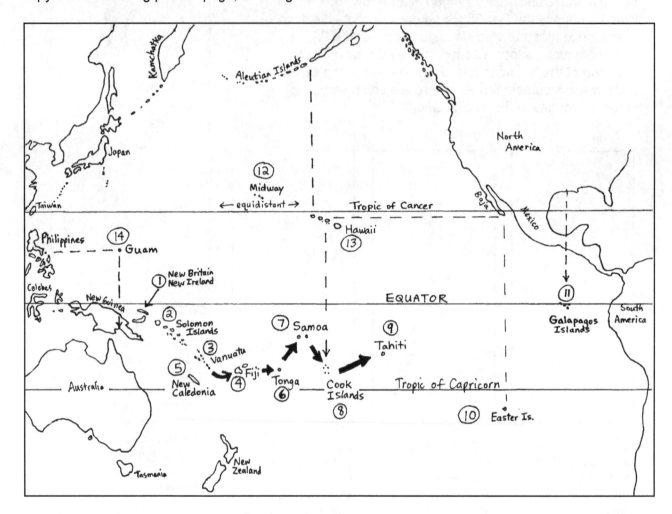

STEP 1: Draw New Britain and New Ireland right above the "tail" of New Guinea.

STEP 2: Now lightly (very lightly!) sketch in a curvy "L" shape (or backwards "J" if you prefer) going down from these islands. In reality, this curve represents an underwater mountain chain. The islands along this curve are simply the tops of some of the mountains. Draw the Solomon Islands at the top of the L.

STEP 2

STEP 3: Add Vanuatu.

STEP 4: Add Fiji.

STEP 5: Now drop down below this curve and draw New Caledonia. It's directly below the gap betwen the Solomon Islands and Vanuatu.

STEP 6: Go back up and add the Tonga Islands just to the right of Fiji. (Abel Tasman called these islands the Friendly Islands, because the natives were overly friendly)

STEP 7: Go up a bit and draw a few dots and label them "Samoa." The Samoan Islands are divided into two political groups. There is Samoa, which used to be a territory of New Zealand but is now independent, and American Samoa, which is a territory of the U.S.

STEP 8: Draw a small group of dots to represent the Cook Islands. Since we learned about Captain Cook, it seems appropriate to include the island group named after him. You can remember its latitude position easily because it is right below Hawaii, where Cook died.

STEP 9: Go up and to the right a bit and make a dot for Tahiti. This island is part of a whole group of islands called French Polynesia. (You might want to add some dots around Tahiti.) Tahiti was made famous by the French painter Gaugin, who lived on the island for a while and painted pictures of the natives.

STEP 10: Easter Island is the only island in its part of the ocean. It's very famous because of the huge stone statues found there. No one knows who made the statues or what purpose they served—they are a complete mystery. The island was named Easter Island by the Europeans who discovered it on Easter Sunday. If you trace a line north, you will see that it lies approximately under the tip of Baja California.

STEP 11: The Galapagos Islands lie right on the equator. Surprisingly, they are right below New Orleans!

STEP 12: Now it's time to go above the equator and above the Tropic of Cancer. The Midway Islands are just above the Tropic of Cancer and—as you might guess by their name—they are exactly halfway between the coast of China and the coast of the U.S. You can even measure it off with a ruler! The Midway Islands were the site of some famous battles during World War II.

STEP 13: Finally, Hawaii! If you imagine a line down from the tip of Alaska's beard, and a line over from the tip of Baja California, you'll get Hawaii in just about the right spot. Remember, that's down from a tip and over from a tip. Easy to remember!

STEP 14: You've probably heard of Guam. It's an important military base for the U.S. It's right across from the Philippines and up from the tail of New Guinea. (There is fool-proof way to remember Guam's latitude, but it's a bit silly. If you don't like this kind of silliness, just ignore this—it's really silly. The word Guam is very similar to the word "guano." *("gwan-oh")* Guano is bat dung. If you draw an imaginary line down from Guam, you end up right under the dinosaur's tail. Enough said?)

STEP 15: Add any other islands you want to add. Use an atlas to pick out some that you've heard of or that sound interesting.

STEP 16: OPTIONAL

Add the International Date Line, if you want to. It goes around the Aleutian Islands so that everyone in Alaska is on the same day as the rest of America. It goes just to the left of the Midway Islands (which are territories of the U.S.) and then when it reaches the equator it does a huge loop to the east, to go around the Kiribati Islands (one of which is called Christmas Island). Samoa is on the U.S. side and Tonga is on the Asian side.

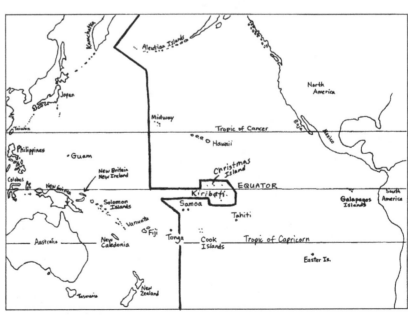

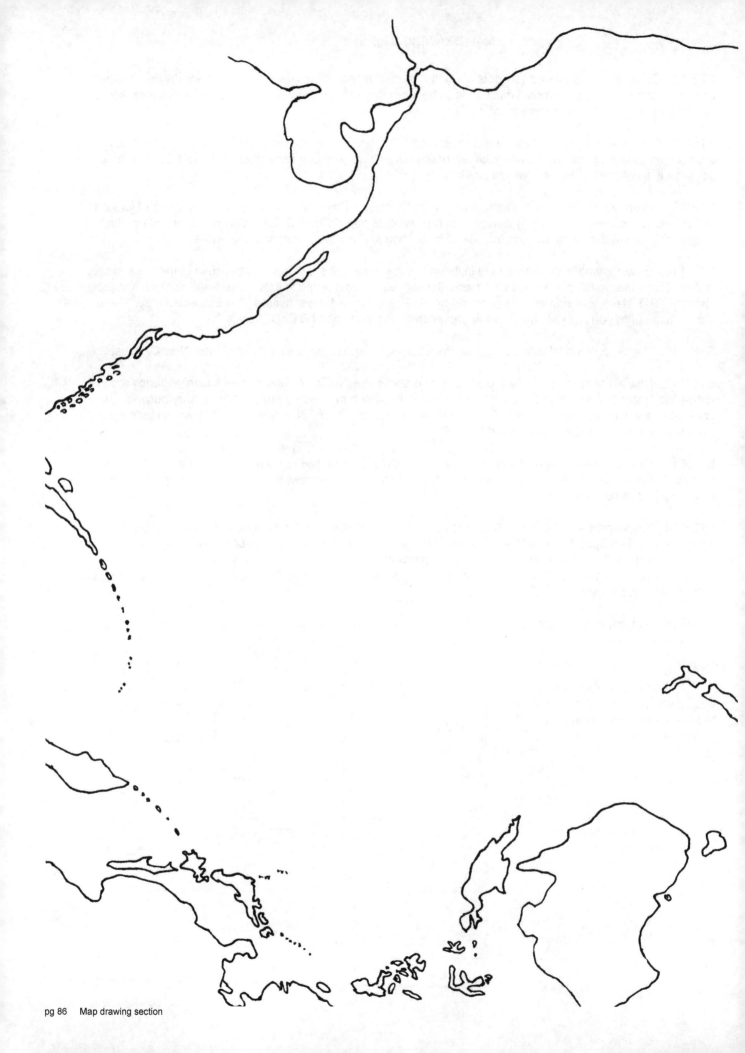

MAP DRAWING 30: Antarctica

When you look at a world map, you don't see Antarctica looking like this (unless it is shown in a little inset box in a corner of the map). You see it as a bumpy, white strip running along the bottom of the map. This is because a world map is almost always a cylindrical projection with the equator in the middle. The north and south poles are stretched out into a line. There's no land at the north pole, so you just see water getting stretched—not a big deal. But at the south pole, there is a whole continent that gets bent out of shape! Antarctica must be cut into pieces and stretched along the bottom.

Here is Antarctica as it really is.

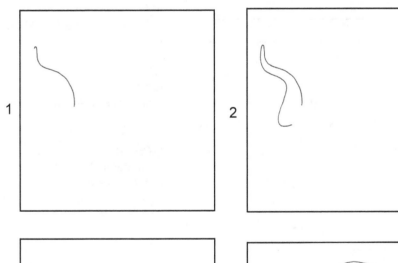

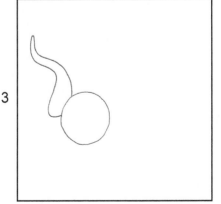

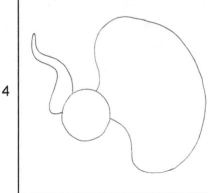

STEP 1: Draw a tiny "hook" following into a slightly S-shaped curve.

STEP 2: Go back to where you started and pick up the line on the other side of the tiny hook. Draw downward, making another S-shape, leading to a bulge at the bottom. What does it look like? A tadpole swimming downward? A flimsy musical note? A giant soup ladle?

STEP 3: Draw a circle on the end of this shape.

STEP 4: Draw a very large mushroomish/kidneybeanish shape. Make sure it is large enough that it goes higher than the tip of your tadpole shape.

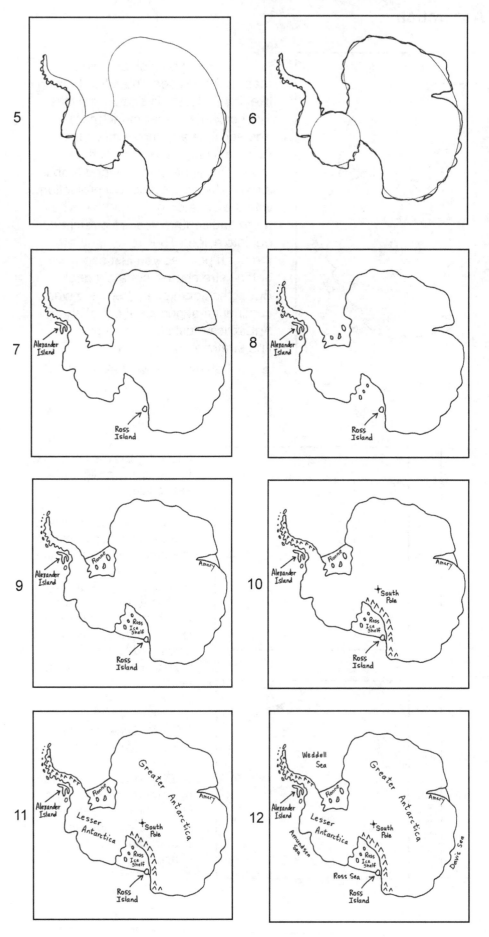

STEP 5: Now begin your outline. Start at the pointed tip. Draw along the underside of the continent, making the line very ripply along the "tadpole" section. Put in some wavy bumps along the large outer edge, as well.

STEP 6: Make a deep "dent" in the "kidney bean," then continue up and over the top. Continue tracing along the edges of the guidelines until you get back to where you started.

STEP: 7: Draw islands in the places shown. Alexander Island looks sort of like a backwards lower case "h." Notice how close Ross Island is to the shore.

STEP 8: Add small islands in the places shown (three in each sea, and a trail of them down along the pointy peninsula).

STEP 9: Draw lines for the edges of the ice shelves and label them (the Ronne, the Ross and the Amery).

STEP 10: Add a line of mountains along the coast of the Ross Sea, as shown. Make an X at the South Pole and label it.

STEP 11: Label the two halves of Antarctica: the smaller side is Lesser Antarctica and the larger side is Greater Antarctica. The greater side is about the same size as Austraila.

STEP 12: Label the seas around Antarctica: the Amundsen Sea, the Ross Sea, the Davis Sea and the Weddell Sea. Each of these is named after an explorer.

ACTIVITY SECTION

The activity ideas in this section are optional and may be used at the parent or teacher's discretion. The review worksheets are highly recommended, however, as they review information learned in the drawing lessons.

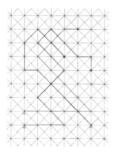

If you purchased a hard copy of this curriculum and therefore don't have a digital copy, you can download many of the patterns in this section. Go to www.ellenjmchenry.com and click on FREE DOWNLOADS, then on GEOGRAPHY & MAPS. There is a special section at the bottom of the page that has many of these pages as digital downloads. This will allow you to print color copies of the game boards right from your home computer. (Or you can take the files to a copy center.) Some of the patterns will provide best results if printed on heavy card stock paper.

ACTIVITY IDEA 1A: An edible Babylonian clay map

The "clay" in this project is a modified cookie dough recipe. (You could also use any of your favorite sugar cookie or gingerbread cookie recipes, but leave out the baking powder or baking soda.) The result will be a little crunchy when you eat it, but it will be edible. Have your students work on a piece of aluminum foil so that their tablets can be easily transferred to a baking sheet.

You will need to provide little wedge-shaped stamps for making cuneiform letters as well as pointed sticks for scratching designs. For the wedge-shaped stamps, you might want to use Sculpey (a clay that you harden by baking in the oven) or if you prefer working with wood, you could use any wood scrap, even the end of a popsicle stick. A piece of dowel rod sharpened in a pencil sharpener makes a good tool for scratching lines in the clay. You may also want to experiment with tools you have around the house, such as plastic silverware.

Edible clay:
3/4 cup sugar
2/3 cup shortening
1/2 cup cocoa powder
2 eggs
2 cups flour   *Bake at 375 F for 10-12 minutes or until done.*

Mix ingredients in order. If the dough is sticky, add more flour. Take a ball of dough and flatten it into a tablet. This recipe makes enough clay for 8 tablets that are about 4" x 5". Here are a few real cuneiform words that your students might like to use on their tablets:

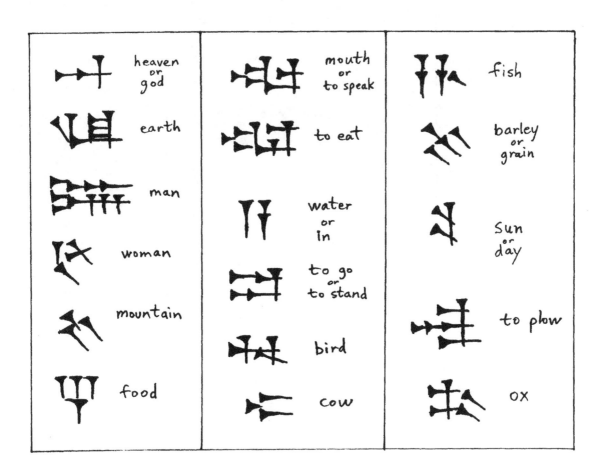

ACTIVITY IDEA 1B: A local map (of your room) on modern papyrus (paper)

Most ancient maps were local maps, like the one on the papyrus. They were made by simply imagining what the area looks like from above, with very little measuring. Have the students make a map of the room they are in, by just imagining it from above and without taking any measurements. Provide paper and pencils and possibly rulers (although the ancients didn't worry overly much about perfectly straight lines).

ACTIVITY IDEA 1C: A Polynesian-style map of your room

Make a map of the room you are in using long, thin pieces of brown paper to represent the reeds used by the Polynesians. If you have a paper cutter, this can make quick work of making strips. Provide a piece of white paper to work on and use a glue stick to tack the thin paper strips at each corner where they cross. Have students cut light brown or yellow "shells" to mark out where important objects are in the room. The "shells" must be on the paper strips (simulating being tied to the reeds), not on the white paper. (The white paper sheet is there just to make your reed map less flimsy. You have to sort of pretend it's not there.)

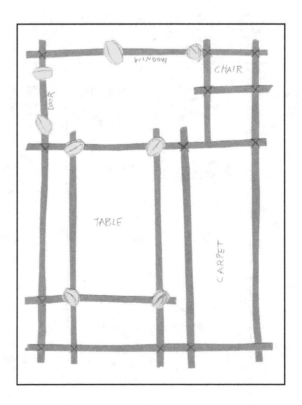

ACTIVITY IDEA 2: Practice using a ruler, a compass and a protractor

This activity prepares the students for future activities. It is important that they feel comfortable using these tools and understand these terms: **parallel, perpendicular, radius, diameter, and degree.**

Each student will need a ruler, a compass and a protractor, as well as a pencil, an eraser, and at least four sheets of paper. Follow the instructions below, in order. Students who have never used a compass or a protractor before may need to have the techniques demonstrated to them. (The best way to hold a compass is to pinch the end between your thumb and forefinger and twirl it while tilting it at a slight angle.)

1) Practice making parallel lines.
Make two parallel lines of any length. Draw the first line using the ruler, then measure off two dots on the same side of the line, the same distance from the line. Then use the ruler to connect the dots. Make two parallel lines that are 2 inches long and 2 inches apart.

2) Practice making perpendicular lines.
Make two perpendicular lines that are each 2 inches long. Draw the base line, then use the protractor to measure the 90 degree angle for the second line.

3) Make these perpendicular lines into a design.
Connect the ends of these perpendicular lines to form a square with an X through it.
Divide each of these triangles in half using the protractor to bisect the angles.
Add a few more lines, either perpendicular or parallel, to make a design you like.

3) Practice making circles.
Use the compass to make circles of various sizes. You will need to work on a surface that allows the point of the compass to stick into the paper a bit.

4) Divide a circle into 32 equal parts.
Use the measuring device on the compass to set the compass radius at 3 inches. Use the compass to draw a circle that will have a diameter of 6 inches across. Draw perpendicular lines that cross in the center, sort of like "cross hairs." (Draw one line first, either straight up and down or straight across. Then use the protractor to measure the 90 degrees for the second line.) Now use the protractor to bisect each wedge into two 45 degree sections. (Put the center of the straight edge of the protractor [the 2 1/2 inch line] right on the center dot of your circle. Make a mark at the 45 degree point, then remove your protractor and connect the dots with your ruler.) Divide these sections in half, then in half again so that the circle is divided into a total of 32 wedges, each a little over 11 degrees (11.25) wide.

Ponder this question: Would your job have been easier if a circle was divided into 400 degrees instead of 360?

5) Follow these directions to make an artistic design:
Make two perpendicular lines that are 6 inches long. Connect the ends of these lines to form a square with an X through it. Find the midpoint of each side, using the ruler. Connect the midpoints to each other to form a square. Then connect the midpoints to the center point. Take your compass and set its metal point on one of those midpoints. Then pull the compass pencil until it touches the center point. Now draw an arc from the center point out to the corner. Draw the same arc with the compass set on the other midpoints.

If you don't have access to protractors for some reason (or can't justify the expense for your class, which is exactly what happened to me and I ended up using paper protractors) you can print this page onto heavy card stock paper and then cut out these protractors. (Don't forget to cut out the inside, too.) They won't have the advantages of clear plastic protractors, but they will get you through the activities for which you need them.

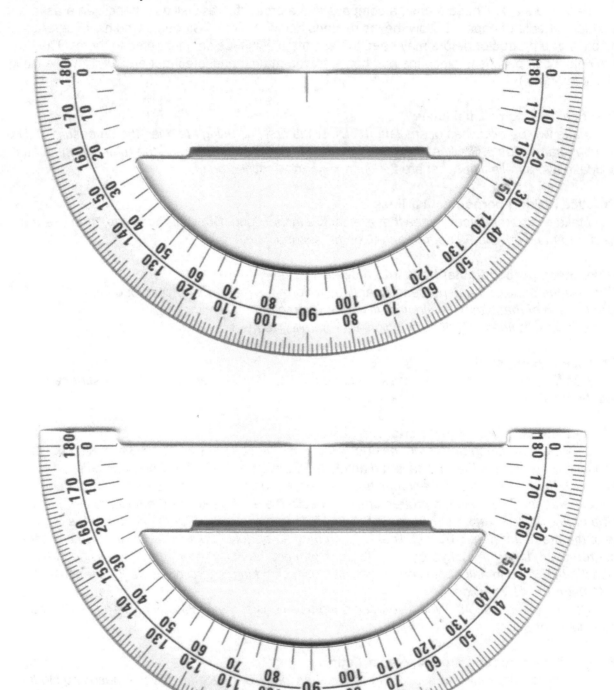

ACTIVITY IDEA 3A: Quick quiz: "Above or below the equator?"

This activity does not require studying an atlas. This is just a quick (and fun) way to do a sort of "pre-test" to find out how much everyone knows about basic geography. (Even we adults will find out we know less about geography than we thought!) Read the list below, one at a time, and have the students guess whether each one is above, below, or on the equator. If you are working with a group, you might want to use the "silent quiz" format. Pause for about 5 to 10 seconds and tell the student to think their answer in their head. Then you say the answer out loud and they see if they were right. You could also have the student write their answers down if you are looking for writing practice. Or you can use a different format that suits you better.

Florida (above)	Australia (below)	Egypt (above)
Spain (above)	the Panama Canal (above)	India (above)
Hawaii (above)	Venezuela (above)	Kenya (on)
Morocco (above)	Ethiopia (above)	Madagascar (below)
Japan (above)	Peru (below)	Ecuador (on)
China (above)	Philippines (above)	Galapagos Islands (on)
Zaire (on)	New Guinea (below)	Sudan (above)

ACTIVITY IDEA 3B: Longitude on an egg

This project demonstrates that lines of longitude can look either straight or curved, depending on the angle of view. Each student will need a hard-boiled egg and a pencil. Have the students put a dot on the top and bottom of the egg, where the north and south poles would be. Then draw lines connecting the poles, as straight as they can, all around the egg. Make a total of about sixteen lines around the egg. Start by dividing it into quarters, then eighths, then sixteenths. Have the students hold the egg straight in front of them. Notice that the line of longitude that appears to be in the middle of the eggs looks straight. The lines at the edges will look most curved. Turn the egg and notice that this perspective doesn't change as the lines move. The line that used to be in the center and looked straight will now be on the edge and look curved.

Add an equator line and two lines for the tropics. Now turn the egg slowly and observe how the longitude and latitude lines always look perpendicular at the places they cross if you are looking at them from a "straight on" view. This is the strange truth about longitude lines: they appear to curve while also appearing to remain perpendicular! (Drawing tip: Use your pinky finger to steady your hand on the egg while your draw.)

ACTIVITY IDEA 3C: Draw your egg on paper

Use a compass to draw a circle that is 4 inches in diameter (set your compass at 2 inches). Put the ruler on the center point and draw the equator. Draw parallel lines 1/2 an inch from the equator to make the tropics of Cancer and Capricorn. Draw a line perpendicular to the equator and passing through the center point. Make three marks along the equator, 1/2 an inch apart, dividing the space on each side of the equator evenly. Make curved lines that go through these points. It should look like the drawing of the egg shown in project 3B, only circular, not oval.

ACTIVITY IDEA 3D: Draw or paint a more accurate map of Greece

<u>To draw a map</u>:

For this drawing, orient your paper horizontally. (This will result in having more of Turkey appear on your map.) Place your hand on your paper as shown. Sketch in the egg and the Aegean Sea outline. Then use the outline map on the next page as you draw in the land forms. You should compare the actual shapes to the basic memory shapes you learned. (You will be surprised how much the real shapes look like what we imagined them to be!) Do the steps, in order, but use the outline map to copy the correct shapes as best you can.

After you are done sketching in pencil, go over your "good" lines with a black fine-point permanent marker, or a black felt-tip pen. Then erase your pencil lines.

OPTIONAL: Use an atlas to add a few more place names. (This option is for students who process information very quickly. If the students have barely managed to get the basic labels, don't add more.)

<u>To paint a map</u>:

You will need: light blue card stock paper, small paint brushes, pencil, eraser, thin-line black permanent marker, acrylic paints (green, tan, cream, maybe dark green) and a physical map of Greece (a satellite image would be the best).   I used a NASA satellite image from the Internet http://www.in2greece.com/blog/uploaded_images/nasa-greece-map-742017.jpg. (A satellite map is available as a free download on the GEOGRAPHY & MAPS page of www.ellenjmchenry.com.)

NOTE ABOUT ACRYLIC PAINTS: These are very inexpensive and can be purchased at any craft store or department store that has a craft section, such as WalMart. Acrylics are permanent and won't smear when dry, unlike poster paints. They can be watered down and used like watercolors or they can be applied thickly like oil paints. They are absolutely the most versatile and easy-to-use paints around. The only drawback is that they won't come out of clothes if you don't catch the spill right away. (If they dry on hands or tables they can be scrubbed out fairly easily.) Wearing good clothes while painting with acrylics is not a good idea, to say the least. However, the advantages of acrylic paint far outweigh this disadvantage.

Sketch in the "egg" and the hand outline. Follow the same steps you did before, but while you do so use the outline map on the next page as a guide for your shapes. Try to make your shapes look like the shapes you see on this map.

After you have completed your map in pencil, use acrylic paints to add color, imitating the colors you see on the satellite map. After the paint is dry, erase pencil lines, then label the map using the black marker.

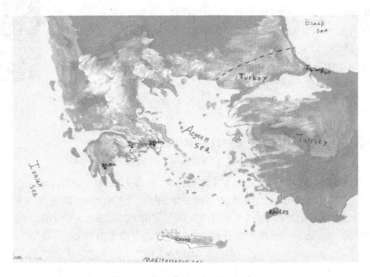

Example of student work

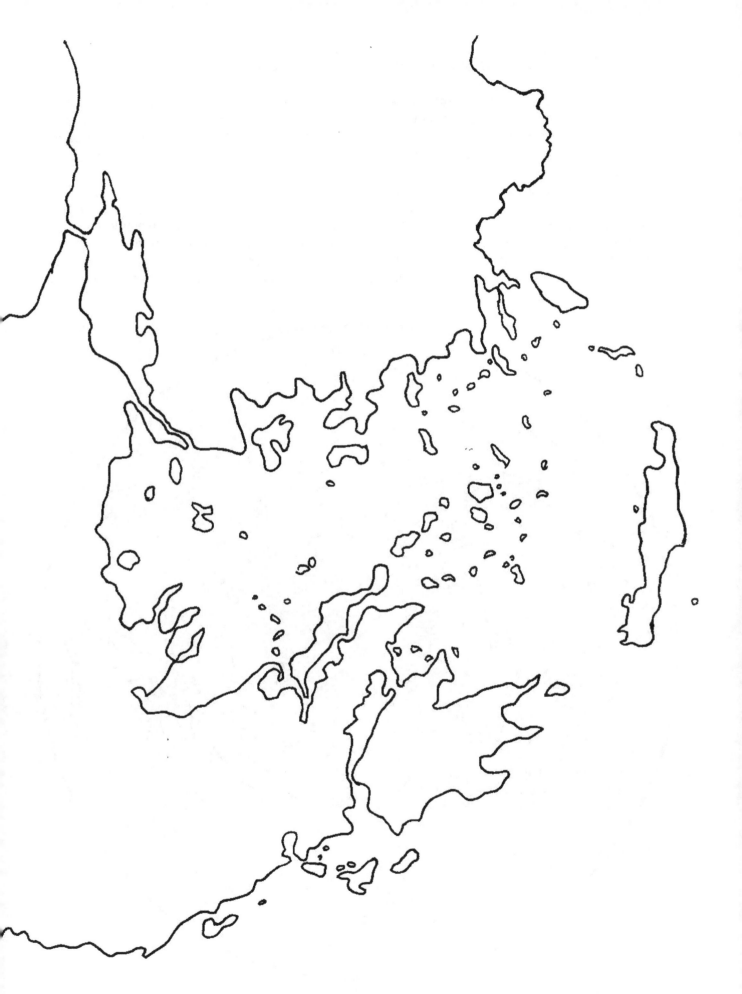

ACTIVITY IDEA 4A: Make a star chart decoration

You will need to photocopy this page onto black paper. (If you use construction paper, trim it down to 8.5x11 before you feed it into the copier.) The black ink will show up on the black paper well enough that you will be able to see the pattern and punch the holes. Use a push pin (or a straight pin) to poke tiny holes where the star dots are. If you want to trace out the constellation patterns, use a white pencil to trace over the lines.

Try this: Put the push pin into Polaris and hold up the star chart over your head. Spin it around so that you can see how the constellations turn around Polaris. If you live in the southern hemisphere, you won't be able to compare this to your night sky, but it will still make a nice decoration. If you are especially interested in sky maps and would like monthly maps for your location (and instructions on how to use it), check out: **www.skymaps.com/downloads.html**

You might want to hang this star chart decoration in a window so that you can see the stars when light is coming in.

ACTIVITY IDEA 4B: Make a navigational quadrant

This is the navigational tool that Ptolemy is shown using in the illustration in the fourth reading. You will need a drinking straw, some clear tape, a piece of dark thread, a needle, a small washer or bolt or fishing sinker (or anything else small and heavy with a hole in it), and a copy of the this page printed onto heavy card stock paper. (NOTE: You could omit the straw and just use the line of sight along the V you will fold.)

After photocopying it onto card stock, cut out the shape below. Do any decoration you want to do before assembling the quadrant.

Tie a piece of thread onto the washer (or bolt or sinker), then use the needle to insert the other end of the thread EXACTLY into the dot (on the bottom dotted line). Tape the thread on the back side of the quadrant so that the washer hangs just below the numbers. The thread should hang down and cross the number line.

Make folds as shown in the drawing below, creating a V on the top of the quadrant, towards the blank side. Tape the straw into this "valley."

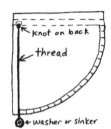

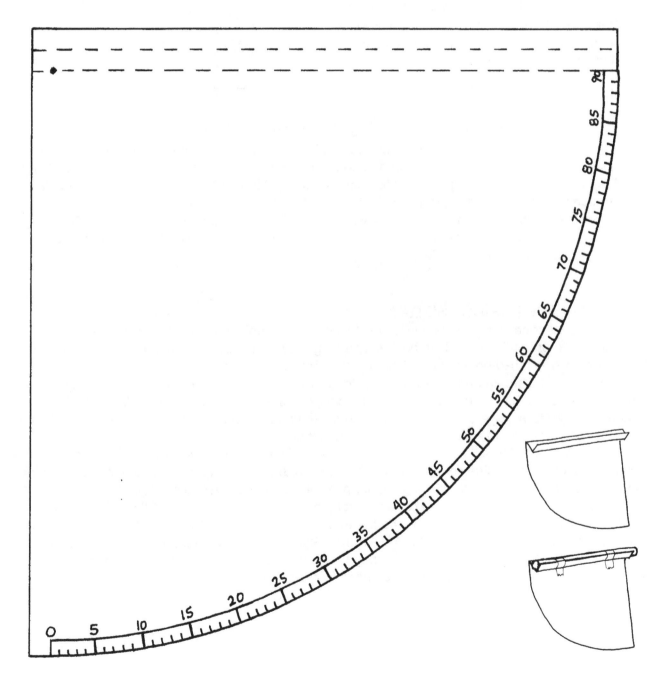

ACTIVITY IDEA 4C: Using the quadrant

BASIC INSTRUCTIONS FOR USING QUADRANT:

Hold the quadrant so that the numbers are on your left. Look through the straw and sight your object. Make sure you let the thread dangle freely, unobstructed by your fingers. The thread should be able to slide along the number line as you tip the quadrant up or down. When you get your object sighted, hold the quadrant still so that the thread eventually stops moving. When the thread is still, pinch it tight to the quadrant and hold it there. Now you can move the straw away from your eye and look at what number the thread is on. This number will be the number of degrees your object is above the horizon.

TRY THIS AT NIGHT:

Point your quadrant at Polaris. Check the reading on the quadrant. How many degrees does it read? This number should also be the degrees of latitude where you are, above or below the equator. Use an atlas to find your latitude. How accurate was your reading?

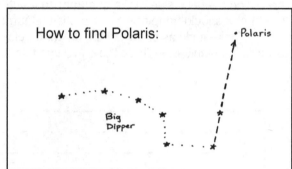

How to find Polaris:

FOR THOSE OF YOU WHO LIVE IN THE SOUTHERN HEMISPHERE:

If you live in Australia or South Africa you won't be able to find Polaris in your night sky. The constellation the explorers used for navigation below the equator is called the Southern Cross. If you would like information on finding this constellation and using it to find true south, (unfortunately it's a lot more complicated than finding true north with Polaris), try this web address or use a search engine with key words "southern cross." **http://www.southernskies.com.au/astronomy/cross.htm**

Even if you live in the southern hemisphere, you will still be able to do this indoor simulation below where you make your own Polaris.

TRY THIS INSIDE DURING THE DAY:

Use a laser pointer to simulate Polaris. Make sure the pointer is absolutely still and doesn't move about. Your hand isn't likely to be steady enough. You will need to improvise some way to have the laser pointer perched on an object, tilted up at an angle.

Pretend you are an ancient sailor trying to navigate out at sea. Sight Polaris in your quadrant and measure its angle. The number of degrees that Polaris is above the horizon will also be the number of degrees you are above the equator. After sighting the star and getting a reading, look at a map and see some possible locations where you might be.

You might want to set up some scenarios ahead of time, giving clues such as the proximity of a group of islands in some direction, or rocky shores just to the east or west. From the latitude reading and the clues, have students search a globe for possible locations where they might be.

You might also want to give a certain starting point and then determine if the ship is keeping a true course east or west. Give them a harbor to leave from and have them find the latitude of that location. Then turn out the lights and shine Polaris. Sight Polaris and determine your latitude. If your latitude is greater than when you left the harbor, you have been sailing to the North and need to head back South. If your latitude is less, then you need to head North.

ACTIVITY 5A: Fill in the gaps on a map of the Mediterranean area

THE MAP FOR THIS ACTIVITY IS ON THE NEXT PAGE.

Photocopy the map on the following page. Fill in each blank rectangle with the appropriate map that you have already learned. The goal is to do it from memory. If students get stuck, you can give them hints or let them take a quick peek, but let them struggle to pull everything they can out of their memory before they resort to peeking. Don't let them wimp out!

Before they start drawing, discuss scale and point out how small the areas are in comparison to drawing the maps on an entire sheet of paper like they did when they learned them. Tell the students to draw lightly at first if they are unsure of scale. Light pencil lines are easily erased. Tell the student to work as quickly as possible. The main point of this exercise is to remember how to draw the maps, not to produce a beautiful finished product. This is just a worksheet.

LABELING: Africa, Mecca, the Black Sea, the Mediterranean Sea, the Strait of Gibraltar, the Red Sea, Rome, Alexandria, Jerusalem, Crete, and any other labels they can fit in

OPTIONAL: You may want to have the students trace over the pathways with two different colors.

ACTIVITY IDEA 5B: Draw some weird people

(This activity is highly optional, a contrast to the first one. You may just want to entertain the students by reading the information aloud if you are short on drawing time.)

During the Middle Ages all kinds of crazy rumors circulated around Europe, telling about exotic races of humans who lived on the other side of the world. Who knows how all these stories got started. Probably every time the stories were told the exaggerations got worse and worse. (Some Bible scholars of that time were very troubled by these stories because if they were true, how could these people have descended from Noah, who was totally human? Those poor scholars would have been relieved to know how outrageous these rumors were!)

It might be fun to draw some pictures of what you think these imaginary races of people looked like. Here are some of the made-up races of people and the characteristics that described them:

Abarimon: backwards-turned feet
Amyctyrae: protruding lower lip, live on raw meat (Ubangi in N. Africa)
Androgini: characteristics of both males and females
Anthropophagi: cannibals who eat their parents when they get old
Antipodes: can walk upside down
Astomi: survive on smells alone; cannot eat or drink; will die if they smell a bad odor
Blemmyae: faces on their chests; no head or neck
Cyclopes: one eyed giants (Watusi in N. Africa)
Cynocephali: dog-headed race; communicate by barking
Gorgades: hairy women who live in Africa (gorillas!)
Hippopodes: race with horse feet
Maritimi: have four eyes
Panotii: ears reach their feet and serve as blankets; also use their ears as wings
Sciopods: one-legged; lie on their backs protecting their heads from the sun with their large foot
Sciritae: noseless and flat-faced race

NOTE: Many of these odd images can be found on the "Hereford Mappa Mundi." This map is part of the "Supplemental Images" free download available at www.ellenjmchenry.com. Click on FREE DOWNLOADS, then on GEOGRAPHY & MAPS. There is also a video about this map posted on the Basement Workshop YouTube channel.

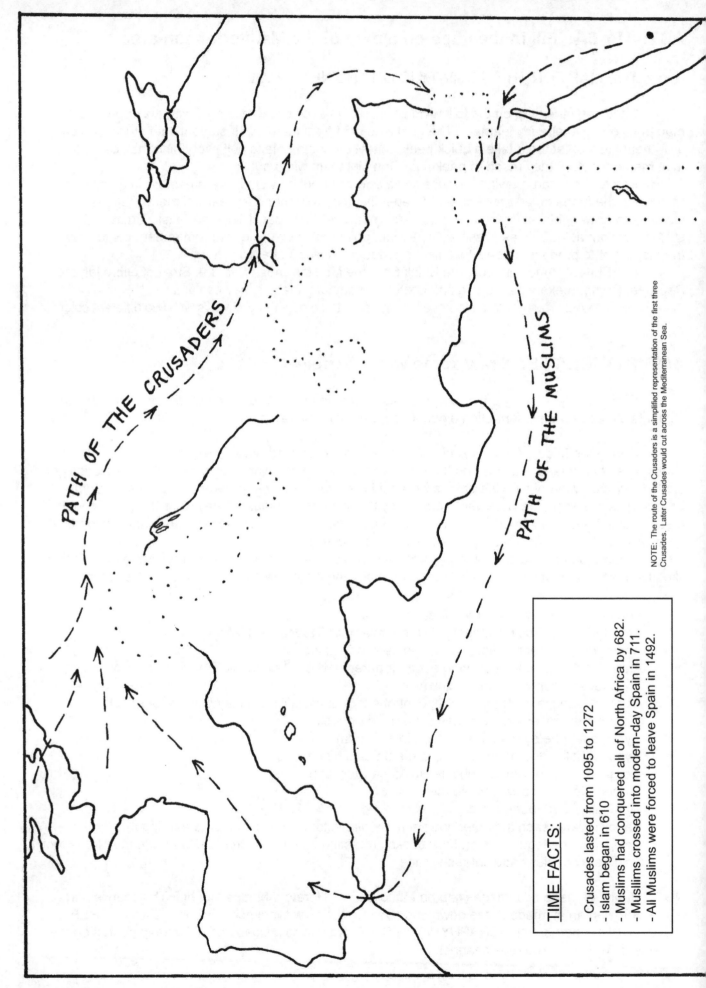

PATH OF THE CRUSADERS

PATH OF THE MUSLIMS

NOTE: The route of the Crusaders is a simplified representation of the first three Crusades. Later Crusades would cut across the Mediterranean Sea.

TIME FACTS:

- Crusades lasted from 1095 to 1272
- Islam began in 610
- Muslims had conquered all of North Africa by 682.
- Muslims crossed into modern-day Spain in 711.
- All Muslims were forced to leave Spain in 1492.

ACTIVITY IDEA 5C: Draw a Medieval T-O map

You will need a compass, ruler, and protractor for this activity, as well as a photocopy of the following pattern page. If you can get calligraphy paper to photocopy the pattern onto it will look more medieval. You will also need a black pen of some kind. A calligraphy marker (with a tip that looks like a chisel) is best, but you could use a felt-tip pen as well.

STEP 1: Begin by making a circle that is 6" in diameter. Make a circle inside this one that is 4" in diameter. Make circles right inside each of these circles, with only about 1/8" or less between them.

STEP 2: Draw a very light horizontal guideline straight across the center of the circle. Then draw a very light perpendicular guideline going down from the center. You can use your protractor to measure 90 degrees.

STEP 3: Draw lines on each side of these guidelines, 1/4" on each side of the lines.

STEP 4: Optional: draw thin lines alongside these lines to make them more decorative.

STEP 5: Go over all your "good" pencil lines with a black marker, then erase any "bad" lines.

STEP 6: Label the outer ring "Mare Oceanum" which means "Ocean Sea." People in the Middle Ages did not have the word "ocean" in their vocabulary the way we do today. The ocean was just a really big sea to them.

STEP 7: Label the large upper half-circle "Asia" and underneath, write the name "Shem." Shem was one of Noah's sons. His descendants were the ancestors of the Jews and the Arabs. When Europeans talked about Asians, they meant Arabs and Jews. They did not know of the existence of the people groups living in the areas we know as China, Korea, Japan, and Indonesia.

STEP 8: Label the bottom left quarter "Europa" and write the name "Japheth" on it. Noah's son Japheth is said to be the ancestor of the people groups we know today as Europeans and Orientals.

STEP 9: Label the quarter on the bottom right as "Africa" and write the name "Ham" on it. Noah's son Ham was believed to be the ancestor of all the dark-skinned people of Africa.

STEP 10: Label the rivers: Don, Nile and Mediterranean. You are already familiar with the Nile and the Mediterranean. Where is the Don? Get an atlas and find out. What great sea does it flow into?

A Medieval Map of the World

This type of map is called a "T-O" map because it looks like a letter T inside a letter O.

Here are samples of some fancy alphabets you could use when labeling your T-O map.

a B C D E F G h I J K L M N O P Q R S T U V W X Y Z

Aa Bb Cc Dd Ee Ff Gg Hh Ii Jj Kk Ll Mm
Nn Oo Pp Qq Rr Ss Tt Uu Vv Ww Xx Yy Zz

Aa Bb Cc Dd Ee Ff Gg Hh Ii Jj Kk Ll Mm Nn
Oo Pp Qq Rr Ss Tt Uu Vv Ww Xx Yy Zz

Aa Bb Cc Dd Ee Ff Gg Hh Ii Jj Kk Ll Mm Nn
Oo Pp Qq Rr Ss Tt Uu Vv Ww Xx Yy Zz

Aa Bb Cc Dd Ee Ff Gg Hh Ii Jj Kk Ll Mm Nn
Oo Pp Qq Rr Ss Tt Uu Vv Ww Xx Yy Zz

ACTIVITY IDEA 6A: REVIEW WORKSHEET

Each student will need a copy of this map worksheet.

This map shows some of the areas traveled by Marco Polo and Ibn Battuta. They both traveled extensively in the regions of the Black Sea, the Caspian Sea and the Aral Sea. Ibn Battuta spent a lot of time in Mecca and North Africa.

The map is fairly self-explanatory. The students are to complete the map as thoroughly as they can. Guidelines have been dotted in to help them get things proportioned correctly.

Label these cities:

Venice (birth place of Marco Polo)
Mecca (favorite vacation spot of Ibn Battuta)
Alexandria
Athens
Baghdad
Cairo
Istanbul
Jerusalem
Rome
Tehran

Label these bodies of water:

Aegean Sea
Arabian Sea
Aral Sea
Black Sea
Caspian Sea
Dead Sea
Mediterranean Sea
Persian Gulf
Sea of Marmara (the little sea in between the
　　　　　Mediterranean and the Black Sea)

Label the line going across the map as the Tropic of Cancer. (Notice again that the Tropic of Cancer goes across Lake Nasser in Egypt.)

ACTIVITY IDEA 6B: Watch a short documentary on the Aral Sea

The Aral Sea is the sea you've never heard of and the sea you'll never forget after watching this piece of video documentation. The Communist government took over the region of the Aral Sea and decided that it would be a nice place to grow cotton. It was a terrible place to grow cotton. Their solution was to try to change the ecology of the region by diverting the streams that flow into the Aral Sea, using the rivers to irrigate cotton fields. With not much water flowing into the Aral Sea, it soon began to shrink. Coastal sea towns soon became desert environments. Huge ships now sit stranded in the middle of a sea of sand. Hot winds now sweep across these dry regions, picking up pesticides from the cotton industry and blowing them into the homes of the people of northern Uzbekistan. These poor Uzbeks are dying of drought and disease.

There is a brief video about the Aral Sea posted on www.YouTube.com/ TheBasementWorkshop. You might also be able to find it on your own by searching with key words "Shrinking Aral Sea."

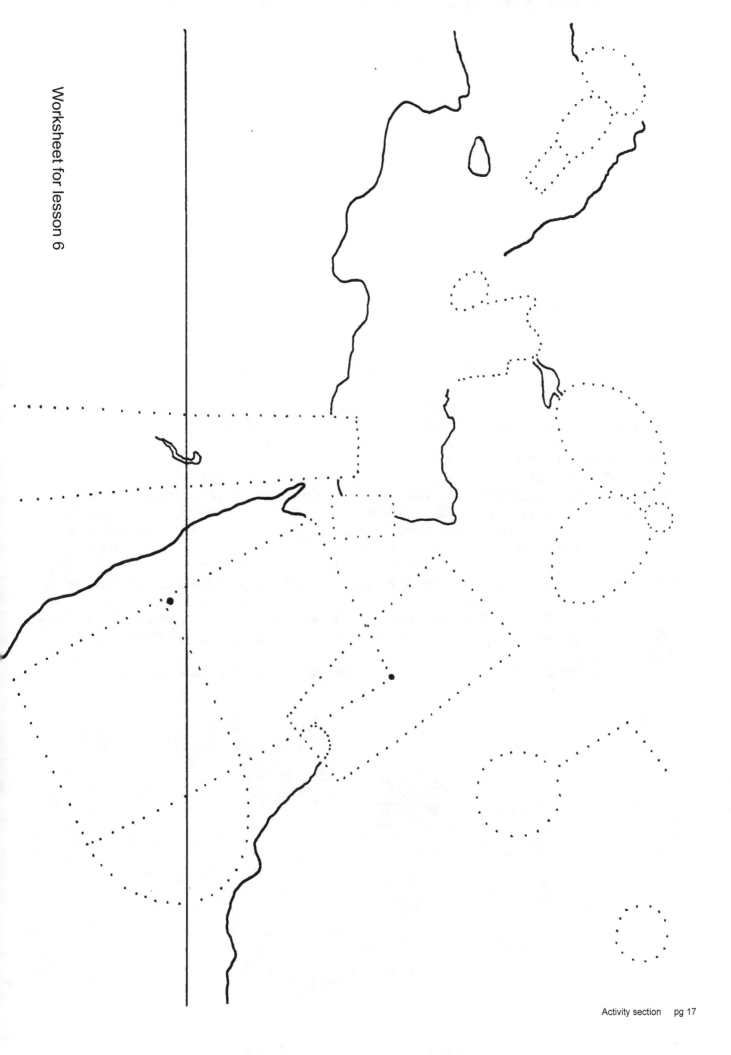

ACTIVITY IDEA 6C: Watch a documentary about Ibn Battuta

The BBC produced a fascinating documentary about the travels of Ibn Battuta, hosted by an English scholar/journalist who lives in Yemen and is an expert on Arabic language and culture. This documentary is usually available on YouTube. You can just use key words "Ibn Battuta documentary BBC." The Basement Workshop channel on YouTube will try to keep this posted, if possible.

ACTIVITY IDEA 6D: Watch a short documentary on Marco Polo

Go to www.YouTube..com/TheBasementWorkshop for some videos on Marco Polo. Some of the videos posted in the past have since been taken down, so it takes constant vigilance to keep something posted. I will try my best to keep the list fresh, but you can always use the search feature with key words, "Marco Polo," or "Marco Polo documentary."

ACTIVITY IDEA 6E: Read about Rabban Bar Sauma

At the same time that Marco Polo was making his way from west to east, another man was making a similar journey, but going from east to west. Rabban Bar Sauma (which is Aramiac for "son of fasting") was born near modern-day Beijing and lived from 1220-1294. His ethnic origin was Mongolian. His people, the Mongol Empire, had just conquered all of what we now call China, plus everything west of China, all the way to Europe (including most of the Black Sea area).   Bar Sauma was converted to Christianity as a teenager (the Nestorian faith, which traces its roots back to the apostle Thomas) and by age 20 he became a monk. In the mid 1200s he decided to go on a pilgrimage to Jerusalem. He met with spiritual leaders along the way, as well as political leaders such as the Il-Khan (Mongol sub-king) of the territory below the Caspian Sea (modern Iran). This Nestorian Christian Khan was being challenged by Muslims from the south and he wished to form an alliance with France. Bar Sauma eventually went all the way to Paris on this diplomatic mission, meeting not only with the French king, but also with Edward I of England. He is recorded as visiting the Pope in Rome on Palm Sunday of 1288. He spent his last years living in Baghdad.   Because of the similarity of his journeys to Marco Polo's, Rabban Bar Sauma has sometimes been called "the reverse Marco Polo."

You can read more about Bar Sauma by putting his name into an Internet search engine.

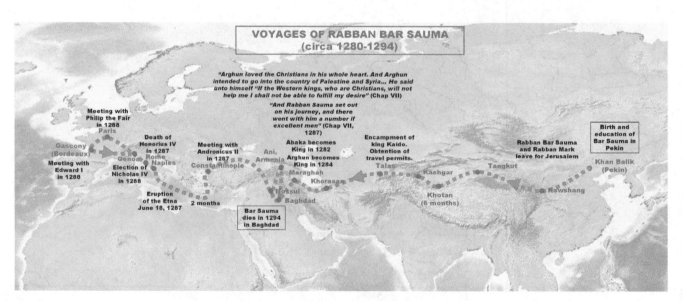

ACTIVITY IDEA 7A: Watch some short video clips

Go to www.YouTube.com/TheBasementWorkshop for a quick peek at historic Lisbon, including a monument to Henry the Navigator, and a travel ad put out by the tourism board of Portugal. (If these videos have disappeared since the printing of this booklet, I will have tried my best to find substitute videos.)

Also, we will try to have some videos posted on Henry the Navigator, but these seem to be less stable and we have trouble keeping them posted. All the videos about Portugal/Henry will be grouped together in the playlist.

ACTIVITY IDEA 7B: Navigation game using a portolan chart

Sailors in Henry's day made and used a type of map called a "portolan." The map at the bottom of the first page of your reading (colored red, white and blue and showing West Africa) is an example of a portolan map. Portolans were covered with lines, called "rhumb" lines, criss-crossing all over the map. Sailors tried to sail right on these rhumb lines, going from point to point using a navigation technique called "dead reckoning." Dead reckoning uses the mathematical concept that distance equals rate times time (d=rt). The sailors knew their position when they started out, then they kept exact records as to how fast they sailed, what direction they were sailing in, and how much time had passed. (To determine how fast they were going, sailors would use simple tools like chip logs. They would throw the log overboard at the front of the ship, then count off seconds to see how long it took for the ship to sail past the log. To determine the direction in which they were sailing, they used an astrolabe or a quadrant, or possibly a magnetic compass.) From these bits of information they estimated how far they had gone in a certain direction and marked their position on the portolan.

In this simulation game, students won't have to judge the speed of their ship; they will only have to count lengths of the ship and judge its direction. They will use a portolan map to try to find three small islands out in the middle of the ocean.

<u>You will need</u>:
 • A piece of poster board 21"x 27" (the sheet I bought was 22"x28" so I trimmed an inch off each side) (NOTE: If you don't have poster board available, you can substitute with anything that can be pricked and is opaque enough to have pencil dots marked on the back that won't show through on the front.)
 • A yard stick (or at least a ruler) and a pencil
 • Copies of the ships at the bottom of this page (printed onto card stock if possible)
 • The portolan chart on the next page (or a copy of it with the lines traced out in color)
If you don't have a digital copy of this curriculum, you can print out these pages using the free downloads on the GEOGRAPHY & MAPS page at www.ellenjmchenry.com
 • A pushpin (or anything that can easily prick a small hole in the poster board)

Cut out one or more ships and fold them so that they can stand up. You'll only need one ship per board per voyage. If you have only a few students and are preparing only one board, one ship will be enough. Younger students may feel strongly about having their own ship to play with afterwards, however, so be prepared with extras.

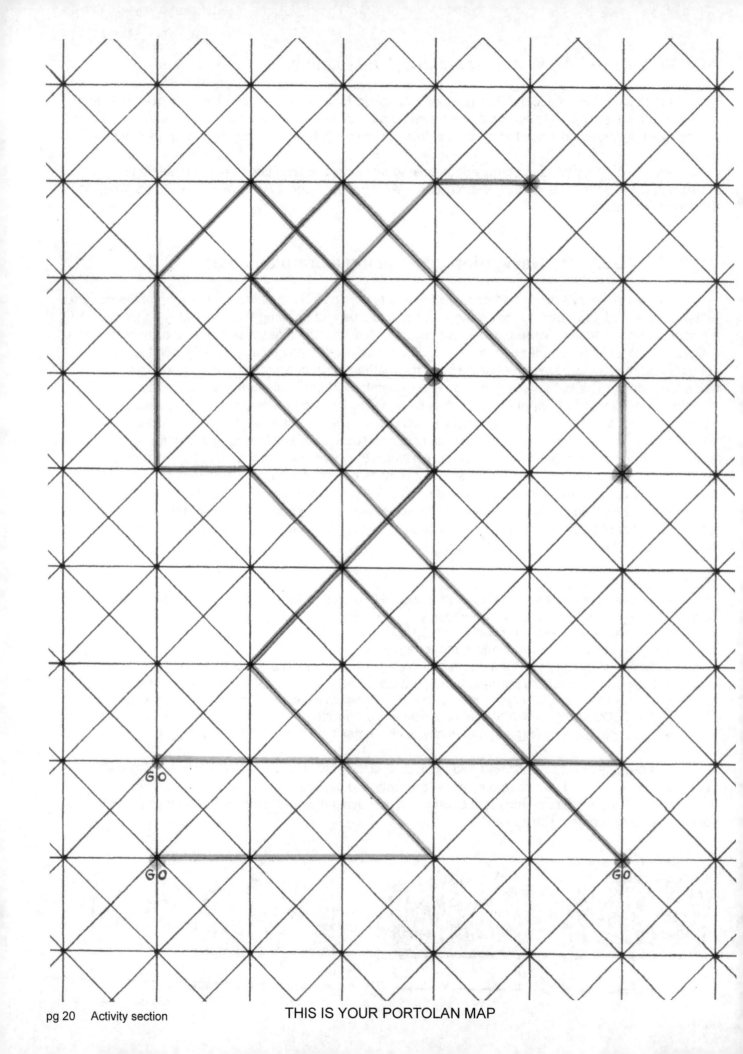

THIS IS YOUR PORTOLAN MAP

Here is a blank portolan pattern you can use to make your own courses.

The piece of poster board will be the "ocean" on which the little ship will sail. Trim the poster board so that it is 21" by 27". You will need to mark the starting points on the front, but mark the ending points secretly on the back. To do this quickly and easily, choose which side will be the back and mark the following points, shown on this diagram.

THIS IS THE BACK SIDE

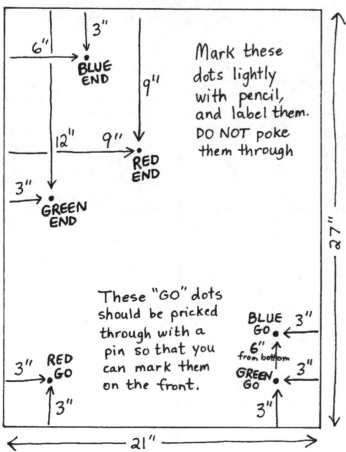

Mark these dots lightly with pencil, and label them. DO NOT poke them through

These "GO" dots should be pricked through with a pin so that you can mark them on the front.

Use a pin to prick holes where the beginning dots are. When you turn the board to the front side, you will see the pin pricks and will know exactly where to put colored dots to mark the starting points. The ending points should not be punched. The players will punch their own ending points when they get to the end of the game, then they will turn the board over and see how close they came to the correct ending points you marked.

To start the game, have the sailors place the ship so that the stern (back) is exactly on one of the starting points. It doesn't matter which color they choose first. The sailors will then look at the portolan map and carefully observe the colored track they have chosen. They must count how many ship lengths they should travel, and in what direction, in order to complete the first leg of the journey. Since the map is smaller than the playing board, they must allow for scale. Here is the key to remember:

THE SIDE OF A SQUARE ON THE PORTOLAN MAP IS EQUAL TO 2 LENGTHS OF THE PAPER SHIP ON THE REAL BOARD.

For example, on the first leg of the green journey, the ship would move 6 lengths to the east. Players are not allowed to make any marks on the poster board ocean. They can use their fingers to "mark" places temporarily, but they may not use pencils or anything else to make a permanent mark. Real sailors can't mark the ocean, after all! (The only way to make a permanent mark in a body of water is to anchor a buoy to the bottom somehow.)

To begin the second leg, very carefully swivel the ship around so that the stern is where you imagine the last dot of the first leg to be. For the green journey, the second leg requires you to sail at a 45 degree angle, to the northwest. This is where it gets tricky because the distance across the diagonal of a square isn't exactly 2 ship lengths. The diagonal distance is (by the Pythagorean Theorem) the square root of 8. The fractional equivalent is 2 5/6. Advise your sailors to make a mark on their ships that is 5/6 from the end. (An easy way to do this is to divide one of the bottom flaps into three equal parts (just draw lines, don't cut), then cross out the one on the end.)

Sailors continue to sail like this, estimating where they think they should be on the poster board ocean. It's not easy, but real sailing was much harder than this! Perhaps this will give them just an inkling of how tricky it was to sail the world without modern navigational instruments.

When the sailors reach the spot where they think the ending point is, they use a pushpin to punch through the poster board at that place. When they have sailed all three courses (or after the first one, at your discretion) they may then turn the poster board over to see how close they were to hitting the correct ending point that you marked ahead of time.

ACTIVITY IDEA 7C: Look at some real portolan maps

Several antique portolan maps are part of the supplemental images free download available at www.ellenjmchenry.com. Click on FREE DOWNLOADS, then on GEOGRAPHY & MAPS. Look for the "Antique maps" download at the bottom of the page.

ACTIVITY IDEA 8A: Watch videos demonstrating printing techniques

Use theses videos to learn about the intaglio print-making, relief printing and lithography. Maps were printed using these processes until the twentieth century. These videos are very well done and well worth your time (and are part of the "Mapping the World" playlist on the Basement Workshop channel).

- An 8-minute overview of intaglio printing (engraving, etching, drypoint):

- A 4-minute overview of relief printing (wood blocks):

- A 5-minute overview of lithography (printing using a stone block):

ACTIVITY IDEA 8B: Learn a little bit about Andorra
(after you've completed Map Drawing 8B)

Andorra is one of the smallest countries in the world, consisting of 181 square miles, with a population of only about 75,000 people. It is so small that it does not have an army and would depend on Spain and France to defend it, should the need ever arise. Its politics have always been linked to those of Spain and France. Currently, its government is more linked to France than Spain.

Andorra is in the midst of the scenic Pyrenees Mountains. The towns are located in the valleys between the mountains. Because it is so scenic, Andorra gets most of its income from running hotels and restaurants for tourists to come to see the beautiful scenery and hike in the mountains.

The official language of Andorra is Catalan, a language that is also spoken in areas of France, Spain, and Italy. Catalan is in the same group of languages as Spanish, French and Italian (the Romance languages). Catalan is also the word used for their culture (music and dance).

YouTube can provide a selection of tourism videos about Andorra, showing the landscape, historic buildings, and people who live there. There will be some Andorra videos posted on the Basement Workshop YouTube channel.

ACTIVITY IDEA 9A: Make the Arabs' navigation device: the kamal

The Arabs had been navigating the Mediterranean Sea centuries before the Europeans began to do so. The Arabs devised a simple, yet highly effective, tool for determining latitude. With this simple tool the Arabs sailed all over the Mediterranean, the Red Sea, the Persian Gulf, and the Indian Ocean. Their ships were the ones that brought the spices from India into ports on the Mediterranean, where European traders could buy them.

The kamal was invented in the 800s. Several centuries later it was being used in both India and China. It consists of a thin rectangle of wood, about one inch by two inches. Attached to the rectangle, right in the middle, is a long piece of string. The sailor would hold the end of the string in his teeth while holding the rectangle straight out in front of him, so that the bottom of the rectangle looked like it was touching the horizon. He would then move the card towards him or away from him until Polaris (or whatever he was sighting) was right at the top of the rectangle. Knots in the string marked degrees of latitude, or possibly the exact latitude of a port city. On some kamals, the rectangle could move along the string, while on others the string was fixed to the card and the navigators slid the length of the string through their teeth.

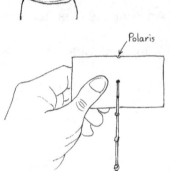

The Arabs measured degrees using the width of their index finger. Their word for degree, "issabah," meant "finger." The Arab degree was equal to about 1.5 modern degrees (which, as you remember, were first determined by the Greeks, who, in turn, had been influenced by the Babylonians). The knots on the string were often pre-tied, spaced out to represent issabahs. This method of using the index finger to measure distance above the horizon is probably still in use anywhere in the world where people don't have modern gadgets.

To make your kamal, you will need a piece of cardboard or thin wood that is about one inch by two inches (it can be a little larger) and a piece of cotton string. If you are using cardboard, make sure it is stiff enough so that it does not bend when you pull on the string. Punch or drill a hole in the center of the card and insert the end of the string. Tie a knot in the end of the string so that it does not pull back through the card. (Your kamal will be the kind where you adjust it by pulling the string through your teeth, not through the card.) At your discretion, you may or may not want to add a tiny notch at the top of the card in which to sight a small object such as a star.

You can use your kamal to sight Polaris at night, or you may want to choose an indoor object. Hold your kamal so that the bottom of the card is touching the horizon (or some horizontal point in the room that you establish as the horizon), then adjust the kamal towards you or away from you until the object you are sighting is right at the top. Make sure the bottom stays right on the horizon line. When you have it at the right place, pull the string taut and hold it in your teeth. When you are sure that the string is at the correct length, let the kamal dangle and focus your attention on marking the spot on the string where your teeth are. Use a marker or very dark pencil to mark the exact spot on the string. Then tie a knot in the string right where the mark is. Sight the same object from different places and make more knots in the string, using the same method.

When you are done, you will have several knots on the string. You can use these knots to determine exactly where you were standing when you made them. Just put one of the knots in your teeth and hold the kamal out tight. Then walk forward or backward until the object appears correctly at the top of the kamal.

ACTIVITY IDEA 9B: Optional: a documentary about Barbary pirates

If you're keen on pirate history, here's an in-depth look at the Barbary pirates— who they were and what they did (focusing especially on their raids along the west coast of England). This documentary is intended for general audiences but please bear in mind that pirates did nasty things. No actual torture is shown, only black and white ink sketches drawn by a historian in the 1600s. Reenactment scenes are taken from a classic black and white Hollywood movie from the early 1900s. It's a brilliant documentary, but parents, please preview this one first to see if it is appropriate for your audience. Search Youtube with key words "Vic Reeves Barbary pirates part 1."

ACTIVITY 9C: Take a virtual vist to one or more of the Balearic islands

The Balearic islands are a self-governing archipelago connected politically to Spain. In times past, they have been governed by Spain. The largest island is called Majorca (pronounced "Mah-yore-kah") and the three smaller islands are Minorca, Ibiza, and Formentera. You can take a quick virtual visit to one or more of these islands using the Basement Workshop YouTube channel. Since tourist videos come and go frequently, I'll try to keep at least a few current ones posted.

ACTIVITY IDEA 9D: Spiced meat recipes

During the Middle Ages and the Renaissance, Europeans didn't use spices such as cinnamon and ginger for desserts. Spices were used almost exclusively for flavoring meats. Here are two recipes that people in the 1300 to1500s would have used (if they could afford them). Why not give them a try?

For either of these mixes, you will need a pound of beef or pork cubed into bite-sized pieces. You may want to brown it first in a frying pan before simmering. Simmer your meat with the spices until the meat cubes reach the desired tenderness (stew meat may need to simmer for several hours).

Mix 1:
2 t. cinnamon
1/2 t. fresh ginger (finely shredded)
2 t. cumin
A cup or more of meat broth or water

Mix 2:
2 t. coriander
1 t. paprika
1/2 t. turmeric
1 t. cardamom
1/2 t. cinnamon
1/2 t. cloves
1 t. fresh ginger
1 t. fresh garlic
A cup or more of meat broth or water

ACTIVITY IDEA 9E: Map worksheet

Copy the worksheet on the following page and fill in all the dotted areas with the maps you already know. India is the only new portion of the map—everything else is review.

Tropic of
Cancer

ACTIVITY IDEA 9F: A board game: "Pirates of the Mediterranean"

      The educational goal of this game is to add just a few more bits of information about Mediterranean geography (Barcelona, Balearic Islands, Malta, coastal towns of North Africa) while also reviewing Mediterranean geography they've already learned. Additionally, some navigational history can be learned in a "hands-on" way, such as the terrible dangers of the "bottlenecks" in the Mediterranean—the narrow places on each side of Sicily. These were especially dangerous places and led to the establishment of a pirate-fighting base on the island of Malta.

      This game can be played by 2 to 4 players (or even solo if the player is willing to play both sides against himself!). One round of the game takes 5-10 minutes.   Play more than one round! You will need to supply a die for each player (but a pair will do), toothpicks, glue, and a small amount of a modeling compound such as Sculpey™ clay, or anything else that can be molded to make a toothpick flag stand up straight.

      The basic idea of the game is very simple. There are 2 European ships, one from Lisbon and one from Barcelona, which are trying to cross the Mediterranean to get to one of these Middle Eastern spice ports: Alexandria, Akka (modern day Acre), or Constantinople (modern day Istanbul). The pirates are trying to stop them from getting to their destinations. There are sea battles along the way. Sometimes the pirates win and sometimes the Europeans win.

<u>To set up</u>:

      You have several options for making the game board. 1) You can cut the following pages out of the book and assemble them. 2) You can make photocopies of the following pages and color them by hand (or leave them black and white).   3) You can print out color copies of these pages using your digital copy of the curriculum. 4) If you don't have a digital copy of the curriculum, you can download a PDF version of these pages by going to www.ellenjmchenry.com, clicking on FREE DOWNLOADS, then on GEOGRAPHY & MAPS, then scrolling to bottom until you see "Pirates of the Caribbean 9F."

      Trim the white edge off the right side of the left map piece (right next to Sicily), then match the two halves and secure with tape.

      Make flag tokens for the players. (If you don't have a digital copy of this curriculum, you can print out this game using the free downloadable files at www.ellenjmchenry.com.) Cut out one of each kind of flag (per game you are making) then secure with a small amount of white glue to the pointed end of a half-toothpick. Stick the thicker end of the half-toothpick into a tiny blob of clay of some kind. The flags should stand up on their own.

<u>Arrangements for numbers of players</u>;

  2 players: one player will play both Spain and Portugal and the other player will play both pirates.

  4 players: each player gets one flag.

  3 players: one person will play either both the Europeans or both the pirates.

  1 player: play all the flags and take turns with yourself playing either side. (I did this many times when I was trying out the game. It's still fun!)

You only need one Spanish flag and one Portuguese flag per game. (An extra of each, just in case.)

These are Barbary Corsair (pirate) flags. You will need just one of each (an extra of each, again).

Rules of the game: (read these out loud to the players before starting the game)

Pirates:
- Start at one of your ports: Tunis or Tripoli. Only one pirate per port.
- You must stay at sea once you have left your port. (You may not land on islands, either.)
- You must use all of your hops on your turn. (For example, if you roll a 6, you must use all 6 hops.)
- You may go in any direction.
- You are permitted to hop over another ship (counting that space as one of your hops).
- You cannot land on a space already occupied by the other pirate.
- To engage a European ship in a sea battle, you must land on it with the exact number of hops. In other words, if you roll a 4, you must be able to count out the hops so that you land on the ship on your fourth hop. Just sit right next to the European ship, not necessarily on the dot, since the dot is so small.
- On the same turn that you land on a European ship, a sea battle ensues. Both ships roll their die. The highest roll wins. The loser is out of the game. A tie means you both go on and keep playing.

Europeans:
- You must start your ships at Barcelona and Lisbon, one ship per port.
- The first stop both ships must make is at the island of Majorca ("Mah-yore-kah"), the largest of the archipelago called The Balearic Islands. This island was home to a community of famous mapmakers and navigators. You must visit the workshop of Abraham Cresques, one of the most famous mapmakers of the time. He will give you the most up-to-date map he has available, which should be a great help in your voyage.
- You may then try to sail to any of the spice ports—Alexandria, Akka or Constantinople—it doesn't matter which one. You don't have to choose ahead of time; you can make your decision once you are out at sea. If a pirate is chasing you, you may have to alter your plans very quickly!
- You may land at any port or island to seek safety from pirates. (Take special note of the island of Malta. There is a European pirate-fighting force on that island so it is a very safe place to land.) In landing on a port or island, you must "waste" any extra hops you didn't use. For example, if you roll a 6 and only need 2 to get to the island of Malta, you must waste the other 4 moves. On the next turn, you may not pass in order to stay on the island. You must move!
- You may hop over another ship, counting that space as one of your hops.
- If a pirate ship lands on you, a sea battle ensues. Each ship rolls its die. The highest roll wins. The loser is out of the game. A tie means both ships keep sailing.

The game is over when one of the following occurs:

- The pirates are gone from the board.
- The Europeans are gone from the board.
- The Europeans reach their destinations.

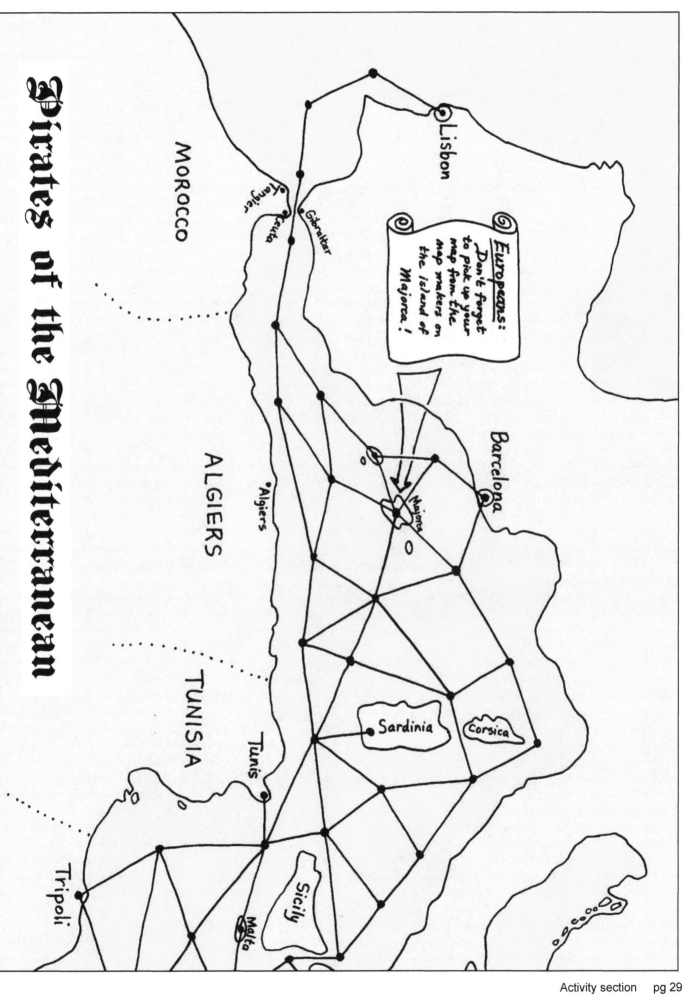

Pirates of the Mediterranean

MOROCCO

Lisbon

Tangier

Ceuta

Gibraltar

Europeans:
Don't forget
to pick up your
map from the
map makers on
the island of
Majorca!

Barcelona

Majorca

ALGIERS

Algiers

TUNISIA

Sardinia

Corsica

Tunis

Sicily

Malta

Tripoli

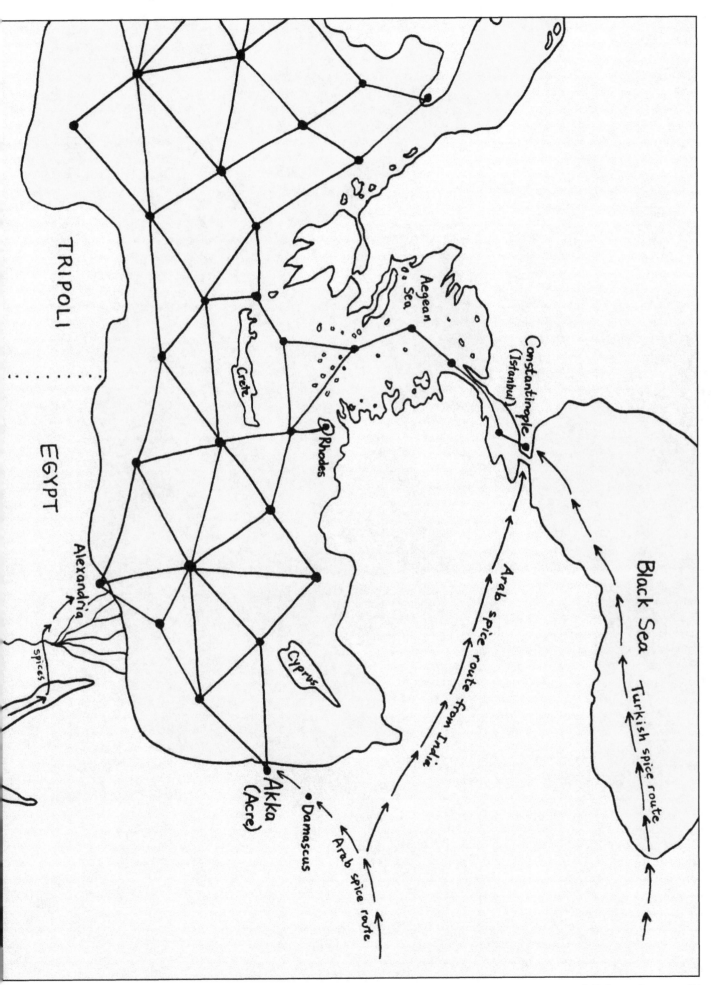

TRIPOLI

EGYPT

Alexandria

spices

Crete

Rhodes

Cyprus

Akka
(Acre)

Damascus

Aegean
Sea

Constantinople
(Istanbul)

Black Sea

Turkish spice route

Arab spice route from India

Arab spice route

Arab spice route

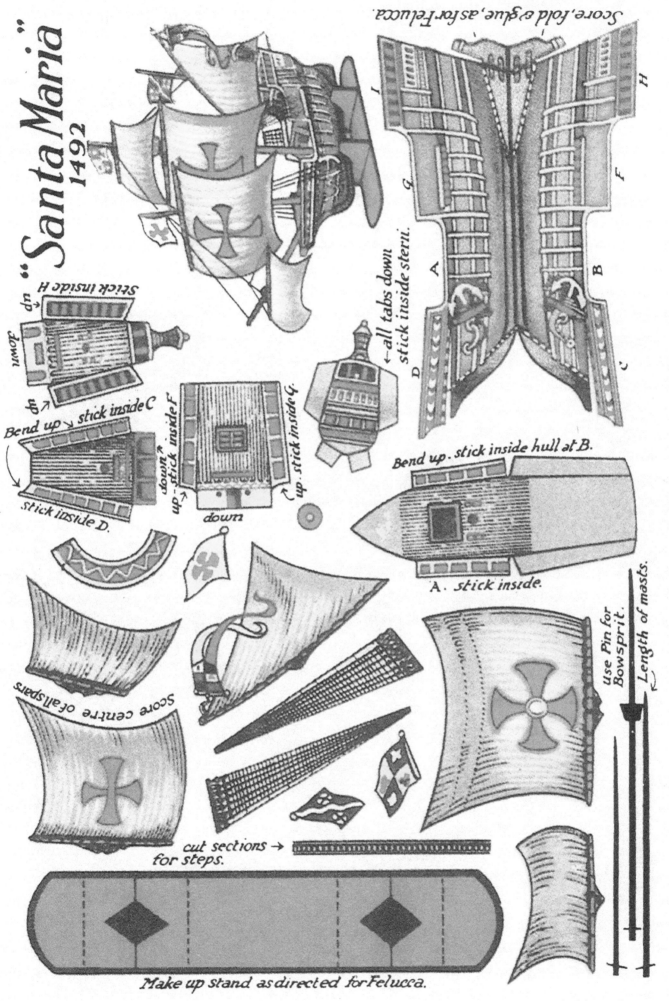

"Santa Maria" 1492

Score, fold & glue, as for Felucca.

Stick inside H

up

down

up

Bend up > stick inside C

stick inside D.

down
up - stick inside F

up. stick inside G.

down

←all tabs down
stick inside stern.

Bend up. stick inside hull at B.

A. stick inside.

Score centre of all spars.

Use Pin for Bowsprit.

Length of masts.

cut sections →
for steps.

Make up stand as directed for Felucca.

ACTIVITY IDEA 10A: Make a model of the *Santa Maria*

Why not make a model of a ship that helped to map the world? There are several paper models available on line, some free, some for sale. The one provided here is not easy, but not ridiculously hard, either. If you have a digital copy of this curriculum, you can just print out the previous page. If you have only a hard copy, you can download this pattern by going to the webstie (www.ellenjmchenry.com) and clicking on FREE DOWNLOADS, then on GEOGRAPHY & MAPS. The pattern is in the list at the bottom of the page.

It's a tiny model, as you can see by comparing the hand for scale.

I assembled the back first. Glue the bottom keel, then insert the back panel.

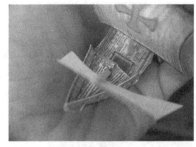

I had to trim the front deck piece to make it triangular. I just couldn't get the pieces to fit in right otherwise.

CONSTRUCTION TIPS:

1) Don't use "school glue." Use regular white glue (good old *Elmer's*).

2) Remember that white glue is actually very strong and you need only TINY AMOUNTS of it on the joints. If glue seeps out of the joint when you press it together, you've used way too much glue. Just a tiny dab will do the job! Press and hold a joint while you count to ten slowly. After releasing your grip, let the joint sit for 30 to 60 seconds.

3) Use toothpicks for the masts. Trim if too long.   Glue two toothpicks together for the main mast, or use a bamboo skewer instead. To glue two picks together, apply glue to the last 1/4 inch of each, then allow them to dry in place, end to end, for at least half an hour. (If you need a fast fix, try Superglue (gel, not liquid) or a tiny amount of hot glue.)

Other models you might want to consider:

http://papertoys.com/santamaria.htm (an easy model, and free)

http://www.model-shipyard.com/html/36uk.html (more complex and costs a little, but is an absolutely fabulous model when finished)

ACTIVITY IDEA 10D: Design a compass rose

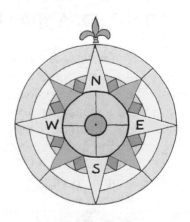

<u>Historical background information</u>:

The fancy design that shows the points of a compass is called a "compass rose." Strangely enough, the four directions of the compass existed long before the magnetic compass was invented. Ancient peoples divided the wind into four directions. They used east and west as their primary markers, based on where the sun rose and set on the days of equinox (March 21 and September 21), then they made halfway markers between east and west, which eventually became north and south. Each country had its own names for the winds that came from these directions, based on what type of weather the wind brought. When the wind blew from certain directions, it brought storms. When it blew from other directions, good weather followed. Eventually they made up stories about the gods and goddesses whom they imagined made the winds blow.

The Greek poet Homer (who wrote the Iliad and the Odyssey) wrote about the four brothers, the gods of the four winds. Their father was Aeolus, the god of all the winds, and their mother was Eos, the dawn. The god of the north wind was called Boreas. He came from the direction of the star called Polaris, and when he came, he rolled up great waves. He was called upon by the other gods to create a storm to shipwreck Hercules. (The northern lights are also named after him: Aurora Borealis.) His brother, Notas, the god of the south wind, brought fog and rain and sometimes sudden small storms, called squalls. Zephyrus was the brother in the west, and his weather was more mild (although he himself was quite a character!). The wind seldom came from the east, but when it did, the last brother, Eurus, brought warmth and rain. These wind gods would show up on maps for centuries to come, shown as little heads with puffy cheeks, blowing as hard as they could.

Here is Zephyrus shown on a Greek postage stamp.

So the first compass roses were actually wind roses, showing the directions of the winds. Then, when the magnetic compass was introduced to Europeans, someone had the brilliant idea of floating the needle above a wind rose chart to make the first real compass. From that time on, the points of the compass no longer had anything to do with the winds.

Even as early as the Middle Ages, navigators began to realize that four directions weren't enough. There had to be names for the points halfway between the four main points. So they simply combined the names to come up with northwest, northeast, southwest and southeast. But these still weren't accurate enough for ship navigators. So they combined these halfway names once again to form directions like "south by southeast" and "north by northwest." Eventually, some compasses had as many as 32 directional points on them!

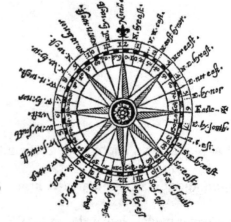

Traditionally, compass roses have always been drawn with a French "fleur-de-lis" on the north point. You can see it clearly on the compass rose at the top of this page, and, if you look very carefully, you can see it on the one here at the right. East often had a cross symbol on it. You can see it on the one to the right if you look very carefully. The principal winds (eventually directions) were always painted in gold, with the half-winds (NE, NW, SE, SW) painted in green, and the quarter-winds (NNE, NNW, SSE, etc.) painted in red. You might want to do a Google image search using the key words "compass rose" and see how many you can find that have this traditional color scheme.

(Use Google image search to find more compass rose designs.)

In this activity, the students will design their own compass rose. They will have to pretend they are Medieval or Renaissance era mapmakers, however, and adhere to the traditional colors for the winds/directions.

Each student will need: a compass, a protractor, a pencil, a ruler, a piece of calligraphy paper, a very thin black marker, and colored pencils in red, green, and yellow (a substitute for gold). If possible, supply a metallic gold pencil or a gold paint marker or a gold gel pen.

Begin by making a circle with the compass, approximately three inches in diameter. Use the ruler (working in pencil, not pen) to draw a line straight up and down, through the center dot. Then use the protractor and the ruler to make a line exactly perpendicular to the first one. These will be your main directional lines: north, south, east and west.

Next, make lines halfway between these perpendicular lines, at 45 degree angles. These will be your half-wind directions: northeast, northwest, southeast, southwest.

Finally, divide the 45-degree angles once again, splitting the angles into 22.5 degrees. These will be the quarter-winds: north-northeast, east-northeast, east-southeast, south-southeast, south-southwest, west-southwest, west-northwest, and north-northwest.

When you are finished, you will have a total of 16 directional lines (all done lightly in pencil so they can be erased later, if necessary).

The next steps will allow more creativity. The students may design their compass roses in any way they wish providing they maintain the main points as the longest ones, the half-points as the next-longest, and the quarter-points as the shortest. They may want to make their points very long and thin, or they may want to contain the whole compass within a circle. Any variation is fine as long as they have 16 points of the appropriate relative lengths.

Put a fleur-de-lis *("flare-de-lee")* on the north point. This has been a tradition for hundreds of years and was always done during the time period we are studying. If you want to be even more historically accurate, you could also add a cross on the eastern point (see sample at right).

When you have all the pencil lines in, trace over the good lines, the ones you want to keep, with a black permanent marker. Then erase any pencil guidelines. To color your compass rose, use the traditional color scheme: gold for the main points, green for the half-points (NE, NW, SE, SW) and red for the quarter-points. You may also want to use extra color to fill in other areas around the points.

Many different designs are possible. This is the time and place to be creative (which doesn't happen too often in a curriculum like this!).

Make sure you put the traditional fleur-de-lis on the north point. To the right are sample fleur-de-lis designs you might want to copy.

ACTIVITY IDEA 11A: Learn a litte about the Arawak language

The word "hammock" wasn't the only word the Europeans adopted from the Arawaks. The English language also got these words from the Arawaks: potato, cassava, guava, papaya, iguana, maize (corn), mangrove and tobacco. Even though there are only about 2,500 Arawaks left (out of 250,000 when Columbus landed), the survivors have kept the knowledge of their native language alive. You can learn some Arawak words by going to the following web address:
> **http://www.native-languages.org/arawak.htm**

ACTIVITY IDEA 11B: Take a virtual vacation to the Bahamas

Use the Basement Workshop YouTube channel to take a quick virtual vacation!

ACTIVITY IDEA 11C: Watch some ads for Lesser Antilles Islands

You can access promotional ads for various islands by using the name of the island plus the word "tourism." After seeing ads for various islands, choose which one you would go to and tell why. What was appealing about their ad? What do you think made you choose that island over the others?

This activity could be done as a group activity if you have an LCD projector. Or, you could assign watching the ads for homework and do the discussion in class.

ACTIVITY IDEA 11D: Focus on Montserrat and its live volcano

Let "YouTube.com/TheBasementWorkshop" take you on a virtual helicopter ride over Montserrat. Then watch a three-minute documentary on the eruption of Montserrat's volcano.

Other similar videos of the island and the volcano will pop up in the side bar menu, as well.

ACTIVITY IDEA 11E: Make a painting showing islands as mountain tops

You will need card stock (or smooth watercolor paper), a pencil, crayons (tans and greens), a large brush, and blue watercolor paint (can use thinned-down acrylic paint if watercolor is unavailable).

Sometimes we can get to thinking about islands as if they are floating in the sea. But of course, islands are really the tops of underwater mountains. Islands that are all in a line, like the Lesser Antilles, are the tops of a long range of mountains.

First, draw your underwater mountains using a regular pencil. Lightly sketch in where the tops of the mountains will be, but leave these areas blank, as you will be coloring them with crayons in a minute.

Here's a tip on using the pencil: Tilt the pencil and use the side, not the tip. Give the mountains texture, making ridges running down the sides of the mountains. Where two mountains overlap, shade the one in the back, near where they overlap. (This will make the rear mountain look like it is really behind the front one.)

Now use crayons to draw in the tops of the mountains, coloring them as islands. Make sure these areas are solidly covered with crayons, as the wax of the crayon will keep the watercolor paint from sticking. Use a large brush to apply the watery paint. Work quickly and stop as soon as the paper is covered. Don't go back and "re-work" the paint. Just swish it on and let it dry. If there are any areas where the paint is sticking to the crayon, gently clean them off with a tissue before they dry.

ACTIVITY IDEA 11F: Make an antique map of the Caribbean

Each student will need:
- a copy of the pattern page printed onto a piece of calligraphy paper (For best results, print it directly from the PDF file. If you don't have a digital copy of this curriculum, you can download this file on www.ellenjmchenry.com, click on FREE DOWNLOADS, then on GEOGRAPHY & MAPS.) For a great antique look, feed calligraphy paper into your printer.
- a pencil
- a permanent waterproof black marker
- colored pencils (TIP: Prismacolor™ makes gold and silver pencils!)
- optional: watercolor paints

Lightly sketch out where the Greater and Lesser Antilles will go on your map. (You will be re-drawing map 11.) Make sure there is plenty of empty space in which to put a large compass rose. Look at the map of the Azores on the next page to see what mapmakers of this time period did to fill in large areas of water. They added lots of compass roses, title frames, ships, and sea monsters in the ocean. In this activity you will be able to add your own artistic touches after you get the technical stuff done.

If you want to make your map into a real sailing chart, you can add portolan lines using a pencil. Make sure the pencil is sharp and use a ruler to draw the lines. Choose various points out in the ocean to be your starting points and draw lines radiating out from them. Keep these lines very light.

NOTE: One of the free downloads for this curriculum (web address listed above) is a file of antique maps to use as examples.

Samples of student work

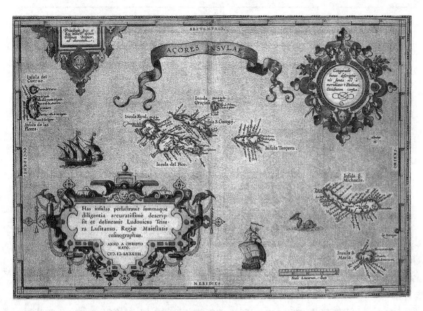

This map of the Azores has lots of empty water space. The artist has added plaques, ships, and a monster to help fill the space.

Portolan maps are covered with criss-crossing lines.

Here are some sample ships you might want to use:

Here are some actual monsters that appeared on real maps made in the 1500s and 1600s:

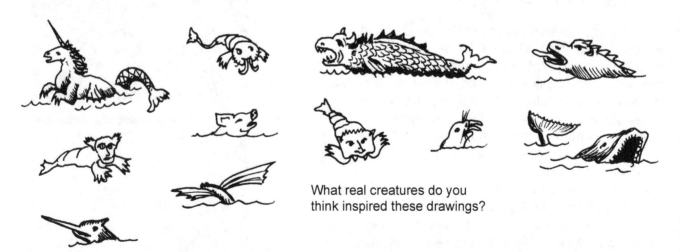

What real creatures do you think inspired these drawings?

If you want to see a page full of sea monsters from an antique map book (including some of these guys), go to this address: **http://historic-cities.huji.ac.il/miscellaneous/sea_monsters.jpg**

ACTIVITY IDEA 12A: Play the "Viking Voyages" game

        To be fair, we need to mention that John Cabot wasn't the first European to discover the coast of Canada. The Vikings had sailed a similar route hundreds of years before Cabot did. (How the native Americans got to North America isn't known for sure, but they probably didn't sail. They probably walked across a land bridge between Asia and Alaska that existed thousands of years ago.) The Vikings were expert sailors. Not many people know the full extent to which the Vikings traveled and traded. They weren't all out pillaging and sacking villages. Many Vikings went east and earned their living as merchants, just like the people of Venice did. This game will let you learn about many of the places the Vikings went.

        To make the board for this game you can either cut the following pages out of the book or you can go to www.ellenjcmchenry.com and print out the pages using the downloadable PDF for the "Viking Voyages Game" (on the GEOGRAPHY & MAPS page of the FREE DOWNLOADS section). Trim off the black edges around the board pieces, then assemble them using clear tape.

        The cards should be printed onto white card stock. Cut them apart then shuflle into a pile and put them (words down) on the rectangle marked WEATHER CARDS.

        You will need to supply your own die, and tokens of some kind.

How to play:

This game is designed for 2 to 4 players.

1) Use the die to determine where each player will start.   The code is:
        1= Trondheim   2= Bergen   3= Oslo   4= Denmark
If you roll a 5 or 6, roll again. As soon as a city has a token on it, no one else can start there. If you are playing with four players, the last person gets stuck with whichever city is left.

2) Use the die to determine which destination each player will go to.
        1 or 2= Vinland   3 or 4= Constantinople   5 or 6= Baghdad
More than one player can go to each destination.

3) The object of the game is to be the first player to reach your destination.

4) If you land on a yellow circle with a dot in the center, you draw a weather card.

5) When you land on a black square, which represents a Viking settlement, you must stop and "waste" any extra hops. For instance, if you roll a six and in three hops you land on a square, then you must stop and "waste" your last three moves. On your next turn, you just continue on again.

6) You do not need to get an exact roll to land on your destination.

GREENLAND

Godhavn

Godthab

Julianehab

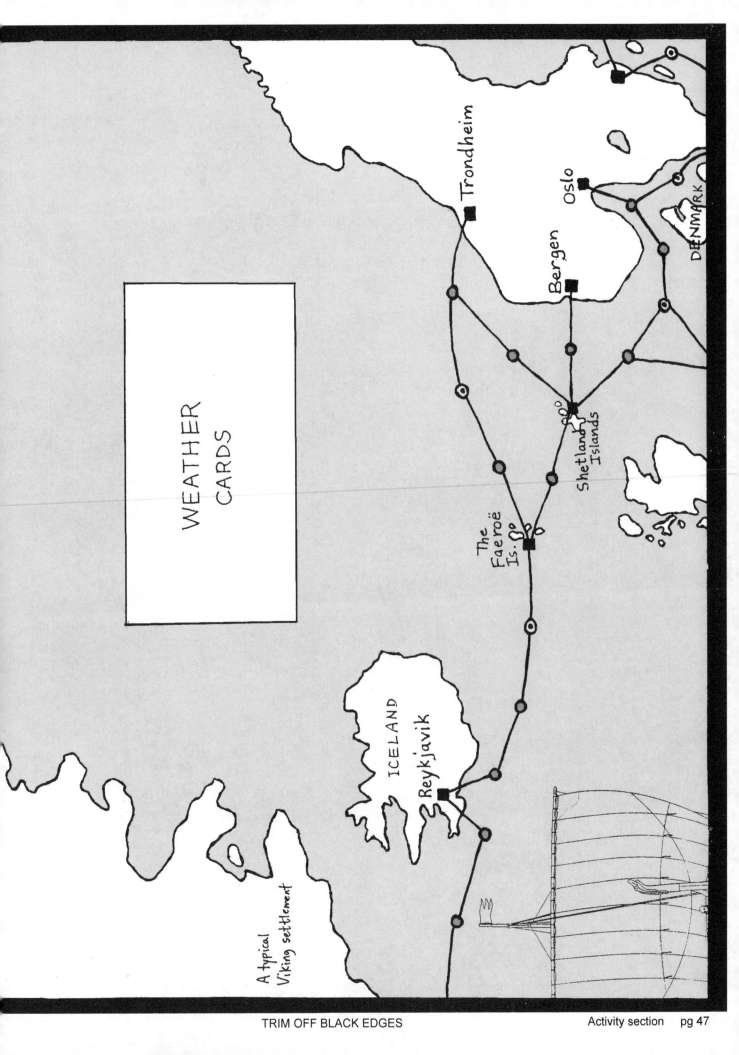

WEATHER
CARDS

Trondheim

Bergen

Oslo

DENMARK

Shetland Islands

The Faeroë Is.

ICELAND

Reykjavik

A typical
Viking settlement

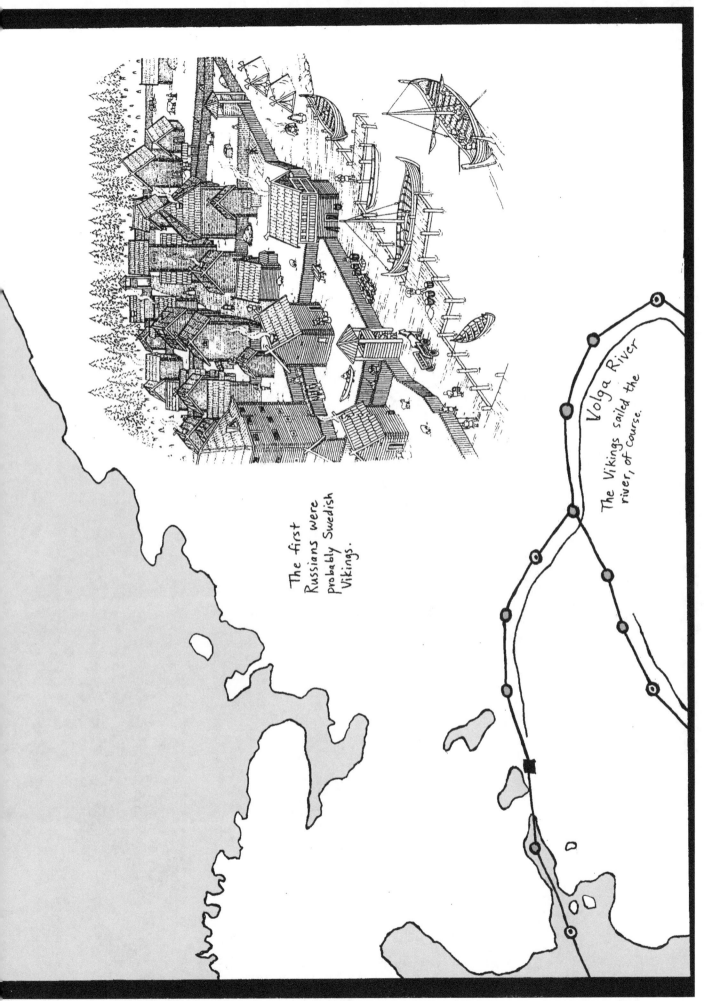

The first Russians were probably Swedish Vikings.

Volga River

The Vikings sailed the river, of course.

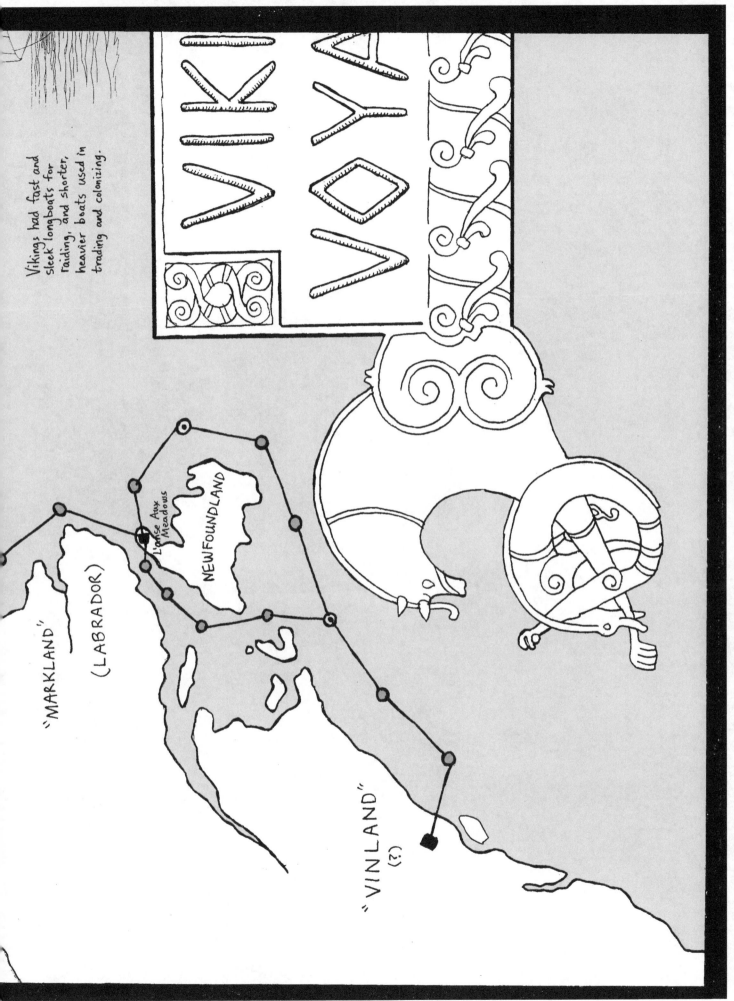

Vikings had fast and sleek longboats for raiding, and shorter, heavier boats used in trading and colonizing.

VIKING VOYA

"MARKLAND"
(LABRADOR)

L'Anse Aux Meadows

NEWFOUNDLAND

"VINLAND"
(?)

Yorvik
(York)

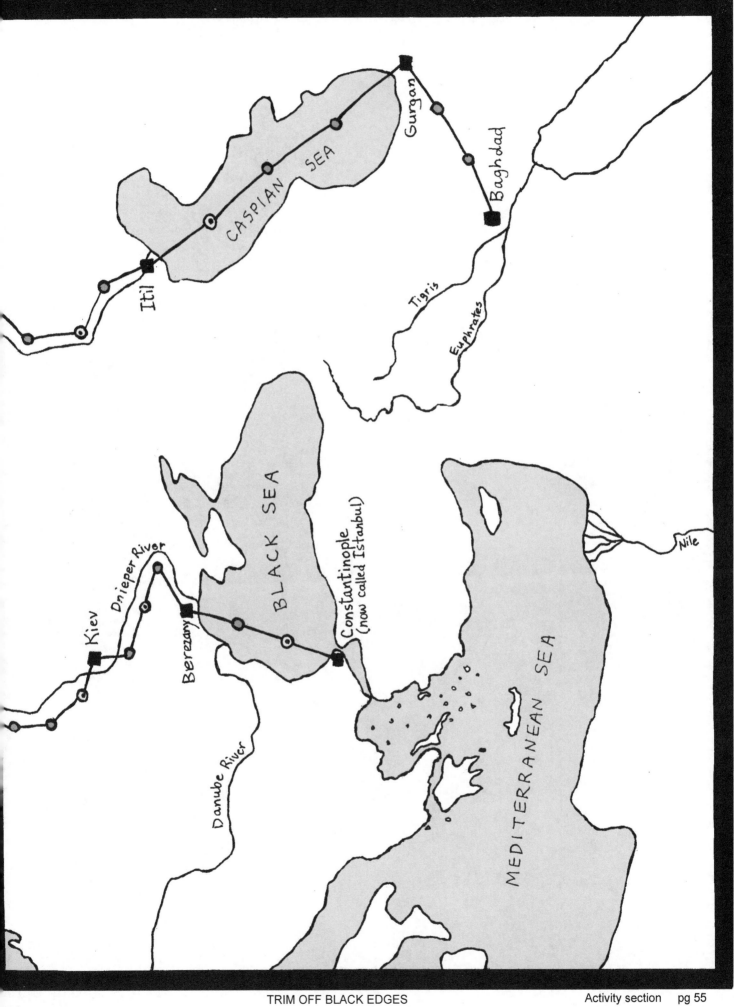

Kiev

Dnieper River

Berezany

Danube River

BLACK SEA

Constantinople
(now called Istanbul)

MEDITERRANEAN SEA

Nile

CASPIAN SEA

Itil

Gurgan

Baghdad

Tigris

Euphrates

TRIM OFF BLACK EDGES

It has been cloudy all week, so you have been unable to use the bearing dial to set your course. This will set you back several days.
Go back 2 spaces.

Four of your best rowers are sick. Since there is not much wind today, you will lose sailing time.
Go back 2 spaces.

There is absolutely no wind today. Your sailors row as much as they can, but you are not going to get as far as you had hoped.
Go back 1 space.

There is a terrible storm and your ship sustains major damage to the hull. It takes ten days to make repairs.
Go back 3 spaces.

The sailors spot a school of fish nearby and since food supplies are low, you decide to spend a whole day catching fish. This was a necessary task, but it did cost you travel time.
Go back 1 space.

Three of your sailors have caught a fever. Because of this, you are unable to go as far as you had liked today.
Go back 1 space.

You are sailing with a current, as well as having a good wind at your back.
Go ahead 2 spaces.

Your lookout has spotted a vessel that could mean trouble for you and your crew. The whole crew puts forth extra effort and makes excellent time.
Go ahead 2 spaces.

The weather is good today.
Go ahead 1 space.

The sun is behind the clouds and it looks like rain, but the wind is blowing in the right direction, so you make good time.
Go ahead 1 space.

There is an excellent wind today. You are making better time than you had expected.
Go ahead 1 space.

Your navigator figures out a short-cut, saving you several days of sailing.
Go ahead 2 spaces.

Today's weather is excellent.
Go ahead 1 space.

There is a storm on the horizon. Your navigator says that if you row hard, you may be able to outrun it.
Go ahead 1 space.

There is a rumor of mutiny. You have to turn your attention from sailing to dealing with your crew. This costs you sailing time.
Go back 1 space.

There is land in sight. The crew would like to go ashore for a day and get fresh food and water. You agree, but it will cost you one day of sailing.
Go back 1 space.

The wind is blowing gently but steadily today. The current is good, as well.
Go ahead 1 space.

You go too far north and get stuck in ice floes. Fortunately, you get out, but it costs you two days of travel.
Go back 2 spaces.

You make an unexpected stop in a trading port. You get some good deals, but it uses up sailing time.
Go back 1 space.

The weather couldn't be better. You have ideal sailing conditions.
Go ahead 1 space.

ACTIVITY IDEA 12B: Draw your maps again, using an exact outline

Here is an activity that will exercise the right side of the brain—the side that sees and copies shapes, like a photocopier. The left side of the brain likes to name shapes. It loves to see Scotland as a rooster head. The right side of the brain can learn to memorize shapes that don't exactly conform to any object. It's the right side of the brain that can remember extra squiggles and lines and shapes without having to name them.

Here are more exact outlines of Britain and of Newfoundland. The students should use the method they just learned for drawing the basic shapes first. Once they have the basic shapes established, they can then look at these drawings to see where to add more detail. This is a general principle of how to draw—sketch in the basic shapes before you add details.

ACTIVITY IDEA 13A: Worksheet showing Africa, Arabia and Europe

Copy the next page and have your students fill in Africa, Arabia, Palestine, Greece, Italy, Spain, France, England, Black Sea, Caspian Sea, Aral Sea, Nile River, and the Tigris and Euphrates Rivers. This may take a while, so encourage patience and perseverence!

ACTIVITY IDEA 13B: Make Africa cookies

Use the recipe from chapter one (the cuneiform cookies) or else a standard sugar cookie recipe. To make the shape of the cookie, you may either roll out the dough, then cut out the shape, or you may pat the dough until it fills out into the right shape. If you are cutting, first cut out the simple outline provided and lay it on top of your rolled-out dough as a cutting guide. If you are patting out the dough, lay the pattern page on the table and place a piece of clear plastic wrap on top. You may then pat the dough directly on top of the pattern. (You don't have to use the pattern. You may want the students to work entirely on their own, using the outline as a visual reference as they sculpt.)

Prepare yellow and green "paint" by mixing food coloring with a bit of egg yolk. Paint in the areas of desert and rain forest before you bake your cookie.

After your cookie has been baked, provide blue icing for rivers and chocolate mini-chips for mountains. To make icing, put about a teaspoon of shortening into a cup of powdered sugar and then add a teaspoon of vanilla and a few drops of blue food coloring. Beat with an electric mixer, adding a few drops of water until the icing is the proper consistency. Put the blue icing in a plastic baggie (freezer or quart size baggies are less likely to break at the seams). Cut off a corner of the baggie (just a tiny snip!) and squeeze the icing into the corner. You should be able to squeeze a thin line of icing from the tiny hole. Use the icing baggie to create the rivers of Africa. Ahdere chocolate chips (or whatever flavor chips you prefer) with a little icing.

The chips will represent the mountains whose streams create the rivers' tributaries.

NOTE: You may want to make the cookies extra large, like our sample cookie shown here. You can enlarge the pattern until it is the size you want. This might require cutting the pattern in half, enlarging each piece separately, then taping them back together. Or, better yet, have the students try it freehand, using the pattern paper just as a visual reference as they sculpt.

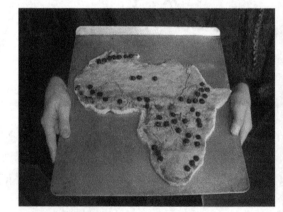

ACTIVITY IDEA 13C: "Above or Below the Equator" Africa quiz game

Provide the students with a map of Africa that shows political boundaries. GIve them a few minutes to study it, making sure they take special note of where the equator is. Collect the maps before you begin the quizzing. Say the name of a country and let the students try to remember whether it was above or below the equator. You can add additional rules of play (for example give points and make it competitive) depending on your situation and your particular students.

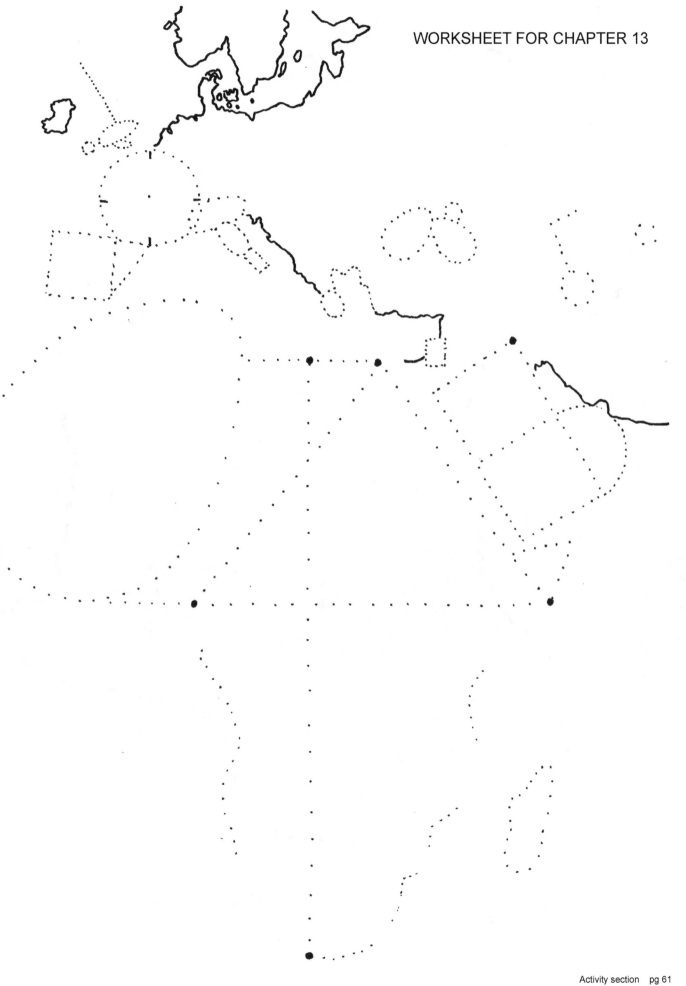

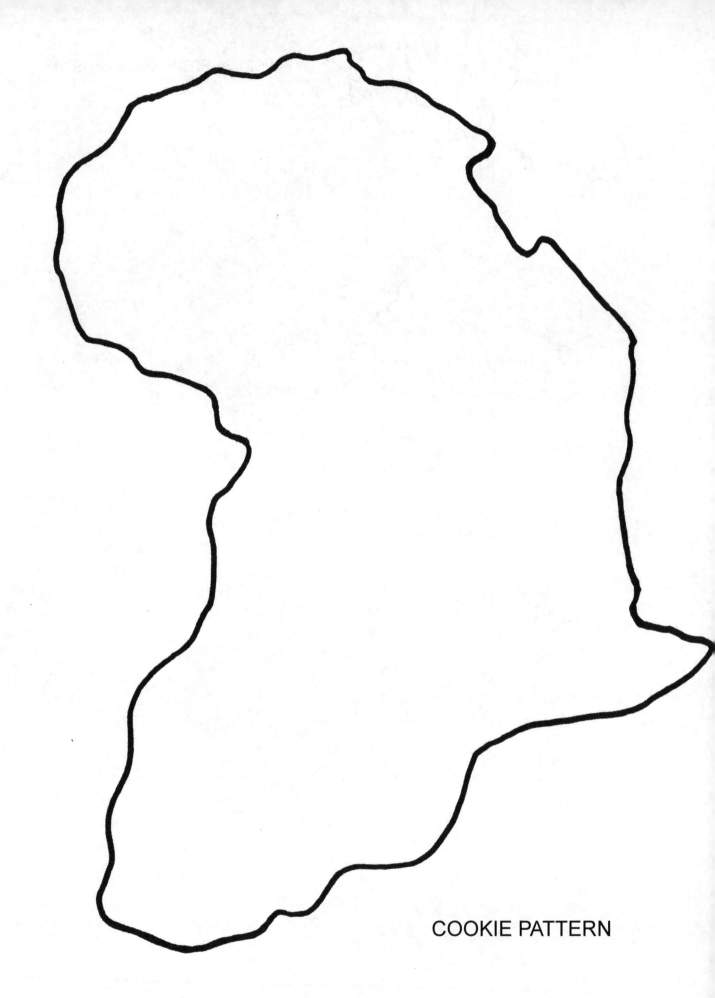

COOKIE PATTERN

ACTIVITY IDEA 14A: Make a star clock

One way sailors could tell time at sea was by using the stars as a clock. The center of the clock is Polaris and the hand on the clock is the constellation called the Little Dipper. The clock shows 24 hours, not 12, so it takes a little getting used to. If the Little Dipper is pointing to what looks like three o'clock, it's really six o'clock.

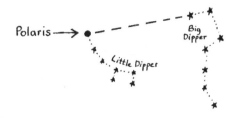

Sailors sometimes used a device called a nocturnal (shown here on the left) to help them estimate the time. It was more accurate than just looking at the stars. You could move the metal arm so that it lined up with the stars, then read the time on the dial. Most nocturnals used Polaris as the key star, although some used the constellation Cassiopeia instead. The nocturnal based on Polaris wasn't any help, however, when they sailed below the equator.

To make your own star clock, copy the pattern on the next page onto heavy cardstock paper. Cut out both wheels, and cut out the black area on the smaller wheel. Use a paper fastener to fasten the smaller circle on top of the larger one.

To use your star clock, go out and look at the night sky. Find Polaris and the Little Dipper. (This is assuming you are in the Northern hemisphere.) Hold the star clock wheel so that the current month is at the top. Then turn the star wheel so that the picture of the Little Dipper is at the same angle as you see the real one in the sky. Then read the time inside the window, right at the pointer. This star clock is set for Eastern Standard Time in the USA. If you are not in this time zone, add or subtract hours accordingly. For instance, if you are in California, subtract three hours since you are three hours behind EST. Also, don't forget to add an hour if you are in Daylight Saving Time (March-November).

How else did they tell time at sea?

If the clouds were not blocking the view of the sunrise in the morning, someone on the ship (often the cabin boy) was given the job of watching intently to see the exact second that the sun became visible over the horizon. At that exact moment, he would turn over the ship's large hourglass (which was usually only a half-hour glass and would run out every 30 minutes). The navigator would have tables telling the exact sunrise times for every day of the year at each latitude. So at sunrise they knew exactly what time it was. Then the cabin boy would have to watch the hourglass for the rest of the day, turning it over at the exact moment the sand ran out. Ships often had two hourglasses, providing them with a back-up.

Eclipses could also be used to tell time, although they didn't come around very often, which made them less useful than the sunrise. Navigators carried books that listed eclipse times for every possible time and place on Earth. Columbus used his table of eclipses to save his life during his fourth voyage. You can read this story in activity 14B.

To the ordinary sailor, who wasn't involved with navigation, knowing the time to the exact minute wasn't important. He could tell approximately what time it was by the position of the sun in the sky or by how tired he was. It was only the navigators who wanted to know the exact time because they could use this information to calculate their longitude. But more on longitude in a later lesson...

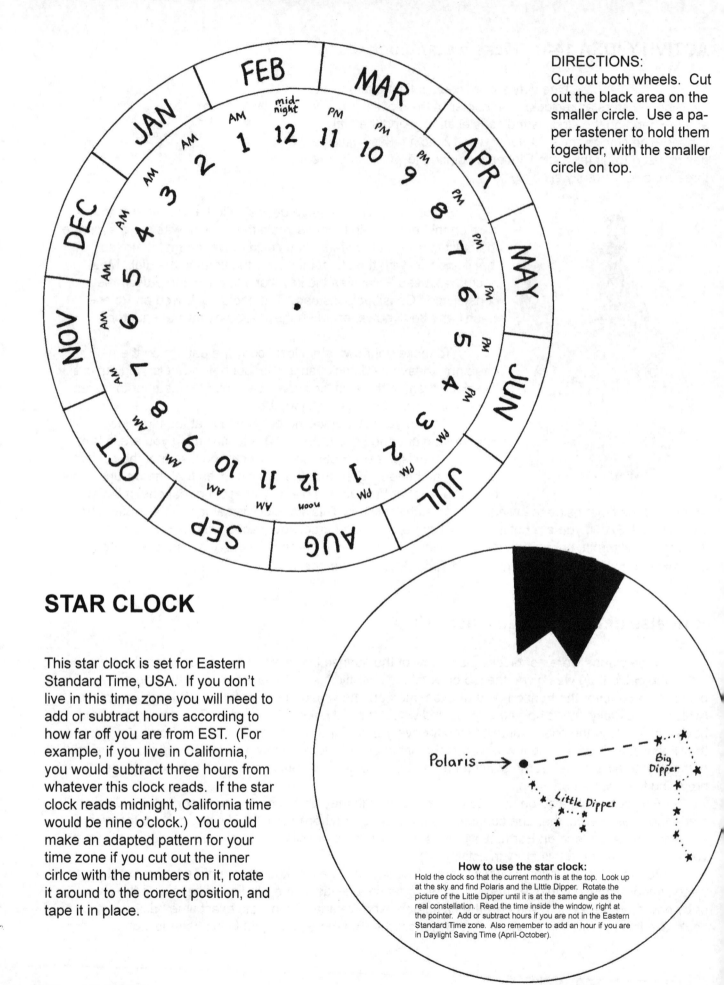

DIRECTIONS:
Cut out both wheels. Cut out the black area on the smaller circle. Use a paper fastener to hold them together, with the smaller circle on top.

STAR CLOCK

This star clock is set for Eastern Standard Time, USA. If you don't live in this time zone you will need to add or subtract hours according to how far off you are from EST. (For example, if you live in California, you would subtract three hours from whatever this clock reads. If the star clock reads midnight, California time would be nine o'clock.) You could make an adapted pattern for your time zone if you cut out the inner cirlce with the numbers on it, rotate it around to the correct position, and tape it in place.

How to use the star clock:
Hold the clock so that the current month is at the top. Look up at the sky and find Polaris and the Little Dipper. Rotate the picture of the Little Dipper until it is at the same angle as the real constellation. Read the time inside the window, right at the pointer. Add or subtract hours if you are not in the Eastern Standard Time zone. Also remember to add an hour if you are in Daylight Saving Time (April-October).

ACTIVITY IDEA 14B: Read about Columbus and the eclipse

Eclipses were very important to navigators. As we learned in our early chapters, records of eclipses had been kept for thousands of years. People discovered that eclipses occurred at very precise intervals. Astronomers found that they could predict almost to the second when an eclipse would begin and how long it would last. Eclipses were sort of like a giant clock that only ticked once a year or so. Navigators at sea could make use of this natural "clock of the heavens." When they saw an eclipse begin, they could check their charts and know exactly what time it was.

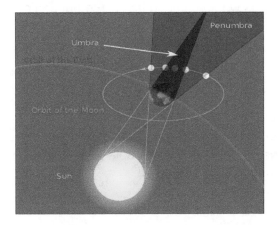

Lunar eclipses happen more frequently than do solar eclipses. In a lunar eclipse, the moon goes through the Earth's shadow. The shadow has two parts: the umbra (total shadow) and the penumbra (partial shadow). (Notice that the word "penumbra" starts with "pen" (Latin for "almost") just like the word "peninsula.") A total eclipse is when the moon is totally inside the Earth's umbra shadow. A penumbral eclipse is when the moon is only within the penumbral shadow and a partial eclipse is when the moon crosses into the umbra, but not totally.

Christopher Columbus had on board his ship a table, like the one below, that predicted the up coming eclipses.

On his fourth voyage, Columbus discovered that his ship was leaking quite badly. Marine worms of the Caribbean Sea were living on the hull of the ship and were gradually eating it up. The ship could not go on without the hull being rebuilt, which would take months to accomplish. Columbus pulled into a harbor on the coast of Jamaica and stayed there for about a year while they tried to fix up the ship. A year is a long time to be stranded, and the crew found it hard to survive. The natives of the island were curious about what the foreigners were doing and they hung around to watch. They could see that the Spaniards were running short on food and were kind enough to bring food for the sailors. For months the natives brought food and supplies to the crew. It started to become quite a job for the natives! The sailors weren't as appreciative as they should have been and they sometimes stole things from the natives. Finally, the natives had had enough and they refused to bring any more supplies. Without these supplies, the Spaniards believed they would starved to death. Some

sailors said they should kill the natives (typical European solution) but Columbus came up with a better plan. He realized that a special day was coming up, and he told the natives to gather in front of him on the evening of February 29, 1504. When they were all assembled he told them that their god was angry at them for stopping the supply of food to the Spaniards. Columbus said that the gods would show their displeasure by taking the moon out of the sky. Sure enough, the moon began to get dim, and then it began to disappear! The natives were terrified and promised to resume supplying Columbus and his crew. Columbus then said the gods would forgive them and return the moon. And wouldn't you know it—the moon came back again!

You can find out when lunar eclipses will occur by searching the Internet for "lunar eclipse tables." The tables will tell you what kind of eclipse it will be (total, partial, penumbral), how long it will last, and what parts of the world will be turned the right way to see the eclipse. (If you are on the side of the Earth facing the sun, you won't be able to see it.)

ACTIVITY IDEA 15A: Maps that show particular information

Sometimes maps are used to convey information such as rainfall, population density, types of climates, altitude, natural resources, or land use. These maps always come with a key telling you what each color or line pattern on the map means. In this activity, the students will colors maps showing rainfall, population density and average temperatures. They will they use this information to answer questions.

Make copies of the worksheet on the next page. Provide the students with well-sharpened color pencils, if at all possible. Next best is thin markers. Crayons would come in last place but could be used if they are sharpened as well as possible.

ACTIVITY IDEA 15B: Map worksheet

Make student copies of the map worksheet (the one that looks almost empty, having just the dotted outlines of a cirlce, semi-circle and large rectangle). The students should be able to fill in all of the Caribbean plus South America. This combines map drawings 10, 11, 14 and 15.

ACTIVITY IDEA 15C: Learn about some South American animals

A whole slew of clickable pictures with info is available at:
http://www.enchantedlearning.com/coloring/southamer.shtml

ACTIVITY IDEA 15D: Make South America cookies

If the Africa cookies were a hit, you can do the same thing with South America.

ACTIVITY IDEA 15E: Videos about the Amazon River and rain forest

An IMAX about the Amazon is posted on the Basement Workshop channel. (There are also many other videos on the rain forests and the Amazon River if you search using key words "Amazon River, rainforest.")

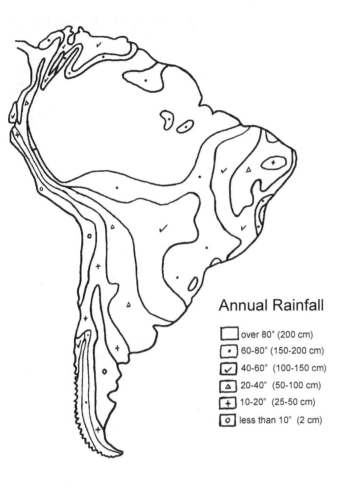

Annual Rainfall

- ☐ over 80" (200 cm)
- ⊡ 60-80" (150-200 cm)
- ✓ 40-60" (100-150 cm)
- △ 20-40" (50-100 cm)
- ✛ 10-20" (25-50 cm)
- ○ less than 10" (2 cm)

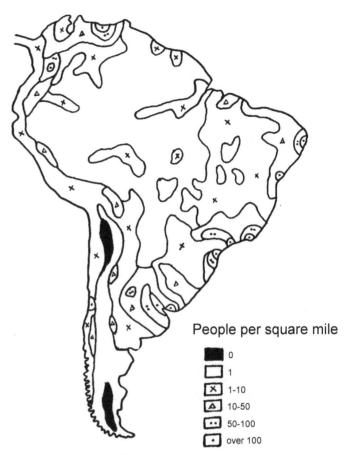

People per square mile

- ■ 0
- ☐ 1
- ☒ 1-10
- △ 10-50
- ⊡⊡ 50-100
- ⊡ over 100

Average temperature in winter (July)

- ☐ 68-85 F (20-30 C)
- ⊡ 50-68 F (10-20 C)
- ☒ 32-50 F (0-10 C)
- ⊡⊡ under 32 F (0 C)

Directions:

Choose colors to represent each type of symbol in the little boxes. (Hint: You may want to choose white as the color for the blank boxes. That way you can save yourself time and effort by not having to color large areas.) Color in the little boxes and their corresponding areas on the map.

Questions

Look at the information presented on these maps and answer the following questions according to that information. (Plus you may use anything you learned while drawing South America, such as where the mountains and rivers are.)

1) Where do most people in South America live? in the mountains? on the coasts? in the river basin?

2) What does altitude do to temperature?

3) What part of the continent gets the most rainfall?

4) Do you think all the water in the Amazon River comes from the mountain tributaries? Why or why not?

5) Where are the deserts of South America? (A desert is defined as a place that gets less than 10 inches of rainfall a year.)

6) Can you tell where tribuary rivers of the Amazon are located just by looking at the population map?

Galapagos Islands

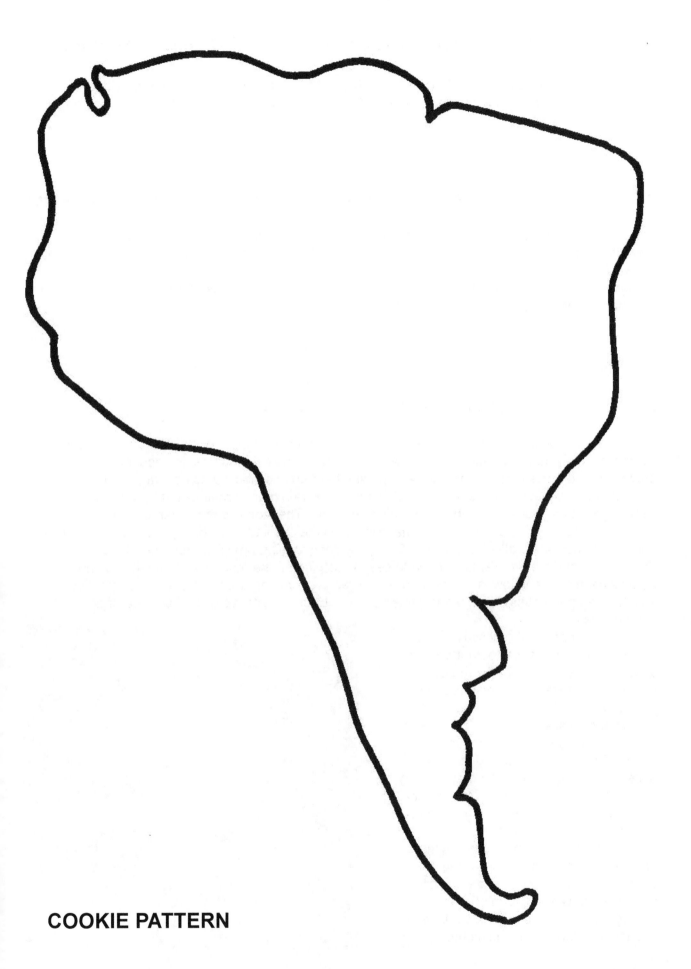

COOKIE PATTERN

ACTIVITY IDEA 16A: Tour an exquisite model of a Chinese treasure ship

Log on to the Basement Workshop YouTube channel and find a video that provides a tour of a model of one of Zheng He's treasure ships. It's fabulous. The person that took the video gives you a mini-tour of the ship.

ACTIVITY IDEA 16B: Watch a documentary about Zheng He and his ships

There is a fabulous National Geographic video about Zheng He: "Treasure Fleet; the Adventures of Zheng He." Totally running time is about an hour. You can access this documentary on YouTube using a search with key words "Zheng He Treasure Fleet" or you can go to the Basement Workshop channel. (There may also be some shorter videos about Zheng He posted on the channel, as well.)

ACTIVITY 16C: Read about Chinese stone maps

The Chinese not only made silk maps, they also made maps out of stone. In the 1100s, some Chinese school directors came up with a way to educate their students about geography: they engraved maps onto very flat stones and set them up in school yards so that students could study them and even copy them. The students could have a map of their own if they put a sheet of paper against the stone then rubbed the paper with ink. The stones were as large as 3 feet on a side. The most famous of these stone maps is called the "Yu ji tu." A rubbing of this stone is shown below. You can see the Yellow (Huang) River, the Yangtze (Chang) River, and the island of Hainan. Though the letters are too small for you to see in this picture, the map makers labeled all the lakes, mountains, rivers, and towns.   The map is covered with horizontal and vertical lines, creating a grid. You can see part of this grid in the lower left corner. Each square represents an area of about 33 square miles.

The shape of the coastline is so accurate that modern cartographers are amazed. No one knows how the Chinese map makers were able to make such an accurate map. They did have magnetic compasses available to them, but little else beyond simple plumb lines and measuring sticks. The creators of this stone map were following guidelines for map making established by Pei Xiu in the 3rd century (the 200s). Pei Xiu seems to have been Ptolemy's counterpart in the east.

Stone carving was used by many ancient cultures and has proven to be the best way to preserve information for thousands of years. Our modern books, photographs, records and CDs will never outlast engravings made in stone!

ACTIVITY IDEA 17A: Take a video tour of Malacca (Melaka)

YouTube has a video tour of Melaka (that's the modern spelling) that showcases the city's beautiful historical sites and diverse ethnic groups. The city of Melaka, along with its "sister" city, Georgetown, are now officially "World Heritage Sites" as determined by Unesco. This means that their history and culture are considered "world treasures" and should be protected and appreciated by everyone in the world. (This video was made to explain how and why Melaka was able to become a Unesco World Heritage Site.) This video (and possibly some others) have been uploaded to the Basement Workshop YouTube channel.

ACTIVITY IDEA 17B: Play "The Spice Islands Game"

This game is for 2 to 4 players (4 is ideal)

You will need:
- Copies of the following pattern pages (For best results, print the pages using the PDF file on the CD and feed card stock into your printer. In a pinch, you can pull the color pages out of this book.)
    - Scissors, glue stick, and tape
    - Tiny balls of clay or dough (Sculpey™ works well)
    - Two toothpicks and paint or markers to color them
    - Whole cloves (about 25 of them) (if you can't get whole cloves, just substitute some kind of object that can be collected by the players)
    - Optional- a small jar lid or container to hold the cloves during the game

NOTE: If you don't have Sculpey™ you can substitute another type of dough that is not too greasy or wet, or you can improvise a different kind of token. If your improvised tokens don't have a removable colored parts that can be transferred to another token, just have your players mentally keep track of when they are on board someone else's ship. (This direction will make sense after you have read the playing instructions.)

To set up:
Cut out the game board sections and assemble them to make the portolan map game board. There are some glue flaps indicated for your convenience if you wish to use them.
Cut apart all the cards.
Roll a pea-sized ball of Scupley (actually a little smaller than a pea) for each player. Cut the toothpicks in half, trim off the sharp end, and paint each half a different color. Put each colored half-toothpick into a Sculpey ball.
Put 25 cloves into a jar lid or some small container and set it somewhere on or near the game board. The number of cloves will determine how long the game goes on. For a shorter game, put in less. 25 cloves will let 4 players play for about 30 minutes. When the cloves are gone, the game is over.

Rules of movement:
The rules of movement seem natural if you imagine yourself to be sailing on a ship. If you are on the open sea, you can keep sailing. If you run into an island, you must stop. If you land at one place on an island, you must also leave from that place because that's where your ship is anchored.
To begin the game, each player places his token on one of the compass roses. (If you need a way to randomly assign the starting places, write the numbers 1 to 4 on slips of paper. Each player will draw a slip of paper. Whoever gets 1 will have first choice, 2 will have second choice, and so on. Or you may want to assign a number to match each rose, starting with 1 in the top left corner and then going around clockwise. You can use this same method for determining who goes first.)

There are no dice in this game. Players make a move by traveling along the rhumb lines. On each move, a player may move as far as he wants to along one rhumb line, and may change direction once. For example, on his first move, a player chooses one of the many rhumb lines leading out from the rose. He starts moving out along this line and may go as far as he wants on that line (unless he hits an island, in which case he must stop and his turn is over). When he comes to an intersection, he has the option of turning left or right (or some odd oblique direction). After making this turn, he may not turn again on that move. He either hits land, or stops at an intersection and waits for his next turn. (On that next turn, his first move onto one of the lines does not count as a change in direction. He may still have a change of direction on that turn.)

If you run into an island, you must stop regardless of whether there are spices on that island. When you land on an island you cannot move about the island (after all, there are natives living on the island and they might not be happy to have you tramping about!). Your ship docks at the point where you land, so you must leave from that point as well. However, very small islands are a special case. If the island is smaller than the diameter of a pencil eraser (you can use one to check) then you may exit the island from the line on the other side. (These tiny islands look almost like "blips" on the rhumb line.)

You cannot return to an island you've already been to. If you do, you don't get a landfall card. Only one ship can occupy a landing site.

Ships can pass each other at sea, whether going the same direction or the opposite direction.

A player may not "sit" on a site for more than one turn. After making landfall and either answering a question or following the directions on the card, he must sail again on his next turn.

What happens when you land on an island:

As soon as you land you draw a Landfall Card. This card will give you instructions to follow. Most of the time the card will say, "Draw a Spice Card." In this case, you then immediately proceed to draw a Spice Card. (Put your Landfall Card on the bottom of the deck.)

If the Landfall Card tells the player to get on another player's ship, the first player removes his colored toothpick from his dough ball and places it in the other player's dough ball. Now there is one dough ball with no token in it (which stays put until the ship can be reclaimed) and one dough ball with two tokens in it. The owner of the double token dough ball moves it just as he would ordinarily. However, when it comes time to answer questions, the "guest" may help out with the answer. If the question is answered correctly, both players get a clove.

When a player draws a Spice Card, he hands it to the player to his right who then reads the question out loud (including the multiple choice answers). If the player guesses the correct answer, he receives a clove. If he guesses incorrectly, the question then passes to the player on his left. If this next player guesses correctly, he receives the clove. If the second player misses the question, it then passes to the third player. If the third player misses the question, no one gets a clove. The fourth player is holding the card and sees the answer, so it would not be fair to let him guess. The question card is then returned to the bottom of the stack.

Winning:

The game is over when all the cloves have been claimed. The player with the most cloves wins. (Try eating one after the game is over!)

Alternate mode of play:

For a second round of the game, you might want to try this variation. Put cloves right on top of the islands. Some islands will be too small for any cloves, others will hold up to 5. Don't put any on Irian Jaya, as it was never considered a source of spices. Don't put a lot on Timor, either. Once the spices are gone from an island, you can't get spices by landing on it.

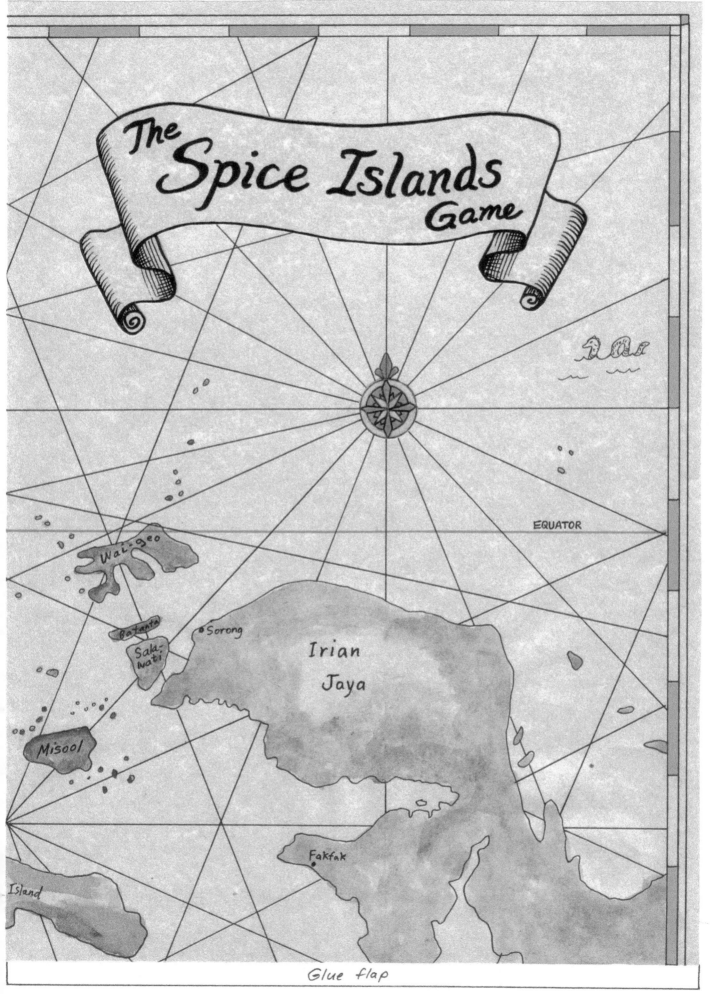

The Spice Islands Game

EQUATOR

Wai-geo

Batanta

Sala-wati

Sorong

Irian Jaya

Misool

Fakfak

Island

Glue flap

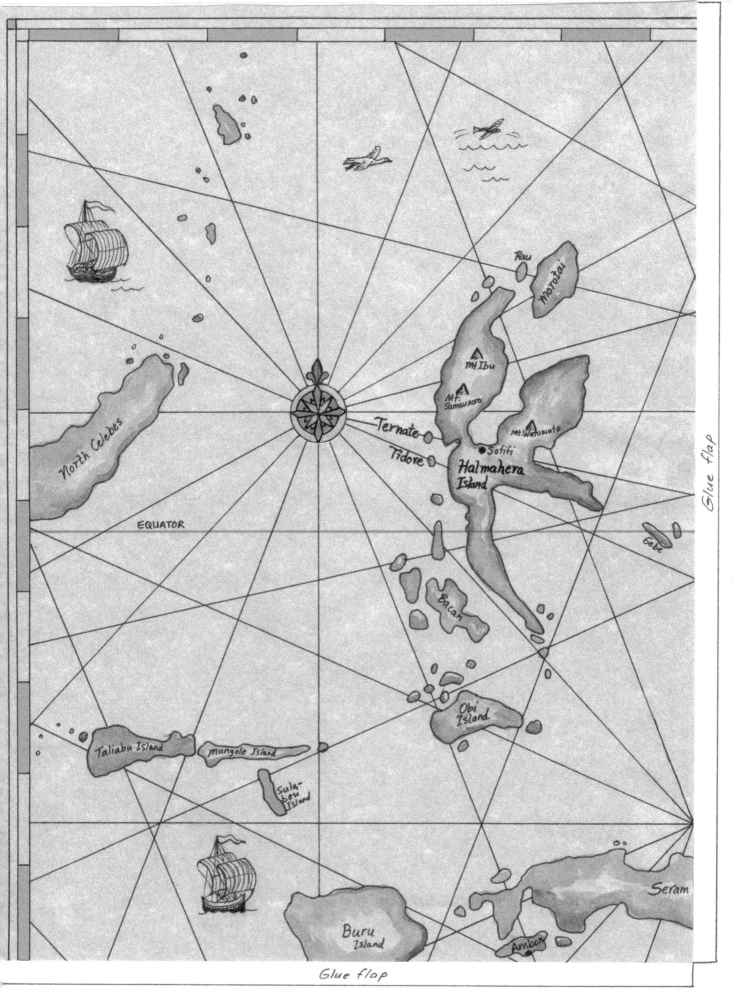

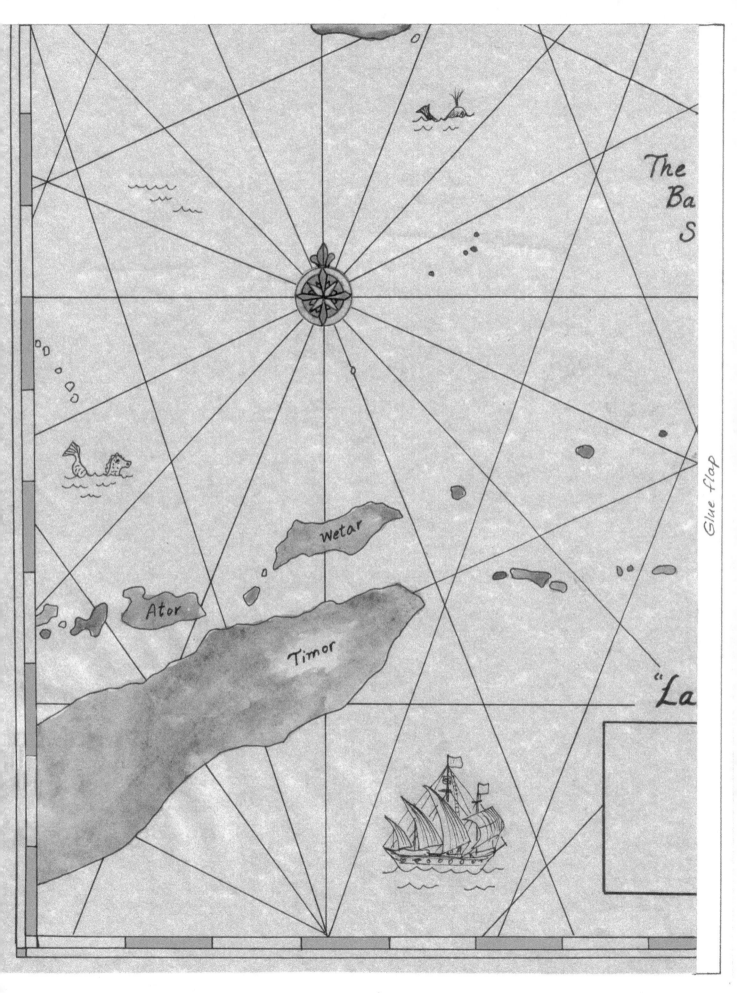

The
Ba
S

Glue Flap

"La

Wetar

Ator

Timor

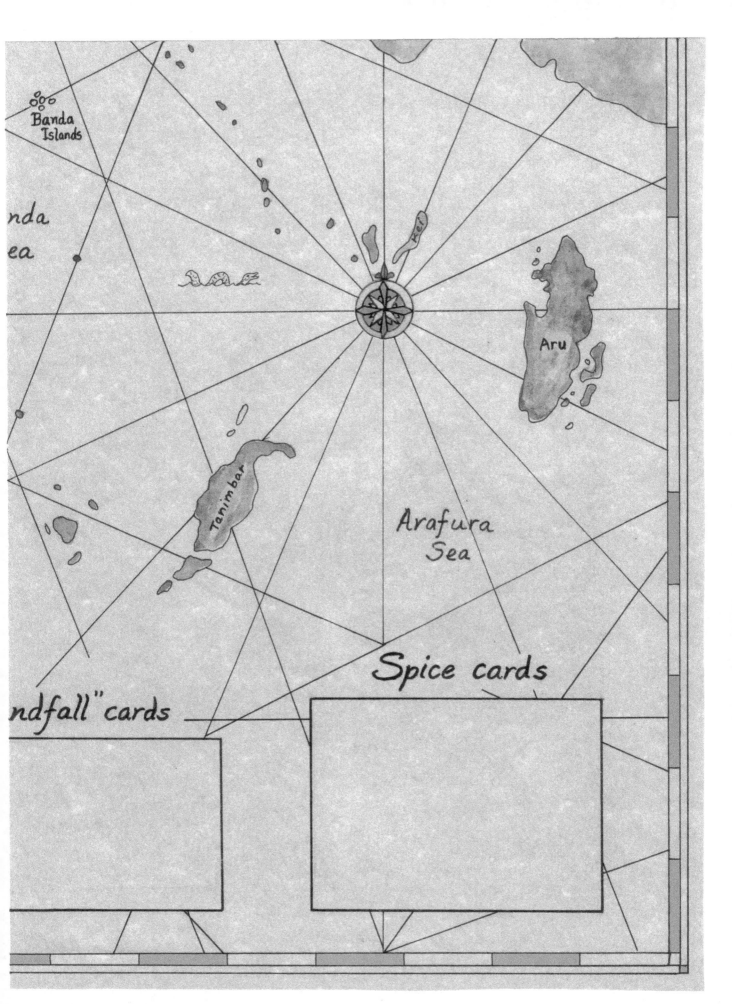

Banda
Islands

nda
ea

Kei

Aru

Tanimbar

Arafura
Sea

Spice cards

ndfall" cards

Your ship has developed serious leaks. Your carpenters will need several weeks to make repairs. All of your crew must get on another ship (the one closest to you) and travel with them for 2 turns. After that, you may return to your ship where you left it.

Your ship has barnacles encrusting the bottom of the hull. They must be scraped off or they will ruin the ship. This will only take a week. You and your crew may sit out one turn or you may hop on board the nearest ship and sail with them for 1 turn.

All of your sailors have come down with a tropical fever, leaving you very busy trying to manage the ship by yourself. You will be unable to answer any question cards until it comes back around to your turn again.

The monsoon winds are at your back and you can sail at maximum speed. On your next turn you may switch directions twice instead of just once. (You may also hold this card and use it on a future turn instead of your next turn.)

There is a rumor that Spanish ships are coming from the north. You don't know if this is true, but just in case it is, you must head north on your next turn. (Once you've touched the northern edge of the map, you've done your duty and you may proceed on your way on the following turn.)

Your captain wants to find other spice islands. No one knows what is on the large land mass to the east (Irian Jaya). Sail there on your next turn. You may change directions any number of times to get there. You won't find spices, so you will be unable to draw a spice card.

There is a rumor that Spanish ships are coming in from the east. You must head east on your next turn. (Once you have touched the eastern edge, you have done your duty and may then proceed to any island on your following turn.)

There is a rumor that gold has been discovered on Timor. You want to be the first to claim the gold (if there is any). Sail there on your next turn. You may change directions as many times as you need to. You won't find gold, so you can leave the island on your following turn.

You ship has sustained major damage in a recent storm. The tropical monsoon rains shredded your sails. It will take 2 weeks to repair them. For the next 2 turns, you and your crew must sail with the ship that is closest to you right now. After that, you may return to your ship where you left it.

The weather couldn't be better for sailing. On your next turn you may change directions twice instead of once. Or, you may hold this card and use it on a future turn.

Draw a SPICE CARD.	Draw a SPICE CARD.
Draw a SPICE CARD.	Draw a SPICE CARD.
Draw a SPICE CARD.	Draw a SPICE CARD.
Draw a SPICE CARD.	Draw a SPICE CARD.
Daw a SPICE CARD.	Draw a SPICE CARD.

Draw a SPICE CARD.	Draw a SPICE CARD.
Draw a SPICE CARD.	Draw a SPICE CARD.
Draw a SPICE CARD.	Draw a SPICE CARD.
Draw a SPICE CARD.	Draw a SPICE CARD.
Daw a SPICE CARD.	Draw a SPICE CARD.

Who is considered to be the founder of the European Age of Discovery?

A) Christopher Columbus
*B) Henry the Navigator
C) Vasco da Gama
D) Bartholomew Dias

From what English port did John Cabot leave?

A) London
B) Dover
*C) Bristol
D) Plymouth

Which one of these would be the least helpful if you are tyring to determine how far above or below the equator you are?

A) astrolabe
*B) compass
C) quadrant
D) kamal

Which of these islands is NOT a part of the Lesser Antilles?

A) Grenada
B) Guadeloupe
C) Antigua
*D) Turks and Caicos

Which one of these islands lies just below the Tropic of Cancer?

*A) Cuba
B) Jamaica
C) Majorca
D) Sri Lanka

Which one of these rivers has a very large estuary?

*A) Plata
B) Niger
C) Ganges
D) Amazon

Which of these rivers does NOT have a delta region?

A) Nile
B) Ganges
*C) Plata
D) Orinoco

Which of the following places was never controlled by the Portuguese?

A) Malacca, Malaysia
B) Calicut, India
*C) Alexandria, Egypt
D) Rio de Janeiro, Brazil

Which of the following places has the largest number of Portuguese-speaking people outside of Portugal?

A) Indonesia
B) Argentina
C) Malaysia
*D) Brazil

Which of these places did the Portuguese never visit?

*A) Mexico
B) India
C) Newfoundland
D) Madagascar

Which of these waterways did a Portuguese ship never sail through?

A) The Strait of Gibraltar
B) The Mozambique Channel
*C) The Magellan Strait
D) The English Channel

Which one of these modern countries does NOT touch the Tropic of Cancer?

A) Egypt
*B) Spain
C) India
D) Saudi Arabia

Which one of these was NOT used as a "pit stop" by European vessels heading west?

A) the Canary Islands
B) the Azores
C) Maderia Island
*D) the Balearic Islands

Which of these is on the equator?

*A) Lake Victoria
B) Madagascar
C) The Kalahari Desert
D) Timbuktu

Which one of these words was NOT taken from the native peoples of the Caribbean?

A) tobacco
B) hammock
*C) tomato
D) potato

Which of these lies on the Troipc of Capricorn?

*A) Rio de Janeiro, Brazil
B) Buenos Aires, Argentina
C) Havana, Cuba
D) Quito ("kee-toe"), Ecuador

The Falkland Islands lie off the coast of the tip of South America. Which country has claimed them?

A) Argentia
B) Brazil
C) The United States
*D) England

How many voyages did Columbus make to the New World?

A) 1
B) 2
C) 3
*D) 4

When were the Barbary pirates finally eliminated?

A) the 1630s
B) the 1730s
*C) the 1830s
D) the 1930s

Which one of these places was never controlled by Barbary pirates?

A) Tunis
B) Alexandria
C) Sicily
*D) Venice

What was Henry the Navigator's greatest contribution to Portuguese exploration?

*A) ship building technology
B) invention of the astrolabe
C) portolan maps
D) military strategy

Which one of these bodies of water dows NOT touch France?

A) Bap of Biscay
*B) the North Sea
C) the English Channel
D) the Mediterranean Sea

Which of these islands is NOT in the Mediterranean Sea?

A) Malta
B) Crete
C) Majorca
*D) Madeira

Which of these does NOT touch the country of Turkey?

A) The Black Sea
B) The Aegean Sea
*C) The Ionian Sea
D) The Sea of Marmara

Which of these islands is farthest from the Italian peninsula?

A) Corsica
B) Sicily
*C) Majorca
D) Sardinia

Which of these spices is not from the Spice Islands?

A) Cinnamon
B) Mace
*C) Vanilla
D) Nutmeg

Which of these is NOT south of the Tropic of Capricorn ?

A) Capetown, South Africa
*B) Lima, Peru
C) Santiago, Chile
D) Buenos Aires, Argentina

In what city was John Cabot born?

*A) Genoa
B) Venice
C) Lisbon
D) Bristol

What body of water is on the western side (left side) of the Malay peninsula?

A) the South China Sea
B) the Indian Ocean
*C) The Bay of Bengal
D) the Banda Sea

Which one of these is NOT a part of the Malay archipelago?

A) the Philippines
B) Java
C) Sumatra
*D) Taiwan

What body of water is between China and the Korean peninsula?

*A) The Yellow Sea
B) the South China Sea
C) the Sea of Japan
D) the East China Sea

Which river flows down the Indochina peninsula?

A) the Yangtze River
*B) the Mekong River
C) the Malay River
D) the Cambodian River

Which of these tiny countries lies between Spain and France ?

*A) Andorra
B) Luxembourg
C) San Marino
D) Monaco

Which of these does Arabia NOT have?

A) a peninsula
*B) a major river
C) access to the Persian Gulf
D) mineral resources

The Caspian Sea touches all these modern countries excpet which one ?

A) Russia
B) Iran
C) Kazakhstan
*D) Uzbekistan

Which of these is NOT part of the Greater Antilles?

A) Cuba
B) Jamaica
*C) Trinidad
D) Puerto Rico

ACTIVITY 18A: Sail with Magellan in this outstanding documentary

      The host of this BBC video, modern day explorer Paul Rose, takes you on board a replica of Magellan's ship as he sails the same route Magellan took five hundred years ago. (This is part of a BBC mini-series called "Voyages of Discovery" which aired July-August 2008.) The total running time is about 50 minutes. If it is available currently on YouTube, it will be posted on YouTube.com/ TheBasementWorkshop. If it is not there, you can try to access it via Paul Rose's BBC site:

http://www.bbc.co.uk/bbcfour/documentaries/features/voyages-discovery.shtml

      (You might have to install a "plug-in" if you don't already have the necessary one installed. They give you the link and all you have to do is click on it.)

ACTIVITY IDEA 18B: Use your imagination to create visual mnemonics

      Strange shapes are hard to remember. Imagining them as something understandable, such as an animal or object, is a way to help you remember what they look like. Anything that helps you remember is a "mnemonic." (The first "m" is silent in this word.) Copy the following pattern page (showing the major Philippine islands) and tell the students to make the shapes into whatever they imagine.

ACTIVITY 18C: Review worksheet

      Copy the worksheet page and have the students fill in Arabia, India, and all of southeast Asia.

ACTIVITY IDEA 18D: More about the Spice Islands

      Magellan's crew also visited the Spice Islands, although Magellan himself never got to see them. The Basement Workhshop channel has some short videos about the Spice Islands.

ACTIVITY IDEA 18E: Read about prevailing winds

Ancient sailors knew a lot about the wind. They knew that in certain areas the wind blew in one direction most of the time. They didn't know why, but they knew it was true. These directional winds are called "prevailing winds." The European sailors of the 1500's learned to keep track of which way the winds blew at various latitudes and they used this information to plan their journeys around the world. They would "ride" a prevailing wind as long as it took them toward their goal. If they came close to the path of a new prevailing wind they could "shift over" and start "riding" this next wind. There were certain places on the globe that were trouble spots, where prevailing winds didn't line up well, such as below the southern tips of Africa and South America.

Can you identify the prevailing winds that Columbus would have use to go to the Caribbean? Was he able to follow that same route back home?

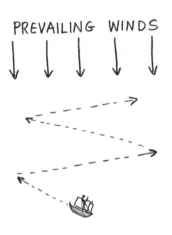

PREVAILING WINDS

Sailors knew how to adjust their sails if the wind wasn't going in quite the right direction. They could swivel them clockwise or counterclockwise to change the angle at which the wind hit the sails. If the wind was going in the opposite direction they had to use an maneuver called "tacking." Tacking involved zigzagging back and forth getting only a little bit closer to your goal each time. It took a lot longer to get where you were going if the wind wasn't at your back!

Triangular sails are better at catching the wind at angles that are less than ideal. They also perform a high-tech feat of air pressure physics by loweri g the air pressure on the far side of the sail, causing the wind to rush even faster into the sail. This makes the ship go faster. Henry the Navigator's ship builders were the first ones to begin putting triangular sails on their ships. (The Arabs had been doing this for centuries.)

The ship's keel also helps to make the ship go in the right direction. Even if the wind is pushing at an angle, the keel keeps the ship from turning, and the wind pressure ends up pushing the ship forward. Rudders were also added to the back of the ships to give even more steering control.

keel
The keel sticks down into the water.

ACTIVITY IDEA 19A: Read a letter Verrazzano wrote to King Francis I

King Francis I of France

You can read a translation of the actual letter than Verrazzano wrote to King Francis I. It's a bit long, but very easy to read and full of interesting information about the native culture that Verrazzano met.

http://bc.barnard.columbia.edu/~lgordis/earlyAC/documents/ verrazan.htm

EXTRA TIDBIT OF TRIVIA: King Francis befriended Leonardo da Vinci in the last years of the artist's life. Leonardo sold the famous Mona Lisa painting to King Francis, though many scholars think that Leonardo was reluctant to part with his masterpiece.

ACTIVITY IDEA 19B: Tourism videos about the eastern seaboard

Watch the Eastern seaboard video posted on YouTube.com/TheBasementWorkshop.

If you like horses, use key words "Wild horses of Asseteauge Island" or "Chincoteague Pony Swim" to find both articles and videos about the wild horses of the barrier islands. No one knows the exact story of how the horses got to the islands, but undoubtedly they were brought over by settlers from Europe, probably in the late 1600s.

ACTIVITY IDEA 20A: Learn about Anticosti Island

      For thousands of years, Anticosti Island belonged to the native peoples of Canada. They called it Natigostec or Notiskuan. Both the Innu and the Micmac peoples used the island as a hunting ground. When Cartier discovered the island in 1534, he named it Assumption Island. In the early 1600s, French settlers came and officially claimed the island as the property of France. The French king, Louis XIV (the famous "Sun King") decided to give the island as gift to one of his nobles, Louis Jolliet. Jolliet built a fort on the island in 1681 and lived there with his wife, four children, and six servants. In 1690, the fort was captured by the British army. Jolliet, however, remained in possession of the island until 1763 when it officially was registered as part of the British Empire. The island was bought and sold several times to various businessmen who were interested in harvesting its timber.

      In 1895, Anticosti Island was sold to a French chocolate maker named Henri Menier. He didn't make chocolate on the island, however—he brought 200 deer to the the island and used it as a personal hunting ground. He established a fish and lobster cannery at a place he called Port Menier, and built a small village for the employees to live in. When Henri Menier died in 1913, his brother took over the island and in 1926 sold it to the Wayagamack Pulp and Paper Company.

      In 1937, the German government under Adolf Hitler expressed interest in buying the island. The Canadian prime minister stepped in and forbade the sale of the island to Germany. In 1974 the government of Quebec managed to buy the island from its last private owner and today it is a national park. It has 24 rivers and streams and is a popular destination for fishermen, hikers, and bird watchers.

      Anticosti Island has a website that will give you a virtual tour, showing you all the splendor of its natural beauty. Its main river, the Jupiter River, is one of the best places in the world to catch salmon.

      http://www.anticostiphotos.com/index-en.html

ACTIVITY IDEA 21A: An artistic review game (similar to "Pictionary")

It's time to review! Here's a game that makes review not only painless, but even fun. This game requires a minimum of four players, but can accommodate as many as two dozen players (split into four or six teams).

You will need copies of the pattern pages printed onto card stock (on regular paper the answers might show through). Make a complete set of cards for each team you will have in the game. You will also need to choose whether to make it a drawing game or a sculpting game. If you choose to draw, you will need paper and pencils, and if you choose to sculpt you will need play dough or clay. Cut apart the cards and stack them so that number 1 is on top and number 36 is on the bottom. The cards start out easy and get progressively harder.

Allow at 30-40 minutes to play all 36 cards. You can play a shorter game by using less cards. You could also make the game harder by giving the players just words with no picture clues. To make it super challenging, give the players terms such as "Tropic of Cancer" or "Bay of Bengal."

IMPORTANT: PLAYERS SHOULD NOT SEE THE CARDS IN ADVANCE!!

Divide your players into small teams. A team can be as small as two players or as large as six players. For each round, one player on each team will be the "artist" and the other players will be the guessers. (Obviously, the players take turns being the artist.) The object of the game is for the artist to draw or sculpt the geographical feature on the card so that someone on his team will be able to guess what it is. The first team to guess correctly scores a point.

You will need a supervising adult to give the "Go!" signal. (The adult should also make sure that all the teams are on the same card each turn and that there is no peeking at the cards in the stack.) When given the signal, the artists draw the top card from the pile, look at it, then put it face down so that none of the other players can see it. The artists then begin to draw or sculpt what they saw on the card. As soon as a guesser on their own team guesses correctly, the artist yells "DONE!" (or whatever word you want them to say). In case of ties or very close calls, the ruling is at the discretion of the supervising adult.

If you are sculpting with dough, an extra dimension can be added to the game by taking a small amount of dough away from the losing teams at the end of each round. Use a small measuring spoon to make sure the quantity is consistent. Some teams might end up with a very small amount of dough by the end of the game. Ages 12-16+ will think this variation is fun. (They'll scream like crazy about it during the game, but afterwards they will say it was fun.) Younger kids might not be so keen on this idea.

TROUBLESHOOTING NOTE: If you run into a situation where a card accidentally gets turned over at the wrong time and other players see it (who were not supposed to see it) just have all teams discard that card and go on to the next card in the stack.

REMINDER: THE GUESSERS MUST SAY THE EXACT WORDS ON THE CARD. For example, if the card says BRITAIN, that means "England" and the "United Kingdom" aren't valid answers. If the card says IBERIAN PENINSULA, "Spain" and "Portugal" are not correct answers.

When you are finished with the last card, the team with the most points wins. (You don't need to keep score, though. Your students might care more about who wins each round than they will about the overall score. You can make it less competitive if that works better in your situation.)

1. AFRICA	2. SOUTH AMERICA	3. NEWFOUNDLAND
4. FRANCE	5. ARABIAN PENINSULA	6. BLACK SEA
6. ITALIAN PENINSULA	8. BRITAIN	9. CUBA
10. BORNEO	11. INDIA	12. CRETE

13. CELEBES	14. CASPIAN SEA	15. NEW GUINEA
Celebes Sea / Celebes		Irian Jaya / Papua New Guinea
16. HISPANIOLA	**17. NILE RIVER**	**18. THE SPICE ISLANDS** (or "Maluku Islands")
		Ternate and Tidore
19. MALAY PENINSULA	**20. BAJA CALIFORNIA**	**21. THE PHILIPPINES**
Mekong River / Hainan / South C. / Malay / Sum	Colorado River / Rio Grande River / Tropic of Cancer	
22. THE GULF OF MEXICO	**23. JAMAICA**	**24. MADAGASCAR**
New Orleans / Corpus Christi / Gulf of Mexico / Bahamas / Cuba / Kingston / Yucatan Peninsula / Caribb		Tunis / Madagascar

25. THE LESSER ANTILLES	26. DELMARVA PENINSULA	27. INDOCHINA PENINSULA
28. GREATER ANTILLES	29. SICILY	30. SRI LANKA
31. IBERIAN PENINSULA	32. NOVA SCOTIA	33. STRAIT OF GIBRALTAR
34. ANDES MOUNTAINS	35. PELOPONNESIAN PENINSULA	36. STRAIT OF MAGELLAN

ACTIVITY IDEA 22A: Visit the Svalbard Islands

What do the islands near the North Pole look like? Surprisingly, they are not covered with snow all year. You can take a virtual visit to the Svalbard Islands via the Basement Workshop You-Tube channel. Almost 3000 people live in capital "city" of Longyearbyen. (It's the northernmost town in the world.) This archipelago officially belongs to Norway, but the population of Svalbard is very inter-national, with folks from as far away as Thailand and Iran. You'll love the stuffed polar bear sitting in the middle of the baggage claim area at their airport.

ACTIVITY IDEA 23A: A supplemental map to use for the drawing lessons

Here is a map you might find helpful for drawing lesssons 23A and 23B. First, fill in France and Britain. Notice that not all of the guidelines have been provided for Britain—the students will need to add some of the guides themselves. Then add the Low Countries and Ireland (using the instructions in the drawing lessons.)

ACTIVITY IDEA 23B: "Unfolding the Earth" video

This short animation (just a few minutes) shows a virtual globe being opened up and flattened in numerous ways. It's not just cut into familiar geometric forms—it's also cut into strange patterns, some of which get as thin as ribbons. It's very interesting and worth watching several times in a row! Check it out on the Basement Workshop YouTube channel.

ACTIVITY IDEA 23C: See how globes are made (a virtual factory tour)

A factory tour of the Replogle Globes factory is posted on the YouTube channel.

ACTIVITY IDEA 23D: Learn more about map projections

Other videos about map projections will be posted on the YouTube channel. (The selection of videos may vary from time to time according to their current availability.)

DRAWING 23A:
REVIEW, then add the
"LOW COUNTRIES"

ACTIVITY IDEA 23E: A globe-tossing game

Here is an interesting game (or rather, a mathematical experiment) you can do with a globe that you don't mind being tossed about. (Inflatables are great for this!) If you have a group, have the students stand in a circle. (For one student, just toss the globe up as high as you can and try to make it spin when you toss it.) Take turns tossing the globe to each other. When someone catches it, they call out whether their right thumb landed on water or land. Keep a tally of how many "waters" and how many "lands" you get. After 100 tosses, check the tally. It should be something like 75 "waters" and 25 "lands." This shows that 75 percent of the globe is water, and 25 percent is land. If you get numbers far different from these, think about how to make sure the globe is being randomly thrown and caught. If it is truly random, you should get something close to 75/25 (could vary from 70/30 to 80/20).

ACTIVITY IDEA 23F: Europe worksheet

It's time to try to draw all of Europe. A few extra islands have been added, but otherwise, the students should know how to fill in the whole map. Make copies of the worksheet on the following page and allow at least 20 minutes for them to fill it in. Encourage them to label everything they can.

WORKSHEET FOR LESSON 23

Faroe Islands
Shetland Islands
Orkney Islands
Madeira Island

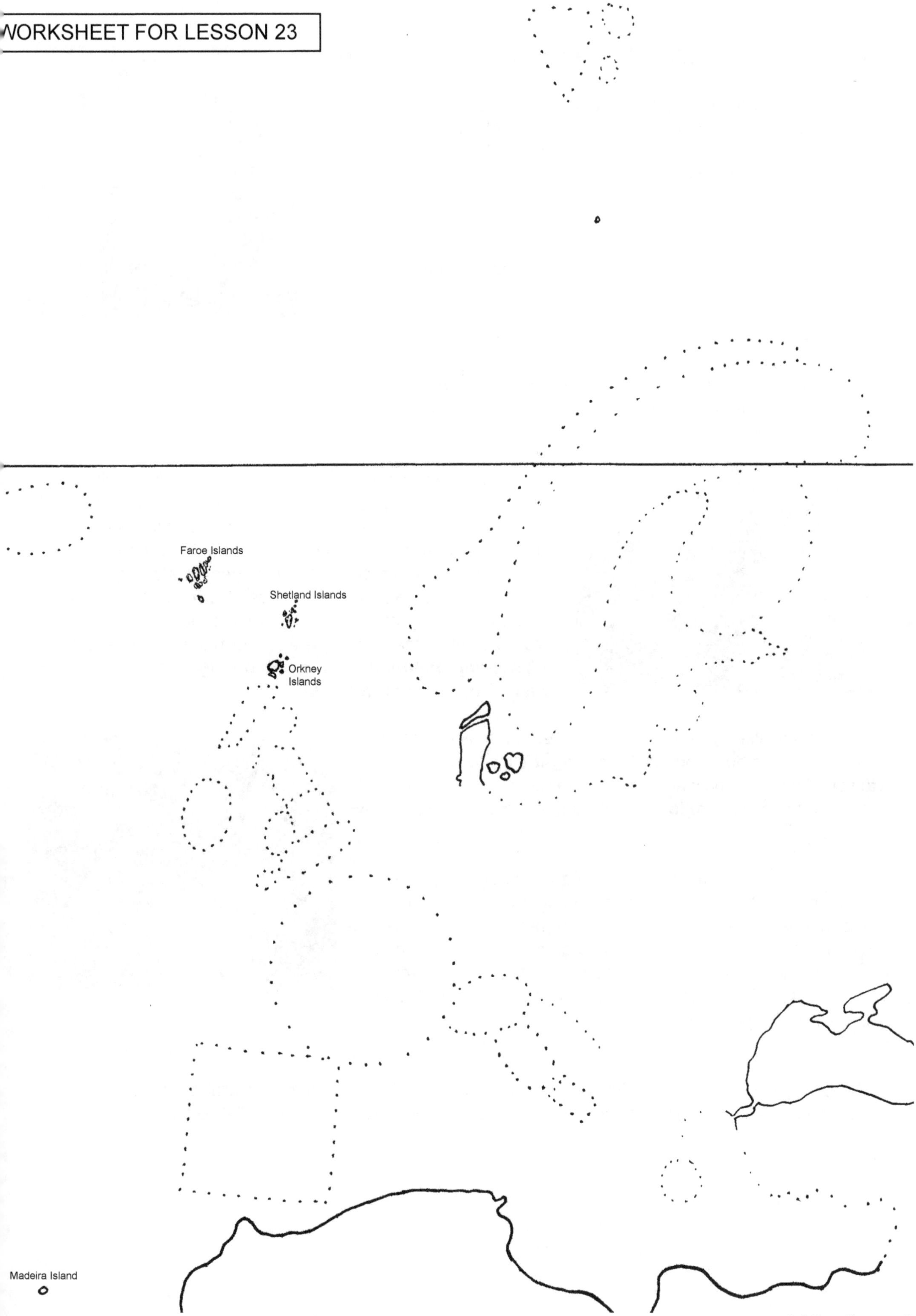

ACTIVITY IDEA 23F: Make an octahedral globe

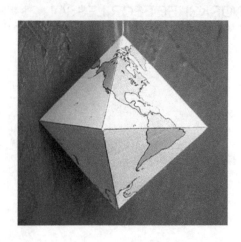

A three-dimensional map of the world doesn't necessarily have to be round. A sphere is the most perfect representation of the Earth, but a three-dimensional shape with flat sides is more accurate than a flat map. In this activity you can make an 8-sided globe.

You will need:
- Copies of the following pattern pages (print the cards onto heavy card stock, if possible)
- Scissors
- White glue (regular, not "school" glue)
- Ruler
- Compass (use the point for scoring the folds)
- Thin string or heavy thread, if you want to make a hanger

Cut out the octahedron. Score all the fold lines by putting the ruler right along the edge and gently running the point of the compass (or the edge of a scissor) along the line. The idea is to scratch the line without cutting through the paper. You might want to practice scoring lines on a piece of scrap paper before doing your good ones. If you are tempted to skip this scoring step, try a fold with scoring and one without. You will notice that scoring is well worth the time it takes! *(A scoring demonstration and a gluing demonstration are included on the third DVD.)*

If you want to add a string hanger, cut a piece of thin string and glue both ends of it to the ***inside*** of the globe before assembling it. If you want the globe to hang with Antarctica at the bottom, make sure to put the string in the corner right above Greenland.

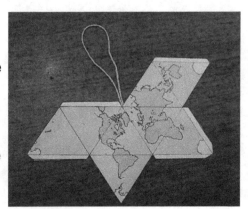

It doesn't matter which glue flap you begin with. Just do them one at a time, pressing and holding each joint for at least 10 seconds before you move on to the next. (If possible, let the joint rest for a mintue before moving on the next one.) Don't use too much glue. Use just enough glue to put a very thin film across the surface of the flap. The whole project should take only a few drops of glue.

NOTE: If you don't have a digital copy of this curriculum, the pattern for this project can be downloaded at www.ellenjmchenry.com. (FREE DOWNLOADS, GEOGRAPHY & MAPS)

This pattern is for you to color. You can make it traditional—blue for water, green or tan for land—or you can use your own coloring scheme. (If you have a very fine ballpoint pen, you might even be able to add rivers and mountains.)

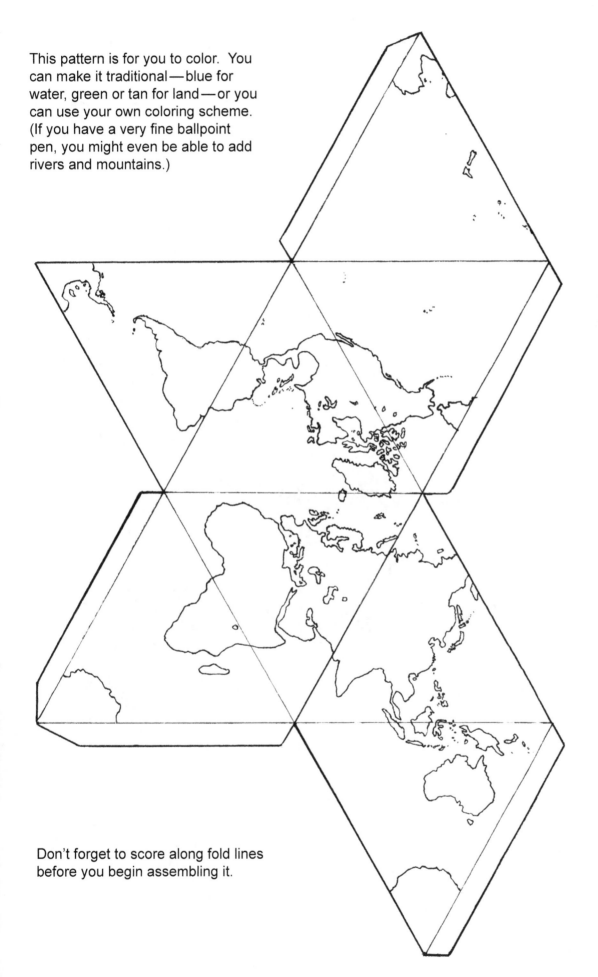

Don't forget to score along fold lines before you begin assembling it.

FOR BEST RESULTS, PRINT THIS PAGE ONTO CARD STOCK.

You can fill in the continents with
appropriate colors (green for lush
areas, tan for deserts, white for snow),
or you can use your own coloring
scheme. You can also leave it blue
and white, if you wish.

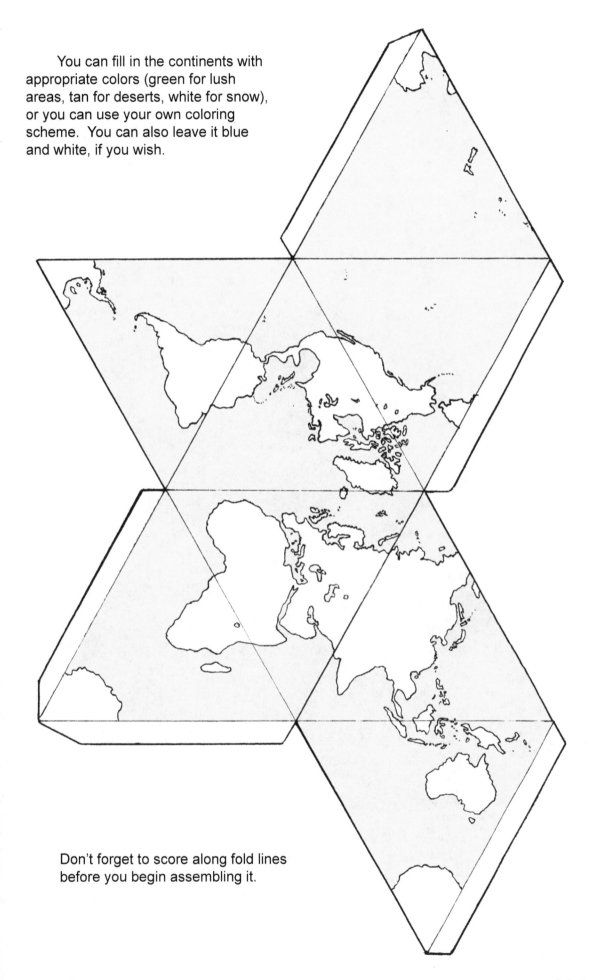

Don't forget to score along fold lines
before you begin assembling it.

Even though this pattern already
has a lot of color on it, you can still
add your own artistic touches, if
you want to.

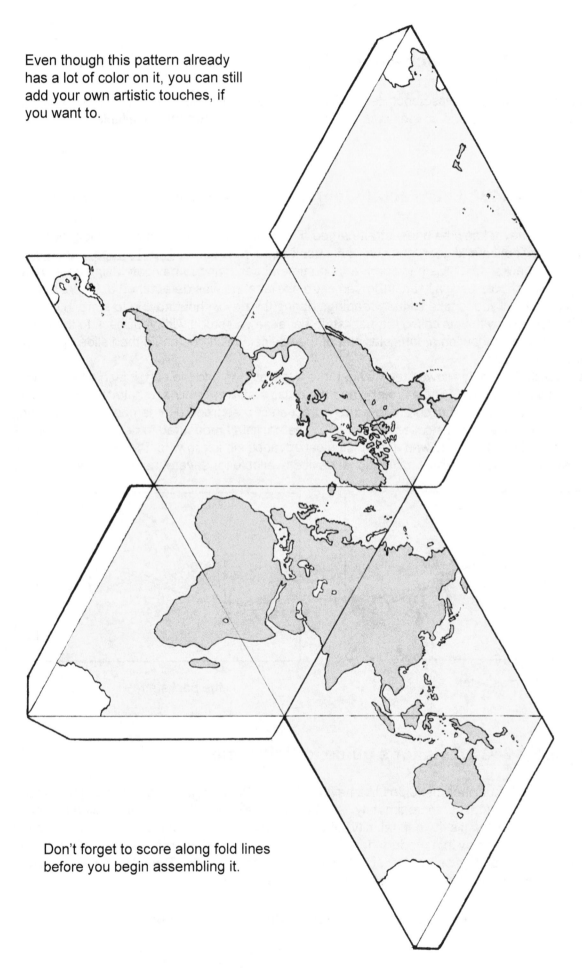

Don't forget to score along fold lines
before you begin assembling it.

ACTIVITY IDEA 24A: Watch a brief video clip about Henry Hudson

There are a few video clips about Henry Hudson posted on the Basement Workshop channel. These types of videos come and go, so whatever is posted is what is currently available.

ACTIVITY IDEA 24B: Learn about John Davis' invention: the backstaff

John Davis never knew he had a strait named after him. As far as Davis knew, his great contributions to navigation and geography were his book about navigation, <u>The Seaman's Secrets</u>, and his invention: the backstaff. Davis had spent enough time at sea trying to navigate using an astrolabe or a cross-staff (which was basically an improved astrolabe) that he was determined to invent a new device that would allow you to take latitude readings during the day without having to stare into the sun. What he came up with was called the backstaff, because you stood with your back to the sun. The sun would cast a shadow on a particular part of the device, which you could then slide up or down to line up with the horizon.

The backstaff not only allowed the navigator to avoid staring into the sun, it also allowed him to get more accurate readings. The astrolabe and the cross-staff were only accurate to within one degree. The backstaff could be accurate to within a fraction of a degree. (Remember, a degree can broken down into 60 smaller units called "minutes.") The backstaff measured in degrees and mintues, not just degrees. At that time, this was a technological advance similar to what the GPS has been to us. The backstaff remained the best navigational device available for several hundred years.

the cross-staff

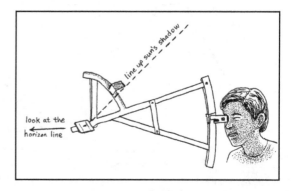

the backstaff

ACTIVITY IDEA 24C: A visitor's guide to Baffin Island

The Inuits that Frobisher met didn't like having visitors. But nowadays, the Inuits of that area are thrilled to have visitors! The approximately 1,000 people that live in the town of Iqaluit have made their town into a tourist site. It's the capital "city" of the Canadian province of Nunavut. In the heart of the Arctic tundra, you can stay in a modern hotel that has cable TV and Internet, eat at restaurants, buy souvenirs at gift shops, and go on nature tours led by professional guides. The web address below lets you download Iqualuit's offical visitors' guide. What a unique vacation!

http://www.city.iqaluit.nu.ca/i18n/english/pdf/iqaluit_visitors2009.pdf

ACTIVITY 25A: Paint a physical map of Japan

In this activity, you will use the same painting technique as in activity 11E. Crayons will be used to cover the surface of the land. The wax will resist the blue watercolor paint when you paint the oceans and seas.

You will need:
- a copy of the following pattern page printed onto heavy card stock paper (smooth water color paper is even better)
- your waterproof black pen (and a blue waterproof pen if you have one)
- crayons in these colors: white, tan, light green, dark green, light blue
- blue watercolor paint
- a large brush (1" is good)
- paper towel (can substitute facial tissue)
- a map of Japan (for an online map: www.freeworldmaps.net/asia/japan/japan.jpg)

Label your map before you start coloring, using your black waterproof pen.   Label the four islands (Honshu, Hokkaido, Skikoku and Kyushu), the bodies of water (Pacific Ocean, Sea of Japan, Philippine Sea), the other countries (Korea, China, Russia), the major cities shown as dots (Tokyo, Kyoto, Osaka, Nagasaki, Hiroshima), and Mt. Fuji. Of course, you are welcome to do as much additional labeling as you want to. (*NOTE: The Koreans prefer "East Sea" to "Sea of Japan."*)

If you have a blue waterproof pen, use it to draw rivers. You could also use a blue colored pencil or a sharpened blue crayon. Rivers always come out of mountains and flow to coasts. If you want to be exact about your rivers, consult an atlas to see where they are. Color the little lakes blue.

Instead of making upside down V's for mountains, we will be indicating altitude by using various colors. White is usually used for very high mountains, tan for medium height mountains, light green for low mountains, and darker green for sea level areas. The dotted lines on this map show you where the highest mountains are. The area inside the dotted lines should be colored white. (If you want to be artistic, you could add some tan lines here and there for crinkly texture.) Just outside the dotted lines should be a ring of tan. Outside the tan will be light green, then darker green along the coasts. NOTE: Make sure you cover all of the land areas with crayon of some color. Any place that is not covered with crayon might soak up blue paint. Go over the areas several times to make sure they are covered.

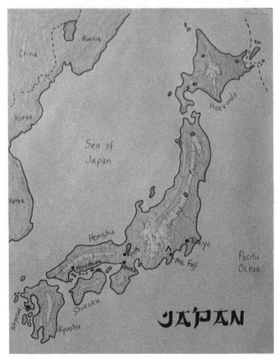

After you have finished with the crayons, mix some fairly watery blue paint. Test it on a scrap of paper before applying it to your map. The blue should be fairly transparent and should not obscure any of the labels. If you want to show approximate depth of the water, make the areas along the coastlines lighter. Shallow water is indicated by white or light blue and deeper water is dark blue. The northern part of the Sea of Japan is deeper than the southern part. To the east of Honshu there is a very deep trench.

As you apply the paint, you don't need to worry too much about getting it on the land areas, because they should resist the paint. Any paint that looks like it is going to settle on the land can be easily removed while wet by blotting it with a paper towel or facial tissue. Allow the map to dry flat. If the map is excessively wrinkled after it is dry, you can flatten it a little bit by putting several paper towels on top and pressing it with a warm iron.

JAPAN

ACTIVITY IDEA 25B: A virtual visit to Hokkaido

You may know quite a bit about Japan in general. But what about that northern island of Hokkaido? What is the weather like? Who lives there? Find out by watching the Hokkaido videos on the Basement Workshop channel.

ACTIVITY IDEA 26A: Read about a few mapmakers' art techniques

Mapmakers like Blaeu had to be artists, not just cartographers. They needed to be experts on working with paints, inks and gold leaf.

Eggs were an important ingredient for several processes. The white of the egg could be used for making colors stick to the paper, and also for making this surface shiny when finished (like a varnish). Sometimes they would add vinegar to the egg white to make it "keep" longer. The yolk could be used when you wanted to have white lettering on a black background. The artist would paint the letters in egg yolk, using a very fine brush. When the yolk letters were dry, black ink would then be rubbed right over the letters. When the ink was dry, the egg yolk would then be gently rubbed off the paper, exposing the white paper underneath.

Two popular types of black color that were used on maps. One was called "fume" black and was obtained by letting a candle burn underneath a metal pot. The candle flame would make a big black spot on the bottom of the pot. This black char would then be scraped off and mixed with a little egg white. The other black pigment was called black velvet and was obtained by burning the antler of a deer until it turned to a black powder. Once again, egg white was then added to the powder to make a paint that could be brushed onto the paper.

Real gold was often applied to maps as a final touch. Gold is a very soft metal and can be pounded into very thin sheets—thinner than a piece of paper. To get the thin layer of gold to stick to the paper, the artist would apply (believe it or not) a layer of garlic juice. The thin gold leaf would be gently laid on top of the garlic juice and allowed to dry. When dry, the paper was then buffed with a cloth and any extra gold would be rubbed off. Only the area where the garlic juice had been painted would have gold stuck to it.

Mapmakers had to be very particular about the quality of the paper itself. They knew that if the paper was not of the highest quality, the map would fall apart in a few decades. To their credit, most of their maps are still in amazingly good shape after hundreds of years. (Of course, once they made it to the 20th century, there was extra special care available, such as cases that control the temperature and humidity.)

ACTIVITY IDEA 26B: A review worksheet for all of southeast Asia

Copy the worksheet on the following page, This is the same worksheet that appeared in activity 18C, only this time Japan and Australia must be filled in, as well as Arabia, India, China, Indochina, and the Malay archipelago.

ACTIVITY IDEA 26C: A video about fine map making in the 17th century

Check the YouTube channel for a BBC film about beautiful maps.

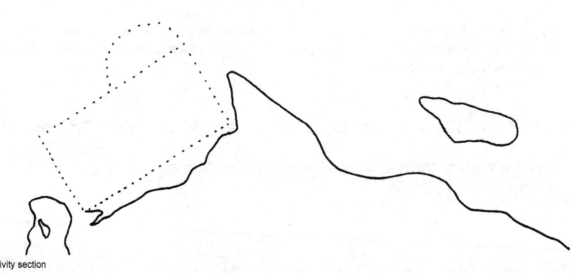

ACTIVITY IDEA 26D: Make your own antique map

You will need a copy of the pattern sheet on the next page (with the rectangular border around it). If you copy it onto calligraphy parchment paper, your antique map will look very authentic. You will also need a pencil, an eraser, your compass, a good quality fine-line waterproof pen, a few colored pencils (for the compass rose), watercolor paints in at least two colors, and a very small watercolor brush (1/8" diameter or less).

NOTE: You can use either watercolor paints that comes in tubes, or the kind that comes in little dry circles in a long tray (pan paints). For tube paints, you will only need a dab about the size of a very small pea. *(There is a demonstration on DVD 3 showing how to shade with paint .)*

1) Use your pencil to LIGHTLY sketch the guideline shapes for Australia. (Keep those lines very light!!) Your map does not have to look identical to the one shown above. You may choose to show Australia larger and omit the islands of Indonesia, New Zealand and Caledonia. It's up to you. You might also want to put New Zealand just a little bit closer to Australia. Remember, this is an antique map and those early mapmakers didn't get all the proportions right. They were not able to accurately measure longitude, so they really didn't know exact distances east to west.

2) LIGHTLY sketch in where New Zealand will go, how much of New Guinea will show on the top, and where any other islands go (if you have space for them).

3) Use the ink pen to draw all the outlines. Use the reference map to see the in's and out's of the coastline and where to add rivers and mountains. Be especially attentive to rivers along the coastlines. These were very important to early explorers because they provided an easy way to get into the interior of the continent. The sketch to the right shows how mapmakers of the 1600s shaded the sides of their mountain symbols to make them look 3D.

4) Label everything you want to label. If you want to add more features to your map, consult an atlas.

5) Make sure the ink from the pen is dry, then erase all the pencil lines.

6) Watch the "how to" video file on the DVD to see how to apply the watercolor paint. (If you can't access the file for some reason, just experiment on a piece of scrap paper first and learn how to control the paint so that you don't get either huge watery blobs or thin dark lines. Look at the sample above and try to make yours similar.)

7) Use a black or brown paint to go around the outside edges of the landmasses.

8) Choose a color to tint the inner edges of the landmasses. The most common colors used by the mapmakers of the 1600s were yellow, pink, orange and green. Keep the colors light so you can see all the ink lines underneath.

9) Add a compass rose in any of the blank areas and color it with colored pencils. Also use one of your colored pencils (black or brown is best, but any color will do) to fill in every other rectangle in the border going around the edge.

10) Add any embellishments you like, such as pictures of sailing ships, whales, sharks, sea monsters, etc. Perhaps you can use actual animals from the appropriate areas of land and sea. Sketch them lightly in pencil first, then go over them in pen. (Then erase the pencil lines.)

Optional step #1: If you want to make your map look like a portolan map, use a very sharp pencil to add lines radiating out from the compass rose, and possibly one or two other points.

Optional step #2: You might want to add a scale. This is a line that tells approximate mileage on your map. Australia is about 2400 miles across. If you mark on a piece of paper how wide your Australia drawing is, then fold that measured part of the paper in half, and in half again, you will get a 600 mile section. Make a little strip on the bottom of the map that shows that distance of 600 miles. (You can mark off 100 mile sections on that strip, if you want to be more accurate.)

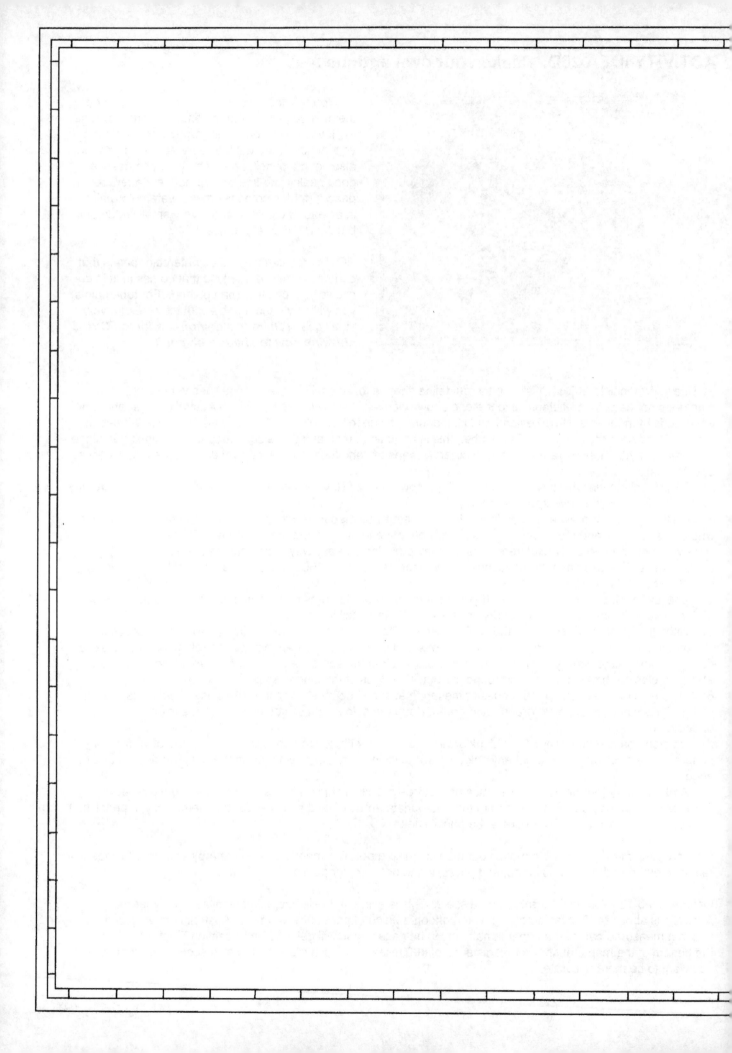

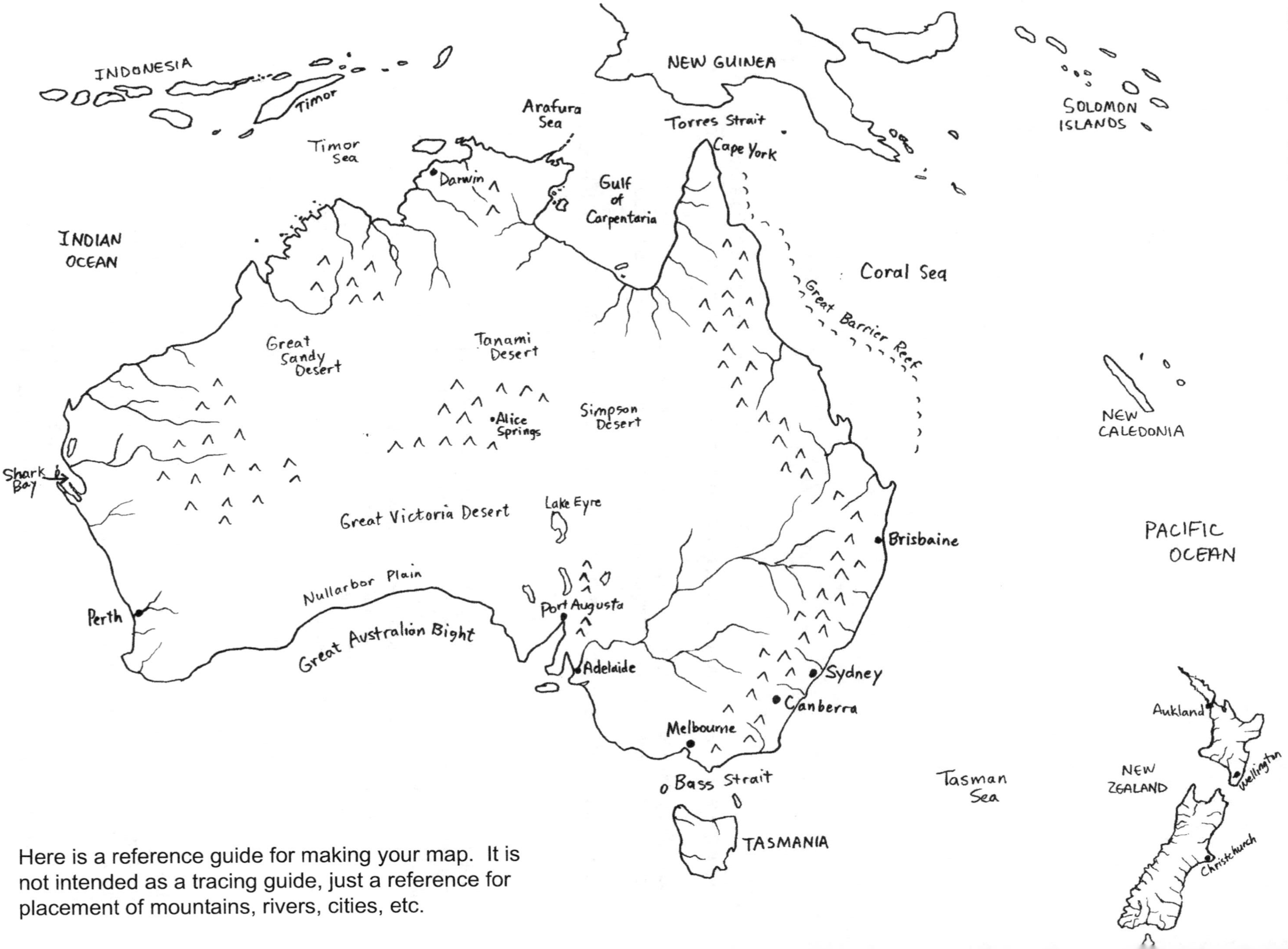

Here is a reference guide for making your map. It is not intended as a tracing guide, just a reference for placement of mountains, rivers, cities, etc.

INDIAN
OCEAN

INDONESIA

Timor
Timor
Sea

Arafura
Sea

NEW GUINEA

Shark
Bay

Perth

Great Sandy Desert

Darwin

Gulf
of
Carpentaria

Torres Strait

Cape York

Great Australian Bight

Nullarbor Plain

Great Victoria Desert

Tanami
Desert

Alice
Springs

Simpson
Desert

Lake Eyre

Port Augusta

Adelaide

SOLOMON
ISLANDS

Great Barrier Reef

Coral Sea

Melbourne

0 Bass Strait

Canberra

Sydney

Brisbaine

TASMANIA

Tasman
Sea

NEW
CALEDONIA

PACIFIC
OCEAN

NEW
ZEALAND

Aukland

Christchurch

Wellington

ACTIVITY IDEA 27A: A documentary about a proposed bridge across the Bering Strait

Is it possible to build a bridge across the Bering Strait? The strait is 55 miles wide and is filled with ice a good portion of the year. Believe it or not, an experienced bridge engineer spent 30 years drawing up plans for a bridge he believes would be able to withstand the harsh Arctic winter. The first part of this video series is uploaded to the Basement Workshop channel.

ACTIVITY IDEA 27B: A review worksheet of the western hemisphere

Try the review worksheet on the following page. You will notice that North America bends up and to the left quite a bit, leaving Alaska pointing up instead of out. Not worry, though—as long as those guidelines are there, you can draw the shapes around them. You will also notice that the Tropic of Capricorn line doesn't go all the way across. This is because it was not an essential part of the South America drawing. The equator is helpful because that's where the Amazon River delta is. But the Tropic of Capricorn line makes the rectangle look too cluttered and might make the drawing more difficult to do. If the students want to extend the Tropic line to go through South America, they are welcome to do so.

ACTIVITY IDEA 27C: Western hemisphere extreme challenge worksheet

Try the second, more difficult, version of the western hemisphere review worksheet. It has only the Tropic of Cancer, the Caribbean circle, the Alaskan square, the Newfoundland triangle and the South American rectangle.

For a super extreme challenge, try a drawing the western hemisphere a third time—but this time on a completely blank piece of paper.

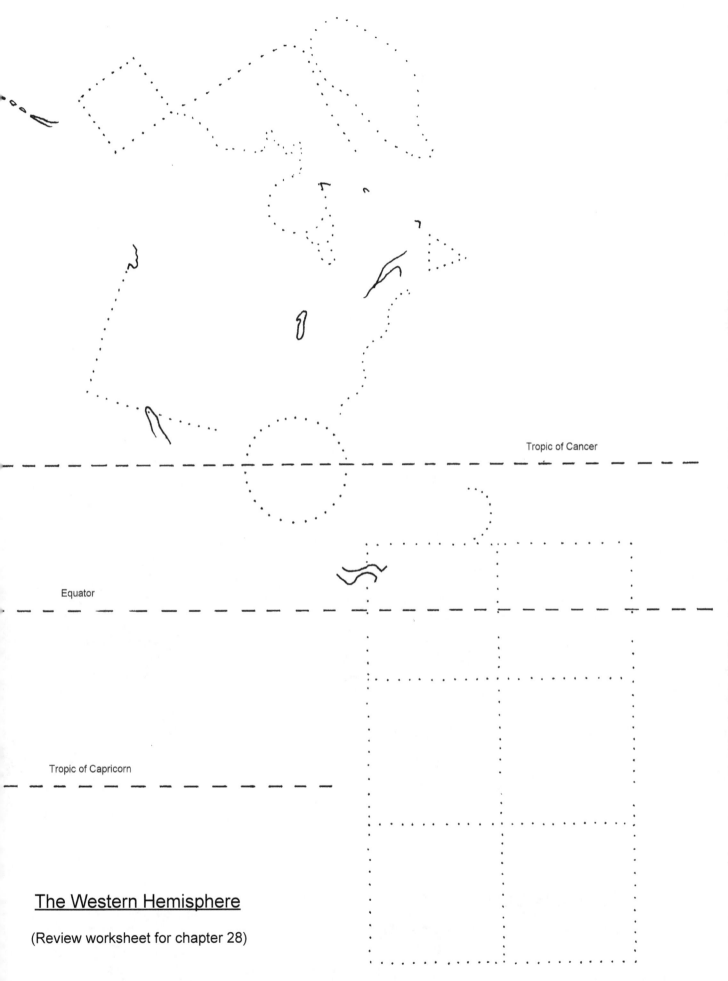

Tropic of Cancer

Equator

Tropic of Capricorn

The Western Hemisphere

(Review worksheet for chapter 28)

The Western Hemisphere

(A more challenging worksheet for chapter 28)

ACTIVITY IDEA 28A: A video about longitude

Enjoy a movie (on the Basement Workshop channel) about the discovery of longitude, based on the non-fiction novel, Longitude, by acclaimed author Dava Sobel. (If this video disappears from YouTube we'll try to replace it with something similar.)

ACTIVITY 28B: Watch a video of H1 in motion

Videos of H1come and go. Whatever is available currently will be posted on the Basement Workshop channel.

ACTIVITY IDEA 28C: Watch an animation of a "grasshopper escapement"

This web address will take you to an animation showing how Harrison's grasshopper escapement works. (It's mesmerizing—or perhaps soothing—to watch!) You can also get to this address by looking up John Harrison on Wikipedia. It's imbedded in the article.

http://en.wikipedia.org/wiki/File:Grasshopper-escapement-005.gif

ACTIVITY IDEA 28D: Photoshop™ yourself onto the Prime Meridian

If you have Photoshop™ capabilities, you can make yourself a souvenir photo of the Prime Meridian without even going there! You can download a picture of this sculpture by either searching for it yourself using Google images, or by downloading our picture (a photo of just the sculpture with no one in front of it), posted at www.ellenjmchenry.com (FREE DOWNLOADS, GEOGRAPHY & MAPS).   Take a picture of yourself against a solid color background, then use Photoshop™ to replace the solid background with the Meridian photo.

This sculpture sitting on the Prime Meridian doesn't serve any practical purpose in determining longitude, although it does point to the North Star. It's mostly to make the tourists' photos look more interesting. The sculpture is called "The Gyroscope " and was made in 1999.

ACTIVITY IDEA 28E: Review worksheets

The following pages have patterns for review worksheets. The second version is more difficult, giving only pinpoints for the corners of the triangles and squares. Take special note of the addition of the two large lakes of Asia: Lake Balkash and Lake Baykal. Lake Balkash is just to the right of the Aral Sea and Lake Baykal is up from the China circle and to the left of Sakhalin Island, the top of the lake being approximately even with the bottom of the Kamchatka squares, although in reality it does go a little higher. The top of Lake Baykal is at the same latitude as the middle "point" of the Kamchatka peninsula.

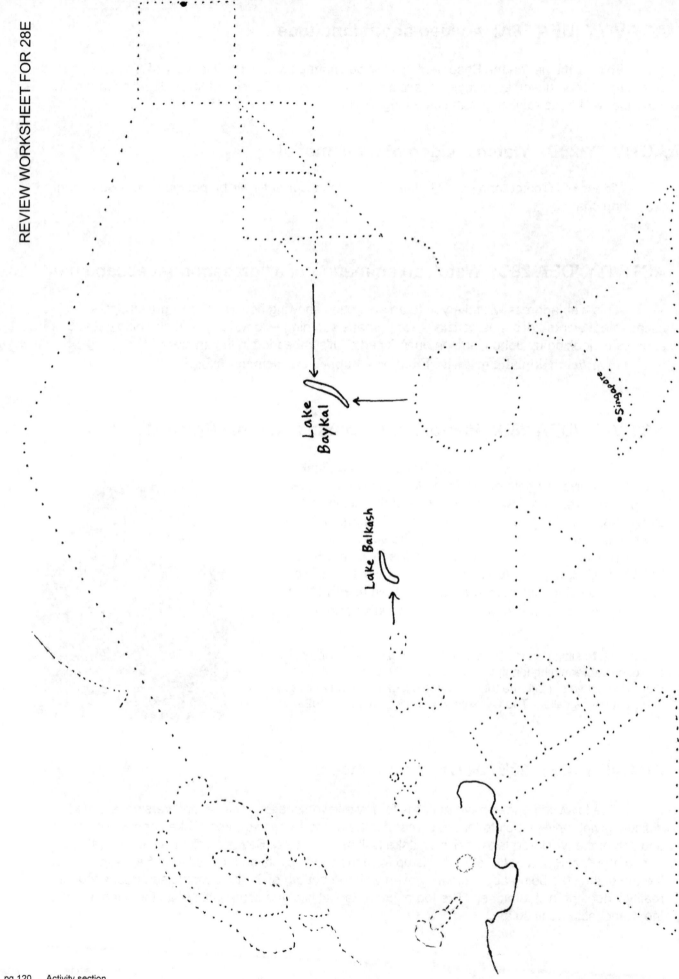

Lake Baykal

Lake Balkash

Singapore

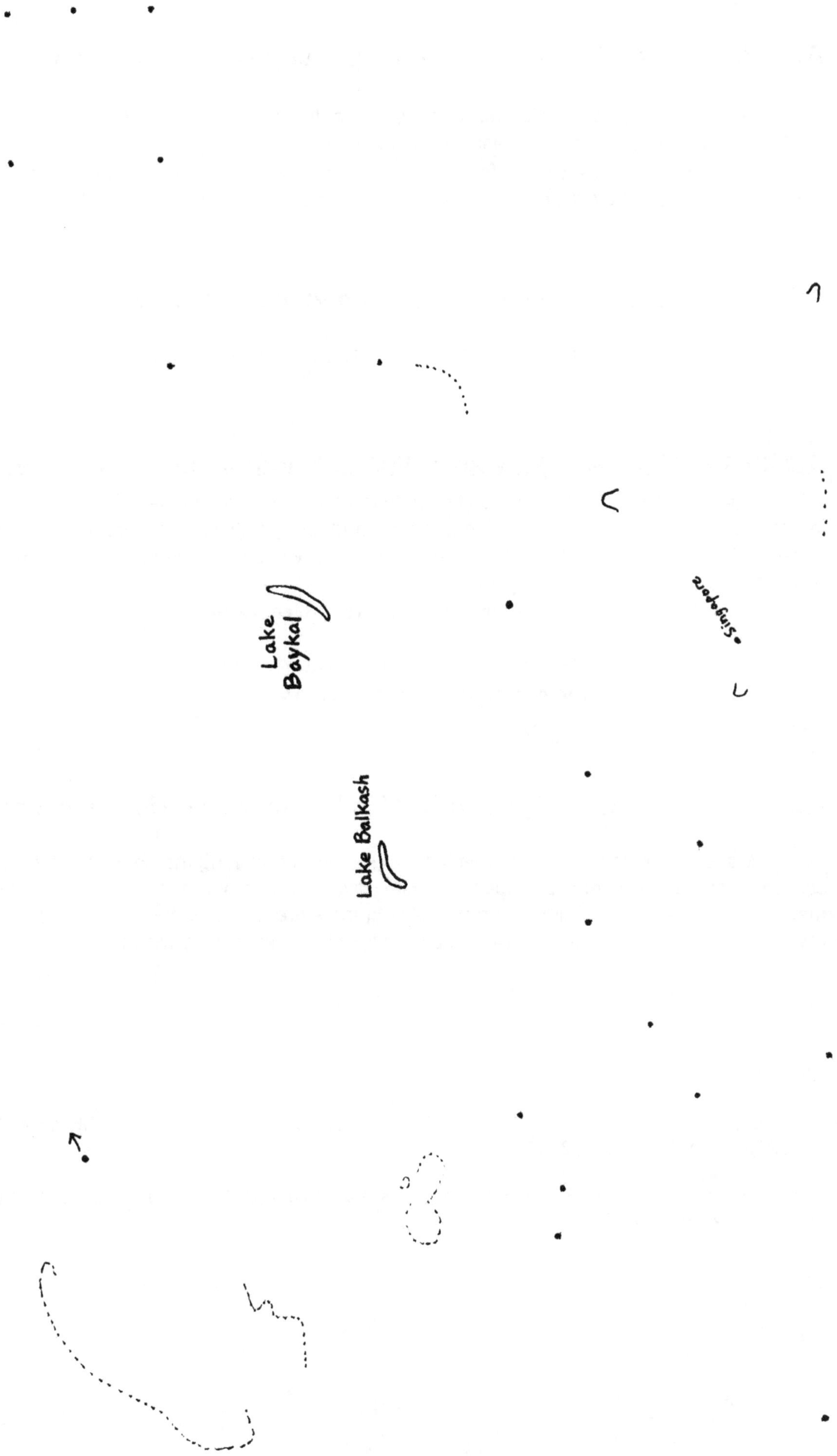

Lake Baykal

Lake Balkash

Singapore

ACTIVITY IDEA 29A: Watch a documentary on James Cook

A documentary about Captain Cook is available on Paul Rose's website. (He's the one that did the Magellan video.) You can access it by going to:

http://www.bbc.co.uk/bbcfour/documentaries/features/voyages-discovery.shtml

If this video is available currently on YouTube, we'll post it on the Basement Workshop channel.

ACTIVITY IDEA 29B: Watch a tourism video about Vanuatu

Take a very brief virtual vacation to Vanuatu via the Basement Workshop channel.

ACTIVITY IDEA 29C: Play an online quiz game about Pacific islands

The islands of the Pacific aren't easy to learn. Here is a site that offers a tutorial and two levels of quizzing to help you learn the Pacific island groups. (They are grouped according to political divisions.) This address will take you to a page with multiple quiz options. To quiz on island locations, use the buttons under the country flag.

http://www.sheppardsoftware.com/Oceania_Geography.htm

Another site that offers a very straightforward quiz game is:

http://www.lizardpoint.com/fun/geoquiz/oceania_quiz.html

ACTIVITY IDEA 29D: Captain Cook's Island Match Up Challenge

Make copies of the following pages and have fun matching the shapes to the names. If the students need a review of the shapes, let them have a certain number of minutes to study a world map. You can set the time limit appropriately. (If the extreme challenge is too difficult to do from memory, you could allow the students to consult a map while they are working.)

ANSWER KEY:

First challenge: 1)S, 2)R, 3)I, 4)D, 5)O, 6)V, 7)B, 8)F, 9)K, 10)U, 11)C, 12)J, 13)Z, 14)E, 15)A, 16)T, 17)L, 18)G, 19)P, 20)H, 21)Y, 22)X, 23)N, 24)M, 25)W, 26)Q

Second challenge: 1)F, 2)D, 3)N, 4)U, 5)O, 6)V, 7)R, 8)A, 9)L, 10)B, 11)G, 12)P, 13)J, 14)Q, 15)I, 16)M, 17)S, 18)K, 19)C, 20)H, 21)T, 22)E

CAPTAIN COOK'S ISLAND MATCH-UP CHALLENGE

They put me on this stamp because I've been to an awful lot of islands! How many of these islands can you recognize?

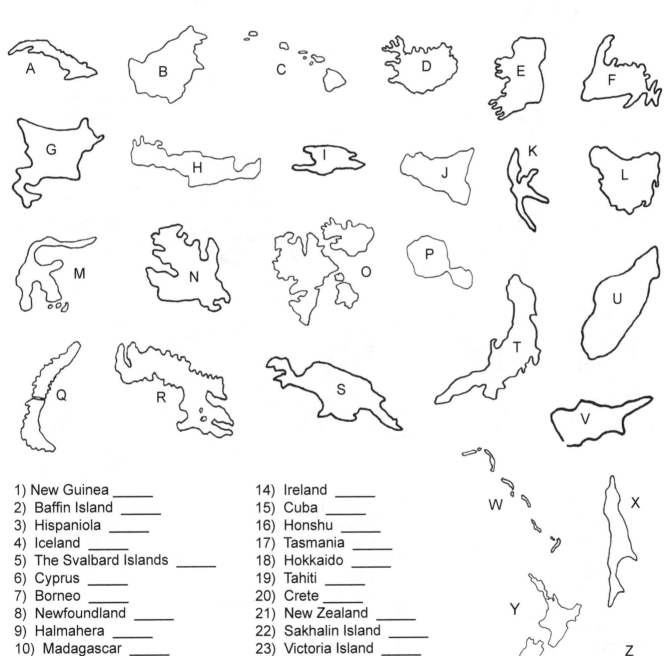

1) New Guinea _____
2) Baffin Island _____
3) Hispaniola _____
4) Iceland _____
5) The Svalbard Islands _____
6) Cyprus _____
7) Borneo _____
8) Newfoundland _____
9) Halmahera _____
10) Madagascar _____
11) Hawaii _____
12) Sicily _____
13) Cape Breton _____
14) Ireland _____
15) Cuba _____
16) Honshu _____
17) Tasmania _____
18) Hokkaido _____
19) Tahiti _____
20) Crete _____
21) New Zealand _____
22) Sakhalin Island _____
23) Victoria Island _____
24) Celebes _____
25) The Bahamas _____
26) Novaya Zemlya _____

CAPTAIN COOK'S ISLAND MATCH-UP - - EXTREME CHALLENGE!
Try these more difficult matches!

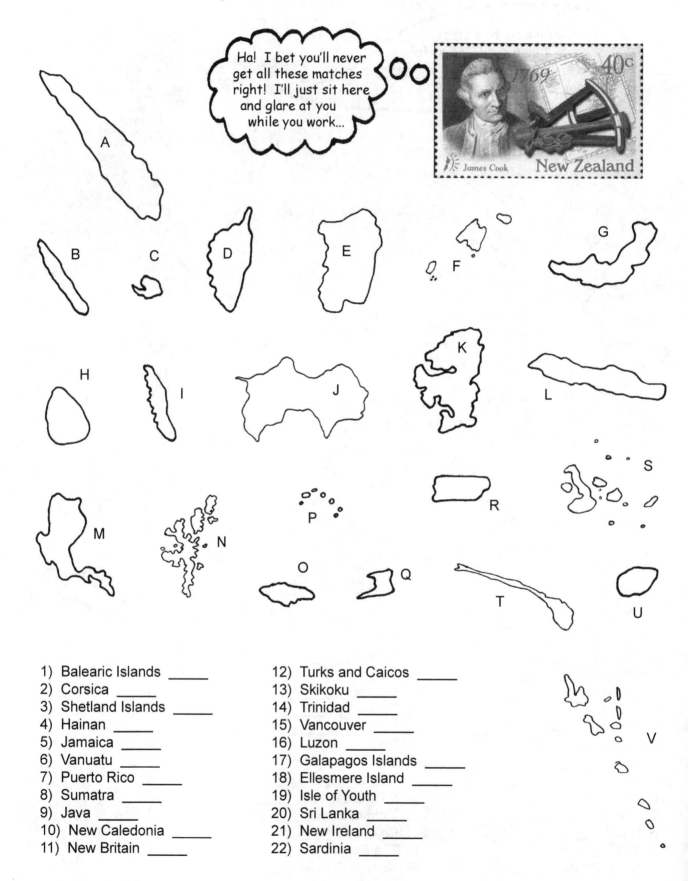

1) Balearic Islands _____
2) Corsica _____
3) Shetland Islands _____
4) Hainan _____
5) Jamaica _____
6) Vanuatu _____
7) Puerto Rico _____
8) Sumatra _____
9) Java _____
10) New Caledonia _____
11) New Britain _____

12) Turks and Caicos _____
13) Skikoku _____
14) Trinidad _____
15) Vancouver _____
16) Luzon _____
17) Galapagos Islands _____
18) Ellesmere Island _____
19) Isle of Youth _____
20) Sri Lanka _____
21) New Ireland _____
22) Sardinia _____

ANSWER KEY TO CAPTAIN COOK'S CHALLENGES:

First challenge: 1)S, 2)R, 3)I, 4)D, 5)O, 6)V, 7)B, 8)F, 9)K, 10)U, 11)C, 12)J, 13)Z, 14)E, 15)A, 16)T, 17)L, 18)G 19)P, 20)H, 21)Y, 22)X, 23)N, 24)M, 25)W, 26)Q

Second challenge: 1)F, 2)D, 3)N, 4)U, 5)O, 6)V, 7)R, 8)A, 9)L, 10)B, 11)G, 12)P, 13)J, 14)Q, 15)I, 16)M, 17)S, 18)K, 19)C, 20)H, 21)T, 22)E

ACTIVITY IDEA 30A: Download a game about Antarctica

You can download all the patterns and instructions for a game called "Science in Antarctica" on the author's personal website: ellenjmchenry.com. Click on "Free products to download," then click on "Geography/Maps."

The board for this game is a map of Antarctica, and the players are given task cards to complete. The tasks are real jobs done by various types of scientists who do research in Antarctica: biologists, zoologists, meteorologists, and astronomers. There are quiz cards about famous explorers that can be used to get extra help in gaining the right kind of transportation: snowmobiles, boats, airplanes and helicopters.

ACTIVITY IDEA 30B: Play a review game: "Where Am I?"

The questions are on the next two pages. These questions can be read aloud as part of a group guessing game, or they can be used as an individual activity (like a quiz).

Answers:

1) Jamaica
2) Lisbon
3) the Canary Islands
4) Honshu
5) the Dead Sea
6) Italy
7) Aswan, Egypt
8) Babylon
9) Corinth
10) Sweden
11) Aegean Sea
12) India, Ganges River, Calcutta
13) Bona Vista, Newfoundland
14) Mozambique Channel
15) Kamchatka
16) Philippines
17) Lake Victoria
18) Aral Sea
19) Buenos Aires, Argentina
20) Istanbul, Turkey
21) Baja California
22) Ellesmere Island
23) Solomon Islands
24) Cape Breton Island
25) Amazon River basin
26) Tangier, Morocco
27) Hawaii
28) Iceland
29) Halmahera (the correct name for the largest of the Spice Islands)
30) Greenland

ACTIVITY IDEA 30C: Do quiz 3A again: "Above or below the equator?"

If you did this activity in chapter 3, go back and do it again. The first time around, the students probably found it fairly difficult. Now, they will probably find it very easy. They will be amazed at how their knowledge of world geography has grown since they started this course.

Where Am I?

1) I am on an island. This island has two islands nearby: one to the north and one to the east. If you use your imagination while looking at a map, those two nearby islands look as though they might be trying to eat the island I am on. Can you guess where I am?

2) I am in a city that is famous for mapmaking. Christopher Columbus had a brother who was a mapmaker here. Sailors and navigators from this city took over the spice trade in the 1500s. Can you guess what city I am in?

3) I am in a small archipelago off the coast of Africa. The Europeans used to stop here routinely whenever they were about to cross the Atlantic Ocean. If you know Latin, you can figure out what animal this place is named after. Where am I?

4) I am on an island that is part of an archipelago that has four main islands. The island just to the north looks like a ray. What island am I on?

5) I am standing next to a sea and the air smells very salty. I can see people in the water trying to swim but finding it difficult because the water is so buoyant. All around the sea is a very dry desert. Where am I?

6) I am standing in a green valley. All around me I can see fields and grape arbors. To the south lies a long, thin peninsula and to the north lies a mountain range. What country am I in?

7) I am just a tiny bit north of the Tropic of Cancer. I am standing on the edge of a lake. The water in this lake came from the mountains of Ethiopia. From where I am standing I can see a large dam that controls the amount of water in the lake so that people who live below the dam don't get flooded. Can you name the city and country I am in?

8) I am between two rivers. The city I am standing in is nothing but ruins, but 3,000 years ago this city was a center of culture and military strength. I am not in Nineveh. Where am I?

9) I am on an isthmus. I am not in the western hemisphere (meaning I am east of the Prime Meridian). There is a large city on one side this isthmus and it has a book of the Bible named after it. Can you name the city?

10) I am in a country that has the Baltic Sea to the southeast and a country that looks like a spoon to the north. Where am I?

11) I am in a sea that is full of islands. One of these islands looks like a Martian lying on his back. Another island used to have a famous lighthouse on it. What sea am I in?

12) I am standing right on the Tropic of Cancer. There is a river delta to the south. The river extends far to the north, with tributaries coming out of a mountain range that contains the tallest mountains in the world. Can you name the country I am in, the river I am standing next to, and a nearby city?

13) I am standing on a hill, looking out over the Atlantic Ocean. There is mostly grass around me, not many trees. Next to me is a large statue of a famous navigator who came here in 1497. The name of this hill means "good view." Where am I?

14) I am in a boat. The waterway I am passing through has a large continent to the west and a

fairly good-sized island to the east. This waterway looks as though it could be called a strait, but it isn't. Can you guess which waterway I am in?

15) I am on a peninsula. This peninsula has three shallow spikes on the bottom, but I'm nowhere near either Mecca or Madrid. Can you guess where I am?

16) I am in an archipelago that was named after a Spanish king. To the south of me there are two large islands; one looks like a bear and the other looks like a cat. Where am I?

17) I am standing on the shore of a very large lake. I am also standing on the equator. To the north of me are mountains. If I traveled east I would eventually come to the Indian Ocean. What lake am I standing next to?

18) I am next to a sea. It looks smaller today than it did yesterday! Where am I?

19) I am at the mouth of a large estuary. This estuary is so large that you can't see from one end of it to the other. The enormous size of the estuary caused confusion for European navigators who were looking for a way through the continent. If I keep sailing into the estuary, I will eventually come to a large river and a large city. South of this city there isn't much civilization, just a cold desert. Can you name the city?

20) I am in a city that is located on a very narrow strait. This city became prosperous because of all the shipping traffic that passed through the strait from one sea to another. The sea to the north of this strait has a finger shape that points to the country of Russia. What city am I in?

21) I am on a very skinny peninsula. The Pacific Ocean is to the west and I'm not sure what to call the sea to the east because it has two names. Where am I?

22) I am on a very cold island. If you sail along the west coast of Greenland you run into this island. What island am I on?

23) I am in an island group that is self-governing yet still technically under a European country. The northernmost island in this group belongs a country that looks like the back end of a dinosaur. What island group am I in?

24) I am on a little heart-shaped island. The landscape looks very much like that of Britain. The mainland to the south was named after Scotland. Where am I?

25) I am in one of the largest river basins on earth. There is so much rainfall here that the plants grow like crazy. The tributaries run into a river that eventually empties into the Atlantic Ocean. Where am I?

26) I am in Africa but I'm closer to Madrid, Spain, than I would be if I was in Paris. A famous explorer was born in this city. What city am I in?

27) I am south of the first Aleutian Island and west of the tip of Baja California. Where am I?

28) I am on a volcanic island just below the Arctic Circle. Where am I?

29) I am on an island that looks like an "X." Where am I?

30) I am on the largest island in the world that is not considered a continent. Where am I?

ACTIVITY IDEA 30C: Make an antique map of the eastern hemisphere

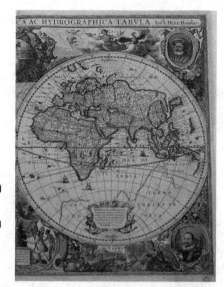

Sometimes mapmakers choose to show just one side of the earth. This activity will focus on what we call the eastern hemisphere, which includes Africa, Asia and Australia (all the "A's").

As you can see in the example to the right, mapmakers needed to fill up the space around the circle, so they added lots of extra artwork. The subjects they drew included mythological gods and heroes, native people or animals from various places on the map, portraits of mathematicians or mapmakers, landscapes and fancy geometrical designs. Sometimes the mapmakers drew in Terra Australis Incognita and other times they left the bottom of the map empty. This particular mapmaker put a plaque over the bottom of the world so it wouldn't look so empty.

To make your antique map, you will need to copy the pattern on the following page onto "parchment" (calligraphy) paper. You will also need a copy of the tracing template on white paper. Place the tracing template under the parchment copy. (If you are worried about the two papers slipping apart while working, use tape or paper clips to keep them together.) Place the papers on a window or clear door so that you can see the template shapes coming through the parchment paper. Use a pencil to lightly trace the shapes onto your parchment. Remind the students that these pencil guidelines are just guidelines. The students may be tempted to just trace over them with pen (Norway, for example) without bothering to think or to consult an atlas. Also, let them know that this is supposed to be an antique map, so they don't have to get overly worried about getting everything perfect. Those old maps were often wrong.

To finish the map, you can use the same technique you did for the map of Australia, or you can use pens and pencils with your own decorating style. You will need a very fine tip pen for drawing Europe and Indonesia. The samples below show the same map with and without added color. The black ink version looks nice even without color. Antique maps were often left uncolored. If you are short on time or if your students don't like to color, leaving it uncolored is just fine.

This student decided to use the four seasons as the theme for the designs in the four little circles.

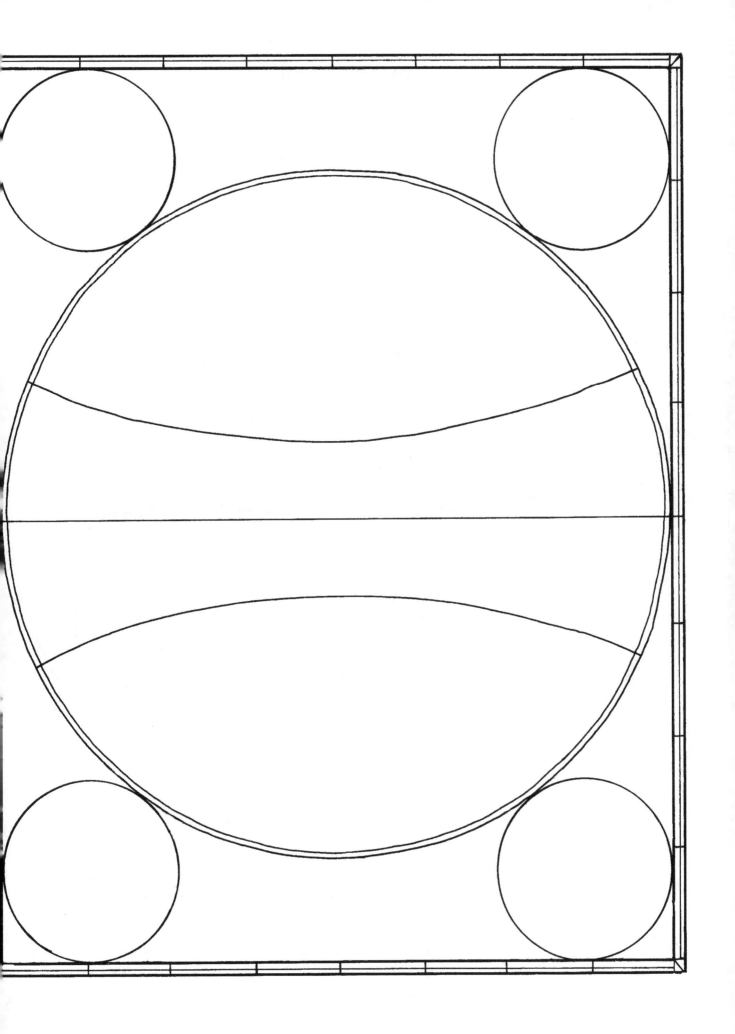

Copy this page onto regular white paper. Place it underneath the parchment blank map (copied from the previous page). Place both on a clear, bright surface so that you can see these shapes coming through the parchment. Make sure the large circles are lined up perfectly. Then use a pencil to trace the shapes (very lightly!) onto the parchment map.

Note the four dots on this template. Make sure you trace them as well. There are two for Africa (top and bottom) and two for the Indochina peninsula (the tip of the hair and the tip of the hand).

ACTIVITY IDEA 30D: Explore some islands using Google Earth™

If you have a reasonably fast Internet connection, check out Google Earth! You can type in the name of a place you want to go, then Google Earth will "fly" you there. Once at your destination, you can click on various sites and see photos and information.

Don't know where to go? Here is a list of islands in order of size, starting with the largest island in the world: Greenland. (Australia doesn't count as an island because it is a continent.)

The 60 largest islands in the world, ranked in order of size:

1) Greenland
2) New Guinea
3) Borneo
4) Madagascar
5) Baffin Island
6) Sumatra
7) Honshu
8) Great Britain
9) Victoria Island
10) Ellesmere Island
11) Celebes
12) South Island, New Zealand
13) Java
14) North Island, New Zealand
15) Cuba
16) Newfoundland
17) Luzon (Philippines)
18) Iceland
19) Mindanao (Philippines)
20) Ireland
21) Hokkaido
22) Sakhalin
23) Hispaniola
24) Banks Island, Canada
25) Tasmania
26) Sri Lanka
27) Devon Island, Canada
28) Berkner Island, Antarctica
29) Alexander Island, Antarctica
30) Tierra del Fuego

31) Novaya Zemlya (northern island)
32) Kyushu
33) Melville Island, Canada
34) Southampton Island, Canada
35) Axel Heiberg, Canada
36) Spitsbergen, Norway
37) New Britain
38) Taiwan
39) Hainan
40) Prince of Wales Island, Canada
41) Novaya Zemlya (southern island)
42) Vancouver Island, Canada
43) Sicily
44) Somerset Island, Canada
45) Sardinia
46) Bathurst Island, Canada
47) Shikoku
48) Ceran (Indonesia)
49) NorthEast Land, Norway
50) New Caledonia
51) Prince Patrick Island, Canada
52) Timor
53) Sumbawa, Indonesia
54) Ostrov Oktyabr'skoy Revolyutsil, Russia
55) Flores, Indonesia
56) Samar, Philippines
57) King William Island, Canada
58) Negros, Philippines
59) Thurston Island, Antarctica
60) Palawan, Philippines

Here's something else to do with this list—play a quiz game where one person names two islands on this list and someone else (or a group of someone elses) tries to guess which is larger.

ACTIVITY IDEA 30E: A fun game about famous places around the world

Here's a just-for-fun board game you can download for free. It's a game about famous places around the world including man-made structures such as the Eiffel Tower, the Statue of Liberty, the pyramids and the Taj Mahal, natural features such as the Great Barrier Reef, Angel Falls, Mt. Fuji and El Capitan, and even some animals such as orangutans, pandas and Komodo dragons. It's very straightforward—you simply get task cards and hop around the board visiting those sites.

This game is called "On Vacation Around the World" and it is listed at the top of the GEOGRAPHY & MAPS page at www.ellenjmchenry.com.

Final Project:

Create a world map

Instructions for creating a world map

There are several ways to approach this project. Your choices will be based on various factors such as whether you need to store the map inside a binder or in a portfolio, which art materials your students prefer to work with, or how much time you want to spend on the project. The following outline is intended to help simplify the decision-making process. First, you will need to choose either Option 1 or Option 2. Then you will need to decide on the sub-options listed below.

Option 1: A poster that will not be folded (intended to be hung on the wall)

Option 1A: Use a piece of white poster board
Poster board has the advantage of being sturdy and cheap. Some art media may not adhere as well to poster board as they will to watercolor paper, but if hot press water-color paper is difficult for you to acquire, poster board is an easy option. If your poster board has a shiny side and a dull side, make sure you use the dull side. Use the shiny side only if you intend to use permanent marker as your medium.

Option 1B: Use a large sheet of "hot press" (smooth) watercolor paper
Watercolor paper that is very smooth is the best paper to use if you want to use watercolor paints on your map. Watercolor paper is designed to absorb moisture evenly, giving a pleasing visual result. Rough watercolor paper (cold press) will be too difficult to label—the ink is likely to bleed. The smoother the paper, the better the lettering will look.

Option 1C: Use a page from a very large sketch pad (poster board-size paper)
Tear a page out of an extra-large sketch tablet. These are easily purchased at any art supply store. (The art section of Wal-Mart might even have one.) Sketch-tablet paper is heavier than regular white paper and will be slightly better for watercolor or marker. However, if the paper is too rough, ink lettering might bleed, even with a non-bleeding pen.

Option 2: A large map that can be folded to 8.5"x 11" size for storage.

Option 2A: Tape together 4 sheets of paper
You can use regular white paper, a heavy cardstock paper (recommended over regular paper), or calligraphy paper. Some office supply stores carry parchment cardstock. If you want the antique look but don't want to sacrifice sturdiness, this is the best option for you.

Option 2B: Tape together 6 sheets of paper
You can use regular white paper, a heavy cardstock paper (recommended over regular paper), or calligraphy paper. Some office supply stores carry parchment cardstock. If you want the antique look but don't want to sacrifice sturdiness, this is the best option for you.

How to tape pages together to make options 2A and 2B:

Machine-cut paper has perfectly straight edges and perfectly square corners, so it should be relatively easy to get them lined up exactly. Line up the edges of two sheets and secure with two small pieces of clear tape. (You will tape them better in a minute.) Add a third sheet and secure it with small pieces of tape; keep adding pages one by one and securing with small pieces of tape. When they are all secured in place, roll out a length of clear packaging tape (or substitute with some other kind if you must) and place the tape along the seams. Packaging tape will give you seams that will stand up to being folded and unfolded multiple times.

For any of these options, you must decide whether to provide guidelines (the same pencil guidelines that were used in the step-by-step drawing lessons) or to require drawing completely from scratch.

DRAWING FROM SCRATCH:

Most students will find drawing without any guidelines extremely difficult. They will undoubtedly start drawing everything too large, leading to great frustration as the drawing progresses. I recommend using the tracing templates to establish minimal reference points such as the equator, Prime Meridian, Tropics of Cancer and Capricorn, the centers of the Caribbean circle and the China circle, and perhaps a few other points. (If they get frustrated they can always add more guidelines.)

USING THE TEMPLATES:

Photocopy the pattern pages onto regular white paper (or print them out from the PDF file on the DVD). Trim off the edges and tape them together with clear tape so that the lines and shapes match up as perfectly as possible. Place the template under the blank map and hold it in place with paper clips or clear tape. Hold it against a light source such as a window or door, and use a pencil to LIGHTLY trace the guidelines. As always, you will be erasing these guidelines and you want them to come off with just a slight rub of the eraser.

ABOUT THE 4-PAGE PATTERN:

This pattern has the equator and the Prime Meridian placed on the cracks between the pages. When assembled, the pattern is 20" wide and 12" to 15" high (50 x 38 cm). The height depends on where you cut off Antarctica at the bottom. (The problem with including all of Antarctica is that the drawing they learned is a view from the south pole, not a standard Mercator view of the world.) You will have extra space around the edges of your map because the pattern is a little smaller than your good paper. You can trim this off or make it into a decorative border.

ABOUT THE 6-PAGE PATTERN:

This pattern has the equator below the center, which results in the omission of a large portion of Antarctica, but allows for an increase in size for the other continents. When assembled, the pattern will be 26" wide and 15" high.

ABOUT THE PROJECTION

These tracing patterns use an adapted Mercator projection, somewhat similar to the "Gall Stereographic" projection. Northern Canada is shifted to the center a bit, while leaving Alaska out to the side. The patterns are not an exact copy of any one projection, and were designed to be the best fit for incorporating all the guideline shapes used in the drawing lessons.

PROVIDING A WORLD MAP FOR REFERENCE (OR NOT):

At some point in the drawing process you may want to provide a large world map for the students to look at. Certainly, as they get the basics filled in and want more detail, they may need to use a map as reference. It's up to you to decide what the main point of this project is. If the main point is to draw from memory, don't let them have a map until the very end. Or skip the map altogether if you are using this exercise as a sort of final exam.

PROVIDING ART MATERIALS:

It's up to you what media to use. This project can be done in pencil, colored pencil, pen, ink wash, watercolor, felt-tip markers, or acrylic paint. The easiest is probably colored pencil. Black ink pen with watercolor wash applied around the edges of the continents (as in the Australia map) is also an option to consider. If you are working with anything wet, use a thick paper.

THIS PROJECT CAN BE DONE AS PREPARATION FOR A FINAL MAP DONE ONLY FROM MEMORY (STARTING WITH 4 BLANK SHEETS OF PAPER TAPED TOGETHER).

Samples of student work

This project could easily take several hours to complete. For school classes, allow 3-5 class periods (assuming 45 minutes per period) to work on it. Younger students will have trouble with the small size of areas such as Italy and Greece. Encourage them to just do the best they can. If they take their time and work patiently, they will produce a final project they can really be proud of.

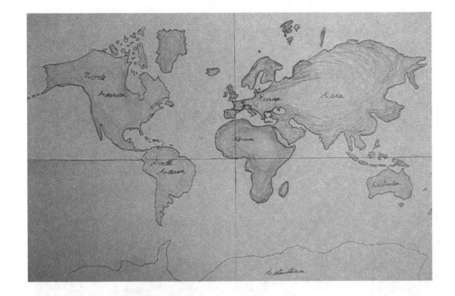

This young student decided to make the shape of the continents the main focus of her project, and to work in colored pencil on parchment paper.

This more advanced student used the same type of colored pencils, but decided to show some basic climate characteristics: vegetation, desert, and snow. The student used a Micron 01 pen to do the labeling. (The best substitute for a Micron 01 might be a ballpoint pen that has a sharp tip.)

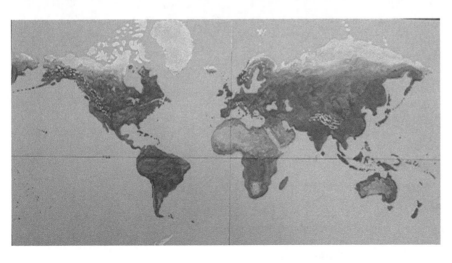

This student also wanted to show basic climate characteristics, but worked in acrylic paint instead of colored pencil. The paper is blue card stock. (This project could also have been done on blue posterboard with the 6-page pattern.)

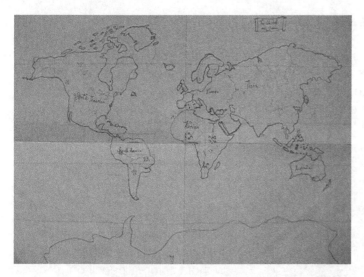

This student decided to work in pen. Class time was limited, so he did just the basic continents.

This map was done on calligraphy paper. The stude added some watercolor highlights to her pen drawing.

Students will be proud of their work. They started with a blank piece of paper and drew the world!

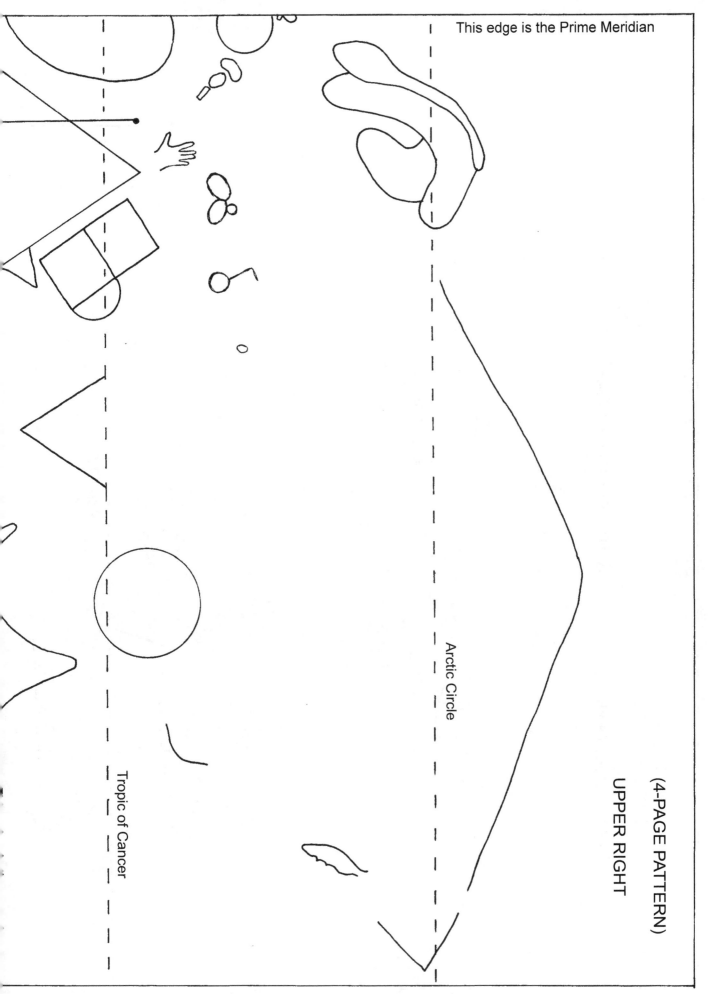

This edge is the Prime Meridian

Arctic Circle

Tropic of Cancer

(4-PAGE PATTERN)

UPPER RIGHT

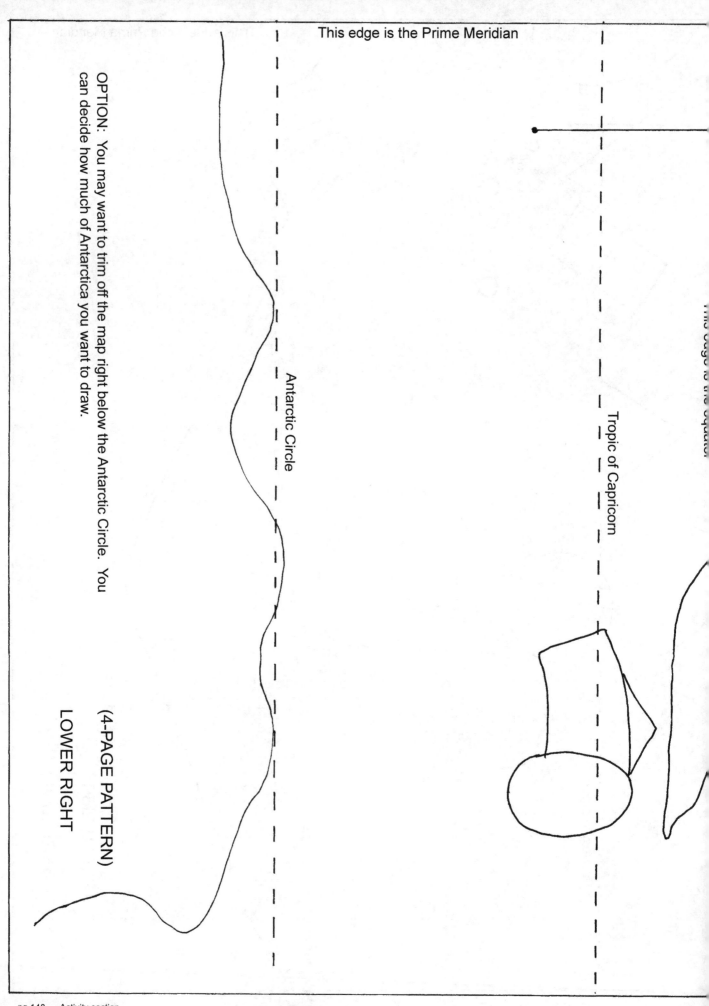

This edge is the Prime Meridian

Antarctic Circle

Tropic of Capricorn

OPTION: You may want to trim off the map right below the Antarctic Circle. You can decide how much of Antarctica you want to draw.

(4-PAGE PATTERN)

LOWER RIGHT

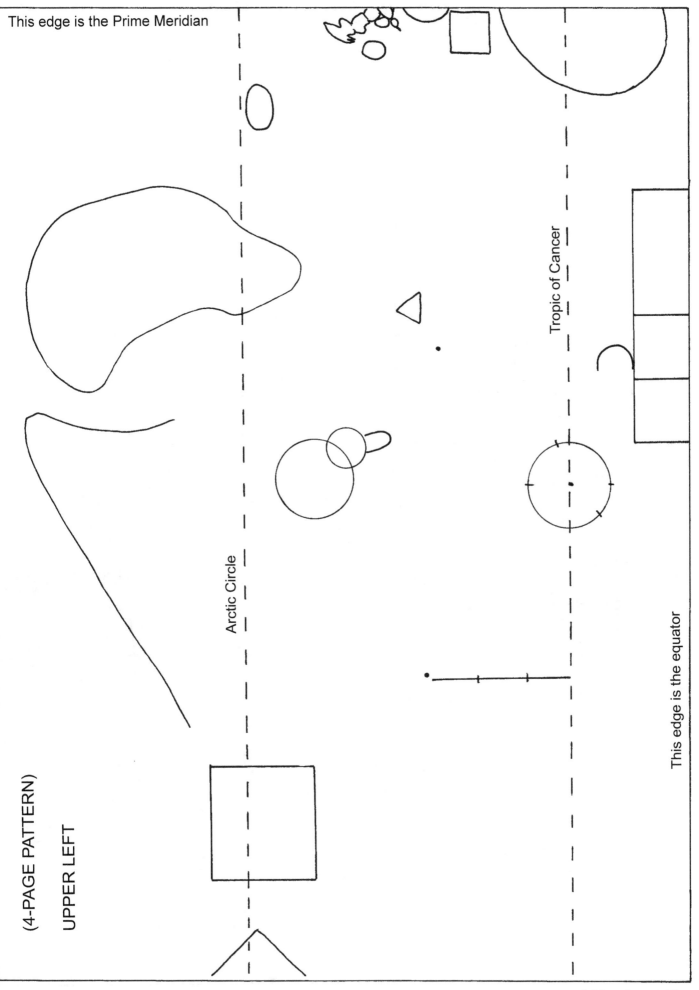

This edge is the Prime Meridian

(4-PAGE PATTERN)

UPPER LEFT

Arctic Circle

Tropic of Cancer

This edge is the equator

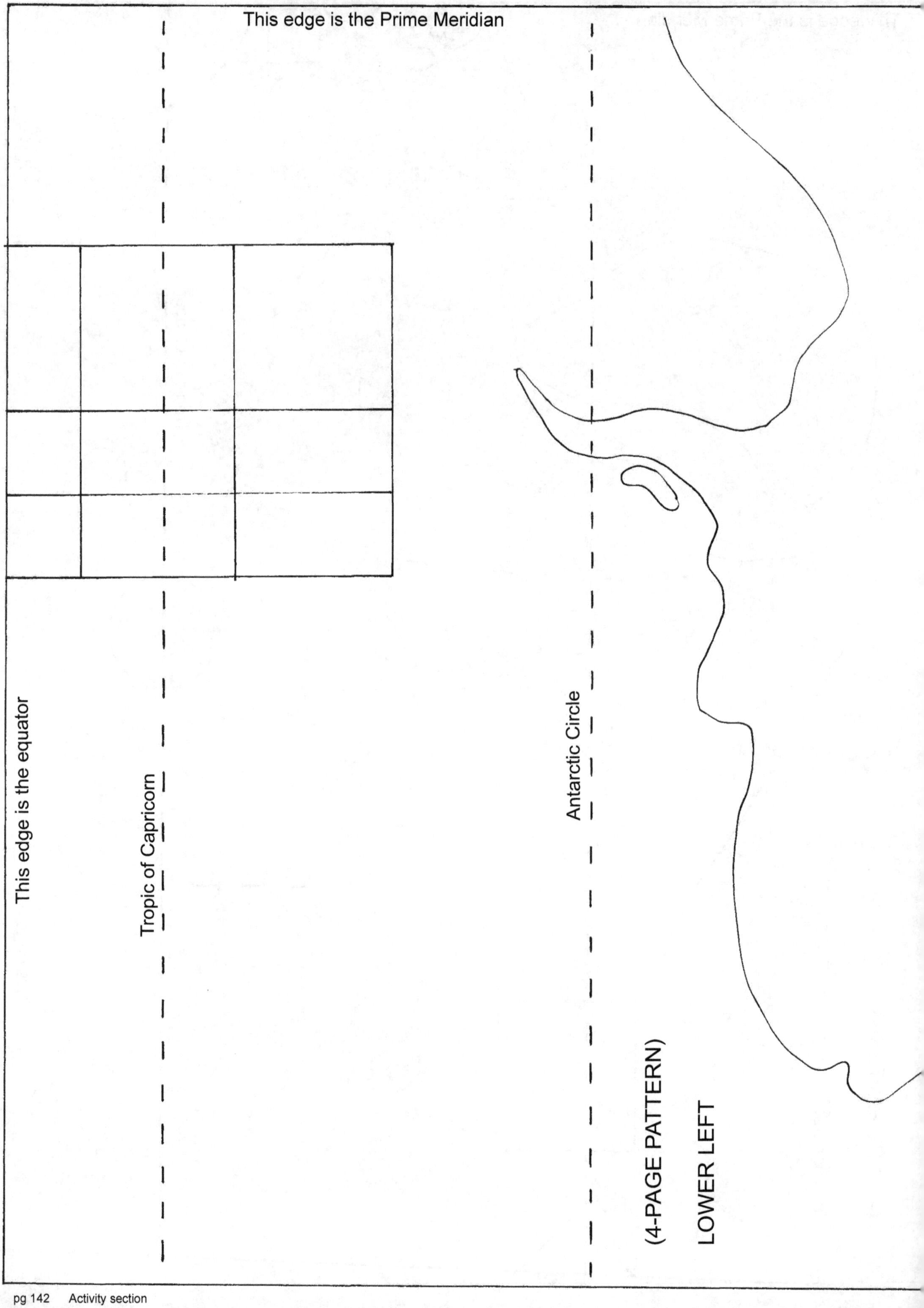

This edge is the Prime Meridian

This edge is the equator

Tropic of Capricorn

Antarctic Circle

(4-PAGE PATTERN)

LOWER LEFT

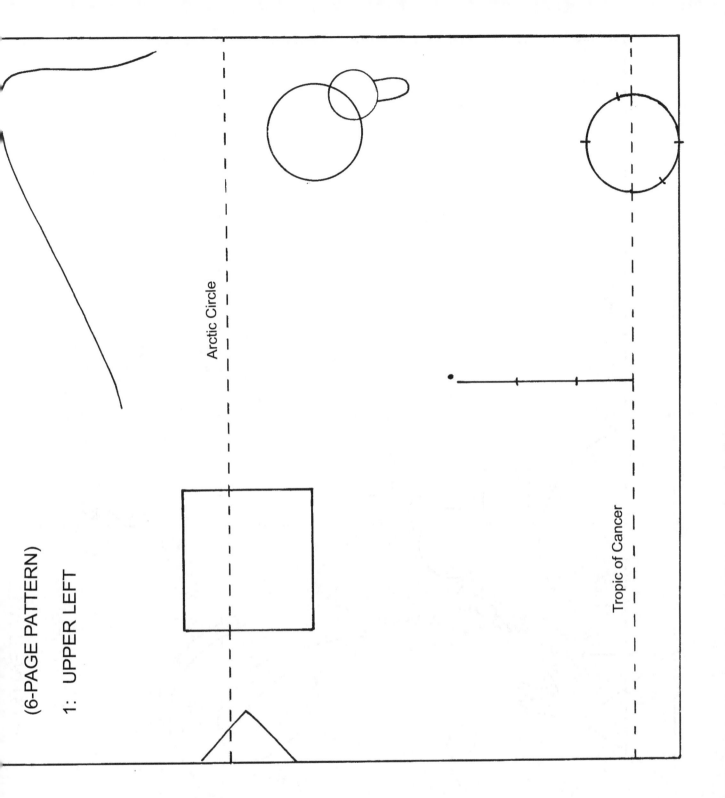

(6-PAGE PATTERN)

1: UPPER LEFT

Arctic Circle

Tropic of Cancer

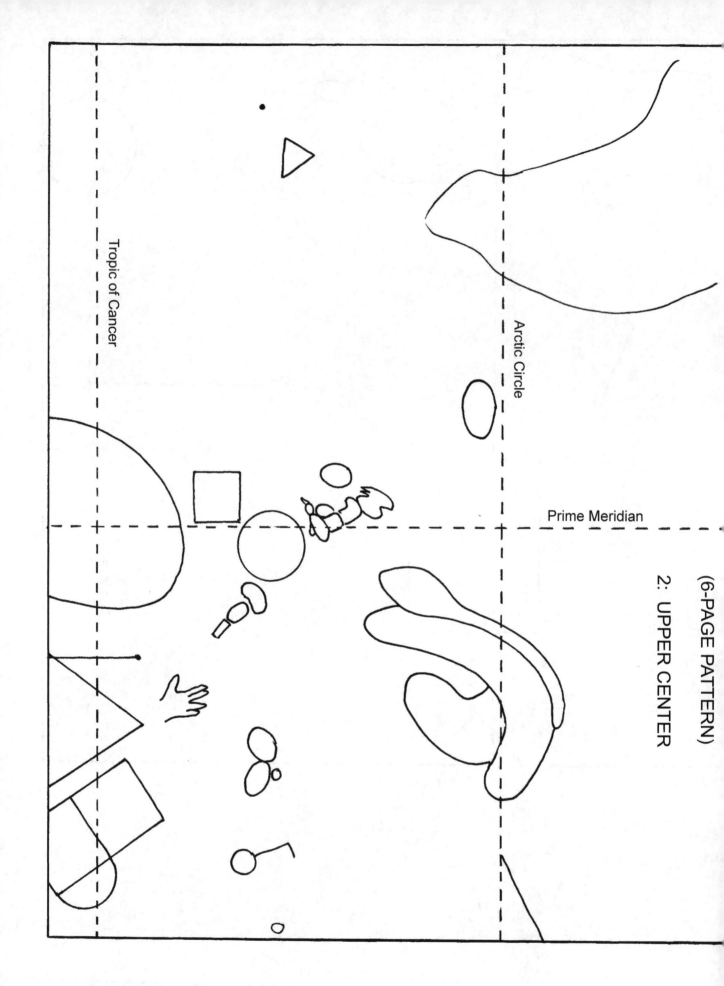

Tropic of Cancer

Arctic Circle

Prime Meridian

(6-PAGE PATTERN)

2: UPPER CENTER

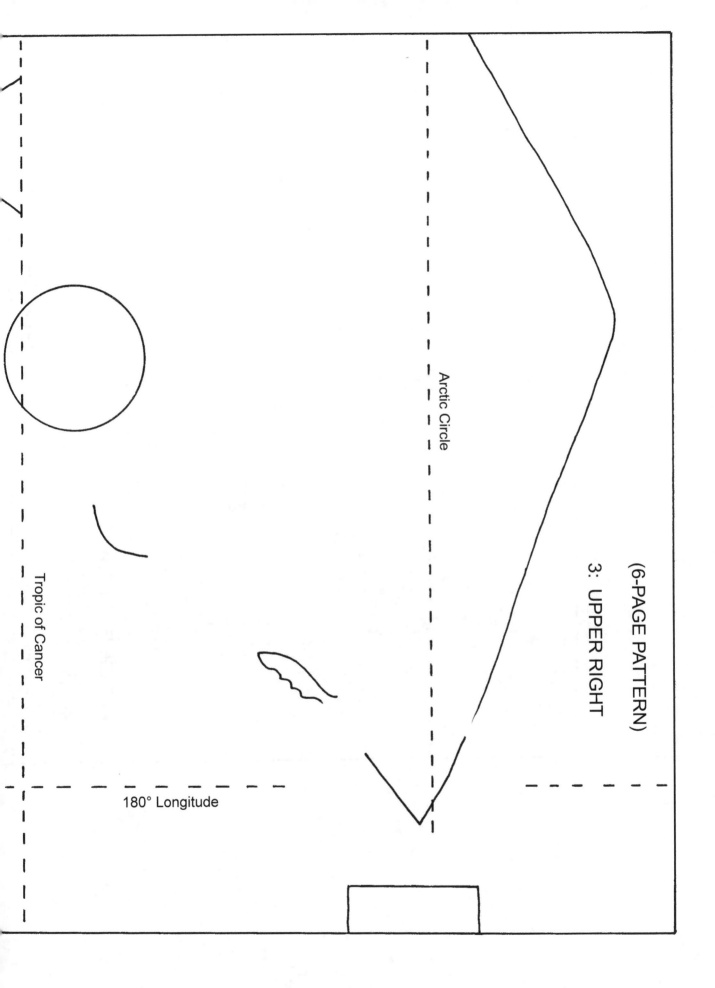

(6-PAGE PATTERN)

3: UPPER RIGHT

Arctic Circle

Tropic of Cancer

180° Longitude

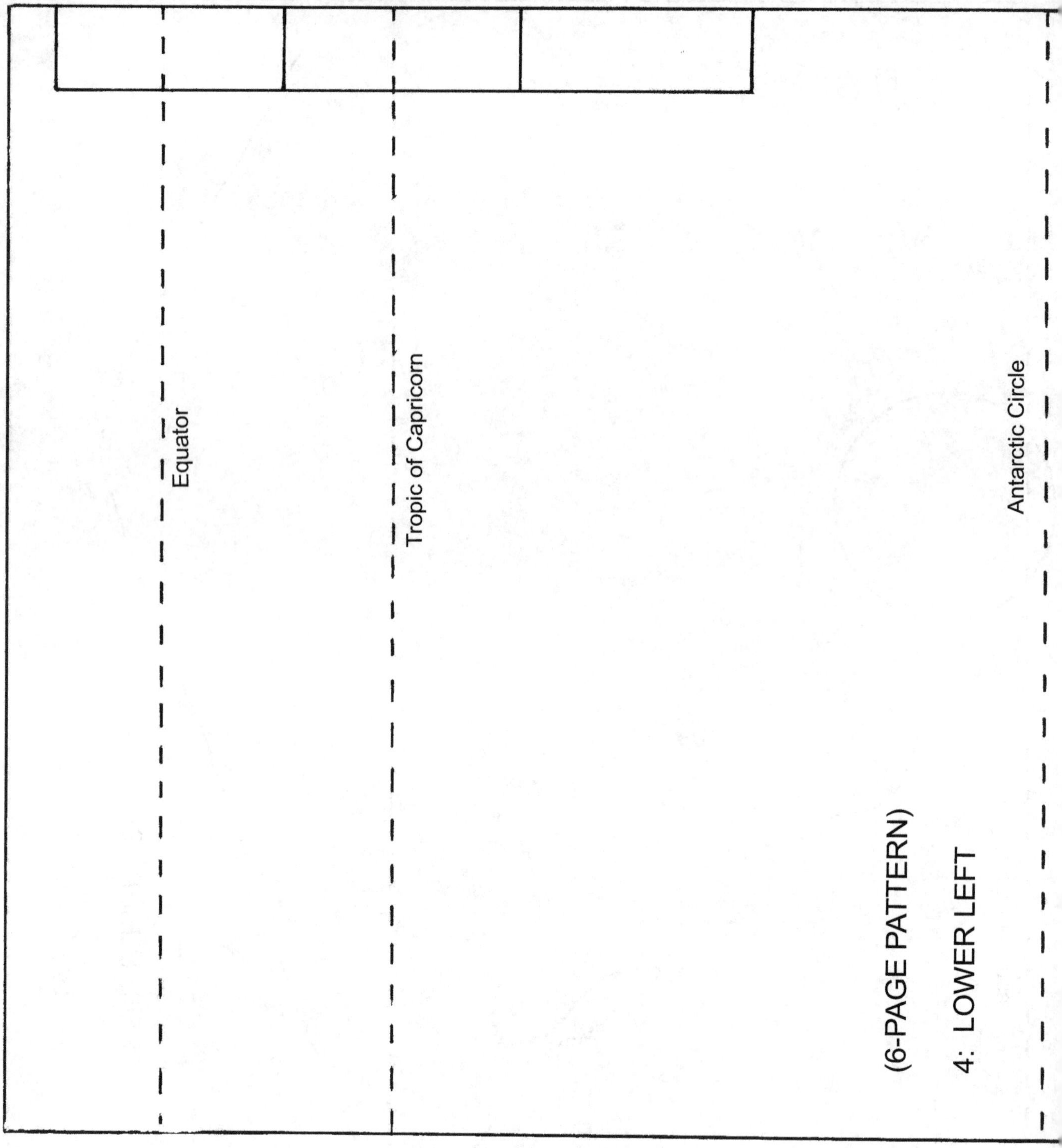

Equator

Tropic of Capricorn

Antarctic Circle

(6-PAGE PATTERN)

4: LOWER LEFT

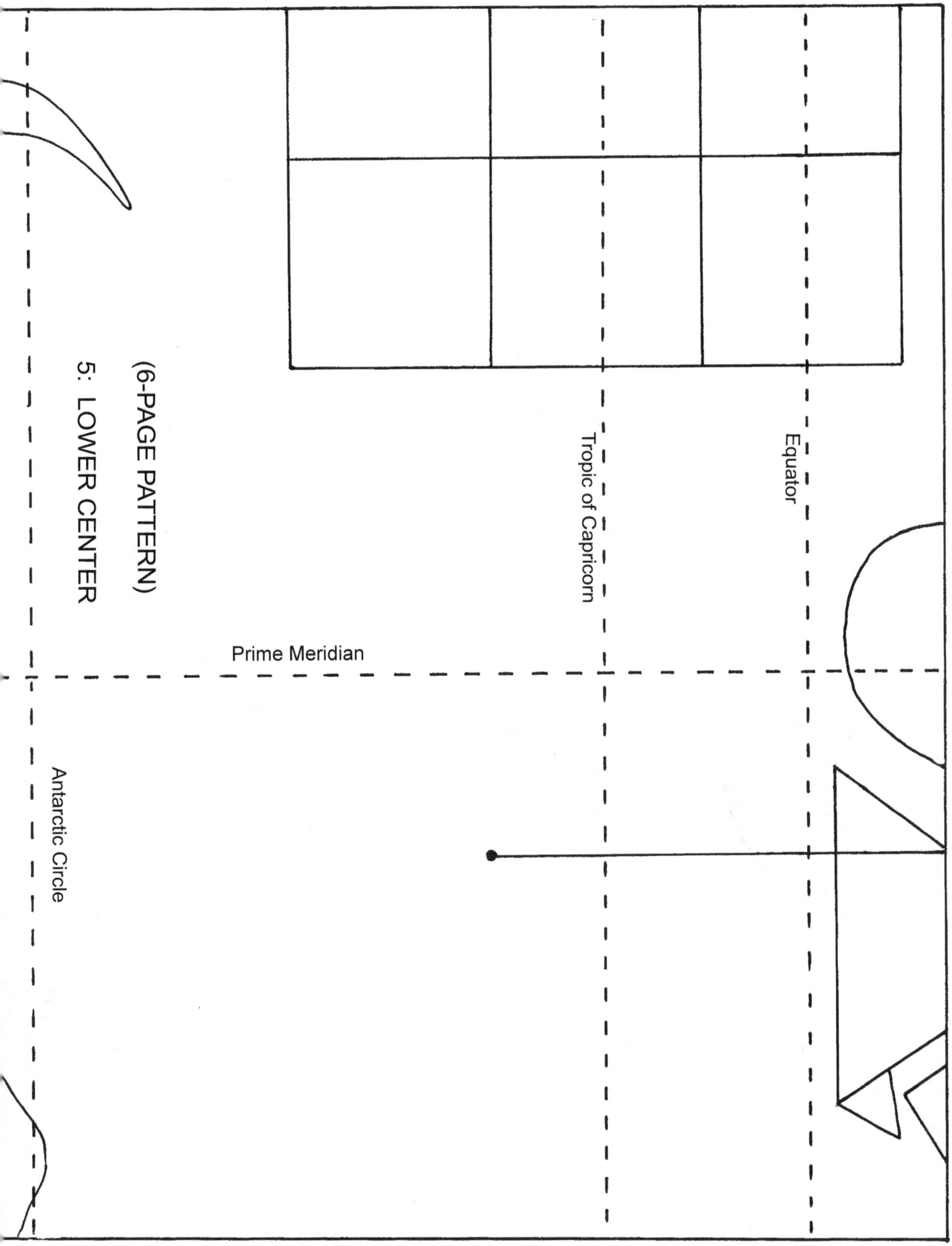

(6-PAGE PATTERN)

5: LOWER CENTER

Equator

Tropic of Capricorn

Prime Meridian

Antarctic Circle

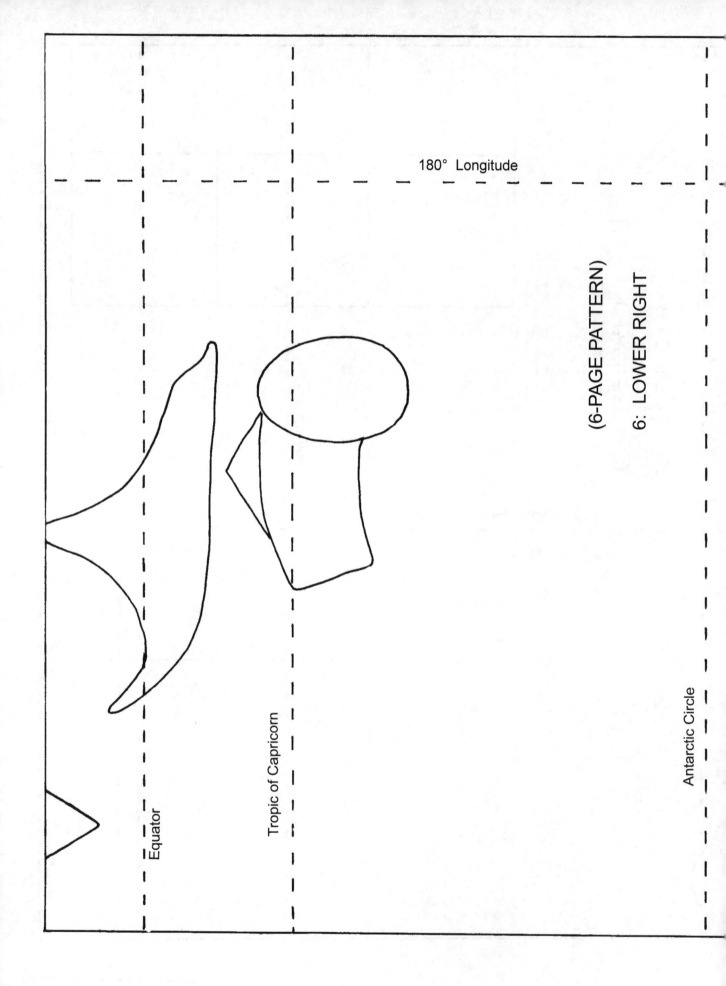

180° Longitude

(6-PAGE PATTERN)

6: LOWER RIGHT

Equator

Tropic of Capricorn

Antarctic Circle

Some recommendations for students who will be drawing completely from memory:

1) Use four sheets of paper so that the cracks will be the equator and the Prime Meridian.

2) Draw in the Tropics of Cancer and Capricorn, about 1.5 inches (4 cm) from the equator.

3) Lightly sketch the African "egg" first. The bottom is just above the equator, and the Prime Meridian goes through the middle of the egg. The Tropic of Cancer also goes through the center of the egg. Make sure the egg tilts to the right a bit.

4) Sketch the African triangle and bottom dot, and very light sketch around where the outline of Africa will go. Keep these lines light so that you can erase them later on if you need to make adjustments.

5) Lightly sketch where you think the Arabian rectangle should go, then add the India triangle hanging right below the Tropic of Cancer.

6) Add the China circle. The bottom of the circle sits just below the Tropic of Cancer.

7) Next sketch where Malaysia's arm stretches down to touch Sumatra, then block in where you think the eagle ray should go. Make some very sketchy shapes showing where Borneo, Celebes and New Guinea will go. (Remember, Celebes' tail is above the equator, his body is below.)

8) Sketch Australia below the eagle ray. The west coast of Australia is right below Borneo's legs and the east coast of Australia is right below the eastern edges of New Ireland and New Britain.

9) Make light guidelines for where you think Japan and Kamchatka and the top of Asia will go.

10) Sketch in the Mediterranean area next. Italy and Greece will seem very small.

11) Mark where Britain will go. Britain will only be about an inch high. Make sure it tilts to the west.

12) Sketch in Scandinavia next.

13) Move to the west and draw in the South America rectangle. The upper right hand corner of the rectangle is (amazingly enough) only about an inch (2.5 cm) to the left of the African egg. South America is only just slightly shorter than Africa. Don't let South America creep too far down on the map. There will be a lot of ocean at the bottom, plus room for Antarctica. Also remember that the equator cuts through the middle of the top square in the South American rectangle. (Remember that the rectangle is made of six squares, two wide and three high.)

14) Draw the Caribbean circle. The center of the circle is on the Tropic of Cancer. The right side of the Caribbean circle is just about directly above the left side of the South American rectangle. The diameter of the circle is a little smaller than the China circle.

15) Draw the Hudson circle. It is at the same latitude as Norway and the Kamchatka peninsula. It is a little smaller than the Caribbean circle and is located right above it.

16) Draw a box for Alaska. There should still be about two inches of space above the Alaska box. Sketch in the top curve for the Canadian islands, then add Greenland. Ellesmere and Greenland will almost hit the top of the paper.

17) Decide what you want to do about Antarctica. Sketch it stretched across the bottom, or else trim about two inches off the bottom of your paper, so you only have to draw the tip of Lesser Antarctica.

Extra facts you may be interested in knowing as you draw:

Britain is on the same latitude as Labrador.
Gibraltar is on the same latitude as the Delmarva peninsula.
Honshu and California occupy the same area of latitude (meaning that they are the same height and at the same latitudes).
Hawaii is right under Alaska's skinny beard.
Iceland is right above the Canary Islands.
The tip of Greenland is just a little bit east of the mouth of the Amazon River (and lot further north!).
The Lesser Antilles are right under Nova Scotia and Cape Breton Island.
Labrador's larger ear is right above Cuba.
Newfoundland is at the same latitude as the Brittany peninsula of France.
Bermuda is right below Nova Scotia.

Finishing up:

After following these recommendations for sketching in your guidelines, then go back and make more solid pencil lines, putting in all the details. Keep these pencil lines fairly light, as well, as you will likely be doing a lot of erasing as your brain struggles to remember the shapes. When you are ready for your final lines, use a very fine tip bleed-proof pen to trace over the pencil lines. Then use your large eraser to remove all pencil lines. (If you are painting, you don't need to do pen lines.) Add any rivers or mountains you want to add, and do any labeling you want to do.

You want to add some sea monsters or ships in blanks areas. You might also want to add a fancy box or scroll with your name and the date.

ONE FINAL RECOMMENDATION:

Relax! Try to have fun doing this project, and remember how many world maps throughout history have been far less than perfect. Some of the most famous and most collectible (expensive) maps today are antique maps that far less accurate than the one you will produce. (At least you know that California isn't an island and you know about Antarctica.) Be proud of your map. Make it a work of art. When you tell people you drew it from memory they will be amazed!

Bibliography

Books:

Allen, Philip. <u>Mapmaker's Art; Five Cenuries of Charting the World</u>. New York: Barnes & Noble
   Books, 1992. ISBN 0-7607-2024-X

<u>Answer Atlas; The Geography Resource for Students</u>. Rand McNally & Company, 2003.
   ISBN 0-528-83872-5

Berthon, Simon, and Andrew Robinson. <u>The Shape of the World</u>. Rand McNally, 1991.
   ISBN 0-528-83419-3

Brown, Lloyd A. <u>Map Making; The Art that Became a Science</u>, Boston and Toronto: Little, Brown and
   Company, 1960. Library of Congress catalog number 60-9338.

Desmond, Kevin. <u>A Timetable of Inventions and Discoveries</u>. New York: M. Evans & Company, Inc.,
   1986. ISBN 0-87131-520-3

<u>DK World Atlas; An Atlas for the 21st Century</u>. New York: DK Publishing, Inc.,1997.
   ISBN 0-7894-1974-2

Ehrenberg, Ralph E. <u>Mapping the World; An Illustrated History of Cartography</u>. Washington, D.C:
   National Geographic, 2006. ISBN 0-7922-6525-4

Fisher, Dennis. <u>Latitude Hooks and Azimuth RIngs</u>. Camden, Maine: International Marine/Ragged
   ountain Press, 1995. ISBN 0-07-021120-5

Greenhood, David. <u>Mapping</u>. Chicago and London: The University of Chicago Press, 1964.
   ISBN 0-226-30696-8

Konstam, Angus. <u>Historical Atlas of Exploration</u>. New York: Checkmark Books, an imprint of
   Facts on File, Inc.   ISBN 0-8160-4248-9

Kurlansky, Mark. <u>Salt: A World History</u>. New York: Penguin Books, 2002. ISBN 0-14-200161-9

<u>Magellan and the Exploration of South America</u>, from the "Great Explorer Series" published
   by Scholastic, Inc. Original copyright is by Barron's Educational Series, 1998.
   ISBN 0-439-11023-8.

Novaresio, Raolo. <u>The Explorers</u>. East Bridgewater, MA: World Publications Group, Inc.
   (White Star S.p.A.), 2002. ISBN 1-57215-485-3

Platt, Richard. <u>Pirate</u> (an Eyewitness/Dorling Kindersley Book). New York: Alfred Knopf,
   1994. ISBN 0-679-87255-8

Sobel, Dava, and William J. Andrews. <u>The Illustrated Longitude</u>. New York: Walker and
   Company, 1995. ISBN 0-8027-1344-0

Tooley, R. V. <u>Maps and Mapmakers</u>. New York: Dorset Press, 1987. ISBN 0-88029-161-3

Tracy, James D. ed. "Structural changes in European long-distance trade, and particularly in the re-export trade from south to north." <u>The Rise of Merchant Empires</u>. Cambridge University Press, 1993. ISBN 0521457351

<u>World Atlas</u>. Hammond, 1987. ISBN 0-8437-1254-6

<u>Film</u>:

"Voyages of Discovery," a BBC documentary hosted by Paul Rose. Aired summer 2008.

<u>Websites</u>:

"A fresh view of Magellan" http://voices.cla.umn.edu/vg/Classroom/Student_writing/1301v-s2005/Group3/Philippines_files/page0004.htm

colonialvoyages.com/malacca

http://thanasis.com/winds.htm

http://www.mdstud.chalmers.se/~md2nicke/MISSUPPFATTNINGAR/magellan.txt
(A Magellan website)

http://www.chenowith.k12.or.us/TECH/subject/social/explore.html#verraz (This is a general website about European explorers, with clickable links to other websites.)

Wikipedia:
I consulted Wikipedia articles when I needed basic facts quickly. I have checked Wikipedia facts against other sources and have found Wikipedia to be very reliable for researching basic historical facts (names, dates, etc.).

CPSIA information can be obtained
at www.ICGtesting.com
Printed in the USA
BVHW09026251119
564524BV00010B/134/P